FROZEN, NOT BROKEN

Master Your Stress, Adapt to Adversity, and
Activate Rapid Self-healing

Mario Godiva

Paperback: 978-0-578-96977-0
First paperback edition August 2021
Cover art and design by Danielle Camorlinga
Printed in the United States of America
Mario Godiva
1223 Wilshire Blvd. #531
Santa Monica, CA 90403
Mariogodiva.com

For Angel, who unconditionally loved, anchored, and co-regulated me. To each of you that chose to support me and read this book, I see you, hear you, feel you, and I'm so grateful for your kindness.

Contents //

PREFACE //

I'M NOT A WIZARD, ALIEN, OR SAINT

After being in septic shock, drowning inside out from my inner fluids, and being given a week to live by my doctors, I went from stage four cancer to complete remission in fifty days. My doctors didn't tell me this initially; I had to figure it out on my own by translating medical jargon from a test. I only say fifty days because that was the time from the diagnosis to a PET-CT scan that showed the cancer had completely reversed. So, who knows how fast it really happened? It was so unexpected that I was stunned, while my doctors quickly shunned.

Note that I'm also a Black man in America, and as such, I was never taken seriously by most of my doctors from the start. Why? Because of systemic medical racism that's overbearingly prevalent in healthcare. It's commonly expressed by a doctor's unwillingness to hear, see, or acknowledge a Black patient's concerns. America is home to stark and persistent racial disparities in health coverage, chronic health issues, mental health, and death. These disparities are not a result of just individual or group behavior but also decades of systematic inequality in the American economy, housing, and health care systems. Conscious and unconscious bias across the medical community is life-threatening to patients, regardless of their socioeconomic status. No matter how many medical professionals believe that all races are equal, they can all harbor different subtle biases.

In my personal experience, doctors and healthcare professionals often assumed that I was poor, uneducated, and indifferent to how I was treated by them, oftentimes in a condescending manner. I endured over 20 different medical errors. One medial error is supposed to be rare, imagine suffering through 20? When the people you trust prove untrustworthy, who do you trust? When the people you run to when you are harmed, are the ones causing you harm, what do you do? Not only that, constantly navigating systemic racism in general adds a massive stress barrier to minorities that makes it even harder to find and realistically sustain optimal balance, health, and well-being. I encountered over twenty-three doctors and their tests, pills, and statistical approaches in a four-month period. Why so many doctors? Because none of them listened to me or took me seriously. I was constantly patronized, minimized, and delegitimized until I almost died. I can tell you with conviction that racial healthcare disparities are very real. I'm still mystified by my ability to heal so fast through such a tremendous amount of stress, resentment, and anger. Most of my doctors didn't care if I lived or died, and I had to become my own health advocate, as I forged my path back to holistic health—a path that was exponentially faster than theirs.

Data and statistics have an important place in our world, but they are not relevant or reliable at predicting how any single person will respond to new information, connections of information, and/or cultivating a healthier inner ecosystem. Did you know it takes an average of seventeen years from the time that research is published for the average doctor to use the information in their practice?[1] A lot of things can change in seventeen years. I didn't have seventeen years to wait for my doctors to understand and approve all aspects of the holistic approach that I took, factor in the impact of my unresolved trauma, or connect that my dysregulated nervous system helped create and fuel my health challenges. I couldn't wait for them to realize that I was frozen, not broken with symptoms. I was too often frozen in states of stress and shutdown that robbed me of the self-healing potential I could have found in a relaxed state. Acknowledging that there is much to learn, and consistently new information being discovered about the body, the mind, and how it's connected to health would be a more honest approach to start working on our limitations, instead of generalizing symptoms and Adverse Reactions (ARs). Statistics are numbers that tell us how the "average" person did in the past during treatment taking allopathic focus. But you are anything but "average," unless that's what you want to be!?! #nojudgement We all have a unique inner individuality, and no two people have an inner environment that is exactly the same. This should be celebrated; instead, it's regulated.

I was frozen, not broken, and it took training micro intervals of awareness to defrost and realize that. Was I hopeful that I would heal? I don't believe in hope, I believe in self-generating. Hope is a great selling point for charities and can work for some people but hoping can make you feel powerless. Hope is a feeling and doesn't really get things done. Motivation, action, strategy, and consistency get sh*t done. Just think about that for a second: are you in a position of power when you hope? When you hope for something, you rely on an external force that you have no certainty or control over to heal you on the inside. I wasn't hoping for my healing, I already knew I could heal myself, and I knew that I alone was standing in my own way. I was frozen in dysfunction, delusion, and disease because I continuously betrayed my mind and body. I had to train myself out of the preconditioned doubts that tried to self-sabotage my efforts. What if I die? What if I'm disabled? What if my illness comes back? The only way to overcome that preconditioning is to recondition yourself out of it. And you do that through the art of self-generating which you learn by integrating my practice called Interval Mindfulness™ and its various Innervals™ into your everyday life.

I'm not a wizard, alien, or saint. My healing journey wasn't all roses, candy, and teddy bears; I suffered greatly during my experience. But suffering isn't a form of punishment, it's a call to action. Even though I went through four months of over 20 medical mistakes, misdiagnosis, and malpractice, I'm not slamming or disparaging doctors. I forgive them for all that I experienced: the constant grief, frustration, and disbelief from being fundamentally misunderstood. The feelings of isolation, negative experiences, and difference of opinions were several of the catalysts that helped activate my rapid transformation, and that's partly because I never liked being told what to do without a proper explanation as to why I should be doing it. I recognize that some people feel they have no other choice than to place blind faith in their lab coat attendants in order to overcome illness. I on the other hand, withdrew and that withdrawal led me back to myself, and the fastest and most dramatic cancer recovery on record. Please understand that I'm not advocating for tearing down or completely avoiding the conventional medicine model. I'm not suggesting that conventional medicine, practices, and procedures don't have value; they do. I am proposing zooming out and looking at how you can integrate various modalities, disciplines, and methodologies to help you holistically self-heal.

Being ill put me out of the spotlight for a while. I became very selective about the people I shared my illness with. It was lonely being at the hospital, even when I had company, I dreaded visitations because I was in extreme denial about the severity of my condition. Having to reassure everyone else that I was doing better than I appeared to be while being filled with fear myself and masking it was at the very least, isolating and exhausting. I had a sh*tload of fear about the future and if I would ever be able to work in the fitness industry again. Most importantly: I was terrified to think I could die. Once the terminal diagnosis came in, I was overtaken by fear about everything: erratically shifting nerve states dancing among hope and hopelessness, I flip-flopped between both worlds, at my most honest trying to make peace with the life I had lived, should I have to accept the end of it.

My quest to heal myself led me to that dark haunted house around the block that no one wants to go to, but it was inside my own mind. I had all the time in the world to think, feel and digest the negation of my unmet needs while in bed rest and at the intensive care unit (ICU). Living in New York and being used to the minute to minute pace, I had to sit down with my frustration and restlessness, and for the first time in my life, I had to befriend my sorrows, the ones I had repressed and piled up after years of being auto-avoidant of my own emotions and running solely on auto-pilot. I had to thaw out the unconscious patterns that were driving my self-suffering thoughts, actions, and behaviors. I had to actively do my own inner work, and there was a decades-long backlog to get through.

With all the time in the world to think, process, and release, I realized this: most of my stress came from inner wounds like childhood trauma, unresolved emotions, and my preconditioned personality full of unhealthy beliefs, behaviors, trauma responses, and coping mechanisms. Subsequently, I developed an emotional addiction to chaos, drama, and adrenaline because that's what I was mainly exposed to when I was growing up. I was frozen in these familiar behaviors from childhood and I would actively and unconsciously seek them out in adulthood. All because I was conditioned to believe that they made me feel "safe". Familiar isn't safe; if you're sleepwalking through life like I was, familiar is frozen. Once you wake up by cultivating self-awareness, you gently raise the temperature and slowly start to thaw out. Although the longer that you have stayed frozen and maybe even become freezer burned, the longer it will take to thaw out. Not only that, I'm an empath, an extremely sensitive person (even when I don't show it) and not only prone to an overload of information, stimulation and distraction but also prone to absorbing other people's energies and denying emotions.

This quality manifested greatly during my time in the fitness industry. My greatest sin was overtraining from a young age, because not only was I addicted to endorphins and feeling good after working out, but I was competitive and wanted to stay relevant. I drank and partied often to stay current. This was the socially acceptable way to network in NYC. We all followed the "work hard, play hard" mentality, but for me it only led to years of exhaustion. Instead of living, I was constantly trying to just keep up and continued to lean on this very unsustainable way to avoid my emotions. I used it to escape. It was my own personal virtual reality experience. Being a procrastinator yet hyperactive led me to rely on stimulants to get things done. Family grief combined with failure and betrayal in work ventures undoubtedly led to a physical manifestation of my own emotional neglect for myself over many years. For me it was cancer, but for you, it could be something entirely different. It could be heart disease, diabetes, autoimmune disorders, or a variety of other chronic health issues that finally express on the outside after brewing on the inside for years or sometimes decades of being frozen.

This book is my opinion based on my experience. It may be controversial, and people will have differing opinions about it. That's great because everyone is entitled to their own opinion. Opinions are a projection or viewpoint from the limited perspective of a person. Opinions are shaped by that person's life experience, conditioning, associations, and perspective. I welcome and hold space for differing opinions. So much of our root suffering comes from being conditioned in environments where our realities were denied. You don't have to agree with me or listen to what I have to say, but that doesn't devalue, delegitimize, or deflect what I experienced, what I feel, and how it may help others. The fact that I'm still thriving after a dance with stage four cancer and multiple snuggles with death should speak for itself.

I'm not here to debate, or to say anyone is right or wrong. I'll leave that to the people who love sharing their opinions on social media and passionately fighting to convince others that they're "right." My methods aren't "right," I'm not a "miracle worker," and I'm not some authority figure on healing that you should blindly follow without question. I did something extraordinary and I'm offering a different path for people than the traditional path through the medical-industrial complex. This path, for me, was faster, healthier, and more efficient. This path won't be for everyone, and that's okay. This is a book about radically regressing unhealthy aspects of your life. Spontaneous mind-body healing doesn't just apply to cancer, it applies to a wide range of chronic health issues like diabetes, heart disease, depression, trauma, and many others. In *Spontaneous Remission, An Annotated Bibliography*, Brendan O'Regan and Caryle Hirshberg provide 334 references for spontaneous remission for diseases other than cancer, as well as a summary of the research on cancer regression.[2]

In this book, I will lean heavily toward addressing your anxiety and stress levels, which includes anxiety, stress, and negativity, because they're the three most powerful precursors to all chronic diseases and the biggest roadblocks to your hopes, dreams, and needs. I talk heavily about rebalancing the nervous system, shifting nerve states, and stimulating your nerves, because no matter what you do, if you aren't in the self-healing nerve state (relaxation response), you simply won't heal, feel safe, detox, or be able to relax. Your nerve state also dictates the stories that you tell yourself. If you're stuck in a defensive (stress response) nerve state, the intensity and speed of your thoughts will increase, and your self-talk will be more defensive, harsh, and combative. However, if you're in a relaxation response nerve state, the intensity and speed of your thoughts will decrease and your thoughts will be more calm, thoughtful, and compassionate to yourself and others. If I could go back in time (although I wouldn't want to), I would go to the times when I was experiencing the highest level of anxiety, stress, and negativity and get them in check to the best of my ability. I would've been more conscious of my inner whispers, which are warning signs, red flags, or my body's car dashboard lights that were telling me that different parts of my life were unbalanced and needed attention.

Mastering my stress, rebalancing my nervous system, and taking a holistic approach to my health were the three most powerful things I could've done to support my body's natural, innate immunity and would have prevented me from even thinking about cancer, let alone experiencing it. Other than that, healing is also about retraining ourselves to our birthright of being healthy, happy, and living a purpose-filled life. Whatever the primary healing method is, it must be sustainable and effective in the long term. We know in life that there are long, slow, and inefficient ways of doing things and shorter, faster, and more efficient ways of doing them. We admire, focus, and obsess over talented, successful, and high-achieving people in every single industry imaginable, yet no one pays much attention to people who have achieved optimal health quickly and sometimes instantly, after devastating disease.

People love innovators who break the rules, shatter the ceilings, and go against the herd. I did all of those things and instead of being met with fanfare, I was met with shooing, shaming, and shunning by my doctors and the medical community as a whole. I'm not a world-class athlete and I'm not a revered Harvard Ph.D. My super skill is that I triggered my spontaneous healing in record time, the fastest of any documented time. Is that not worthy of being world-class? Is gaining and sustaining health not a skill worthy of being recognized, championed, or celebrated? I don't want a trophy, title, or f*cking cookie (maybe a gluten-free one), what I want is more people to start taking a balanced and holistic approach to their life, as well as taking their health and well-being more seriously before they get frozen and it's too late. Too late is when a crisis, emergency, or trauma happens from your frozen preconditioned behavior. Too late is also when your body is internally screaming SOS. Too late is when you go through life on autopilot frozen in dysfunctional, damaging, and delusional behavior patterns.

Too late is when your family and loved ones have to bury you too soon. Our stubbornness has a way of turning very masochistic when we wait for the bucket to appear in order to gather the will to live.

This book isn't just about me, it's about how I can help you unfreeze yourself. Retrain you to cultivate more awareness and take responsibility for your mostly subconscious thoughts, habits, and behaviors. Retrain you to raise the temperature so that you start to gently thaw out from some of your unhealthy, negative, and self-sabotaging behaviors and tendencies. We have a hidden epidemic of superficial suffering in the world that's propagated by our mainstream-suffer-culture. Whether it's sports, entertainment, music, or business, we are led to believe from a young age that when it comes to succeeding, winning, or gaining attention, those positives will come with a price and are synonymous with "suffering."

We think that if we suffer it automatically changes us or makes us better, and those who have mastered suffering the best (who didn't die in the process), are the people whose stories inspire us the most. They have endured suffering for so long that they create a legacy in their respective field, and they become the "gurus" we revere, the only people that inspire us after death. The truth is that people bring about most of their own suffering without really knowing that they do. Many of our problems are self-generated and people make many of their own surface-level challenges, frustrations, and changes bigger, worse, and more overwhelming by ruminating about those problems non-stop. They ruminate about those things non-stop because they are in their stress response state. When you change your state, you will change your mind. Most people stay frozen in a stress or shutdown response nerve state or oscillate between the two, and unknowingly trigger self-suffering with their conditioned thoughts, feelings, and behaviors. And when we trigger suffering consistently, we are sending endless RSVPs to our toxic guests of honor: disease, illness, distress, more suffering. Yes, it's our party but they're our uninvited guest of honor, because it's the paradox of self-generation.

There are a lot of people who are walking around thinking that they are broken and permanently stuck in whatever illness, state, and circumstance that they are currently in. Broken is often a label that people tend to over-identify with. To be broken is hopelessness. Breaking, mostly associated with glass, often results in things breaking into a lot of different pieces that can never be put back together again. What's the first thing we do when we break glass? We throw it away. If someone says and feels like they are broken, they are also probably thinking, consciously or unconsciously, that they deserve to be thrown away or discarded by others. The extreme "take it or leave it" outlook on life. So, they just stay frozen in their unhealthy lifestyle habits, self-sabotaging thoughts, and destructive coping patterns. I'm here to tell you that you're frozen, not broken. Frozen in a defensive stress response nerve state, fighting or running unconsciously from your issues in life. Or you're frozen in a shutdown response nerve state, hopeless, depressive, and on autopilot to numb your inner pain. Or you're frozen oscillating between these two extreme states. Frozen in the unconscious habit and addictive patterns of self-suffering. Frozen in the same cycles that you desperately want to escape, but seemingly never can.

So many aspects of society are reinforcing most people's deep freeze. For example, let's take a look at the beauty industry and how they market to people. The way you get people to buy something, especially women, is you tell and show them they are not good enough. Then you offer them a solution for it. Make-up, skin creams, hair care products, etc. If you watch just about any beauty-relief product or any health-related product for women. It's all tied into on some level "You ain't good enough". You're not lovable as you are. Whether you are male or female you grow up with these imprinted images that you didn't invent that you're getting from everywhere. You're being inundated with how you're supposed to be; and feeling guilt, shame, and resentment when you realize: Dam that's not me. Nutritional confusion is the new eating disorder. The media bombardment of "eat this" or "eat that". The demonization of wellness diets. People have so many choices that they don't know what to do for themselves. That happens when we are in our heads and we are not connected to the wisdom of our bodies. We aren't listening to what our bodies truly need. When we attach ourselves to an Influencer. The need to measure up to that perceived image can be devastating to somebody that already has a negative self-image. And that in itself can be traumatizing to someone who doesn't have the self-esteem or wherewithal to figure out what's right for them.

You're frozen, not broken, and it's because of your inner and outer conditions that have caused your deep freeze. But you have the power to defrost to a happier, healthier, and more holistic life. However, people keep themselves frozen by keeping secrets, isolating, judging themselves, escaping their feelings, blaming themself, blaming others, or ignoring or minimizing their inner pain. This is in no way an issue of blame, it's simply what we do and I'm not placing a judgment or a value on it. One major way we reinforce being frozen is through self-limiting beliefs, negative self-talk, or our thoughts that reinforce keeping us stuck in our defensive nerve state. If you truly think that change isn't possible, there's no point in feeling your feelings, right? You aren't consciously choosing to have limiting beliefs, they are simply there and serve a function. And they are directly connected to which nerve state you're in.

When you do some of those things above, they just keep you frozen, hard, and rigid in how you behave, think, and show up in your world. But there's hope for you, you can improve your life, and things can literally get better for you. I'm not saying this to be dismissive or insensitive, I'm telling you this because I've personally been there and have helped thousands of others become unstuck. It all begins with a simple reframing. You aren't trying to pick up a million pieces and glue them back together, you're simply slowly raising the temperature and thawing your subconscious thoughts, actions, and patterns to consciously create new, healthy, and productive ones. Thawing helps increase your flexibility, flow, allows you to see more options, and access more resources. A lot of solutions out there want you to go directly from frozen to cooked, but those are often short-term solutions and leave most people more frustrated than before they started. To defrost is a slower, manageable, and more long-term solution. To finally start thawing out is to make lasting change. I know it sounds like an enormous undertaking, but I am here to guide you step by step through the process.

Life moves fast in the 21st century, and most of us are programmed to avoid difficult things. That includes emotional and personal growth. It's exponentially easier to bury our traumas than it is to face them. To drink, doom scroll, smoke, snort, or binge eat them away. But at what cost? All too often we don't take action to address our traumas until the symptoms or behavioral adaptations have overwhelmed us. I know firsthand what happens when you ignore, minimize, or avoid your unresolved issues, traumas, and inner pain, it snowballs, oozes out of you, and gets exponentially worse. It doesn't just sit there waiting patiently until you address it; it slowly hijacks your body and infects other areas of your life like work, health, social engagement, and your relationships until you have no other choice but to face it.

The inner pain you may be going through, the fear, panic, anxiety, and depression is trying to tell you something. But are you ready to see it, hear it, and finally listen to it? You have a personal responsibility to listen to it instead of fighting, repressing, or avoiding it. I am here to help you do that work, but at the end of the day, you have to decide to begin improving yourself. Before you dive inward it's better to strengthen your relaxation response and build resilience to anchor yourself in safety. Once anchored and with your nervous system properly balanced, you can then start to explore more inwardly. If it seems like it's too much to bear all at once, you can take micro-moments to explore it calmly and curiously without feeling the need to judge or evaluate it. This is why I wrote this book and created the practice of Interval Mindfulness™, so that you can have a toolbox full of micro doses of learning, doing, and defrosting to help you anchor to the present, feel safe, and find stillness for short intervals of time. We aren't monks, nor will we ever be in the environment that monks thrive in. We are collectively submerged in a never-ending loop of continuous chaos. Our world has gotten so stimulating, overwhelming, and information overloading, that we have lost our ability to easily relax. To combat this, we must become inner athletes to retrain ourselves to relax amid chaos; or at the very least, adapt to navigate chaos more efficiently.

INTRODUCTION //

TOO BUSY TO RELAX

I created Interval Mindfulness™ and its various Innervals™ because you and I, and everyone else on the planet are overworked, overwhelmed, and extremely busy. #BreakingNews. The people who aren't are in the 1% (can I please borrow your privilege card?). By now we all know and can acknowledge our own issues as well as the issues of others. However, we don't have time to put our faith in learning traditional, long, and sustained relaxation, mindfulness, and stress-relief practices, hoping that after weeks, months, and years down the line of practice, we'll finally see the benefits. Also, those methods don't work for people who are frozen in a stress response nerve state. If you're frozen in fight-or-flight, running from a tiger in the woods, the last thing you want to do is sit still in a chair or lay down and go to sleep. Am I right? You want to use the defensive energy that is inside of you.

There are only a few mindfulness, meditation, and relaxation modalities that people are told that they should try and practice. Many of these mainstream modalities simply don't work for most people. No one has thought to put short intervals of multiple modalities together in one unique experience. What works for one person doesn't always work for another, just like a diet. What works for you, makes you feel good, and keeps you consistent varies, so it makes sense to me that you should try and practice a method that has many modalities, variety, and novelty. Also, most people generally want to see benefits right now! We live in a click, get, and right-now instant-gratification culture. Social media gives you instant dopamine hits now, with every like, share, or follow. If I can order a product on Amazon and get same-day delivery, that sets a precedent not only for everything else in my life but also for reducing my anxiety and stress levels and dealing with any and all chronic health issues. It's okay to acknowledge that you want quick, bite-sized activities and quick results.

Interval Mindfulness™ gives you a short mental, emotional, and physical wellness break that will clear your mind, lower your anxiety, and reduce your stress. Because your brain loves novelty, curiosity, and efficiency, Interval Mindfulness™ puts a variety of mindfulness, breathing, and other nerve stimulating exercises into short Innervals™ (Inner Intervals). Innervals™ are powerful tools for stress mastery, mental clarity, and more energy, easily injecting well-being into your busy and stressful workday. Since each Innerval™ workout is no longer than 3 to 12 minutes, it shouldn't be difficult to incorporate into your daily life; even on days that you need to skip your actual workout. We essentially do 30 seconds of something and follow it with 30 seconds of doing nothing. The more energy you put into doing something, the easier it will be for you to do nothing. To "innerve" is to proactively stimulate your nervous system so that you reflexively shift back into better balance. A balanced nervous system supports healthy brain function, and improves physical health via healthy digestion and immune function, minimizing pain and calming inflammation.[3]

A lot of people don't want to learn what to do and just prefer being told what to do (by a big buff Black man) and seeing immediate results. That backs up why traditional interval training is so popular in the fitness and sports world. People experience interval training and it's efficient, they reap the benefits and soreness immediately. Talk is cheap; training is everything. Concepts, ideas, and methodologies for change are great, but what good are they if most people who need them don't use them? People today need to be trained to change, otherwise, they'll stay frozen in a stress or shutdown response nerve state, and keep telling you how good they looked in college or the "good ole days" when presently they look a mess. Practice makes permanent. With this methodology, we're trying to retrain years and decades of being frozen in a stress or shutdown response nerve state. When you're lifting weights in the gym, the weight doesn't get easier to lift, you get stronger to lift it more. Life's frustrations, stressors, and challenges don't get easier to handle, you train to become better equipped to handle them.

Unfortunately, health is not valued until health issues come. Infection, illness, and disease are a multidimensional progression as a result of being frozen in defense or shutdown nerve states. But this progression does not have to be permanent, and by taking the appropriate steps, you have the power to change. You can always undo what you overdo, even if it's been going on for a long time in the back of your mind. I viewed getting sick from the energy-progression perspective, and that allowed me to understand that in order to efficiently, effectively, and easily get better, I had to take a multidimensional, multifunctional, and multifaceted approach to radically regress what had progressed. Just like what goes up must come down, what gets started can be stopped, and what moves forward can also move backward. In other words, the content of this book is for absolutely anyone and it meets you where you are. There is no negative mental or physical health condition that you cannot decide to take power over. There is hope for you, I promise.

I was frozen, and I had to get myself unfrozen. So how do you get unfrozen? The master key is rebalancing your nervous system. Your body already knows what to do and the tools are already inside of you, you just have to activate, stimulate, or innerve them. A new smartphone is useless unless it's activated by a service provider. Let me be your T-Mobile!

Whether you chose to believe this right now or not, you have the power to start thawing yourself out and get unstuck, but something is blocking that from happening. And it's YOU. This gets complicated because it could very well be the subconscious or preconditioned version of you that's holding you back. What is blocking your progress isn't always clear unless you can tune into a deeper level of self-awareness. This can sound intimidating, but it doesn't have to be. It can be accomplished by simply practicing micro-moments of awareness every day. This is why I made it easy for you by creating Interval Mindfulness™. Rebalancing the nervous system happens when you reconnect the mind and body. Specifically, in the brainstem where the most primitive, protective, and survival mechanisms lie.

It's hard work, I know. But it's easier when you commit to a short amount of time every day or every other day. Looking inward and expecting to deal with all of your issues all at once isn't doable, safe, or practical. The good news is that you don't have to do any of that. You just have to strengthen your relaxation response nerve state. Yep, that's it! Focus on the positives, focus on what energizes you safely. Focus on doing things that help anchor you into the present moment. Things that bring you some energy, joy, and connection. This book provides eye-opening wisdom, practical resources, and micro tools that provide a more direct route of looking inward and allowing stress, relaxation, or shutdown energy to release or return.

This is also a book about overcoming extraordinary challenges in record time, simply by taking a holistic approach with your mind, stress, and inner environment. Healing literally means "to make whole again," so why wouldn't you first want to take a holistic approach? This is also a book about awareness, faith, action, training, and empowerment. It's a book about realizing your inner potential once you connect your mind to your body and shift to a self-healing and safe nerve state. This will help you start listening to your authentic self over your preconditioned self, your lifetime of unconscious trained thoughts, actions, and behaviors.

Most importantly, this is also a book about doing inner work and will give you easy-to-follow, digestible, and powerful tools that make you want to do it. When you take a micro approach to change, your mind, body, and nerves are less likely to resist. We all have issues, traumas, unresolved emotions, and inner wounds that have been stored in many areas of our bodies. If you aren't actively doing inner work to resolve, dissolve, and release this energy, the anxiety, stress, and negativity will permeate and progress to chronic health issues. However, as I have proved profoundly through my own story, what can progress, can regress. You have so much potential to get unfrozen and unstuck that it's ridiculous. The energy is inside of you laying dormant and just waiting to be activated. But you must become an inner athlete and train to be in the self-healing nerve state where you feel safe and give your body permission to use it.

You are fully capable of mastering your stress, adapting to adversity, and activating rapid self-healing. How fast you do all of those things depends on how strong your relaxation response nerve state is. Stress, anxiety, and negativity trigger the states of emergency that freeze them and hold people back from healing, losing weight, having energy, living fully, thinking clearly, and achieving the many hopes, dreams, and needs they want to achieve. Interval Mindfulness™ and its various Innervals™ of relaxation, meditation, and stress-relief will help you to strengthen your nerves so that you can efficiently rescue yourself from yourself. If we train your mind, body, and relaxation response to be a consistent, strong, and reliable emergency break to your unlimited daily stress response triggers, all your hopes, dreams, and needs will be easier to accomplish. It won't be easy; it will be training. And don't even think about getting shady on my watch.

Are you ready Inner Athletes? Let's begin.

How to use this book

This book combines my personal journey with informative theory and practice and doesn't follow a traditional format or structure. This hybridity is intentional. You'll notice that most chapters have a memoir and prescriptive parts braided together in a very balanced way. Each chapter should read, feel, and flow like a short, timed interval. You have the option of reading the whole thing from start to finish or reading through a chapter at a time, taking in this theory in a micro format, just like the theory of Interval Mindfulness™ itself.

We're going to get pretty theoretical at times, but don't worry and bear with me. Every bit of theory and research is interconnected, important, and intentional. I've also done my best to synthesize it in a way that everyone can understand, so by the end of your time with this book you will have not only an action plan, but also an understanding of WHY you're doing what you're doing. Let me tell you, as someone who has spent a lot of time in the health, wellness, and fitness spaces, that is not something you see every day. You should feel empowered through the knowledge I share to implement these practices into your life.

Every now and then, your reading will be interrupted with an actionable activity such as an Active Innerval™ or Mindful Innerval™. These Innerval™ interruptions serve as nightlights, micro-moments, and safety beacons to help anchor you in the present, master your stress, cultivate awareness, and activate thought-provoking self-reflections as you read. With each Active Innerval™ you are simply following directions and doing the first part intensely or with energy (something) and the second part passively or easily (nothing.) Try to be mindful to the best of your ability and that simply means being present in the now judgment-free, not thinking about yesterday or tomorrow. With each Mindful Innerval™, you are simply trying to authentically answer each question to the best of your ability.

Before you do each Innerval™, rate the intensity of your current anxiety and stress levels on a scale of 0 (none) – 10 (nervous breakdown). After you finish each Innerval™ exercise, rate the intensity of your current anxiety and stress levels again. Did the number drop? Also, as you go through this book, try to notice internally what triggers you, resonates with you, and relates to you. Your mind, body, and nerves are trying to direct message you.

The foundational "passive" or "rest" breathing of Interval Mindfulness™ is called "Core Breathing." Core breathing is when you take long, slow, and deep inhales, feeling the bottom of your lungs and all 360 degrees of your core expand, and then take longer, slower, and deeper exhales, feeling the bottom of your lungs and core deflate. Taking long, slow, and deep core breaths during any activity will help to strengthen your diaphragm, one of your major breathing muscles for deep breathing. There are two types of foundational rest breathing Innervals™.

1. CORE BREATHING FREE INNERVAL™ // 60 seconds

Take long, slow, and deep inhales and take longer, slower, and deeper exhales for 60 seconds or 6 times each if you don't have a timer. How long each of your inhales and exhales are freestyle and up to you. As you breathe in, your core goes out, as you breathe out, your core goes in.

STIMULATION: The phrenic nerves, vagus nerves, motor cortex, and posterior thoracic nerves.

2. CORE BREATHING INNERVAL™ // 60 seconds

Take long, slow, and deep inhales and take longer, slower, and deeper exhales for 60 seconds or 6 times each if you don't have a timer. As you inhale for 3 seconds your core goes out, and as you exhale for 6 seconds your core goes in.

STIMULATION: The phrenic nerves, vagus nerves, motor cortex, and posterior thoracic nerves.

Core breathing is also called diaphragmatic breathing and is an easy tool to stimulate your vagus nerve, activating your relaxation response, and helps quickly lower your stress responses. When your breathing is shallow in your chest, it keeps you frozen in your stress response. Long, slow, deep, and balanced breaths permeate nourishing oxygen into your body, blood, and cells. The more oxygenated your blood, the more healing, rejuvenating, and cleansing it is for your body.

The Active Innerval™ combo workouts include two Innervals™ together that repeat. Each Innerval™ combo starts with a type of action and is followed by something passive like core breathing (CB), which is long, slow, and deep diaphragmatic breathing. The more effort and energy you put into the active part of the Innerval™, the easier it will be to drop in the passive parts, just like in traditional interval training. This pendulation, or back-and-forth, is the natural pulsation between states of expansion and contraction in the nervous system. It's one of life's fundamental principles of ebbing and flowing. The ebb and flow of waves, nighttime and daytime, and a bird's wings going up and down in flight. A healthy, resilient, and adaptable nervous system is one that can move between alertness and action, and calm and relaxation easily or efficiently, without getting frozen at either of the extremes.

The format of the Innerval™ combos are as follows:

1.   The name and length of the Innerval™ combo.

2.   The name and length of the specific Innervals™ (1 & 2) that make up the combo.

3.   The directions of how to properly do each Innerval™ written in long-form.

4.   How many times the Innerval™ combo repeats.

5.   The details of how to properly do each Innerval™ written out in long-form

6.   The nerves, neurotransmitters, or actions that are stimulated with the Innervals™.

ENERGY BALANCE COMBO. (3 minutes)

1. FAST BREATH INNERVAL™ // 30 seconds.

Inhale and exhale through your nose equally for as fast as you can. Do this for 30 seconds or 60 times if you don't have a timer.

2. CORE BREATHING FREE INNERVAL™ // 30 seconds.

Take long, slow, and deep inhales and take longer, slower, and deeper exhales for 60 seconds or 6 times each if you don't have a timer. How long each of your inhales and exhales are freestyle and up to you. As you breathe in, your core goes out, as you breathe out, your core goes in.

3. Repeat 2 times

STIMULATION. The phrenic nerves, vagus nerves, and posterior thoracic nerves

1 //

SPONTANEOUS HEALING, PLACEBOES, AND STATISTICS

Spontaneous remission is the fast and unexpected remission of a disease that's expected to progress severely or fatally. Instead of progressing, it sharply turns around, reversing, regressing, and disappearing. What has progressed can always be regressed, because it had to start somewhere right? People live past their "death day," cancer dissolves into thin air, and tumors melt like ice cream on a summer day. It can be partial or complete, permanent or temporary. The very few people who experience it are often surprised, excited, and overjoyed by the development while getting chilly receptions from their doctors, because these extraordinary events go against their preconditioned beliefs and how they were trained to view illness.

People are surprised and oftentimes simply shocked about their recovery, because anyone that has been severely ill has heard at least once in their life that one of their conditions was "incurable." Or what most people hear is "you'll be on these pills for the rest of your life." To those who had their life span severed by the "accurate predictions" of the Western medical world, I see you, I hear you, and my heart goes out to you. To the top players of this structure: I respect your field but don't always agree with you. I have value. I'm alive today because I defied you. My struggle, story, and resilience have value, and that's why I'm sharing my story.

I got written off as some kind of "once in a blue moon anomaly" and quickly disregarded. I didn't make their list of positive recoveries (PR), and I still owed my hospital bill. Why would I receive such a negative response from my doctors? After all, isn't this exciting news?!? What I did is extremely touchy, taboo, and controversial for many reasons. When it comes to Western medicine, I'm allegedly one of those fairy tale, rare, and "miracle" cases that are unworthy of real scientific investigation. As a result, my recovery was never reported, I'm not included in the cancer cure rate statistics, and my case is ignored by an entire medical community simply because I didn't approach the diagnosis "by the medical book." I'm okay with that, but still, I get the struggle, if any of you were ever able to access your own healing and your primary caretakers saw it like a "casual coincidence," not a product of your awakening, intelligence, and hard work.

Not only that, but I also literally had every possible thing going against me being a Black male. I endured over 20 different types of medical errors. Typically, one medical error can kill you. I was constantly patronized, ignored, and they tried to make many major decisions about my health and treatment without consulting me or explaining to me what they were doing. With every clarifying question that I asked, I was met with a demeaning valuation of my life. I saw firsthand how deep subconscious beliefs could deprioritize Black life. I noticed all the small ways that racism was covertly built into the medical system and normalized through repetition and routinization. Subtle racism harms people, causes accidental deaths, and leads to distrust in the health care system. The third leading cause of death is medical error. Who do you think the majority of those deaths are? Black people.

Many studies show that Black people (and other minority groups) experience more illness, worst outcomes, and premature death compared to White people.[4] I don't think all doctors and registered nurses are overtly racist, however, I do think and feel that there are subtle, invisible, and hard-to-detect workings of racism and microaggressions in health care encounters and the healthcare industry. It's well established that they operate in a system that is inherently racist.[5] A common way that Black patients receive different care is called cumulative deprioritization.[6] If a white doctor has to decide between giving a lifesaving treatment to a white patient or a Black patient, who do you think he's going to pick? A white doctor or nurse can't easily relate to or identify with a Black patient. So, they will prioritize unconsciously the patients that they can easily identify with or relate to.

It is what it is. I experienced this firsthand. Cumulative deprioritization is when implicit bias unconsciously affects smaller decisions, and it's deadly. As a society and in our respective professions, we must do a better job of being socially aware of our own biases. What are your biases? Have you even thought about this question and how it affects your day to day?

Even with this massive racial stress barrier, I was still able to activate rapid self-healing. The cancer didn't just get tired, change its mind, give up, and throw in the towel. I trained as an "inner athlete," rebalancing my nervous system, and allowing me to make an inner change that built resistance to what was internally attacking me. I focused on my inner strength to activate my rapid self-healing. The human mind and body are too complex to try and describe in a minimalist way, and one action can trigger thousands of different outcomes depending on a person's inner environment and immune system. Doctors, although defiant of self-induced recoveries, already understand how powerful the mind can be over the body from a pesky scientific annoyance called the placebo effect. The placebo effect is defined as a phenomenon in which some people experience a benefit after the administration of an inactive "look-alike" substance or treatment. Placebos are given to convince patients into thinking they are getting the real treatment, most commonly referred to as a sugar pill. Placeboes have been shown in endless medical studies to produce a 35-45% improvement in whatever medical condition is being treated.[7] So people are getting better and healthier simply from "thinking" they are getting treatment. Even doctors who are otherwise skeptical about the psychological aspects of illness accept, and often utilize, the power of placebos. So why are spontaneous-remission cases treated so differently?

What the medical field can't explain or understand, they dismiss. Then these exceptional healing feats, like Olympic game times and records, are treated as anomalies, pushed to the wayside, and mostly forgotten by the mainstream. Spontaneous remissions aren't that rare at all, doctors just don't really talk about them. There are over a thousand case studies in literature and some say it happens to roughly one of every 100,000 people.[8] Critical analyses of spontaneous regression cases date back more than a century to physicians like Dr. William

Coley, Dr. G.L. Rohdenburg in 1918, landmark studies by Drs J.J. and J.H. Morton in 1953, and the widely cited review by Drs T. Everson and W. Cole in 1956.[9-11] Medical literature is now filled with observations of biopsy-confirmed malignancies with CT scans or MRIs showing widespread disease that spontaneously regresses, which encompasses nearly every cancer type like leukemia[12,13], lymphoma[14,15], breast cancer[16], lung cancer[17,18], testicular cancer[19], prostate cancer[20], cervical cancer[21], colon cancer[22,23], sarcoma[24,] and melanoma.[25] The mechanisms most often implicated in facilitating the spontaneous regression of cancer and other diseases related to immune system function.[26]

Why does the world get excited, inspired, and in awe when Usain Bolt breaks the world record in the 100- and 200-meter dashes, but indifferent when someone goes from terminal cancer to cured instantly? Bolt will get credited with doing the hard work, consistent training, and having an optimistic mindset to break records, while spontaneous remission won't be credited to the person who heals, but is seen as an act of God or a higher being. I'm not trying to trash Bolt or say that I'm somehow better, I'm simply saying that we have different skill sets that are both worthy of being equally recognized. We're also human and have free will. We can say "no." You can't heal someone that doesn't want or think they deserve to be healed. You can't help someone who doesn't want to help themselves. And this resistance to healing could be conscious or subconscious. This ties back to people triggering their own self-suffering. Have you ever tried to help someone who didn't want to receive it? I took personal agency of my healing and if I didn't want to heal, I wouldn't have, especially as fast as I did. Healing is a skill, and I had to work just as hard as Bolt with strategy, pure hard work, consistent training, and maintaining an optimistic mindset.

Another reason that spontaneous remission isn't really acknowledged is that Western medicine is mostly directed by a molecular medicine paradigm. Most doctors don't know how it happens and don't care to find out. This is strange to me because the very logic behind immunotherapy and its treatments is that they can supercharge your immune system to fight off cancer and other chronic diseases. But rather than talking about training people to focus on training their inside, the focus is directed at something on the outside to help heal the inside. We can naturally boost and fortify our innate immune system from the inside, and inner athletes like me who activate spontaneous self-healing are living proof of that.

When I was struggling with cancer, I never owned the disease. Meaning I never called it "My cancer." It wasn't "mine", it was an unwelcome guest internally trashing my body. You are NOT the diagnosis, symptoms, or challenges you currently have or will face. You are frozen in them at this moment but you are not them. Retraining our mind can go both ways, we can either own disease (claiming that it's yours, that you deserve it, or that you're broken) with "genetic inheritance beliefs," incurable illness, or we can envision healing and actively participate in bringing that scenario forth intentionally as opposed to allowing a diagnosis to determine our "due date." Just like the placebo effect and the long-standing debate: is it that it's in pill form or the fact that we believe a certain something can heal us? It makes us rethink if we'd be able to access the same level of healing through sound therapy or talking to a monkey in a sacred site. Lourdes is a well-known place for "miracle healing." Every year, burdened sufferers make their pilgrimage to this site in France where it's believed that people are cured of their sins and illness, by the magic powers of the waters on site. And this belief has its origins all the way back to the year 1858.[27] How long have we started identifying ourselves as a diagnosis and owned illness for? Was it with the rise of the pharmaceutical industry into the corporate advertisement magnate that it is today?

Nature doesn't have accidents and my journey was no accident, coincidence, or stroke of luck as many are quick to comment. What I discovered, like so many other inner athletes before and after me, is that when your mind and body unite, it can trigger a powerful symphony of immunity. A perfect storm of immunological events that can overpower cancer or any type of chronic health issue you're facing. Just because you don't understand how something works doesn't mean that you shouldn't acknowledge, accept, or try to recreate it. I'm living proof that cancer and all chronic health issues are reversible, at least in most circumstances. These concepts also apply to those that do not have a terminal illness but may just be suffering from depression, or indigestion. The connection of the mind and body with intentional awareness is universally beneficial, so why not try it? And for those who are severely ill, don't underestimate the power of the concepts I'm putting forth.

You don't need to be a doctor to understand that there are many ways to get an efficient, faster, and stronger health outcome for any chronic health issue you're facing. A shotgun approach to all things can be more harmful when the situation calls for a precision sniper. Collateral damage should be unacceptable when it comes to you, your health, and well-being. Why constantly use a bulldozer when all you need is a small shovel? Conventional doctors, like all experts in their respective fields, have a singular, conditioned, and limited perspective. This creates several blind spots. They're trained to view things minimally: linking one action, a procedure, protocol, or drug, to an outcome or response, which can be great for some things but not effective broadly for all things. It's like immediately declaring war on other countries no matter how big or small the disagreement. As I discovered, there is nothing minimal about your mind, body, its connection, and your inner capacity to self-heal.

The second you start chasing symptoms and ignoring the secret source of your health issues, you hop on the "elliptical of symptom management" as I'll call it, bouncing up and down, doing the same boring movements, staring at a screen, and going nowhere fast for life. You aren't regressing what progressed, you're simply managing it. Just doing the bare minimum of what you need to get by and survive with as little pain and discomfort as possible. I didn't manage the symptoms of cancer, I quickly reversed it. If you really want to arrest, reverse, and resolve the secret source of your health issues, the answer is mastering your stress, rebalancing your nervous system, and taking a holistic approach to your health. Regarding rebalancing your nervous system, I'm specifically talking about stimulating your vagus nerve, the relaxation response part of your autonomic nervous system. After conception, when a fetus enters the embryonic stage, the nervous system including the brain, spinal cord, and nerves are the first thing to develop and they directly govern your ability to reach and sustain optimal health.[28]

I'll be going over this more in detail as we move along, but simply stated, if your nerves aren't connected, communicating, and coordinating or you are frozen in a defensive or shutdown nerve state, you'll never find the permanent relief for any health issue you face, ever. Nerves that connect and communicate together, coordinate better. And they must be strong enough to help you shift into your self-healing nerve state, the relaxation response. I will help you learn to master your anxiety, stress, and negativity before it wreaks havoc on your nervous system (which communicates to your entire body).

My doctors unwittingly led me to discover firsthand that human beings are limitless, our bodies are designed to self-heal (and rapidly), and that our brain has the lifetime ability to create new nerve pathways with awareness, commitment, and training. We can unlearn our frozen unhealthy behaviors, start thawing out and relearn healthier ones. We can defrost out of our frozen self-suffering. Self-healing is self-empowerment, and we can move slowly away from our past conditioning that can self-sabotage us and recondition ourselves to accelerate healing. However, we must choose it and be willing to step into a proactive approach to our health instead of a reactive one. Reactive means taking action when you start getting really sick or dying. Which is what most people today tend to do. Do you know anyone who finally took action to improve their health after getting sick, a crisis, or a brush with death? Waiting can be fatal…literally. Please don't wait.

I love, support, and appreciate the expertise and work of conventional doctors, they have saved many lives, and I think they are highly appropriate for many acute issues like breaking your arm or leg or getting into a car accident. I understand that they must adhere to the standards of care, medical guidelines they must follow for all patients even if they think a different treatment option is more appropriate or beneficial. However, I feel differently when it comes to chronic health issues like I had, as you'll soon discover. Chronic health issues are modern, more prevalent today than they used to be due to our lifestyles, and often misunderstood. Many standard remedies miss the mark, manage symptoms, and don't factor in the immune potential of the individual. These remedies seem to work as if an individual doesn't have an immune system at all. But we f*cking do! It's just frozen.

Imagine the disbelief when my path was faster than theirs? How could this random Black man that didn't follow our specific instructions, guidelines, and warnings activate spontaneous remission when we were just trying to treat him to live longer than a week? How can a guy that we patronized, ignored, deprioritized, and didn't take seriously accomplish such a mystical feat? I'm not a doctor or medical professional, I'm a human who chose to focus primarily on myself and my inner defenses, and not exclusively on cancer and textbook outer procedures (things I didn't know much about). I did know my potential and my willingness to take responsibility for my situation and do whatever it took to get healthier. My doctors were treating me like I was all the Joe Schmos before me, who had cancer and went through the motions. But I'm Mario, not Joe Schmo, who I assume is some mediocre (basic) White guy. I have different eyes, hair, nails, DNA, immunity, strengths, and weaknesses than Joe Schmo, but clearly that never mattered to them. It only mattered to me.

My doctors were focused on the past with their various statistics, but I didn't want to meet them there. I didn't want to hear about what Joe Schmo did, I wanted to know my personal potential and what I could do at that moment to give me the best possible outcome and fast. I wanted them to meet me in the now. No one wants to be sick; sick isn't sexy! Faced with doctors who only provided me with extremely limited options, potential, and bias, I had to embark on a limitless healing journey to figure this out all by myself, in real-time. My healing journey was exceptional, yet I was treated like it was criminal. No rehearsals, scripts, sound checks, or run-throughs, I was 24/7 live, often broadcasting on social media trying to figure this all out on my own.

My life was on the line, but there was no negotiation about what medical professionals should do. They wanted to traditionally treat me with cancer therapies that would suppress my immune system, indiscriminately kill my healthy cells, and potentially lead to more complications or death. But if I had stage four cancer, didn't I possess some sort of immune deficiency already? It didn't make sense to me. My immune system is my first line of defense for cancer, viruses, bacteria, and all other foreign invaders. Why would I want to hurt it more with outer chemicals that I would have to detox when I could fortify my immune system instead of with natural and inner strategies?

My spontaneous remission came with a cost. I had to cultivate awareness, train my attitude, deal with my inner wounds, face my unresolved traumas, and clean up my backlog of emotional garbage. I had to observe my thoughts, feelings, and behaviors, unlearn the unhealthy ones, and retrain healthier ones. I had to take a good look at my ego, inner child, and how I was conditioned to behave over my lifetime. I had to shine a light on my deep-rooted trained beliefs about myself, others, and the world, and fall face-first into all my fears. I had to defrost being frozen in my stress response nerve state, which kept my mind and body anxious, hypervigilant, and thinking I was always in an emergency. It was really hard and it f*cking sucked!

The mind exerts extraordinary influence over the body and inner environment in ways that science can't understand. But you don't need to understand something to see, know, and feel that it works. I've seen it, felt it, and I know that it works, don't take my word for it, jump in and try it. I had to make the conscious and consistent decisions to take back my power, navigating a for-profit healthcare system that made me feel powerless. I had to look inward instead of outward, present instead of past, and at the whole instead of a bunch of disconnected parts. I had to figure out what truly made me happy, alive, and made life worth living. I had to focus on the positives and what safely energized me. Things like music, dancing, singing, and cooking, fitness, and playing. Safety anchors that brought me energy, joy, and connection in the present moment.

I had to find safe people. Not just people to complain or talk about my pain with, but people who I feel truly safe with. Like my friends Kayla, Tess, and Jonathan. People that I could smile, laugh, and be vulnerable around. I had to create more safe spaces where I could retreat from the anxiety and stress levels of lifelike gyms, hiking, beaches, and even mindfully shopping. Places that weren't overwhelming where I could be comfortable, mindful, and at peace. Once I rediscovered the real story of who I was, my authentic self, I activated my spontaneous healing. It wasn't easy; I trained myself for it just like an athlete trains for a race or a game. My placebo was the "delusion" (laughing as if holding a secret no one knows) that I could self-heal. Not only did I self-heal, I self-healed really f*cking fast.

SIGH BREATH COMBO. (3 minutes)

1. SIGH 2.1 INNERVAL™ // 30 seconds.

Inhale through your nose 2 times and exhale through your mouth 1 time making an audible sigh sound. The higher the tone the better and feel the vibration at the back of your throat. Do this for 30 seconds or 15 times.

2. CORE BREATHING INNERVAL™ // 30 seconds.

Take long, slow, and deep inhales and take longer, slower, and deeper exhales for 30 seconds or 3 times each if you don't have a timer. As you inhale for 3 seconds your core goes out, and as you exhale for 6 seconds your core goes in.

3. Repeat 2 times

STIMULATION. The phrenic nerves, vagus nerves, and posterior thoracic nerves.

2 //

RETRAINING: CHANGE YOUR STATE, CHANGE YOUR STORY

The human body is an incredible biological machine made up of thirty-seven trillion cells with ovher twenty thousand genes.[29] Our inner world is vast, complex, and connected, performing millions of tasks per second. Imagine working for a company with twenty thousand employees where everyone is in constant communication to produce millions of tasks per second. Intense I know, but the point is that this leaves a lot of room for misfires, miscommunication, and missteps of our inner workings if we aren't mindful of how our outward actions affect them. What you "think" you see, feel, or experience on the outside directly affects your inside. How? Because of your nervous system whose primary objective is for you to survive. You never objectively encounter the outer world, everything you experience is filtered through your nervous system.

From the moment we leave the womb, we are hard-wired to connect or protect. Starting with our first breath, we embark on a never-ending journey to feel safe in our inner world, outer world, and interpersonally through our relationships. Like an overprotective mother, your body does a variety of things it thinks are in your best interest, all in the name of survival. Connection, protection, and risk are subconsciously decided moment-to-moment by our autonomic nervous system, a segment of the peripheral nervous system. Sometimes these subconscious habits, actions, and patterns lead to self-sabotaging behavior that can be and needs to be retrained. Your nervous system responds to the challenges of daily life by telling you not what you are or who you are, but how you are. Your past experiences shape your nervous system, but it's your ongoing experiences that reshape or retrain your nervous system. Understanding your nervous system helps you become an active operator of it and therefore have more power over your own wellbeing. Once you understand the role of your nervous system in shaping your

11

life, you can never again see the world without that lens. Befriending and understanding the unique responses of your nervous system is a powerful antidote to the dysregulation that can arise from macro (chronic) stress, trauma, or unresolved issues.

This next section may get a little technical, but please bear with me because it's super important to have a foundational understanding of your nervous system. Your life story is written into your neuro-architecture, especially in the difficult times when your stress levels are at their highest. Your brain and nervous system aren't passive receivers of information: they're actively shaping themselves through what they learn from your inner world, outer environment, and relationships. A single nerve cell (neuron) will maintain a chemical history of the events it has dealt with. Each one has thousands of spines that allow it to connect with other neurons so that each neuron is in the web of feedback. Depending on what you experience, certain connections will form between individual neurons and some will be inhibited. This web and the way it communicates is your unique neuromatrix.

Depending on your history, your nervous system governs how you'll respond to stressors: it could be with anxiety, reactivity, or anger whenever there's a conflict. It could be feeling helpless, freezing, or shutting down any time you need to make a hard decision. It could trigger an intense fear of abandonment when you feel ignored by someone. Although there may be alternative ways of responding to a situation, certain defensive strategies get imprinted into the brain and nervous system. And the more positive your outlook on the situation the less likely you'll suffer the negative effects of it. In the article, *Resiliency on the Battlefield*, recent research demonstrated that "soldiers with a positive outlook in the most traumatic situations were less likely to suffer health problems such as anxiety and depression."[30] Like I mentioned before, our nervous system will do whatever it believes is best to protect us, and those instincts are informed by past occurrences. These occurrences can be times of chronic or traumatic stress that will create hypersensitized connections that arise in future reactions. This may be the automatic path that your nervous system takes when you face stressors today despite the different context from the original stressor that created the connection in the first place.

You may become frozen in limited programming loops, inflexibly using only one or two specific defense strategies whether they're appropriately matched to the situation or not. Without creating other neural pathways, your brain is likely to take the same path in the future whenever you try to step out of your comfort zone, drastically limiting your potential. Your neuromatrix and the ways your brain and nervous system have learned to respond to adversity is not who you are. It's simply what your nervous system has learned from the people in your life and the environments you were in.

The good news is that you can consciously retrain your deeply ingrained habits, create new neural pathways, and change the way you react to situations. What you experience today will actively influence these connections, as they're in a state of constant change. There is extraordinary possibility in the coding behind the connections and combinations between neurons. Your behaviors and responses to stress are a result of this coding as well as the sensations you experience, emotions, and thoughts. The potential you have to reshape your brain and nervous system is unlimited. There can be room for both past traumas and a present moment with new possibilities. There's room for new chapters in your story because your book of life never ends. You just need to consistently keep choosing to create new chapters and stop rereading, reliving, and reflecting on your old ones.

The sensory details that we take in helping us process, navigate, and experience our outer world. Our outer stimuli is its own language. And our body has its own language that predates any written or spoken language in the world. There's no possible way that we can communicate every single thing our body is trying to tell us. Our inner translator, a complex network of nerves, signals, and brain areas that form our nervous system, helps us make sense of what we perceive. But what happens when our inner translator gets tired, confused, or sends the wrong messages? Have you ever sent or received a mistext or wrong number call?

Your body goes into instant lockdown/shutdown, fight/flight mode, or an overreaction based on faulty information.

Your nervous system serves as your personal surveillance team, is always on alert, and constantly asks the question: "Do I feel safe?" The moment-to-moment answer to that question produces a cascade of effects in your body that affect you mentally, physically, emotionally, and biologically; and can be either helpful or hurtful in your day-to-day depending on the situation. Neuroception is one of three pillars of the Polyvagal Theory created by Dr. Stephen Porges.[31,32] According to Dr. Porges, your body uses your senses to detect cues of safety or danger from your inner or outer world and then shifts into defensive (stress response), safety (relaxation response), or depressive (shutdown response) nerve states. Whether you feel safe or not is not a conscious choice, safety is felt in your body, not your mind. It has everything to do with your preconditioned responses to safety or danger that happen below your awareness. If you have trauma or unresolved issues, you will more than likely have a harder time feeling safe, being authentically social, and activating rapid self-healing. But don't worry; I believe my practice can help you reroute those subconscious patterns.

Neuroception is our neurons' (nerve cells) reaction to stimulation and is different from, but works alongside, perception. Neuroception is our body's safety radar and inner sensory system that, unlike perception which includes a thought process, is a whole-body reflex reaction. These inner reflex actions quickly shift our operating nerve state. When we neurocept safety, we then engage in prosocial behaviors like laughing, playing, and connecting, and when we neurocept danger or high risk, we shift into an adaptive survival mode and engage in defensive behaviors like running and fighting. And when we neurocept that our life is in extreme threat, we engage in shutdown, depressive, and disassociation behaviors. Your mind may disagree with whatever you neurocept and may want something else to be true, but safety is felt in your body, not your mind.[33] You can't intellectualize, rationalize, or theorize yourself to safety. Neuroception will always have the last word.

The signals from our environment as well as within our mind and body are automatically processed within our nervous system. These neuroceptions of safety, danger, or life threat hijack the nervous system, rapidly shifting our nerve state, emotions, and thoughts. If you're having a great day and feeling good, all it takes is a trigger that you may not even know is a trigger for you to turn your connection off and your survival mode on. Our stress response is, unfortunately, where many of us spend most of our time. Disconnected from our self, others, and the beauty of life. Although it's easier to shift into your stress response at the first danger cue, it's a lot harder to shift into your relaxation response. There have to be more cues of safety than danger in your inner and outer world in order for you to shift into your relaxation response. And living in the world we live in today, that's definitely a tall and complicated order.

Safety or danger cues will instantly and unconsciously shift your nerve state. This is most often referred to as being "triggered." For the outer environment, the trigger could be a danger cue of someone screaming or a safety cue of someone warmly smiling. For the inner environment, a danger cue could be from hunger, illness, or pain or a safety cue of being properly hydrated, satiated, and relaxed heart rate. Whenever you neurocept danger or safety, your nervous system readjusts mentally, physically, and emotionally for what it's assessing the needs for connection, protection, or survival to be. A massive number of unconscious cues are being always filtered through you. None of these automatic nerve shifts are planned. Like apps on your smartphone or software programs on your computer, they are reflexive and subconscious reactions via your body's automated systems that are going on behind the scenes. For most people, there are some universal things that trigger nerve state shifts like tight spaces, darkness, loud sounds, unsafe touch, wide eyes, monotone voices, violation of personal space, and trolls on social media. These are more of a generalization and will ultimately look different based on things like culture, resilience, and whether a person is frozen in a nerve state or not. In other words, the stress response is not meant to be avoided completely as it is a helpful mechanism to remove us from danger. However, as humans, we spend far too much time in the stressed state unnecessarily. Change will begin to come when we move more often from the stressed state to the relaxed state. There, our body and mind can function more optimally until an actual danger comes along.

STATE STAIRS

As I mentioned above, your nervous system runs all the involuntary systems in your body that are not under your conscious control; they are automatic. Things like your heart rate, blood pressure, digestion, respiration, cell activity, and even body temperature are automatically regulated. Your autonomic nervous system is made up of two main branches (parasympathetic and sympathetic) and it responds to sensations and signals via three different primary nerve pathways, each with a unique pattern of responses that follow a specific chain of command. I'll be going into more detail on each primary and hybrid nerve state later, but here is a little preview.

Pathway 1: Relaxation Response

Rest-and-Digest / Safe-and-Social / Ventral Vagus Nerve / Parasympathetic Nervous system

This newest or last to develop and ventral part of your parasympathetic nervous system state allows you to rest, digest, repair, and self-heal.[34] I call this the relaxation response and it makes you feel safe, allows for connection, executive functioning, creativity, play, stillness, optimal health, and growth. Being in a relaxation response nerve state looks like feeling calm, peaceful, being able to relax easily, being socially engaged, making gentle eye contact, smiling, full breaths, vocal prosody (rhythm, stress, and tone of speech), and eye crinkles.

Pathway 2: Stress Response

Fight-or-Flight / Sympathetic Nervous System

This is the second to oldest sympathetic part of your nervous system.[35] It originates in your spine and is responsible for priming your body for aggressive response and defense to a perceived threat, stress, or danger. I call this the stress response and it's most commonly called the fight-or-flight response; an adaptive survival mode that allows for the arms and legs to be used for evasion or aggression. Being in a stress response nerve state looks like your heart rate going up, anxiety, shallow breathing, digestive issues, emotional flooding, tense muscles, chronic pain, sleeplessness, ruminative thoughts, and scanning for danger.

Pathway 3: Shutdown Response

Down-and-Depressed / Dorsal Vagus Nerve / Parasympathetic Nervous System

This is the oldest primitive and dorsal part of your parasympathetic nervous system that causes rapid shutdown, slow-down, and other depressive behaviors. Dr. Porges calls this the shutdown response.[36] This typically takes place in extremely stressful situations where you cannot perceive any possible escape. It's a life-threatening response and active when the outer or inner world is perceived as life-threatening and there seems like there is no escape. Being in a shutdown response nerve state looks like depression, chronic fatigue, disconnection, digestive issues, hopelessness, disassociation, auto-pilot, body numbing, and low blood pressure.

Think of these three primary nervous system states as separate muscles that can be strong or weak, functional or dysfunctional, and trained or untrained. This trio of primary nerve states work together to regulate your body's balance, or what is also called the state of homeostasis. They follow a chain of command in the way that the circuitry is stacked in the body. Your neurons never work alone and do specific functions in networks or circuits. The specific actions that happen will always follow a specific order no matter what. Deb Dana, a clinician, consultant, lecturer, and expert on the Polyvagal Theory and trauma, calls this the "polyvagal ladder,"[37] but in my book, I will refer to this chain of command as "state stairs."

In safety, we walk up or ascend the stairs to relaxation, social engagement, and self-healing, whereas in defensive states we walk down or descend to the middle of the stairs to fight or run, and if we feel trapped and like we can't escape danger, we trip, fall or descend to the bottom of the stairs where disconnection, dissociation, and shut down happens. The bottom of the barrel is literally the bottom of the stairs. We shut down to conserve energy, to survive, and it's a long and painful journey back up to the top of the stairs and to feeling safe, social, and self-healing again. Our traumas and unresolved issues live in the stress and shutdown responses. Whenever we end up in these nerve states, our trauma and unresolved issues come alive and latch on to us. Trauma and unresolved issues reshape our nervous system so that we prefer protection over a connection, which keeps us in a survival state instead of a thriving state.

Do you feel at "home" inside of your body right now? Your relaxation response is what makes you feel at "home" inside of your body. Macro stress, adversity, unresolved issues, and trauma all make it hard for you to come "home" to your body. When you feel at "home" in your body, you feel safe, social, secure, and joyful naturally. You don't feel the need to do things to try and feel at "home," you peacefully and authentically already do. When you don't feel at "home" inside of your body, you mobilize with feelings of fear, defensiveness, and anxiety or you disappear feeling depressed, numb, or flat.

Home is the state where your body rests, relaxes, recovers, repairs, and grows. Can you imagine not being able to return to your physical home after a long day of work or school? Without being able to be home, your emotions, immunity, digestion, and endocrine systems are out of balance, and this is how many chronic health issues arise. When you're disconnected from home and don't have space to recharge, it's harder to connect with others. It's hard to form and maintain relationships when you don't feel safe and trusting. Your nervous system has evolved to help you survive and is quick to take you away from "home" when it believes that you're not safe. If you're never at "home" and constantly in a stressed response state, you won't be able to relax and enjoy life, and your mind and body won't be optimally prepared to heal, process, and grow. The entire human experience changes depending on whether or not you feel at home inside of yourself.

The nerve state that we should all be in the most is the relaxation response. Ironically this is also the hardest nerve state to get into and stay in. This is the rest, relaxation, and regenerative state of our body. It's also our safe and social state that allows us to authentically connect with others. All of our body's energy is focused on self-regulating, refreshing, and self-healing in this state. Creativity, play, stillness, and optimal health happen in this nerve state. When we are anchored in this nerve state, we can quickly visit our stress or shutdown responses and not get hijacked by either of them. The problem is that unless you're constantly practicing and working at being in the relaxed state, i.e. strengthening that state's muscle, this state is hard to get in and stay in. Mainly because the nerve fibers are thicker, slower to activate, and lose their activation faster than other nerve fibers State shifts happen automatically, faster even than a thought enters our mind, and we don't get to choose whether our systems will move us up or down toward connection or into defense. But the more we look around and notice where we are, the easier it becomes to trace how we got there, as well as manually use tools to move ourselves around the state stairs.

Most people are frozen in either a stress response or a shutdown response. You can also oscillate between being frozen in these two specific states. Unlike activating the stress or the shutdown response, it's stimulating and strengthening the relaxation response that is the easiest, quickest, and most powerful way to help self-regulate and start being in the relaxation response nerve state more and in the other nerve states less. This is what Interval Mindfulness™ and its various Innervals™ are designed to do. A weakened relaxation response is the most common imbalance in nervous system dysregulation and this method will attack this issue head-on.

According to the American Psychological Association, your nervous system plays a vital and direct role in your stress response.[38] A healthy and balanced nervous system is not always calm. It's adaptable, flexible, and resilient. According to a 2018 meta-analysis and review published in Psychiatry Investigation, heart rate variability (HRV) may be a great indicator of psychological stress and finding your stress load sweet spot.[39,40] Your HRV is a non-invasive and simple way to check for nervous system imbalances. If you are frozen in a stress response nerve state due to chronic stress, your HRV will be low. However, in a healthier and more relaxed state, your HRV will be high. The healthier your nervous system is, the faster it will be able to switch gears and relax after experiencing acute stress. High HRV means more resilience to stress, better mental health, greater cardiovascular fitness, a healthier body, and a lower risk of mortality.[40] A low

HRV may be associated with depression, anxiety, and symptoms and risks of chronic stress. Checking your HRV several times a week to look for patterns can be an insightful and helpful tool. A low HRV shows that you need to improve your resiliency to stress to improve your mental, physical, and emotional health.

According to physiotherapist Jessica McGuire, "a well-functioning nervous system isn't built through relaxation: it's healthy when it can respond with the correct levels of activation to help you meet the demands you face."[41] She also says that a resilient, adaptable, and flexible nervous system needs to experience some stress, challenges, adversity, and even failure. When you're pushed outside of your comfort zone, your nervous system learns to function more effectively under stress, provided it gets to fully recover from the stress activation. In other words, it's good for us to be pushed into stressful situations sometimes, but we must have ample time and the appropriate neural pathways built in order to recover from that stress and nimbly move back into relaxation. The stress response should also be activated at appropriate times. This idea typically falls on deaf ears in a society that seems to never stop demanding more and more productivity. We often end up sacrificing our physical, mental, and emotional health to meet its endless requirements. We do not give ourselves enough time to recover from stress and this is mainly by choice.

If you experience stress that's too far outside your comfort zone you also move outside your "window of tolerance." Coined by clinical professor of psychiatry Dr. Dan Siegel, the term "window of tolerance" describes your capacity to manage your emotions even when under stress.[42] This window is the space where you can approach day-to-day life most effectively, handling emotions without losing control, and making clear-headed decisions with rational thought. Imagine a day when you're coping well with the ups and downs of life when your thoughts are rational and your emotions are calm in response to daily stressors. In general, on this day, you can experience emotions without being overtaken by them. You may be pushed to the edge of your window when experiencing anxiety or anger, but you can confidently rely on a range of inner resources and strategies to keep you within your window. You manage stress and return easily to a relaxed state.

Our body is always releasing hormones to try to keep us as balanced as possible. When our hormones are more level (within our window of tolerance), we feel more able to handle situations appropriately because we have the inner resources to deal with them. Within this window, we are adaptable, able to emotionally self-regulate, and deal with triggers more harmoniously. However, we all have a limit of what we're able to tolerate at any given time. When things become too much for us to tolerate, our hormones respond in one of two ways out of our window: either down to the middle of the state stairs to our stress response where we'll experience overwhelming anxiety, anger, reactivity, and hypervigilance, or fall to the bottom of our state stairs to our shutdown response where we'll experience exhaustion, numbness, and withdraw. Either way, your resilience is depleted. Chronic or traumatic stress tells your nervous system to activate and leave stress responses turned on when there may only be a challenge, not a true threat. This is how nervous system dysregulation arises.[43] Stress inner whispers of dysregulation can include prolonged anxiety, racing thoughts, overworking, overdoing, starting arguments, and an inability to switch off. On the other hand, shut down inner whispers could also include procrastination, avoidance, withdrawing, and lack of motivation.

How big or small our window of tolerance is will depend on our inner and outer influences. If we are feeling sad, stressed, sleep deprived, or having trouble self-regulating, our window of tolerance gets smaller. The smaller the window, the less we are able to tolerate things and the more easily we can get triggered out of that window. Sometimes unresolved issues, childhood trauma, and other traumatic experiences can shrink our window of tolerance. Smaller windows also mean difficulty managing emotions, stress, and overall resilience. If you haven't developed effective coping strategies or the ability to self-regulate from a young age due to childhood trauma, you may be frozen and struggle to deal with stressful things in the present and be able to stay in your window.

Re-regulation and resilience tools like Interval Mindfulness™ help the nervous system widen its window of tolerance, rebalance, and recalibrate. This is especially important following periods of macro or traumatic stress. Dysregulation makes the nervous system less able to cope with stressors, and in turn, your comfort zone and window of tolerance shrink. This means it takes less to make you feel stressed. With the right tools, you can expand your comfort zone and window of tolerance so that you're less likely to move into your stress response when you experience times of adversity. Re-regulation and retraining of the nervous system lies at the heart of having an adaptable, resilient, and flexible nervous system that can respond flexibly in the heat of the moment. The ability to stay regulated means you can still think clearly and make good choices that align with your deepest values.

STATE STORIES

We know from the Polyvagal Theory coined by Dr. Stephen Porges that our nerve state is the driver of our thoughts. Our state dictates our stories, what I will call "State Stories." Depending on our nerve state, our thoughts and their intensity alter. In different nerve states, you may think about the same thing very differently. You may even think about yourself very differently.

Different State Stories change in different nerve states. For example:

- Relaxation Response – "I am loved, supported, and appreciated."
- Stress Response Fight – "No one loves, supports, or appreciates me, so I'm going to cause conflict and force them to."
- Stress Response Flight – "I feel like no one loves, supports, or appreciates me, so I'm going to be distant in all of my relationships."
- Shutdown Response – "No one loves, supports, or appreciates me, so I'm just going to give up trying and on life."

As our nerve state changes, our thoughts and their intensity change, too. Not only that, but how we filter and react to the world shifts along with it. For example, if we neurocept that we are in danger, our body becomes more mobilized for running away: heart rate goes up, hearing is more attuned to dangerous sounds, breathing becomes shallower, and we think more fear-based and negative thoughts. In this nerve state, social engagement becomes much more of a challenge. We all have different stories that we tell ourselves in our heads. But where do those stories come from? Because we humans are meaning-making beings, what begins as the wordless experience of neuroception, drives the creation of a nerve State Story that shapes our daily living. Changes in our nerve state create discomfort in our bodies. The brain then tries to make sense of what is happening in the body by making up stories in our minds. It's these stories that our mind uses to explain our nerve state shift when we are triggered. The kind of stories you tell yourself will always depend on which nerve state you're in.

These state stories are there to explain the world and attempt to make sense of what caused the nerve state shift. However, these state stories do not necessarily reflect reality, they simply serve the function of creating an explanation and possibly minimizing the sometimes overwhelming emotional nature of the nerve state shift. So, in essence, some of the thoughts you have, especially in the stress or shutdown response nerve state can be complete bullsh*t, but you will never realize that in the middle of a hypervigilant or depressive nerve state. These narratives can also add to the problem by keeping the person in their defensive nerve state. The narrative can unintentionally act as a reinforcer, triggering self-suffering. There's the actual event that happens, the nerve state shift in response to the event and our perception of the event, then the narrative that the person creates to explain the nerve state shift.

Our nerve states also directly influence our thoughts throughout a normal day. These state stories are not just in relation to traumatic events. In our relaxation response nerve state, our thoughts will be more calm, peaceful, empathetic, understanding, playful, validating, and normalizing. In a stress response nerve state, thoughts will be more intense, anxious, catastrophizing, avoidant, or aggressive. And in a shutdown response nerve state, thoughts will be small, pessimistic, helpless, lacking hope or belief, and devoid of purpose.

And as our nerve state changes, how much access we have to our higher brain functions changes as well. Our ability to think clearly and critically, to plan, to weigh pros and cons is entirely dependent on the strength of our relaxation response. When we neurocept safety, we activate the relaxation response pathways and unlock access to our prefrontal cortex; the most integrative structure of our brain that supports resilience.[44] Your ability to sustain focus is driven by your prefrontal cortex. This is the part of your frontal lobe that's located in the front portion of the brain, behind your forehead—and its job is an important one. The nerves in your frontal lobe help your brain sort through stimulation to decide what information is relevant and what needs to be ignored. This helps you regulate movements, control impulses, use language, focus attention, make decisions, and correct errors.[45] This means that all the aforementioned functions are inhibited when one is not in the relaxation response.

This ability to hold back certain behaviors helps your brain focus on important tasks, improving your thinking and processing speed. Your prefrontal cortex is responsible for executive functioning, which includes thinking, organizing, problem-solving, memory, concentration, and decision making. Without your prefrontal cortex, you would have trouble finishing reading this book, remembering to pay your bills, or doing things on your daily to-do list. Research shows that decreased firing of messages from the frontal lobe results in lower levels of motivation, mood issues, behavioral problems, and a decreased sense of well-being.[46] This helps to explain why most people who get depressed also have a hard time concentrating, focusing, and remembering details.

According to Linda Graham, MFT, author of *Resilience: Powerful Practices for Bouncing Back from Disappointment, Difficulty and Even Disaster,* your prefrontal cortex integrates experiences from the past, present, and future to create a coherent narrative of who you are and how your life makes sense.[47] It's these many modes of neural integration from the prefrontal cortex that promotes resilience. Your prefrontal cortex also helps calm your stress response by chemically moderating or holding back signals from the emotional area of your brain known as your amygdala. When this prefrontal-amygdala connection is weak, excessive anxiety can result.[48] This is why many of the Innervals™ are specifically targeted to strengthening the connection to your prefrontal cortex. When we are regulated by the relaxation response of our pre-frontal cortex, we turn to people near us to help, for co-regulation, or we turn to memories of people where we have felt loved, understood, and supported. We do this to try and make ourselves feel safe and feel that everything is going to be okay. When you actively stimulate your prefrontal cortex, you enhance your brain's ability to plan, organize, and see the big picture; you create the awareness of more options for the challenge or struggle at hand. However, when the prefrontal cortex is not strong, it loses processing speed as well as a tendency for procrastination, a short attention span, distractibility, disorganization, and hyperactivity. According to Graham, strengthening the prefrontal cortex also exerts a moderating influence on the more impulsive and less flexible structures of your limbic system, helping you calm repetitive thought patterns and anxiety.

Survival is the priority, not critical and rational thinking, when we are in a stress response nerve state. In defense, the primary goal is to identify, dodge or counter what is deemed dangerous. We become super-efficient at scanning for threats, but not necessarily better at recognizing actual danger. It's easy to see how this little nuance can directly influence our daily functioning and our underlying sense of "self".

The answer lies with your nerves, and the more you get a handle over your nerve state shifts, the more you'll have conscious control over your health. Learning: is making new nerve connections. Remembering: is maintaining those connections, and training is making those connections stronger. It's like meeting new friends, keeping in touch with those friends, and getting closer to those friends over time. Just like any relationship, the more you communicate, maintain, and strengthen, the more bonded you'll become. Your nerves are the same way. Chronic health issues are simply the disconnection, divorce, and division of your mind, body, and nerves. Are you ready to jump in and become more bonded with your mind, body, and nerves? I f*cking hope so, enough should be enough already.

We were ALL created with a powerful, innate, and self-healing ability with limitless latency. It's an infinite intelligence hidden away deep inside our cells. The power to ambush anxiety, stress, and negativity and accelerate your healing is already inside of you, however, you must retrain, reset, and recharge your nerves to use it. What good is having a million dollars in the bank if you don't know how to access it? Most people wait until they're struck by a crisis, trauma, or emergency before they seek help. I want to help you figure out how to access your limitless potential with my Interval Mindfulness™ method. There's no telling what insightful information or juicy gossip your body has waiting to share with you! But simply opening your mind to it, has already created a new pattern where you're retraining your mind, unlearning what you know, and embracing what you don't. I'll be moving into the concrete information on how to practice Interval Mindfulness™ very soon, but first I need to lay the groundwork on a few more important concepts.

FAST HAND SLIDE MOTOR COMBO. (3 minutes)

1. FAST HAND SLIDE INNERVAL™ // 30 seconds.

Start with the bottom of both of your hands touching; keeping both hands touching slide your hands back and forth as fast as you possibly can. Do this for 30 seconds or count to 30 if you don't have a timer.

2. CORE BREATHING INNERVAL™ // 30 seconds.

Take long, slow, and deep inhales and take longer, slower, and deeper exhales for 30 seconds or 3 times each if you don't have a timer. As you inhale for 3 seconds your core goes out, and as you exhale for 6 seconds your core goes in.

3. Repeat 2 times

STIMULATION. The phrenic nerves, tactile stimulation, vagus nerves, motor cortex (14), and posterior thoracic nerves.

3 //

YOUR BODY WHISPERS BEFORE IT SCREAMS

Our nervous system is in a never-ending chat text chain with our subconscious mind. Sub means below, below our level of conscious thoughts. The subconscious mind is like an advanced software program (think Windows) that stores programs, patterns, and core beliefs. Our core conditioning, which Dr. Nicole LePera, the holistic psychologist, calls the preconditioned self, is patterned responses that most people don't realize can be retrained.[49] When I say frozen, I mean frozen in your subconscious conditioning. Most of us are not conscious of our preconditioned patterns, this is why conscious awareness is the foundation of holistic healing. Without it, we can feel frozen, and we can technically be stuck from a biological perspective.

One of the primary things that Interval Mindfulness™ does is strengthen your conscious awareness and allow you to bring those negative patterns and conditioning to the fore. You can't correct what you can't see, so the ability to shed light on what is in the subconscious is of utmost importance to your healing. Have you ever tried to fix something in pitch-black darkness? Once your self-awareness muscle is stronger, it will serve as a night light, helping to create a bigger space between what triggers, stimulates, or surprises you, and your response. The more space you create between a stimulus and your reaction to it, the more ability you have to acknowledge what you're feeling and choose how you react. You're increasing your body and mind's ability to be resilient. After all, your body can be a bit overly dramatic, and whenever you trigger your stress response, it releases a chemical cocktail (cheers mate) like it's going to die; regardless if you actually are or not. The subconscious mind removes a lot of the decision-making and reactions from the brain and completes them automatically. This is why we can do so many things without really being "there." This saves time and can be great if you haven't picked up any self-sabotaging habits, patterns, and behaviors. Have you? I will tell you now that most people have.

Your stress response is activated in everyday life and when your mind or body "thinks" you're in immediate physical, mental, or emotional danger. It responds to danger cues and activates the release of adrenaline, cortisol, and other stress hormones to fuel your fight-or-flight response. If you shift into this nerve state, you are powered up to respond to threats with an almost superhuman effort and it makes energy available to your muscles to mobilize, fight or flee.

It's your stress response that speeds up your heart, creates anxiety, and makes you hyperreactive while your relaxation response, slows down your heart, calms you, makes you feel safe, and gets you into a self-regulating and self-healing state. Your relaxation response turns on your digestion, but when you feel anxiety, your stress response kicks in and turns off digestion, which is one of the many reasons why so many people have a variety of gut-related issues.[50] There is a constant gear shifting between the stress and relaxation responses with one or the other having a stronger role at any given time. They both can be dominant but not at the same time, and it's more likely that you will get frozen in your stress or shutdown response, dysregulating your nervous system.

Optimally, we should all be in the relaxation response state most of the time, but it's not easy to get into and stay in this nerve state and shouldn't be expected to happen the majority of the time. What's more realistic is to train and access this nerve state more and more until you have strong roots there and understand how to access that space. Many people struggle to be in this state at any point during their day, because their anxiety and stress levels inhibit the relaxation response. And who is not chronically stressed in this day and age? A major barrier to people getting in this nerve state is that stress often isn't small and short term, it's massive and prolonged; seemingly never-ending like the pandemic. When your relaxation response is compromised or weak, you can't drop into a self-healing and safe nerve state.

Three things that compromise your relaxation response are physical and emotional trauma, physical toxins, viruses, and infections, and toxic thoughts or stress. When our stress response is triggered and we feel under threat, we lose the capacity to engage and feel connected with one another. Many abrasive interactions may stem from both parties being frozen in a stress response, which is not an ideal state to be in when engaging with others especially about emotionally charged and belief-based conversations. When you have two people rooted in their stress response trying to engage, rational and high-order thinking is disabled and the conversation will never lead anywhere productive. This is why I never argue with someone online or who is having an emotional reaction. You first have to connect, defrost, and make them feel safe. Always connect before you correct. We all have the same nervous system responses, but how they present themselves is uniquely different depending on the person.

When you're frozen in your stress response or it's out of balance, it's important to retrain your nerves to activate the relaxation response that brings your nervous system back into balance or regulation. This isn't a one-and-done thing, though; you need to consistently keep training your mind just like a muscle until it gets stronger. This optimal state of balance between our stress and relaxation response is facilitated by the vagus nerve, the longest nerve in the body which originates in the brain and wraps through almost every organ in the body. Whenever you see me say "train your nerves," I'm referring to activating, stimulating, and strengthening your vagus nerve functioning or increasing your vagal tone. This is some super technical sh*t, and I'm trying to make it as digestible and easy to understand as I can. To put this concept simply, the stress and relaxation responses are always operational, but there should be a balance between them. The yin and yang pull of these two systems keeps our body in its natural balance or homeostasis. Together they ensure that we have sufficient resources, to deal with life's challenges. For many, these responses are out of balance and therefore remove them from an optimal mind and body to heal and live as healthily as possible.

Why is focusing on your nerves so important? All processes of your self-healing and sustaining optimal health, including digestion, breathing, detoxification, immunity, tissue regeneration, and being aroused, happen in the relaxation response nerve state. Often, it's just a minor tweak, a gear shift, from the stress response to the relaxation response that limits your ability to heal. The problem is most people have a hard time accessing and staying in this state because of trauma, modern life, unresolved emotional issues, and so much more. So instead of healing happening, chronic issues are made WORSE by a frozen stress response.

Another downside is if your stress response triggers too much and too often, you'll get frozen in that nerve state which weakens your immune function and opens the door to pathogens and chronic health issues. This also creates a vicious cycle as chronic health issues put us into inflamed states which further trigger our stress response. When your body is frozen in a stress response nerve state, certain chemicals are released like cortisol and adrenaline. These chemicals are meant to be released in certain situations, but they begin to cause a lot of problems when they're being released constantly. You have opportunistic pathogens that are lurking in your body, and once they sense an opportunity, like the continual release of stress hormones, they start to multiply and hijack your health. Being frozen in a stress response also disrupts homeostatic mechanisms like blood pressure, heart rate, and digestion. When we're frozen in a stress or shutdown response, the nerve state will become so familiar that it becomes normalized and our new normal. We don't realize that we are operating primarily from this state that is supposed to be temporary. Nervous system balance and regulation is the ability to easily move in between all three states, and what we do, think, and neurocept can draw us in and out of nerve states. Nervous system imbalance and dysregulation happens when we shift to a nerve state, get frozen there, and the disconnection is sustained.

When you have any type of sickness or chronic health issues, you're on fire. Your nerves are stuck in a stressed state that keeps your inner fire going. Literally a wildfire of inflammation incineration that can be felt inside and sometimes outside of your body. Every thought, decision, and action you take is either fueling the fire or containing it until you can handle putting it completely out. You can only contain and eventually put out your inflammation fire by strengthening your relaxation response. When you stimulate your relaxation response or vagus nerve, you activate your body's natural anti-inflammatory mechanisms. Almost all disease, dysfunction, chronic stress, and runaway inflammation stem from you not being able to drop into the relaxation response state because you're frozen in a stress response.

Retraining my nerves by activating, stimulating, and strengthening my vagus nerves, which I'll discuss further in chapter five, using my Innervals™ is one of the primary reasons why I was able to self-heal at record speeds. Why? Because your body's nervous system follows a chain of command. Your brain may be the King of your body but your nerves are the queen, and they have to work together to get things done efficiently. Once the king and queen unite and give your body direct orders to get back to balance as fast as it can, the body and its systems follow suit. Here's the kicker though, the body can only receive those orders when you're in the relaxation response state. You can't heal if you're anxious, worried, or don't feel safe. When you're in the stress response or fight-or-flight, your body disables higher-order thinking, goes rogue, and does what the f*ck it wants all in the name of survival, defense, and efficiency.

When we regulate and strengthen the relaxation response, it regulates and normalizes our stress response, we start gently defrosting and we are less likely to hyper react, overreact, be aggressive, or get defensive. It allows us to get those master commands from the King and Queen to get back to balance if we have any imbalances. It also helps to support our holistic growth, health, and regeneration. You can only self-heal when you feel safe. Safety is felt in your body and not your mind. You cultivate inner safety by strengthening your relaxation response. We want our body to do its job internally, not be fighting other people externally.

Your physiological (nerve) state is the intervening variable between trigger and response. The state of your nervous system will fundamentally determine how you react to stimulation, stressors, and triggers in your environment. When we have a strong relaxation response, we are in a state of great resilience and the stimulation, stressors, and triggers can seemingly ricochet right off of us. However, when we're frozen in stress and the fight-or-flight response, the stimulation, stressors, or triggers result in a hyper reaction, defensiveness, aggressiveness, and a sense of being hurt. Or if we're in our shutdown response, we are dissociated (checked out) and don't even recognize what's being said to us.

Your relaxation response is the emergency brake to your stress response, the thing that puts us into "emergency mode." When it's weak and you keep triggering your stress response repeatedly, your body will default to become frozen in an emergency state because it thinks that is the "new balance." The problem is that many people are frozen in this emergency mode based on what they "think" they see, feel, or experience, not always what is there or true. This default hypervigilance makes them emotionally reactive and hypersensitive to everything.

For example, let's say you're walking in the woods and you think you see a snake. You immediately freeze or jump, then your brain (prefrontal cortex) double-checks to see if it was an actual snake. It turns out that it was just a stick. You feel relieved, you've calmed down, and now you're continuing your hike. Your amygdala is the part of your brain that gathers info from your senses to determine if you're safe or if something is a threat.[47] Once it gets hijacked by false alarms it can get hypersensitive and every time you see a big stick you may automatically think and react like it's a snake.

When you're in a stress response, everything is heightened, and even neutral things seem like a threat. This makes "common" concerns build up because you're pouring gasoline on your internal fire and inflammation starts to wreak havoc inside and outside of your body. The constant triggering of your stress response creates a web of repetitive thoughts and triggering emotions, which lead us into a material-based focus where we find ourselves subconsciously scanning our environment for threats, strategizing safety, and prioritizing survival. When you're trapped in an emergency, even non-emergencies are perceived as threats. That means that for most of us, the daily Modus Operandi (MO) is none other than a "daily emergency mode." When you are constantly anxious, negative, and frozen in your stress response, you're in a default emergency mode.

If you're drowning in your stress response nerve state, you can shift into your relaxation response easier with some sort of mediator. Co-regulation is the inner realm of connection. The environment impacts itself and we are all impacting each other. When you smile at me (or a friend or loved one), authentically pleased to see me, my nervous system picks up the safety cue and we have co-regulated; this happens automatically. In nature, our neuroception picks up on all the safety cues of life. Go for a walk or run, spend some time in nature, go for a hike, go to the beach, tend to a garden, and find moments of awe in your day. All these things and more can support our capacity to turn off our stress response, and through co-regulation, the sense of the natural environment as well as the mediators soothing, compassionate accompaniment, can redirect us to marinate once again in the beauty of life, connection, and calm of our relaxation response.

YOUR INNER WHISPERS

Concealing and healing are two completely different things. Western medicine uses toxic and sometimes invasive strategies to conceal the inner whispers of chronic or acute diseases and this can slow or prevent your body from fully healing. They seek to suppress the way your body naturally looks after itself. We have been conditioned to think that healing looks different than it actually does. If your body is doing it, it's not an accident, it's by design. Every inner whisper is a perfect response and representation of how your body is trying to compensate and heal from what it's currently experiencing, what's been done to it, or what's been held inside of it. How intense your body's inner whispers get depends on the need and/or how long the inner whisper, your body's self-talk, has been suppressed.

The truth is, healing isn't glamorous, sexy, or trendy; healing is healthy. Healing is often ugly, uncomfortable, and unpredictable. Healing is a cough, mucous, sore throat, and runny nose. Healing is also a fever, tumor, acne, and an immune response. Healing is taking such a massive sh*t that you have to breathe like you're giving birth. Healing most notably is painful. Healing is all the ugly things that we don't want to see or experience, but it's so incredibly beautiful at the same time. Your body's healing response is an effect. And effects don't cause things. Effects aren't foreign spies, airborne, they don't hang out on surfaces, and you can't wear a face mask to stop an effect. An effect is always preceded by a cause. You can either ignore the cause and just focus on reducing or managing the effects or investigate the cause and eliminate the effects completely and permanently.

You don't want to stop these effects, as they are all ways that your body is trying to get your attention, you want to uncover and know why your body is trying to get your attention in the first place. You should be learning how to listen to your body's inner whispers and help it while it tries to heal you instead of demonizing or concealing every symptom that you feel. As an example, if you have a headache, most people's instinct would be to take an Advil and move on with their day. I urge you, instead, to figure out why you are getting headaches in the first place. Poor posture? Screen time? Something else? Take the appropriate time to become aware of the causes and work on removing the cause as opposed to concealing the effect.

Being "sick" is such a confusing term to describe what the body does to self-heal. Not to mention all the negative associations with being sick, and the pressure and urgency when you are sick to "Get Well Soon." No, I want you to get well when you figure out what you need to get back to balance. However, things are viewed differently if you're a part of the industrial medical industry. They technically aren't in public service and it's just a conglomerate of companies that care exponentially more about making people think they need medicine to boost profits than actually caring for the health and well-being of the people.

When you ignore your body's inner whispers, they graduate to outer screams. Outer screams are louder warnings that point to pain, inflammation, or other imbalances in your body. If people were like cars, their outer gas pedal is too strong while their inner brake pedal is too weak, resulting in speeding, chaos, crashes, and confusion in life. We see this scenario play out in many different variations from the many people in our lives. Your body whispers before it screams, but people don't recognize their inner whispers, talk, or feedback because it's a foreign thing to most. They resort to rationalizing, ignoring, or misinterpreting their inner intel, making their mind-body connection weaker, divided, and silent. They silence the one thing that's innately designed to help them.

We all have uncomfortable, strange, or painful sensations in our bodies from time to time. These sensations are inner whispers and are a source of information. Most of the time people ignore these inner whispers, writing them off as a daily inconvenience, and they assume that they will go away on their own. Hell, I ignored mine for over a decade! However, if these aches, pains, and weird sensations of the body get worse, they will become indications of chronic health issues. What we call "symptoms" are simply an energy expression of an internal imbalance. Inner whispers, visceral alarms, and crippling screams tell you that you're pushing your body out of balance way too much. After blood work, tests, and scans are done and conventional medicine is unable to identify a physical cause of common symptoms, they're called "medically unexplained symptoms." This leads us to ignore the possibility that there could be a mental, chemical, biological, or emotional origin of the symptoms: an internal root cause, an imbalance from which everything stems before it becomes a physical expression. What is your body trying to whisper to you right now?

Inner whispers are the expression of mental, physical, emotional, and biological inner wounds that are dirty. If your inner soil (biology) is already dirty causing symptoms, what sense does it make to feed it dirty chemicals like pills, making it even grimier for short-term relief? Why would you try to clean something with a dirty towel, water, and soap? A dirty inside can't be cleaned or corrected by something chemical on the outside that your body must get rid of. There's a reason why we have nutrient deficiencies and not toxic chemical deficiencies. Toxic chemicals aren't supposed to be in our bodies. All toxic chemicals must get evacuated from our body, and those that don't, build up causing inflammation until they are transformed from inner whispers to bodily screams of some type of chronic health issue. Your body always inner whispers before it outer screams. So what do inner whispers look like? I'm glad you asked!

Inner whispers look like:

- Sleep issues

- Energy issues like fatigue, lethargy, and demotivation
- Digestive issues like bloating, gas, heartburn, constipation, diarrhea
- Sinus issues like congestion, excess mucous, infections, and chronic post-nasal drip
- High or low blood pressure
- Skin issues like eczema, psoriasis, rashes, acne
- Hormonal issues
- Mental issues like brain fog, focus problems, and depression
- Nerve issues like tremors or dizziness
- Weight issues like unexplained weight gain, weight-loss resistance
- Aches and pains like joint pain, muscle aches, and headaches/migraines

These are all telling signs of your body being pushed too far out of balance or a toxin overload. Some of these inner whispers are similar to what people report when they are suffering from some sort of autoimmune issue. The great thing about autoimmune issues is whatever has progressed, can be easily regressed. You are in far more control of your health than you think, and all it takes is a few Innervals™ and lifestyle tweaks to get you on the path to self-healing. Thousands of people have healed autoimmune issues by cleaning up their personal environment and changing up their lifestyle habits. Even simple things like cooking and shopping changes add up.[51]

In addition to our personal health, our holistic health is also the sum of our relationship with our environment—what we drink, eat, absorb, think, breathe, put on our skin, and how and where we live—and how well our body can detox chemicals naturally. As our outer world gets more toxic, our bodies become submerged in an overload of toxins making us collectively the sickest we have ever been. In 1930, there was virtually no large-scale manufacturing and, in turn, almost no man-made chemicals.[52] According to the Natural Resources Defense Council (NRDC), we have over 80,000 synthetic toxic chemicals in the US and most haven't been tested for their effects on human health.[53] Right now, you most likely have at least 700 chemicals in your body that are not supposed to be there. If that wasn't bad enough, the synergy of all of those chemicals mix with each other to create the so-called "cocktail effect", so we don't know how they truly affect us.[54] It's also estimated that the average American adult is loaded with 700 contaminants. Why do you think that is? What can you do about it?

We are swimming in a sea of toxicity from the things we eat, inhale, see, and put in our bodies every day and over our lifetime. Even though technically everything can have a lethal dose, toxins build up over time, keep your body inflamed if you can't eliminate them, and causes you to get frozen in your stress response due to inner stress. Chemicals in our food and water, air pollution, and chemical cocktails in our home and personal care products. Scientists call it "total toxic load" when they are describing the total amount of toxic stressors in your system at one time.[55] Over the years toxins, emotional traumas, unresolved issues, infections, and other stressors accumulate in your backpack or purse of stressors until it starts overflowing causing a cascade of negative health issues like chronic inflammation, autoimmune issues, DNA damage, cancer, dementia, leaky gut, and other digestive issues.

Some toxins that are in our air, food, and water include heavy metals like mercury, lead, aluminum, arsenic, cadmium, and medications including many prescription drugs, antibiotics, and vaccines. Other toxins include food additives, preservatives, and sweeteners like monosodium glutamate (MSG) and artificial sweeteners (aspartame, sucralose) and many genetically modified organisms (GMO) contain built-in pesticides or herbicides. Many foods that trigger allergic reactions like gluten, dairy, soy, etc., can be especially toxic to people prone to autoimmune issues and air pollution, including second-hand cigarette smoke and vehicle exhaust.[52] We can't forget mold, which produces poisonous mycotoxins[56], chemicals used in industrial production and farming, water treatment, dry cleaning, home cleaning, and body-care products. And finally, chronic or heavy exposure to electromagnetic frequencies (EMF) and "dirty electricity"—high-frequency voltage variations/spikes on electrical wiring.[57] We are electromagnetic beings that can be influenced by frequencies, so it's silly not to consider that some frequencies could harm our body, cells, and health.

Inner toxins are sometimes produced by your body or living inside of you. Unresolved, repressed, or lasting emotional pain like grief, anger, and resentment can get stored in our nervous system keeping us frozen and can promote and or fuel chronic health issues. Chronic stress, anxiety, and negative thinking can disrupt your neuroendocrine system and your gut balance; killing off your good bacteria and causing an overgrowth of bad bacteria that will hijack your health.[58] A high amount and or certain species of fungus, yeast, and bad bacteria can be harmful to your gut and be toxic. Improperly detoxed hormones like xenoestrogens can recirculate, bind to estrogen receptor sites, and trigger hormonal imbalance.[59] Lipopolysaccharides (LPS), bacterial toxins, can leak into your bloodstream and even cross the blood-brain barrier, causing an outsized immune system reaction in your body and brain.[60] Yeast and *Candida* produce a toxic analogous to formaldehyde (used in embalming fluid) called acetaldehyde.

I want you to understand that your holistic health is in your hands. Here are some simple ways that you can start lowering your toxic load right now.

1. FIBER. Fiber feeds your good gut bacteria and binds to waste products to help gracefully escort them out. Some good sources of fiber are organic and freshly ground chia or flax seeds and organic fruits and vegetables like avocados, artichokes, coconut, and raspberries. Aim for 35 - 45 grams of fiber per day and ramp slowly to avoid digestive discomfort.

2. FILTER. Tap water contains toxins like fluoride, chlorine, aluminum, arsenic, herbicides, and even traces of prescription medications. Consider a solid carbon block filter as a countertop device or a whole-house water filter if possible.

3. MINIMIZE. Work with your doctor to gradually reduce your dosages and quantities of medications as you experience the beneficial effects of healthful lifestyle changes.

4. CHEMICAL-FREE. Use body care products and cosmetics without chemicals to the best of your ability. If you don't recognize the ingredients, I wouldn't use it or don't put it on your body if you wouldn't eat it.

5.   GLASS. Use glass food storage containers. Plastic leeches chemicals into your food, especially when heated.

6.   ORGANIC. Most toxins are in your food. If you can't afford to go all organic, at least buy organic versions of meat (100 percent grass-fed and grass-finished) and what Environmental Working Group calls the "Dirty Dozen" fruits and vegetables.

7.   SWEAT. Using a sauna or exercising can help cleanse the body of toxins like lead, cadmium, arsenic, mercury, and BPA. Far- or near-infrared saunas support detoxification safely without the high heat of a regular sauna.

8.   COOK. Cook with lower heat. High-heat cooking and barbecuing damages oils and proteins, which can lead to "AGEs, "advanced glycation end products. Because AGEs can age you prematurely[61], be sure to simmer, bake, and gently steam/sauté your food and add oils after your food is on your plate.

Your body is the only thing that can allow you to arrest, reverse, and resolve sickness. No amount of external chemicals can intervene in an internal chronic condition. It can help you manage it, but wouldn't you rather reverse it?

SONG HUM COMBO. (3 minutes)

1. SONG HUM INNERVAL™ // 30 seconds.

Start humming one of your favorite songs. If you can't think of any you can also hum "Happy Birthday" by default. Do this for 30 seconds or count to 30 if you don't have a timer.

2. CORE BREATHING INNERVAL™ // 30 seconds.

Take long, slow, and deep inhales and take longer, slower, and deeper exhales for 30 seconds or 3 times each if you don't have a timer. As you inhale for 3 seconds your core goes out, and as you exhale for 6 seconds your core goes in.

3. Repeat 2 times

STIMULATION. The phrenic nerves, vagus nerves, motor cortex (0), and posterior thoracic nerves.

4 //

YOUR NERVE STATE AND HEALTH ISSUES

Your nerves directly influence your immunity. According to Healthline, 70% of your immune system is in your gut and modulated by your vagus nerve, your relaxation response muscle.[62] Your nerves are the communication and translation that connects your mind, body, and all your body's most intimate relationships. The state of your nerves can accelerate, stop, or delay your self-healing. One of the goals of this book is to help you understand that your nerves are the key to your overall well-being. Training my nerves to rebalance my nervous system was one of the three main strategies I used to activate my rapid self-healing and it's a critical component to health that most people are missing. All the people that are doing everything right; You're eating healthy, you're exercising, you're meditating, you're taking supplements, you're sleeping well and yet you feel like you're just treading water and not swimming to shore. You feel stuck, on a plateau, and like you're just spinning in circles. This feeling of being stuck can be attributed to the emergency state where higher-order thinking is shut down and you're focused on survival. This state makes your brain believe you have limited options, and ultimately you feel defeated, depressed, dissociated even if you're doing everything objectively right. However, as I've mentioned, between stimulus and response there is space. In that space is our power to choose our response. In our response lies our growth and our freedom.

As I've mentioned, when you train your nerves or strengthen your relaxation response, you create and widen that space or window between whatever is triggering you and how you respond. This is not a sexy quick fix, but it is the most effective way to counteract and train your body to handle higher amounts of anxiety, stress, and adversity with grace. The best and most powerful way to normalize your stress response is by activating, stimulating, and training your relaxation response, which is also known as the ventral vagus nerve part of your parasympathetic nervous system. Don't be intimidated by the big words. I will show you exactly how to implement this concept in the coming chapters.

How can the nervous system have so much influence over your health and healing? Here's the thing: your nerves don't know the difference between real life and things that you intensely imagine. Your thoughts, especially when they are frozen in a preconditioned negative and dominant downward spiral, can stop, slow, or delay your healing. The quickest way to change your thoughts is to change your nerve state. When I was fighting the good fight, I didn't own cancer. I proclaimed daily that "I will win—cancer will lose." I said it, saw it, felt it, and believed it. Regardless of if I ever achieved it or not, my belief was the down payment to my success, especially since we know we never get down payments back. My doctors wanted to treat me for years or life, I wanted to be healed in weeks or months. This completely opened the door to my accelerated healing. I created the neural pathway for healing and reinforced it day after day after day until it became a more likely possibility.

Believing is part of the big rewiring as well as taking on positively inclined beliefs. Why? Because you can't heal someone who doesn't believe that they can be healed. Belief is the foundation to motivation or the down payment for your success plan. Even if you miss a monthly payment here and there, eventually you'll pay off the debt with consistency. Can you imagine if LeBron James didn't "believe" he was one of the world's most talented basketball players? People would be like Lewho??? Hopefully, you have already learned this lesson in life (and not the hard way), but you can't change someone who doesn't want to change. Belief works both ways. Belief can fuel your motivation and make you do heroic and extraordinary things, or if the belief is negative, it can quickly extinguish any hope you had for doing just about anything. You honor your down payment and success plan by doing the work and consistently sticking to what you want to achieve. Sometimes that belief yields you something tangible like a car, house, or personal loan helping you accomplish one of your dreams. Or you can say f*ck it, give up, and default losing your down payment, motivation, f*cking up your credit, and having bill collectors harassing you and reminding you of your failures.

I'm sure you've heard about manifesting. According to Oprah Daily, manifesting is about turning your dreams into reality and requires that you take proactive steps towards whatever it is that you desire. It's something that thought leaders, including Deepak Chopra[63], Eckhart Tolle[64], Gabrielle Bernstein[65], Iyanla Vanzant[66,] and Oprah[67] have spoken about. Manifestation can be tricky and seem taboo, but manifesting, or the practice of thinking inspirational thoughts to make them real has never been more popular. However, if you think too hard about it, none of it makes any logical sense. And yet its ideas have stood the test of time. For example, you may have heard of the law of attraction. It's the belief that all thoughts eventually become things, and if you think positively, positive things will come to you. The law of attraction has existed since the "New Thought" spiritual movement of the 19th century.[68] I do feel there is some truth to it, but like a lot of things in this world, it's also largely out of context and out of touch with the reality of many people. We have an overwhelming amount of "manifestation gurus" all over the internet with most of them seemingly off with their brand of Law of Attraction talk. Most are thin, white, rich, and beautiful asking you to drink some poison-laced red Kool-Aid. This colorful mix of capitalism (toxic individualism BS), ableism (trusting people because they fit in with western beauty standards), and classism (equating wealth to goodness and integrity) have made many people do some crazy and f*cked up sh*t, all in the name of "Manifesting."

As a rare cancer survivor, the idea that you can just "think" cancer away with positive thoughts as it's hijacking, beating, corrupting, and looting your body is kind of a stretch. Yes, belief was my foundation for my healing. I have free will and I believed I could heal because I wanted to heal. But you need more than a foundation to build a house or any other structure. You need motivation, tools, a plan, execution, and consistency. You can't just think "I am cancer-free!" and BOOM the cancer is gone. This is why I prefer to use the term "self-generate." When you self-generate, your belief may start it, but it's your energy, actions, and consistency that finishes it.

Here's the thing: You are not your thoughts, but your thoughts are a part of you. Positive thinking alone will not change your material circumstances and may actually do the opposite. There are decades of scientific research and countless studies proving that, often, positive thinking makes us more complacent and therefore less eager to achieve our goals. We get so excited and motivated when we make our manifestation down payment, but lose energy, focus, and consistency of making those monthly payments to create our reality. A recent meta-analysis highlighted four studies that show fantasizing about the future increases the symptoms of depression.[69]

What is a goal without effort? A f*cking wish. You can't sit on your *ss all day and manifest a new car. If you're living on the south side of Chicago, you can't just manifest that the bullets stop flying around from drive-by shootings. If you've lost your job due to the pandemic, you can't just manifest that you're going to pay your rent every month. If your loved one was unarmed and murdered by police, you can't manifest that they come back to life. If you're a doctor or healthcare worker, you just can't manifest away the COVID-19 surges. If you were a migrant that was separated from your child at the US border, you can't just manifest getting your children back. If you're a single mother of five who can't put food on the table, you can't simply "think your way into food, freedom, and happiness." There are multidimensional barriers in place that actively prevent each of these people from doing so. So yeah, you can miss me with that manifestation theory.

If you are in a place of societal, economical, and fundamental privilege, it's much easier to manifest things that help you get further ahead with fewer barriers of resistance. For example, wealthy people can manifest their problems away by writing a big check. Umm... hello college admissions scandal! A trust fund baby can virtually manifest anything. But technically that's not manifestation, it's bribery and privilege. Personally, I think manifesting is a newer, more modern way of praying. Praying can seem outdated unless you're religious or had a religious upbringing. But praying is the same thing as manifesting. Speaking what you want into existence. Affirming what you want to happen or what you feel to be true. They say the original way of praying was to say, "Thank you for (insert prayer or desired goal)" and acting and feeling like it has already happened. Like many new-wellness practices that are popping on the scene today, I think the newer interest in manifesting arose out of an absence of needs once filled by organized religion. And with chronic stress and anxiety running rampant, many people don't have access to a therapist or psychotherapy. So they try to use positive thoughts, memes, and social media inspiration as painkillers.

But manifesting can also backfire for some people and toxic positivity is a thing. Too much positivity, like anything, is bad for you. Toxic positivity is the feeling of acting happy or cheerful when you're not. It's that fake kind of happiness people say to you like "Just cheer up!" or "It'll get better, don't worry," when something really bad happened to you. Do you know anyone that expressed toxic positivity? Toxic positivity can make you inauthentic, distance you from others, and lose touch with reality. You can experience toxic positivity from someone, give it to someone, or inflict it on yourself. You're a human with up to twenty-seven distinct emotions. Emotions are like waves and come and go. We are not supposed to be in one emotion all the time no matter how wonderful that may sound to some to always be super happy. We typically think anyone that is always happy is on drugs. Am I right?

If you're battling depression, anxiety, or other mental health issues, your thoughts could be inherently negative, but that is primarily because you're frozen in either a stress or shutdown nerve state. You could be forecasting doom and gloom and feel you're stuck in this life of misery from all the negative outcomes because of your negative thoughts and expectations. While optimism can be helpful in situations that are out of a person's control, those who focus solely on a dream outcome in their own lives, such as a new job, new car, or finding a soul mate, are perhaps setting themselves up for failure. It's not that our wants, needs, and desires don't matter. To make our daydreams, fantasies, and wishes come true, we must first believe and cultivate the energy, execution, and consistency to see it through. You can't simply think that; you have to actually do that.

Belief is important but you need to feel safe to reinforce your belief. As you've learned already, in order to feel safe, the body needs to be in the relaxation response. It's a lot easier to hold on to faith when you don't feel like you need to fight, run, or shut down to deal with overwhelming issues. Retraining your stress response is important because it's deeply related to our sense of safety. When people are anxious, stressed, negative, and don't feel safe, they get in their heads, speed up their minds, making them feel (even) less safe and more anxious, stressed, and negative, because safety is felt by the body, not the mind. If you can't shift into your self-healing nerve state or your nerves aren't sending the signal that you're resting, repairing, and safe, you won't heal, period. Your healing door will be closed, locked, and chained. And this is the very reason why so many people experience chronic health issues that are managed for years, decades, or a lifetime. Your frozen stress response is keeping your self-healing door closed, locked, and chained.

Think of your body as your car. If you get in your car with no keys to turn it on, you're going nowhere, right? You could "hope" that the car starts on its own without the key or hope that you get to where you need to go in time. Understand that no amount of theorizing, intellectualizing, or strategizing will get you where you want to go without the keys. No keys, no car, and no self-reliance. If healing will happen in 300 miles, would you rather walk to healing or drive to healing? Western medicine puts you on a stationary bike, treadmill, or elliptical and points you in the direction of perceived healing. Most people on the Elliptical of Symptom Management could do 1,000 miles on that elliptical and still not heal, because the machine is literally going nowhere. Sure, you could hitch a ride to healing, but then you aren't in control of your own body and healing—someone else is. The only person that should be in control of you is you. Healing then becomes a possibility that is only harvested by will, accompanied by energy, action, and consistency.

Now brace yourself for a fun fact that's not alternative: Your healing, happiness, holistic health, career, relationships, fun, friendships, and every single aspect of your entire life, all desperately depend on one thing, the balance of your nervous system, which dictates the balance of your biology. This book makes it easier for you by proactively retraining your negatively preconditioned nerves that may be frozen in that state. The quickest, easiest, and most effective way to reset, repair, and recharge your nerves is to retrain them, specifically why I developed Interval Mindfulness™, to help you easily, efficiently, and powerfully retrain your nerves to build resilience. People are not born with resilience; it is trained.

Nervous system imbalance or dysregulation can make you feel like you're at war with your body. You may become frozen in stress or shutdown nerve states or oscillate between the two with minimal time spent feeling at home inside your own body. In your stress response you may feel restless, on edge, have prolonged anxiety, and irritability, and be emotionally reactive. You may use excess caffeine, sugar, or stimulants. You may overwork, exercise too much, overtrain, or have insomnia. In your shutdown response, there may be extreme procrastination, depression, fogginess, chronic fatigue, excessive sleeping, or avoidance. You may crash with a cold or migraine. When you learn to recognize and bring compassion to your own unique nervous system responses, you can dissolve any shame that you may be holding on to. You can see them as patterns shaped by your past, and that anyone could experience dysregulation with too much adversity, no matter how resilient they seem.

Rather than seeing yourself as broken by being too emotional, reactive, or needy, you can see that your internal surveillance system has become sensitized to cues of danger because of being under too much stress. More understanding and less shame leads to reduced levels of stress. These feelings and behaviors came about in service of your survival from what happened in your past. Just like you update the software on your smartphone or computer, it may be time to update your patterns so that your nervous system isn't so sensitized and you can come home to the state where you feel the most safe, secure, and loved your relaxation response. Just like you'd use rehabilitation exercises for an injury that caused you pain, you can use Interval Mindfulness™ and its various Innervals™ to help your nervous system function well again and respond appropriately to what's happening in the present moment. This is how you learn to reregulate your nervous system. You can spend more time in the state of feeling calm and trusting. Where rest and rejuvenation happen. Where you can think, feel, and function at your best.

You can accomplish this, but it's not easy—it takes training. If you're one of those people who are lazy AF, you should probably stop reading now. I'll pray for you though. #realtalk In case you're having some negative thoughts right now, here's a quick Innerval™.

Gratitude 3 Innerval™ (Object/Attribute. Person. Feeling.) // 60 seconds

Close your eyes; using the finger of your non-dominant hand, write three phrases (more than three words) of what you are grateful for on your dominant hand. The first phrase should be an object or attribute, the second phrase should be a person, and the third phrase should be a feeling that you are grateful for right now. After you write all three phrases, start drawing a slow circle and see how long you can spend reliving and feeling the emotions of each phrase.

STIMULATION: Tactile stimulation; prefrontal cortex; visualization; dopamine and serotonin release.

ACCELERATE YOUR SELF-HEALING

The mind-body connection is our most intimate relationship, and like all relationships, it takes honesty and communication to maintain it. Your mind and body can only communicate through your inner translator (your nerves). Your nerves must be connected, communicating, and coordinating, for balance and alignment to happen. If you're honest and communicate with any relationship in your life, whether it's with friends, family, or lovers, what can ever go wrong? It's safe to explore our inner dialogue and remember conversations don't have to be confrontations, perhaps it's time we change the opening lines. Remember we must be in the relaxation response nerve state to always have a productive, compassionate, and thoughtful dialogue. You must connect before you correct to prevent people from shifting into a stress response nerve state. I imagine this is why someone created the sandwich feedback technique so that you start with praise or a compliment, then layer in criticism, and finally end with praise or a compliment.

You activate rapid self-healing by spending the most time activating and staying in your relaxation response. This means you are: resting, relaxing, and regenerating at least 60% more than you are stressing, which seems impossible in this day and age unless you are training for it. We go to school to train for life. We train for professional jobs The military has basic training, and we train for sports, music, and entertainment events. If training is one of the fundamental things we do in life, why are we not efficiently training our nerves to combat rampant anxiety, stress, and negativity that permeates us at all hours of the day? Those things will never change, however, how you react, respond, and rebel against them can.

If you're frozen in a stress response or your emergency mode, it doesn't matter what external methods you use to heal, they won't be effective, because your body isn't making healing a priority, so your healing will either not happen at all or it will occur at a glacial pace. Healing at a glacial pace means more money for medicine. External pills, protocols, treatments, and surgeries don't heal you— YOU heal you.

If you're frozen in an emergency state, your body is mostly focused on survival so it doesn't want to relax, sleep, or even eat. Trying to relax while in your emergency state is equivalent to trying to sleep through a fire alarm. Even if you do manage to sleep, it won't be restful, restorative, and you'll keep waking up. Additionally, when you're in a stress response nerve state, you're going to get frustrated easily trying to relax, meditate, or be mindful, because your nerve state literally won't allow you to. New research by Michelle G Newman and Hanjoo Kim on relaxation-induced anxiety says that these relaxation methods, although proven to be beneficial, can make anxiety worse for some people who have relaxation-induced anxiety.[70] That's not all; do you want to burn fat or build muscle? It won't happen in an emergency nerve state no matter how much you lift. Do you have big hopes, dreams, and needs? You will not achieve them while your inner fire alarms are ringing. The inner fires will always have priority over resources more than anything you may "want" to happen.

We have an abundance of traditional relaxation, mindfulness, and meditation practices (and prescription pills for days!) that are proven to help reduce anxiety, but for many they are intimidating and can be counterproductive when attempting them leads to failure. In my case, some of these mindfulness and meditation methods were nearly impossible because I was hyperactive and was diagnosed with ADD. I realized that a more unique micro method was needed to restore myself, where I could use baby steps to build my resilience and stamina without overextending myself. Where I could use short, timed intervals to look inward to prevent myself from getting easily overwhelmed by emotional energy. Anxious, Type A, busy, and on-the-go people need to be eased into calming their nervous system before the damage of running around all the time catches up with them.

If you don't take action to counteract the damage, you'll get frozen in your stress response, and the new default state of emergency will turn into something chronic, and the thing about chronic health issues is that they don't discriminate. As a health enthusiast and world-renowned Fitness Coach, I had always been extremely self-disciplined in nutrition, fitness, and personal development. That is until I got sick. I was so angry at myself and the world, constantly asking myself *how did I get sick? Me?* People tend to think that only the worst eaters, sleepers, and people with more demanding, high-stress jobs are the only ones that get sick. And then you read a news article like "the death of Steve Jobs," and you wonder *WTF? The guy was a millionaire, brought great technological advancement to the world, he was even a vegetarian and yet he still died of pancreatic cancer?*

One thing that I learned from all of this was to view health and wellness from a more holistic awareness, which defied all previous conditioning I had about being "healthy and happy." I realized I had just been trained by default just like everyone else, and most importantly, that we all have something to heal, which is why illness can really become the warning sign to start the self-quest: of restoring harmony in our lives.

More than a daily emergency, I was living in a frozen state of permanent emergency, can you imagine what that does to the body? To the overactive mind? Having all fire alarms on at the same time at all hours of the day? That's right! No room for healing or recovery there. For me to truly wake up and realize the mental, emotional, physical, and biological damage I was doing daily to myself, I needed a big nervous wake-up call. During the lows of my healing process, all it took was me taking mindful intervals of stepping outside of my experience to focus on the now, judgment-free. This allowed me to activate my relaxation response, listen to my inner intelligence, and guide myself into making the right decisions. I shifted my focus to rehearsing, practicing, and training my positive outcome. It may sound like fluff, but naturally, if we lack awareness and we're always on edge when taking action, we're unable to make the most centered decisions, the ones that not only benefit our short-term but also long-term health.

I self-generated my healing by training my body mentally, physically, and emotionally to feel what the future felt like in the present. I declared my healing in the present. I saw it, felt it, embraced it, and marinated in it. I practiced it, trained it, and rehearsed it. I didn't wait to be healed to feel whole, I already felt whole, and this paved the way for my accelerated healing. The old mental model of reality is cause-and-effect. Because this happened, the effect was that other thing. That old mental model was true when it came to how I became sick. Because of my lifestyle, behavior, and choices, I battled cancer. However, that old mental model wouldn't have served me in my accelerated healing because the effect would have been very far away or unachievable. Traditional conventional methods use the cause-and-effect model, because you take chemical chemo, radiation, or surgery, the effect is that you can reduce your cancer and prolong your life. I didn't want to just reduce the cancer and prolong my life; I wanted to radically self-heal and be able to truly thrive in life. Be a SurThriver! The new mental model that helped get me through my accelerated healing was the Law of Self-Generation. You can self-generate anything you rehearse, practice, and train for. But it doesn't stop there. Rehearsing, practicing, and training may be the down payment, but energy, motivation, and consistency were needed to truly execute my plan.

However, to self-generate, I had to access and stay primarily in my relaxation response. As you've learned from this discussion so far, it is not possible to accomplish this self-generation in a stress response state or a shutdown response state. Self-generation works because of neuroplasticity, which is the muscle-building part of your brain. Right now, you have very different thoughts, habits, and behaviors than you had 20 years ago. The reason is that the nerves and nerve networks in your brain change their connections and behavior in response to sensory stimulation, development, damage, dysfunction, or new information. It changes the way your brain is organized and structured as you experience, learn, and adapt. This is the methodology behind "affirmations" and why repeating a thought or action over and over again increases its power until it becomes automatic and a part of you. You have the power to become what you rehearse, practice, and train yourself to do. Instead of using affirmations, I like to use "activations" where I use one single word, or "A Words" to train or initiate some type of action. You'll see later during my story there were moments where I brought myself back down to earth using a series of words to active breathing, and thinking more clearly before making a decision, or to distance myself from negative emotions.

I didn't naturally have a mindset of a positive outcome in my circumstance (who would?!?); I had to consistently train myself in small intervals each day to reach it. I was scared and fearful AF! However, I never owned illness, and you should never own any health issue you ever face. It's happening to you, it's not a part of you, and if you keep repeating preconditioned negative outcomes in your head, negative outcomes will continue to happen to you, because you are literally practicing, training, and rehearsing negative outcomes to happen to you. 95% of what you think in your head is preconditioned, meaning that it was trained and can be retrained. As I've said, it's not easy; it's training.

Your every thought, action, and behavior is a "rep" as if you are completing an exercise, and the more reps you do of certain thoughts, actions, and behaviors, the stronger they get. On the flip side, if you don't use it, you lose it, literally. All your thoughts, actions, and behaviors that you don't do reps of can grow weaker, fade, and completely go away. Do you have negative tendencies that you don't like doing? Choose one tiny thing you can change about that negative tendency, something manageable, and do that over and over again. Once it becomes routine, you can add in another thing to get you further away from the tendency. All it takes is training bit by bit to create new neural pathways and habits that are reinforced in your mind. Everything is training, and when it comes to your thoughts, actions, and behaviors, they were trained and can always be retrained. With every emotion and thought, you reinforce a nerve pathway, and with each new thought, you can start to create a new way of being. When these micro-changes are rehearsed, practiced, and trained enough, it leads to a change in how your brain works. Younger people can change easily because their brains are very plastic, however, as you get older, (sorry millennials and boomers!) it doesn't come as easy. You become more stubborn in how you think, learn, and perceive. It's never too late, it's just harder as you get older. More reason to be training your nerves as soon as you can.

Here are a few examples of some negative thought patterns that may be strong in you or someone you know.

- Overthinking: Trying to plan for and think of every single possible outcome for a situation. Trying to control things that are out of your control to avoid disappointment, pain, or failure. "What if this happens?" "What if that happens?" "What if this AND that happens?"

- Negative Rumination: Constantly focusing on negative outcomes that eventually lead to anxiety, stress, and feelings of being stuck. "Omg, the sun is out this morning and my pale *ss is going to burn!" "What if they say no, what will I do?"

- Catastrophizing: A drama king or queen. Assuming the worst will happen, thinking the worst of everything, and often exaggerating the challenges you face. This is also amplifying your imperfections and fears and making things into a bigger deal than they really are. "I failed my exam because I'm a horrible student and I'm going to fail college," "My manager is totally going to write me up or fire me over this mistake," "I can't believe how idiotic I sounded in front of my crush. They totally hate me." Etc

- Should Triggers: When you use "should" as a way of motivating you but then you eventually leave you feeling pressured, frustrated, and shame when you don't follow through. "I should be eating healthy today." "I should work out this morning." "I should be productive today and return some of my work emails."

- All-Or-Nothing: Thinking on the opposite extremes or that everything is always black or white.

- Overgeneralization: Inaccurately concluding that one bad experience will lead to a negative future filled with many more bad experiences.

Reflect on the list above and identify if you struggle with one or more of these negative thought patterns. A great start toward healing is the awareness of your negative thought patterns. Regular practice of my various Innervals™ will help you start to strengthen more positive thought patterns. The more reps you do of positive thought patterns the less strength your negative thought patterns will have over you.

LOL INNERVAL™ COMBO. (3 minutes)

1. LOL INNERVAL™ // 30 seconds.

Laugh hysterically out loud continuously for 30 seconds or 10 times if you don't have a timer. Fake it if you need to, it's just as effective.

2. CORE BREATHING INNERVAL™ // 30 seconds.

Take long, slow, and deep inhales and take longer, slower, and deeper exhales for 60 seconds or 6 times each. As you inhale for 3 seconds your core goes out, and as you exhale for 6 seconds your core goes in.

3. Repeat 3 times

STIMULATION. The glossopharyngeal nerves, vagus nerves, facial nerves, hypoglossal nerves, and posterior thoracic nerves.

5 //

TRAIN YOUR VAGUS NERVE (Relaxation Response)

Interval Mindfulness™ and its Innervals™ are unique because they specifically target regulating your nervous system. A lot of people's anxiety, stress, and suffering can be traced back to a dysregulated nervous system. If your nervous system is out of balance, no matter what you do, you won't heal and you'll be frozen, or stuck in the same cycles of suffering, again and again. Every time I have said "relaxation response" in this book, I am describing the ventral vagus nerve portion of your autonomic nervous system. In this chapter, I'll be calling it simply the "vagus nerve" as I get into more of the technical details about it. This is one of those times where we are going to dive deep into the nitty-gritty of a concept. This is because the vagus nerve is so integral to the Interval Mindfulness™ theory and is also deeply interconnected with many systems in our body. By absorbing this information, you will have more power over how the vagus nerve functions in your body. With how important this concept is, it's shocking how few people know about it! So, let's dive in.

When you actively stimulate your nervous system via the vagus nerve, your body responds with a relaxing reflex and optimal self-regulation. Ever wonder why it feels so good after you cry, laugh, or scream? Or have you felt super relaxed after a big yawn and stretch? Those things are actively stimulating your nerves with strong energy and when you're done, your vagus nerve kicks in reflexively even though those actions were active. When you stimulate or push your various nerves, the counter-reaction will typically be a pulling back and calming effect. The key to how much of a calming effect is the strength, time, and dose of the push. We use this dichotomy as the foundation for Innervals™.

Have you ever sprinted as fast as you could for a minute? Or done anything with an all-out effort for a minute? What happened afterward? Were you thinking? Could you even talk? Probably not because your body was too busy trying to internally get you back to balance before you gave your all-out effort. The work may have been intense and stressful, but when you stopped you felt this calming and relaxing wave come over you. We use this stretch and relaxation reflex but creatively, and we focus it on your nerves. Innervals™ work by giving you rapid-fire intervals of different activities to focus your mind for short specific periods. While other traditional methods and practices want you to be calm, still, and steady your mind, we want the exact opposite. We keep your mind active in a strategic, synergistic, and scientific way until you naturally, reflexively, and easily shift inward to catch your breath basking in calm, peace, and quietude, the warm space of your inner perspective. Stress is additive and cumulative, and your strategy to master your stress should be as well.

REFLEX RESPONSES

To understand how and why Interval Mindfulness™ training works, it's important to have a foundational understanding of your nervous system. Your nervous system helps your body perform two types of actions: those you can control and those that you can't. As you read this, small readjustments are constantly being made between the muscles of your back and core to keep you in balance. Your eyes make micro readjustments for every shift of your head and your pupils dilate appropriately to adjust to the level of light and to focus on what's in front of you. Every time you swallow, your throat automatically closes off your airway to prevent saliva from going down the wrong tube. Every breath you take is automatically readjusting to give the right balance of oxygen and carbon dioxide in your blood. These are just a few examples of the unconscious and automatic responses that keep you running daily.

Most of the functions that are critical for life (like digestion and blood pressure) are outside of your conscious control and managed by reflexes. Carried out by the autonomic nervous system (ANS), a reflex is an involuntary or rapid movement to a stimulus or something that causes a reaction.[71] It's a simple (but critical) way your body relays information that never reaches your conscious awareness. The most familiar reflex is the patellar reflex, in which the knee jerks when a doctor taps it with a hammer.[72] Have you ever tripped but managed not to fall on your *ss? (Or maybe you fell, sorry.) When you stumble, your brain tells your body to quickly try to recover from that stumble to keep you from falling; it's your reflex response. Have you ever touched a hot stove, curling iron, or heater? When you accidentally touch something hot, your brain instantly commands your body to quickly pull your hand or body away before you get burned. Not only that, but it also sends a message to another part of your brain to help you remember not to do it again, even though you probably will.

This neuro, instant message exchange happens in a fraction of a millisecond, traveling along your alpha motor neuron in your spine at 268 miles per hour and is the fastest transmission in your body.[73] Porsche has nothing on your nerves! We have "electric-powered" brains, and all of our thoughts and perceptions make up complex networks of electrical signals and electromagnetic fields that pulse and sweep throughout the brain. Most of us take a lot of what the body does for us for granted, and that's a good thing. It would be extremely difficult to have to plan and actively execute every micro-movement we make. Most reflexes protect the body and are coordinated by nerves that go to and from the spinal cord without the brain's direct involvement. Have you ever been surprised by a loud noise? In an instant, the muscles in your arms and upper body probably jerked from the startle reflex. It alerts you to the possibility of danger and makes you aware of your surroundings.

These are just some of the reflex reactions we know about—imagine all the reflex reactions that occur internally that we don't know about. Different Innervals™ play into your body's natural reflex reactions by triggering you to reflexively relax after short intervals of intense, active, and focused effort. This allows you to deeply drop in more and more, each time you experience an inner workout. Reflex actions are important because they are unconscious and hard to notice if you aren't cultivating awareness. When people get "triggered" or emotionally reactive, this is a reflex response brought up by unresolved issues or trauma. With Innervals™, we are training new positive and productive reflex responses, so your old, negative, and unproductive reflex responses get weaker and eventually disappear. If I ask you a thought-provoking question, you will reflexively think of the answer to that question. By tailoring some Innervals™ to asking questions that involve self-reflection, gratitude, self-love, and more, I help you reflexively lean into these mindsets when you probably otherwise wouldn't or know how to get there from a stress response state. There's a faster way to get from a stressed state to a relaxed state, and I'm training you on how to use it.

When we don't know what to do, we do nothing. I want to be your night light in dark times and give you a multitude and variety of Innervals™ to give you something to do and stay ahead of your body adapting to them. When a stimulation is repeated regularly, two changes occur in the reflex response, sensitization, and habituation. Sensitization is an increase in the response; in general, it happens during the first 10 to 20 responses. Habituation is a decrease in the response; it continues until, eventually, the response dies out. When the stimulus is irregularly repeated, habituation doesn't occur or is minimal. Although this habituation takes several weeks, it shows that, with daily stimulation, one reflex response can be changed into another. Repeated activation of stimulating nerves increases their efficiency, causing a lasting change. For example, a negative and unproductive reflex response that you have can be changed to a positive and productive reflex response. When this repeated stimulation ceases, nerve functions regress, and reflex responses return to their original form, just like in regular training you must keep doing the work to hold on to the resilience that you build using this method.[74]

WHAT HAPPENS IN YOUR VAGUS, DOESN'T STAY IN YOUR VAGUS

The vagus nerve (cranial nerve X) is one of the most important nerves in your body. It's critical to your overall health, and without it, the key functions that keep you alive (like breathing) wouldn't be maintained.[75] Unfortunately for most people, the state of their vagus nerve is deeply dysfunctional: like your family arguing around the Thanksgiving dinner table and getting nowhere fast. It's often called your body's "air traffic controller," because it helps regulate all your major bodily functions, plays the role of the direct channel of your mind-body connection, and helps you absorb, process, and make meaning of the daily information from your personal experiences.

Pronounced just like that famous city in the U.S., vagus means "wandering" in Latin, and it literally does kind of wander all over your body, interconnected with your most important organs.[75] Your vagus nerve is a two-way messenger that exchanges electrochemical signals between your brain and body. You could also think of it as your self-love or self-care nerve, because pretty much all things associated with self-love and self-care stimulate your vagus nerve![76] Images of suffering stimulate your vagus nerve (for the worse), and when you hear inspiring, motivating, and resilience-based stories or read uplifting books, they also stimulate your vagus nerve (for the better).[77]

Your vagus nerve is a self-inducing tranquilizer dart that you can use simply by stimulating it. When your vagus nerve is strong, stable, and mobile, it acts like a "hard reset" button for your body after your internal threat alarms have been set off, in response to some internal or external stimulus. It is the emergency brake that can be pulled when you want to stop your stress response. Your vagus sends the "all-clear" to the rest of your body when it gets safety cues that things are okay again, and then shifts your body back to a relaxed, normal, and self-healing nerve state.

Your vagus nerve is so important that when it's not working properly, a variety of digestive and eating disorders may arise, including inflammatory bowel disease, anorexia, ulcerative colitis, and bulimia, just to name a few.[78,79] Plus, if you suffer from food sensitivities and anxiety, have brain fog, or depressive behavior, your vagus nerve is almost always affected.[58,80] If you've been plagued with acute and chronic health issues that have taken control of your life, you have the power to regain control efficiently by stimulating your vagus nerve, and I'm going to show you how with my different Innervals™!

Your vagus nerve is also one of the main players of your social engagement systems. Have you ever noticed that you've been naturally drawn to certain people? Something about their energy, attitude, and presence just pulls you in? Turns out people with a strong, stable, and high vagal tone have these super-traits that make them very attractive to people with a weak, unstable, and inflexible vagal tone. Being around them or even thinking about them can strengthen your vagal tone. They lift you up, literally. How's that for some nerve superpowers?

Processing and managing your emotions occurs with the help of the vagus nerve connection between your gut, heart, and brain. When you feel emotional and are still compassionate, this indicates a stronger vagal tone. However, if you are emotional and negative, prideful, and egocentric, that's a lower vagal tone. No matter the number of micro reasons that doctors, scientists, and researchers come up with for your experience of certain expressions and symptoms, the macro (top-level) reason will always go back to how strong, flexible, and mobile your vagus nerve is.

Four out of the five vagus nerve information superhighway lanes carry info upstream from your internal organs to your brain, while the other lane flows downstream, relaying info from your brain to the rest of your body and internal organs.[81] The more important functions of the vagus nerve include regulating your blood sugar, detoxification, emergency break to your stress response, and regulating your blood pressure.

These are some of the motor functions of your vagus nerve:

• Governs the muscles of your heart, specifically helping to lower your resting heart rate and making you feel calmer.

• Regulates your motility, or involuntary contractions in your digestive tract, including your intestines, stomach, and esophagus, allowing food to move from station to station during digestion.

• Activates muscles in your soft palate, pharynx, and larynx, keeping your larynx open for breathing while feeding your diaphragm and lungs with air

• Stimulates the secretion of your saliva and bile.

• Contracts your bladder.

- Sends messages to your brain to produce and release the "love hormone," oxytocin, to help you love, bond, and feel good.

The sensory functions of your vagus nerve are a little more complex and are divided into two different categories:[75]

- Visceral, where the sensations are felt in your organs.
- Somatic, where the sensations are felt in your muscles, or on your skin.

These are some sensory functions of your vagus nerve:[75]

- Relays powerful visceral sensory information for most of your digestive tract, your lungs, heart, trachea, and larynx.
- Communicates somatic sensation information for parts of your throat, the outer part of your ear canal, and the skin located behind your ear.
- Heightens the sensation of taste near the beginning of your tongue.
- Increases your immunity and longevity.

HONE YOUR VAGAL TONE

Known as vagal tone, your vagal response may be higher or lower depending on a host of factors, including genetics and your level of stressors.[82] It's technically the functional or dysfunctional status of your vagus nerve activity. Your vagal tone is critical to optimal physiological functioning, and a measurable way of gauging a person's resistance to high-stress levels.

The higher your vagal tone, the stronger, more stable, and more flexible your vagus nerve is, and the higher the capacity you have to manage stress efficiently. People with a higher vagal tone tend to be healthier, happier, and more empathetic, while people with a lower vagal tone tend to have digestion problems, chronic inflammation, and are unstable mentally, physically, and emotionally. They are more sensitive to stress, hyper-reactive, frequently sick, and consistently experience depression, anxiety, chronic stress, and pain.[83]

HIGH VAGAL TONE

Everyone has a vagus nerve, and it can be strong or weak. A higher vagal tone is directly linked to physical, emotional, and psychological well-being. A high vagal tone means that your body has an easier and quicker time going into a relaxed state, following an excited, anxious, or stressed state. If someone was being bullied, and you intervened on behalf of the person being bullied, chances are: you have a strong vagal tone. Good for you! Those with a higher vagal tone have increased positive emotions, more resilient responses to stressors, challenges, and adversity, are more often trusted by absolute strangers, express more pro-social tendencies, have stronger social relationships with peers, and regularly exercise, meditate, and do other self-care practices.

From a physiological standpoint, the benefit of a higher vagal tone alone can dramatically reduce the onset of stroke, diabetes, and heart disease. People with a high vagal tone are also psychologically stronger, have better memory and concentration, and are typically more empathetic.[84] Athletes also tend to have a higher vagal tone because aerobic breathing creates a healthy vagal tone.[85,86] Even a healthy, happy, and harmonized heart is directly linked to stimulating your vagus nerve. Way before modern-day researchers began studying more aspects of the work of the vagus nerve, scientists were mostly interested in how vagal tone affected heart physiology. In 2010, researchers discovered a positive feedback loop between positive emotions, good physical health, and a higher vagal tone. Based on their findings, the more you increase your vagal tone, the more your physical, mental, and emotional health will improve and vice versa.[87]

LOW VAGAL TONE

Many people have a low vagal tone or nervous system dysregulation without knowing it. When you have a low vagal tone, you could be in otherwise good health, then all of a sudden get an injury, catch a cold or flu, or hit some type of health wall, and BOOM, it could take months and sometimes years to recover from it, all because you have a low vagal tone. Most symptoms of low vagal tone are very similar to irritable bowel syndrome (IBS), and it makes it harder for conventional medicine to diagnose because these symptoms don't show up on standard testing unless your condition has reached a chronic tipping point. One prominent sign of low vagal tone is how long it takes you to achieve neuro-flexibility, meaning: how quickly do you calm down after stress?

Low vagal tone can lead to anxiety and depression from the imbalance of our neurotransmitters and inner coordination. We can experience stomach problems, motion sickness, liver issues, memory or focus issues, etc. But, great news! the cure for any low vagal tone to simply strengthen your vital vagus nerve. If you're experiencing gut issues, brain fog, anxiety, food sensitivities, depression, and more, your vagus nerve is most likely connected to it, because it innervates all the parts of your body that are implicated in these health issues. People with these types of issues (normally) have a lower vagal tone, which means it's sleeping and slow to do what it's supposed to do. Damages to your vagal tone can be caused by diabetes, alcoholism, upper respiratory viral infections, or having part of the vagus nerve severed accidentally during an operation. Stress can inflame the vagus nerve, along with fatigue and anxiety, and even something as simple as bad posture, shallow breathing, and blocked airways can negatively impact the vagus nerve.

When you have a low vagal tone, you are basically a big ol' hot mess! A lower vagal tone is directly linked to sickness, negative moods, depression, and heart issues. People with a low vagal tone are typically unhealthy, lonely, have negative moods, and are sensitive to stress and disease. A lower vagal tone has also been associated with chronic inflammation, and if your vagal tone stays low, your management of inflammation can become inefficient, leading to autoimmune disorders. Inflammation is not all bad because it helps your body heal after an injury or helps your body kill bacteria, viruses, and pathogens in your system, but when it's chronic, or in an autoimmune state, it can make you bloated, damage your internal organs and blood vessels, and upset hormonal balance. One of the functions of your vagus nerve is to reset your immune system and switch off the production of proteins that keep fueling your body's inflammatory responses, in that sense, imagine: that your vagus nerve is completely offline.

STIMULATE YOUR VAGUS NERVE

You may be wondering how your vagal tone is doing and what you can do to improve it. There are several ways besides regularly practicing my Innervals™ and inner workouts that you can do to hone your vagal tone. Vagus nerve stimulation (VNS) is used in the conventional medicine world to combat seizures, arthritis, drug-resistant depression, and more.[88] Research shows that when you're practicing active exercises that stimulate your vagus nerve regularly, they can be just as effective as conventional methods of stimulating it.[77]

The following are ways to stimulate your vagus nerve:[77,89]

- Deep sleep
- Lying on your right side
- Cold exposure, like cold showers, drinking cold water, cold lake or ocean plunges, and ice baths
- Whole-body cryotherapy and cryo-facials
- Humming, singing, or chanting
- Gargling
- Yoga, Pilates, or Tai Chi
- Positive social connections and face-to-face interactions
- Mindfulness and meditation
- Core breathing
- Pulsed Electromagnetic Field Therapy (PEMF)
- Consuming Probiotics
- Fasting and intermittent fasting
- Coughing
- Laughter
- Music
- Prayer
- Aromatherapy
- Yawning
- Chewing gum
- Moderate physical activity

- Third-person self-talk
- Narrative expressive writing
- A sense of awe and wonder
- Sunlight
- Coffee enemas
- Acupuncture
- Reflexology
- Massage therapy
- Vibration technology
- Visceral manipulation
- Chiropractic care and Cranio-sacral therapy

When you work to increase your vagal tone, you simultaneously increase your capacity for friendship, empathy, and authentic connection. One way to instantly boost your vagal tone is to look for micro-moments of love, happiness, and gratitude during your day. These moments will serve as nutrients for your body, mind, and overall health. Another way to boost your vagal tone is to use the various Innervals™ of Interval Mindfulness™ daily. It's important to know that your vagal tone isn't static, and it fluctuates based on your lifestyle, moods, and daily activities. It's a good idea to work on increasing the activity in your vagus nerve to optimal levels and keeping it functioning at that level because it has so many benefits.

In other words, your vagus nerve is the master of your relaxation response and a powerful nerve pathway that governs your body's ability (or inability) to find calm in stormy waters. Think about the times when you were the most stressed out or experienced a tragedy. How did you react? Were you calm, cool, and collected, or were you anxious, fearful, and constantly worried? Even if you did fly off the rails, how long did it take you to get your composure back and calm down? The answer lies in your vagus nerve.

TONGUE CIRCLE MOTOR COMBO. (3 minutes)

1. TONGUE CIRCLE MOTOR INNERVAL™ // 30 seconds.

Place the tip of your tongue on the roof of your mouth and start drawing a continuous circle shape. Do this for 30 seconds or draw 15 circles if you don't have a timer.

2. CORE BREATHING INNERVAL™ // 30 seconds.

Take long, slow, and deep inhales and take longer, slower, and deeper exhales for 30 seconds or 3 times each if you don't have a timer. As you inhale for 3 seconds your core goes out, and as you exhale for 6 seconds your core goes in.

3. Repeat 2 times

STIMULATION. The phrenic nerves, vagus nerves, motor cortex (1), and posterior thoracic nerves.

6 //

SUFFER CULTURE AND SELF-SABOTAGE

Coming into July 2021, in the US, we're in an unnerving state of a national mental health emergency and it has deeply dysregulated the majority of peoples' nervous systems. The COVID-19 pandemic has had a dramatic impact on the lives of all Americans and it will continue for years to come. It has deeply disrupted the economy, work, education, health care, relationships, and more. In particular, it's negatively impacted Black, BIPOC, and marginalized groups more than others. The unfortunate loss of life, and the feelings of isolation, loneliness, and mental strain that strict lockdowns have caused are deeply affecting large groups of people.[90] The immense trauma and stress for families and friends of those who have died, become infected, or face long recovery hauls can feel insurmountable. The people whose lives have been thrown into a hurricane in countless ways including financial distress, job loss, and uncertainty for themselves and the country struggle to get back on their feet. The extremely divisive politics, the racial reckoning, and white fragility are just added layers of deeply traumatic, heavy, and stressful experiences that people are facing daily.

And this is just talking about people's personal reality and experiences, not factoring in what's going on collectively. The world is a much smaller place now due to the internet and the speed at which information travels and we are constantly being bombarded with information about everyone else's experience. And what's going on in the world and a lot of places we may never see physically or ever be, we can see what's going on for those people. What we begin to see is that not only is there a personal sense of trauma, in terms of interacting with the world and too much coming in, but there's also the social sense of trauma. That people are recognizing now that groups of people are sharing traumatic experiences.

Because we're trained to focus on the different aspects of the outer world to survive, we default to reacting to our environments automatically with conditioned thoughts, feelings, and behaviors. Most of this happens subconsciously below our level of awareness and trains us to innately be reactive instead of proactive with most aspects of our life. As a result, people are sleep-walking through their own lives with an exclusive outward focus. Being focused primarily on the outside isn't good or bad, it's simply limiting. The catch-22 is that while we're on high alert looking for problems, we unwillingly create more problems out of the people, places, and things that are otherwise neutral, safe, or no threat at all. When you're wearing emergency shades, you see and act like everything is an emergency. Every time you trigger your stress response nerve state, you're looking at the world with emergency shades on. With the background hum of a pandemic that's showing no signs of abating, it's safe to say that many people have been wearing emergency shades for the past year or so.

We have this built-in inner guidance system that's designed to help keep us in balance, or homeostasis, what our bodies crave the most. Our inner guidance loves to whisper, call, email, DM, and sometimes scream to get our attention. It does this by expressing different symptoms like a fever, cough, or pain. It's constantly trying to communicate with us, but many people don't understand the language and get confused by it. People are so reliant on responding to their ever-changing outer environment, stimulus, and cues, that they don't recognize inner information, whispers, alarms, or feedback that can serve as a voice of calm, peace, and reason. Or they quickly try and conceal (drugs, drinking, phone addiction, etc) the symptoms of whatever they are feeling without doing any further investigation.

Concealing and healing are two completely different things. Western medicine uses toxic and sometimes invasive strategies to conceal the symptoms of chronic or acute diseases and this can slow or prevent your body from fully healing. They seek to suppress the way your body naturally looks after itself. We have been conditioned to think that healing looks different than it actually does. If your body is doing it, it's not an accident, it's by design. Every inner whisper is a perfect response and representation of how your body is trying to compensate and heal from what it's currently experiencing, what's been done to it, or what's been held inside of it. How intense your body's inner whispers get depends on the need and/or how long the inner whisper, your body's self-talk, has been suppressed.

The truth is, healing isn't glamorous, sexy, or trendy; healing is healthy. Healing is often ugly, uncomfortable, and unpredictable. Healing is a cough, mucous, a sore throat, and a runny nose. Healing is also a fever, tumor, acne, and an immune response. Healing is taking such a massive sh*t that you have to breathe like you're giving birth. Healing most notably is painful. Healing is all the ugly things that we don't want to see or experience, but it's so incredibly beautiful at the same time; kind of like witnessing childbirth. Your body's healing response is an effect. And effects don't cause things. Effects aren't foreign spies, airborne, they don't hang out on surfaces, and you can't wear a face mask to stop an effect. An effect is always preceded by a cause. You can either ignore the cause and just focus on reducing or managing the effects or investigate the cause and eliminate the effects completely and permanently.

You don't want to stop these effects, as they are all ways that your body is trying to get your attention, you want to uncover and know why your body is trying to get your attention in the first place. You should be learning how to listen to your body's inner whispers and help it while it tries to heal you instead of demonizing or concealing every symptom that you feel. As an example, if you have a headache, most people's instinct would be to take an Advil and move on with their day. I urge you, instead, to figure out why you are getting headaches in the first place. Poor posture? Screen time? Something else? Take the appropriate time to become aware of the causes and work on removing the cause as opposed to concealing the effect.

Being "sick" is such a confusing term to describe what the body does to self-heal. Not to mention all the negative associations with being sick, and the pressure and urgency when you are sick to "Get Well Soon." No, I want you to get well when you figure out what you need to get back to balance. However, things are viewed differently if you're a part of the industrial medical industry. They technically aren't in public service and it's just a conglomerate of companies that care exponentially more about making people think they need medicine to boost profits than actually caring for the health and well-being of the people.

When you ignore your body's inner whispers, they graduate to outer screams. Outer screams are louder warnings that point to pain, inflammation, or other imbalances in your body. If people were like cars, their outer gas pedal is too strong while their inner brake pedal is too weak, resulting in speeding, chaos, crashes, and confusion in life. We see this scenario play out in many different variations from the many people in our lives. Your body whispers before it screams, but people don't recognize their inner whispers, talk, or feedback because it's a foreign thing to most. They resort to rationalizing, ignoring, or misinterpreting their inner intel, making their mind-body connection weaker, divided, and silent. They silence the one thing that's innately designed to help them.

SELF-SUFFERING

People also unwittingly self-inflict stress, anxiety, and negativity. They create most of their own problems by assuming that they are their preconditioned thoughts, feelings, and behaviors. Your preconditioned self is layers upon layers of subconscious memories, emotions, reactions, traumas, habits, and behaviors that have been trained over a lifetime. Your preconditioned self's three priorities are survival, safety, and efficiency. It will automatically do this at all costs despite how unhealthy it may turn out for you.

Luckily, we aren't utterly oblivious. People notice what overwhelming suffering is, and many want to bring about change when they feel that they are suffering. But most of the time those changes are short-lived. Why is change so hard for people? Because the brain, body, and nerves view change as life-threatening, and you're trying to work against a lifetime of trained behavior and learned beliefs, which can throw a thousand pounds of resistance to change (if not done properly). The resources we rely on to make change happen are also limited just like how long you can hold your breath, your attention, self-control, motivation, etc have limits. When you're trying to change too much at one time it places unrealistic demands on those limited resources.

People also forget that other areas of our lives keep going and need those important resources as well. Your body and all of its interconnected systems aren't a dictatorship, but instead an ecosystem. For many people, regret, fear, guilt, and shame cycles are powerful catalysts to make changes in their life, but negative emotions are terrible fuel for making life changes that stick. Desperation never yields great results, unless you're on the reality tv show "Survivor." Just ask most dieters who fail, the number of wasted daters who try and get "lucky" on the first date, or the people who cancel their gym memberships two months after their new year's resolution.

We all have personal behaviors that we want to stop, start, or alter, but since change is heavily associated with fear, anxiety, and risk, people would rather default to what's familiar, comfortable, and deemed safe, even if it causes unrelenting suffering. Better the devil you know than the one that you don't. Rather than authentically feel what they have been avoiding and move to a healthier place, they will go back into autopilot because it feels safe, comfortable, and it's what they know.

Suffering for most people is very familiar thanks to sports, TV, movies, and news media. We live in a subconscious silent suffering culture where suffering is normalized, glamorized, and monetized to the point that we have become desensitized to it. Suffer culture has made us complacent, numb, and emotionally addicted to all things that involve some type of suffering. The news is severely traumatizing, just a never-ending loop or clickbait of everything wrong going on in the world. Suicides, deaths, pandemics, police brutality, conflicts, mass shootings, election information and misinformation, homicides, and more negative headlines. As soon as there is a mass shooting, we quickly click and read or watch the details of it, as it's played over and over again. Personally, re-traumatizing ourselves with someone else's experience. The news is like "Trauma On-Demand!" The same goes with anything that's a tragedy, as soon as the news hits, like clockwork we are consuming and trying to suck up every single detail of it as well as the opinions of it not only from all the different experts and pundits, but from our family, friends, and coworkers that LOVE sharing their opinions about the latest news.

If you turn on the radio, what do you hear? A majority of pop, contemporary, and top 40 songs about trauma, f*cked up relationships, break-ups, makeups, cheating, lying, and abuse. All suffering. If you listen to rap and hip-hop, what song is NOT about any kind of suffering, grudges, shootings, death, conflict, violence, or trauma? Don't even get me started on rock and roll and heavy metal which triggers an instant stress response the moment you start listening to it. You can argue that some artists turn their suffering into art, and that's valid. However, although that may help them feel better, it's a different effect on the people who are consuming their art. They are pouring all of their pain, suffering, trauma, and worries into a trauma cake and sending it out to the world for everyone to see and eat. Creating trauma and consuming trauma are two different things. You don't have to eat what you made! Have you ever thought about the mental health of the people on the receiving end of art that's rooted in frustration, suffering, trauma, conflict, and abuse? You can't resolve, relieve, or reverse these traumas for yourself effectively when you're constantly consuming it, swimming in it, reliving it, and developing an addiction to it from repetition and routinization.

So what do I mean when I say that we now live in a subconscious silent suffer culture? The turn of the twenty-first century has seen a radical shift in the way we view mental health issues. Previously, it was viewed as a taboo and those that struggled with it, when brave enough to reveal their struggles, were labeled weak, scorned, and forced through traumatizing medical procedures like lobotomies (removing a part of your brain.) Today our prior reservations with it have been replaced with empathy and our judgment has been cleared through coming to a better understanding of it. Even though social media has contributed to the rise in insecurities, thanks to it the discussion surrounding mental health is at an all-time high.

One could argue that it was the past that valued perfection; now, it is admirable to be vulnerable. From meditation to medication, all methods are applauded today as ways people heal themselves from mental health issues. But the conversation has started to shift from healthy discussion around creating awareness and helping people who suffer from mental health issues to the total glamorization of it. A new silent subconscious suffer culture has emerged where people wallow in sadness, despair, and choose not to seek help in various social media communities. Having someone to relate to is always helpful, but misery loves company and certain unhealthy narratives become perpetuated. These communities create a positive feedback loop where the glamorization of those who suffer is rewarded, encouraging that behavior and steering those who suffer away from long-term solutions that will ultimately benefit their mental health. So they default to feeling supported in their silent suffering.

With COVID-19 clouding the world with uncertainty, more people than ever before are prioritizing their mental health. Societal, racial, and political divisions are colliding. Confronting these raging, rampant issues has both drained and energized all of us. And while social media has been instrumental in facilitating conversations about our mental health, it's also necessary to point out the consequences of such openness. Pop culture has glamorized, romanticized, and glorified what it means to have a mental illness. If you use social media, you are familiar with the idea of the "aesthetic" of posts, be it the color scheme of your Instagram photos or the poetic theme of your captions.

Mental illness cannot be stylized or portrayed in aesthetic fonts. There is nothing trendy, nothing cutesy, about it. Mental illness is a devastating, insidious thing, wreaking havoc everywhere. Some people even go as far as to think some mental health issues are "cooler" than others. They want to have anxiety, depression, or OCD, not bipolar disorder, schizophrenia, or psychotic episodes There's even some racial bias when it comes to mental health disorders. People empathize and want to be associated with the mental health issues of Lana Del Rey while calling Kanye West "crazy" because he struggles with bipolar disorder. The question arises: who is allowed to be mentally ill in our country? And what presentation of that illness is appropriate and sexy? What presentation goes too far into a reality that people are not interested in consuming the content any longer?

In the digital age, a new culture has started to glamorize the notion of anxiety, suicide, violence, domestic and drug abuse, depression, and countless other mental health issues. If you look on social media, you can find tons of memes that minimize mental health issues like anxiety and depression to a temporary feeling capable of being portrayed through simplified text and dark edits. "Look at me depressed, gracefully crying, and looking out a window." While the internet offers the opportunity for people to build community around shared mental struggles like never before, these romanticized portrayals seem alarmingly more dedicated to "flexing" one's inner turmoil through likes and follows than seeding a community. Even those that don't suffer from mental illness mine their experience for something troublesome to hook followers. This has been coined as "trauma porn," a tactic that influencers use to elicit engagement.[91] This invalidates real mental illness, makes it seem relatable and even desirable. Social media removes us from the reality that mental illnesses are ugly, serious disorders that people should be encouraged to receive help for if at all possible. Suffering is not beautiful. Mental illness is not something to be admired and glorified. This becomes a difficult conversation, too, when much of the "help" prescribed in the traditional medical world is medication, a band-aid for a much larger problem.

Countless memes, merchandise, and marketing are really money-making ploys and subliminal manipulation aimed at seeming relatable. Don't even get me started on our collective obsession with relatability. Society has normalized mental illness, which is suffering, as well as commercialized, glamorized, and romanticized it, which has created this subconscious silent suffer culture. We obsessively indulge in the personal stories of celebrity overdoses, the promotion of anorexia, relationship break-ups, and self-harm among other things. Anxiety and depression have become trendy on social media because pop culture has portrayed it as "beautiful suffering" that can be rectified quickly just by meeting some basic human need that one is lacking.

It's great to see mental illness more accepted and discussed in movies and pop culture overall, but it is essential to make sure we know the facts behind these mental health issues and not just what Hollywood shows. No one is going to save you from your anxiety, depression, abusive relationship, drug problem, or any other mental health struggle, but you. In particular, depression is scary, dirty, tragic, sad, and all around you. Depression should not be glamorized or romanticized. The real effects of depression should be talked about and discussed.

Depression is something that millions of people suffer from every year. Another way pop culture misses the mark is by portraying depressed characters as low-functioning and struggling in life 100% of the time. This is not always the case. There are tons of high-functioning people suffering from depression. Many people can effectively manage their bills, career, social life, commitments, and other people all while silently suffering from depression. These commitments can play a role in how depression is brought on, but those who suffer from it try to function well enough to take care of their basic responsibilities, and some with high functioning anxiety and depression are even lauded as the highest performing in their departments at work, the most social, the best parents. This dangerous trend of falsely portraying anxiety, depression, and other mental health issues threatens the already fragile well-being of more people than ever before.

We weren't born to suffer, we were born to survive, adapt, and thrive. Intervals of suffering are expected in human life. If you are a human being that is breathing and living, you can't escape intervals of trauma, sadness, terror, and pain. That's what makes us human and our experiences in life unique. But why are people constantly consuming, swimming in, and re-living suffering? Why do people constantly complain, vent, and emotionally dump on friends, family, and co-workers the WORST things that happen to them? The root of most people's suffering that's hidden below their superficial suffering, is the fact that they don't realize they have a preconditioned self that is self-sabotaging. They think their personality full of unconscious behaviors, thoughts, reactions, and emotional addictions is really who they are. Even if it's constantly causing repetitive cycles of frustration, stress, disease, or pain.

As we've discussed, your brain, nerves, and preconditioned-self love to cling to what's familiar, efficient, and avoids risk. So, any type of change is viewed and treated like possible death. It doesn't want to die so your brain and body will do whatever they can to automatically resist, as soon as willpower and motivation run out. And make no mistake, willpower, and motivation do run out. No matter how motivated you may seem to make changes in your life, if you're just relying on motivation, you're setting yourself up for failure. Motivation is a feeling, and just like other feelings like being sad, happy, or angry, they don't last. Don't get me wrong, motivation can be a great thing; it helps us to energize, focus, and take action. When we're motivated, we can feel invincible, resilient, and do extraordinary things; but it's a fleeting feeling. Eventually, motivation starts to go away so that you can feel something else, and that's when people get shady, lazy, and shift back into their sleeping freeze response, or auto-pilot mode.

Have you ever heard someone say "This is just who I am?" No, it's who you have trained yourself to be. Most people are sleepwalking and don't realize that they are so much more fundamentally than their preconditioned personality. We've been told false stories that our personality is a fixed system of "who we are" or "who we're supposed to be," making it difficult to want, seek, or hope for any type of change to unhealthy thoughts, feelings, and behaviors. Changes then feel life-threatening no matter how you try and go about doing them. Your personality is your "personal reality" of how you experience the world from your limited perspective. Your personality is the "you" you learned to be from the earliest years of your life, based on the perceptions of those whose love, attention, and care you desperately needed.

One of the people I admire, Dr. Nicole LePera (The Holistic Psychologist), talks a lot about the idea of the preconditioned Self.[49] From the moment we are born, our outer world trains us to live, breathe, feel, and perceive in the first and most superficial layer of our awareness. In an attempt at survival and creating safety, we're told a massive number of stories of who we are, what we're supposed to do, and how we're supposed to act in the world by our parents or caregivers. Our mothers, fathers, and caregivers, whom we trust and love deeply, mean well, but with a limited perspective, they can only teach or model things that they've learned themselves. They serve as our mental, emotional, and physical examples of behavior, and our preconditioned self never questions anything it learned or witnessed growing up. However, if they don't know how to properly manage emotions, deal with stress, engage in healthy behaviors, or possess any other critical life skills, they can't really pass them on to you.

We learn more than we realize from our parents and caregivers. We're like little sponges soaking up gigabytes of information like how to communicate, manage emotions, cope with challenges, and how to be in different relationships. It's the start of the ego concept of who you are. "I am fun." "I'm not good at sports." "I can't be a doctor." etc. These are all mental constructs or internalized beliefs about who we are. We call it our personality and really believe that that's who we are. Our parents and caregivers are just human and doing the best that they can. See them as unconscious participants in a cycle of generational and inherited trauma. Repeating what they know, doing what has been done to them, and acting out their own past.

Even though our parents and caregivers play a huge role in the stories we tell ourselves about ourselves, the media and the various systems we access in society do as well. A term that has been featured often in media and politics lately is the "glass ceiling." It's a metaphor referring to an artificial barrier that prevents women and minorities from being promoted to managerial- and executive-level positions within an organization. We live in a male-dominated society and often the barriers that women face in the workforce are unwritten and a normalized form of implicit bias. This term has been especially relevant this year with Kamala Harris being the first Black, Indian, and woman in history to ever be elected Vice President. This means that for the first time Black, Brown, and Indian girls can see the Vice Presidency and Presidency as possible for them. Before that moment, they would only see those two top positions as men and not possible for them. These patterns and limitations condition us as a society, influencing what we believe is possible for us, and ultimately, who we believe ourselves to be.

As we get older and into our teen years, we start to observe those around us with great admiration and a desire for emulation. We tend to copy the mannerisms of the people we look up to, especially celebs, TV/movie stars, and people on social media even though these people are presented in a very superficial way. Because of our social media-crazed society, teens are conditioned to feel that how they look is one of the most important aspects of who they are. It's these early life assumptions, relationships, and experiences in childhood that carry over to dysfunction and self-suffering in adulthood. Things like not having basic needs met, self-betrayal, emotional abandonment, and insecurity on different levels can express themselves in your actions and personality later in life without you even realizing it.

It's this combination of conditioning that forces our brain and nerves to create a task force to cope. A task force that has daily briefings and meetings, and only wants to hear, talk, or think about familiar things. A super survival mode where the body is always in a state of emergency. A state that's externally focused, alert, and makes you never feel safe. A default emergency that has your brain repeating cycles of intrusive, obsessive, and negative thoughts. A state where most people are looking through dysfunctional, distorted, and narrow trauma glasses in how they experience life, situations, and other people. Everything that everyone does is personal, and everyone is a threat. "They did this to me" "They did that to me" "Why is this happening to me?" etc. One of the illusions of living in an emergency state is that the things people do to us are our fault, for being who we are and how we are. It may not make sense to certain people on the outside looking in, but our preconditioned self doesn't question anything it witnessed or learned growing up, it just goes, does, and reacts.

Then, instead of growing into adulthood, we are jolted into a self that is structured solely on conditioning that we had no power over. We go on, day to day, like robots, asleep in our own lives and with no awareness of the conditioning and influences that landed us there. We create layers upon layers of coping mechanisms, personality patterns, and negative behavioral adaptations to help us survive as adults. Many of these were needed when we were younger but no longer serve us now, and we can't seem to let them go. From the stranger who cut us off in traffic, to a family member who forgot our birthday, to our partner who should have "just known" better, we assign meaning and narrative to every one's behavior.

And more often than not, that narrative is rooted in our past conditioning and how our psyche chooses to protect us.

We behave based on our past and project it onto everyone we meet. We automatically act based on how we learned to treat people, process emotions, and cope. I speak from a place of experience, not of judgment; I walked around frozen and unconsciously sleepwalking for over a decade. I was on autopilot until cancer woke me up. Awakening is coming to the painful realization that we've been deeply conditioned. I had to sit with myself and unpack all the hurtful, traumatic, and trained beliefs and start slowly shedding them. The old parts of me had to die for me to live. At the core of my pain and suffering in this world were my inner wounds, unresolved trauma, and the false beliefs I carried about myself because of it. My body was inner screaming because I was so exhausted and deep in my suffering that I had no choice but to wake up and stop sleepwalking through life. I had to practice witnessing myself and being present in my body to feel everything that I had been avoiding, everything that I had been distracting myself from. Pain, shame, and other emotions came rushing in. This is actually protection; an inner alarm going off telling me that this is new, I feel unsafe and uncomfortable.

Before cancer woke me up, I was frozen going in the same negative circles, engaging in the same dysfunctional patterns, and having the same undesirable outcomes no matter how hard I tried to change. Then I started to slowly realize that I was unwittingly seeking out what was continually causing me pain. I had an emotional addiction to stress, chaos, and emotional abandonment stemming from my unstable and chaotic childhood that included losing both of my parents. Many people are (unknowingly) emotionally addicted to stress, chaos, and emotional abandonment. I was addicted to all three for most of my adult life until I woke up. Whenever you feel these emotions, they cause a strong chemical cocktail to be released and create hormonal responses in the body. The mind and body learn these emotional states, get addicted to them, and then covertly seek to recreate them, because they feel familiar. A false sense of safety.

Chaos is one of the biggest collective emotional addictions. Chaos is complete disorder and confusion and it's a general term for feeling emotionally, mentally, and physically activated. Judgment, gossip, drama, uncertainty, and more can be involved in activating chaos. Chaos is mainstream but it is also a form of suffering. I gave many examples earlier of the different types of suffering. The Trump presidency, regardless of how you personally feel about him, was undeniably chaotic at all times. Conflict, trauma, drama, gossip, bullying, firing, lying, cheating, gaslighting, and more are all elements of chaos. TV, movies, reality TV, music, the news, and a majority of entertainment is created around chaos. It's so normalized that if you're aren't aware, like most people, you don't understand the subtle grip it has on you. It creates a massive distraction from ourselves, from our ego, inner wounds, and unresolved trauma. Chaos allows you to feel alive while also allowing you to avoid your inner pain. One big reason why all things chaos sells is because people have grown fond of chaos, it's an outlet and form of escape for most people. Chaos is the most brilliant coping mechanism. At our core, most of us are so deeply disconnected from ourselves and others, that we get desperate for any type of connection despite it being the extension of familiar chaos.

Now, if chaos, stress, and other negative emotions are so bad for us, why do people keep engaging them over and over again? We have something called the homeostatic impulse, a part of the nervous system that regulates things like breathing, heartbeat, and body temperature. It regulates hundreds of chemicals in our billions of cells so that we can operate physically in optimal balance. It also regulates us mentally. Our mind is constantly filtering and bringing to our attention information and stimulation that affirms our preconditioned beliefs, also known as confirmation bias in psychology. This keeps us thinking and repeating familiar thoughts, behavior, and emotions that mimic and mirror that of our past. So, people are subconsciously repeating these emotional states of stress, chaos, frustration, and pain, getting trapped in a hurricane of suffering that makes us feel stuck and powerless to change. The trauma of experiencing chronic levels of these emotions makes us unable to feel other emotional states. Therefore we (unconsciously) seek out the stress, chaos, and frustration so that we can finally FEEL.

After experiencing trauma, what follows is generally a dull and numb existence until we are in the familiar of stress, chaos, frustration, and pain, then we become emotionally activated and feel again. Feeling anything, even if it's negative, is better than feeling nothing to most people. I used to always seek out relationships where I would experience emotional abandonment because that's all I knew. Of course, I wasn't aware that I was gravitating toward these relationships, but subconsciously, they felt comfortable to me because they matched the definition I already had of what a relationship looked like, and so confirmed a bias I didn't even know I had. I learned relationships in a dysfunctional way. I learned that I won't be seen, heard, and connected with emotionally, so I always repeated that pattern in cycles. It's a misunderstood addiction that requires work to release. Many people don't feel safe and are sleepwalking with red "check engine" lights going off for all different areas of their bodies. This book is about becoming aware of those lights, pulling over, and slowly addressing the root issues that have those lights going off in the first place. Resolving stress, watching your thoughts, eating healthier, and living a more balanced life.

The reason chronic health issues and their symptoms arise is to make your body aware of the imbalance and the necessary healing, not suffering and death. However, for you to heed their powerful messages, you must take responsibility for the experience and transform fear into faith, faith that you have the inner resources to create your own healing path that's unique to you. You don't need to follow someone else's book or path. You can do what feels right to you.

I've lived in this cycle for almost my entire adult life. If I felt peace, or that there wasn't some drama, stress, or crisis in my life, I'd feel annoyed, restless, and anxious. I'd pick fights with friends, stir the pot with my partner, or I'd connect with people to whom I could vent, complain, and re-live stress. Your brain is built to reinforce and regulate your life. You will always reinforce unhealthy thoughts, feelings, habits, and reactions until you become conscious. You will always trigger self-suffering until you become aware that you are not your past, your patterns, or the coping mechanisms you needed to survive. Don't wait until cancer or some other chronic health issue tries to kill you before you wake the f*ck up.

SHOULDER DROP COMBO. (3 minutes)

1. SHOULDER DROP INNERVAL™ // 30 seconds.

As you inhale through your nose lift both shoulders as high and forward as you can tensing them up, and as you exhale drop both of your shoulders down and back. Do this for 30 seconds or 15 times if you don't have a timer.

2. CORE BREATHING INNERVAL™ // 30 seconds.

Take long, slow, and deep inhales and take longer, slower, and deeper exhales for 30 seconds or 3 times each if you don't have a timer. As you inhale for 3 seconds your core goes out, and as you exhale for 6 seconds your core goes in.

3. Repeat 2 times

STIMULATION. The phrenic nerves, vagus nerves, motor cortex (17), and posterior thoracic nerves.

7 //

WHY THE INTERVAL APPROACH?

If you're reading this book, I suspect that you resonate with this idea of feeling frozen or used to think that you were "broken". Maybe you're sleepwalking through life on autopilot or spinning in circles and going through the same cycles even though you're desperate for change. Maybe you know you need to change or you know you need transformation, but just don't know exactly what that could look like for you because you feel like you've tried everything. Maybe some type of trauma, crisis, or emergency has happened to you or a loved one recently or at some point in the past. I imagine maybe you have googled like crazy, tried all the things, went down several rabbit holes, maybe even taken medications to manage symptoms, and still haven't found something that truly works for you or something that you feel like you can consistently stick to.

Are you feeling tired, unfocused, and burned out? Do you have a hard time giving yourself mental, physical, and emotional breaks during your busy day? Or at the very least, maybe you're just looking for a non-traditional solution that will give you an easier, faster, and more efficient way to reduce your anxiety and stress levels for whatever challenge you are currently facing. An easy-to-follow, digestible, and sustainable method without all the woo woo, rituals, rules, and belief systems. Whatever the reason you are here, I'm really glad that you are. Know that however hard things may be for you right now, if you're committed to your own self-healing, your breakdowns will become breakthroughs. You can be a hot mess and a masterpiece at the same time; I call that a "hot masterpiece." You may look and feel like you don't have your sh*t together right now but with a little bit of inspiration, creativity, clarity, and consistency, you'll be a Hot Masterpiece in no time! The first step to getting unfrozen is shifting into your relaxation response nerve state and I prefer using an interval-based approach over a traditional one.

If you have anxiety, stress, and unresolved trauma, there's no shortage of unhealthy and healthy ways to address them. You have shopping, video games, tv/movies/streaming, alcohol, sugar, food, or recreational drugs. Or on the healthier side, you have exercise, meditation, mindfulness, yoga, nature, and other mindful practices. All of these different strategies are great, but many of these solutions reveal in the end how they are simple symptom management techniques that are often short-term, superficial, and end up doing more harm than good for some people. For all the vast amount of tried-and-true traditional approaches out there for addressing anxiety and stress, there are very few innovative solutions that exist that meet people in the middle of where they are.

Before you try and sit down and watch your thoughts for 30 minutes or an hour for the first time, you probably need a little steppingstone approach to ease into that type of intense self-reflection. That's where my micro method fits in; I would much rather have you watch your thoughts for 30, 60, or 90 seconds and eventually work your way up to longer periods. Isn't that how we typically do things in life? Start smaller and work our way up? Interval Mindfulness™ meets you in the middle in a way that's immediately evident if you want to complete longer, more sustained, traditional approaches to ambushing anxiety, mastering your stress, and releasing negativity. We use short time interval-based exercises, called Innervals™, as powerful tools for stress mastery, mental clarity, and more energy. Just like your smartphone, laptop, or browser, your mind operates best after a quick refresh.

Going through what I went through, I had to create a technique that could help me train my nerves to not only stay on the course of my healing journey, but to effectively distract me into relaxing, being mindful, and relieving stress when my mind, body, and nerves couldn't find a way to do so on their own (or never wanted to do so on their own). And believe me when I say that my case was always that my body NEVER wanted to relax and relieve stress. My mind, body, and nerves had somehow gotten me into the challenges that I faced, and I knew deep down that they could also get me out of them if only I could find the best ways to direct their ability to heal me. Because what I was going through was so extremely overwhelming in every way imaginable, I had to create something that could help me slow down and take small bites of my thoughts, emotions, and bodily sensations.

As I mentioned, I was also diagnosed with ADD and that means I have a hard time sitting still, I forget names the second people say them, and I must walk or move (in some capacity) at least every 30 minutes, among many other things. I'm something I call a "functional hot mess" at times. Nonetheless, I'm relatively successful and good at what I do. I get by with my big heart, smile, and ability to covertly clean up my micro messes, so no one notices but me. So this method I am going to teach you will work for people like me that don't have the ability or attention span to do this type of work on the macro level.

As a fitness expert, I am fully aware that I should be relaxing, practicing mindfulness, and completing self-care activities daily, but I'm also really busy and I have a lot of hopes, dreams, and needs that I want to accomplish and for that reason, I never really "make time" to relax, practice mindfulness, or do self-care like all the gurus say we should be doing. All the authorities on pretty much everything that has to do with personal development and self-care in the world, always tell people what they "should" be doing. As a private personal trainer, holistic health coach, and life coach to a variety of clients, I definitely preach about all the things you should be doing and quickly call them out when I notice they aren't. Yep! #toughlove

So, there we go, we should all be doing a lot of things, but rather than telling you just what you "should" be doing, I actually want to train you so that you naturally realize what you should and shouldn't be doing in your life. There's a big difference from being told what you should be doing because at the end of the day, you're only going to do and follow through with what YOU think you should be doing, not what some authority, guru, or Francie Fancy Pants is telling you to do. I don't want to just tell you what to do, I want to train you to self-generate what you should do. Another way that Interval Mindfulness™ meets you in the middle.

Short Innervals™ train you to reflexively self-produce feelings of calm, balance, and inner peace triggering a powerful state of physical relaxation, mental clarity, and enhanced well-being. We do this mainly by doing something super active that triggers your stress response for a short time period, and we use the reflex action of that stimulation to help you easily drop into your relaxation response. We use a variety of Innervals™ to help you oscillate back and forth from your stress response to your relaxation response. This deliberate back and forth of your defensive and safe nerve states is like lifting weights for your nerves. It boosts your resilience and increases the capacity of your nervous system to tolerate anxiety and stress.

Our brains love novelty and there's so much variety, stimulation, and efficiency it's hard NOT to want to do it. The Innervals™ are mix-and-match and help you actively stay mindful, present, and intentional navigating an uncertain, chaotic, and uncomfortable world. With a micro-investment of your focus, energy, and time, you will realize what you should be doing and with that, there's a greater chance that you would get around to doing it. When we don't know what to do, we do nothing. Rather than spend a few hours or even days drowning in a state of fear, tension, and anxiety after getting triggered, doing one or more of these Innervals™ can help your nervous system shift into a different nerve state sooner. Each time you do an Innerval™ or Inner Workout, this teaches your nervous system to be more flexible and rebound from being triggered sooner.

When we use different Innervals™ to go back and forth, we are gently guiding the nervous system to remember its natural process of going between a calm and settled nerve state (relaxation response) and being activated (stress response). This begins the process of teaching your nervous system that it can experience stress and then easily shift back to a state of calm. This trains your nervous system to be more flexible and restore its natural rhythm and flow after being badly injured by trauma, inner wounds, and other unresolved issues. A resilient nervous system can move back and forth between alertness and action, calm and rest, and down and depressed without getting stuck at either extreme.

Any time you're injured, or if you take time off of working out, your muscles get weak, atrophied, and you may need to go to physical therapy or start exercising routinely again to strengthen your muscles. With trauma, inner wounds, and other unresolved issues, your nervous system is completely thrown out of whack and its muscles of resiliency become extremely weak. It's practicing resilience exercises like Innervals™ regularly that is going to help them get stronger again and allow you to have a more balanced nervous system.

Maybe you're like me and you're a Type-A personality, go-getter, and stress-inclined overachiever? Do you have a short attention span, bore easily, and have a hard time calming your mind? Are you more of an active type and have a hard time sitting still? Have you tried traditional mindfulness, meditation, yoga, and relaxation practices, only to fail, get frustrated, and think that it's simply not for you?

If you answered yes to any of those questions: I'm sure you love interval training workouts; a non-traditional technique that involves alternating short, heart-pounding bursts of intense exercise with equal, shorter, and less intense recovery periods. These workouts are a highly efficient way to exercise because they get your heart rate up fast, increasing your body's demand for oxygen, and thus allowing you to burn a maximum number of calories in a minimum amount of time. You've done countless Interval Mindfulness Innervals™ and inner workouts throughout this book, and I think it's incredibly important that you read the origin story and the "why" of the method. It's a modern-day fusion method. I didn't reinvent the wheel, I just put a lot of wheels together in an efficient, effective, and innovative way to address the pressing needs of this unprecedented time.

HOW I CREATED INTERVAL MINDFULNESS™

Not surprisingly, my love of intervals came from high-intensity interval training (HIIT). According to the American College of Sports Medicine's (ACSM) annual survey on fitness trends, HIIT has had the fitness industry buzzing from the jump. It ranked as the top fitness trend in the United States in

2014 and 2018 and is now a mainstay in the top 10.[92] The hype comes for one good reason: it's a time-efficient strategy that promises the best workout in the least amount of time. People often want to be fit (or at least say they are), but at the same time say they're too damn busy. *eye roll*

If you sprint across the street and walk back or do some rapid-fire jumping jacks for 20 seconds and then hold a squat, it would be a HIIT. The key is THE INTERVAL and something most people don't understand is: that the reason why HIIT works is because of your nerves! HIIT is a training technique that involves alternating short, heart-pounding bursts of intense exercise with equal, shorter, or less intense recovery periods. This style of training boosts your speed and endurance and strengthens your heart. Think of it as HARD-SOFT or FAST-SLOW. It's a highly efficient way to exercise because it gets your heart rate up fast, increases your body's demand for oxygen, and allows you to burn a maximum number of calories (in a minimum amount of time).

HIIT is super-efficient and the ideal approach for people with busy schedules who want to fit it in during lunch or before work in the morning or need to get in shape fast for any type of special event. When you do a high-intensity workout, it creates an oxygen shortage during the intense effort and triggers your body to ask for more oxygen during recovery. excess post-exercise oxygen consumption (EPOC) is the after-burn effect, and the main reason intense exercises will always allow you to burn more calories and fat than regular and longer aerobic and steady-state workouts; this allows you to burn more calories not only during your workout, but also up to 48 hours afterward.

Your body works a lot harder than it normally would if you were completing steady-state cardio or other aerobic training. It quickly increases your fitness level, and you don't have to spend long hours at the gym as you might with a traditional workout. In the case of interval training, we exchange energy efficiency for intensity. Intense workouts last for very short intervals, for example, 30 seconds on and 30 off, 1 minute on and 1 minute off, and so on. If you go into any gym in the world or any athlete's training center, you'll see some form of HIIT training being done; it's the gold standard for training for all its incredible mental, physical, and physiological benefits.

Interval training is also incredibly convenient because it's highly customizable, you can do it anywhere, and you don't always need special equipment. Most workouts last 30 minutes or less and can be done at home, in a public park, at the beach, in a hotel room, or your office if you've got some space in it. Interval training is the most popular training methodology in the fitness and sports worlds, and it is so well-known because of its leniency for time constraints, infusions of variety, and the "get it over and done with" mentality that people typically attach to completing the workouts. It's also very user-friendly. No matter what your fitness level or experience is, you can easily do it!

In a 2016 SIT study, two different groups of people were followed for 12 weeks. One group worked out for 50 minutes at a continuous steady-state pace, while the other group worked out for 10 minutes, which included several intense intervals, adding up to 1 minute. One of the craziest things about the study was that both groups saw the same improvement in their VO_2 max, even though they worked out at different time lengths. The most consistent benefit of interval training is that it improves your VO_2 max. Scientists have found that VO_2 max is one of the best predictors of overall health, and interval training can boost your cardio-respiratory health with shorter time investment.[93]

Here are other benefits:

- o   Increases your metabolism up to 48 hours post-workout
- o   Quick and convenient
- o   Improves blood sugar balance
- o   Improves aerobic function
- o   Boosts muscle growth
- o   Burns fat a higher rate
- o   Moderates the marker of type-2 diabetes
- o   Improves cognition
- o   Boosts insulin sensitivity
- o   Good for heart health

o   Creates more cellular proteins with oxygen

o   Increases blood flow to your brain

o   Combats depression

Most of these benefits occur with traditional workouts but the benefits with HIIT have been described by many people as: much better and last for a much longer time.

What's lacking about this methodology is the fact that without an "inner workout," your "outer workout" will only give you half of the wellness benefits. You see, many people have hundreds or thousands of inner wounds; traumas, unresolved issues, and cuts that are still bleeding and never healed. Think about this for a few seconds: when you don't properly digest food, you can get gas, bloating, or explosive diarrhea. You know this already, so what do you think happens to undigested emotions? Undigested, unprocessed, and untouched emotions build up, harden, and must be deposited somewhere inside your body. Have you ever thought about where these emotions end up? They end up wherever you're experiencing the most imbalance, tension, or pain. When left unattended, they can even lead to chronic illnesses. They weigh you down, pull your attention and focus away from what you're facing in the present, and work on your last nerve, magnifying the feelings of anxiety, stress, and negativity that you have.

Fusing my love of interval training workouts with my desire to efficiently, easily, and effectively master my stress and activate rapid self-healing (or simply my desire to just chill the f*ck out...) in an active and accumulative way, I created Interval Mindfulness™. Interval Mindfulness™ uses short Innervals™ as powerful tools for stress mastery, mental clarity, and more energy that will improve your life mentally, physically, emotionally, and biologically.

We are electromagnetic beings that produce electrical currents to start all of our internal processes. Energy can't be created or destroyed; it can only be converted from one form to another, and it can also become congested without proper connections that can ensure these conversions. Your nerve signals form a sort of highway that connects everything inside your body, so they need to be online, optimized, and operating at 4 and 5G speeds. How do you do that? Simple; by using the Innervals™ in my Interval Mindfulness™ method to stimulate various nerves to help rebalance your nervous system. Or what I like to call "Innerval™ Training."

Interval Mindfulness™ is similar to the traditional interval training methodology that we know of in the fitness world, but instead of applying it to the usual running, strength training, and sports conditioning, my micro method is applied to relaxation, mindfulness, and stress relief. It's simple, easy to follow, and can be practiced consistently anywhere and at any time, and that ease of practice is how it aligns with Interval training in the fitness world. Each active Innerval™ is like a fitness interval. They can be done on their own, mixed and matched, repeated, and or put together for a specific bigger inner workout. Repeated practice of these Innervals™ and inner workouts are what make you an Inner Athlete.

I originally created these Innervals™ for my use but soon discovered how powerful this could be for more people! You can ambush anxiety, stress, and negativity with a new, active, and non-traditional way to HIIT relaxation, meditation, and stress relief. When you HIIT relaxation, meditation, and stress-relief, they hit you right back with reflexive relaxation, positive outcomes, and progress, making it easier to keep up with it (for us aggressive types)! If you want to practice relaxation, meditation, and mindfulness but are skeptical because you have a hard time calming your mind, but you also like efficiency which you've seen as an outcome when you're able to relax, then, Interval Mindfulness™ is for YOU.

HOW DOES IT WORK?

Interval Mindfulness™ uses nerve stimulation, brain activation, and the body's natural relaxation response to counteract anxiety, stress, and negativity. Innervals™ stimulate various nerves to help balance your nervous system and keep you healthy. Interval Mindfulness™ has been compared to traditional yoga, breathwork, hypnosis, and meditation because it influences the body's autonomic nervous system. The primary goal of Interval Mindfulness™ is to train people to use their nerves and natural relaxation response on their own as needed. The Innervals™ can be used to help master your emotional responses to anxiety, stress, and negativity and control physical aspects like blood pressure, heart rate, and fast breathing. If you tend to be a nervous or anxious person, Interval Mindfulness™ can help you find an inner place of calmness and emotional peace. If you are an overly sensitive person, with Interval Mindfulness™, you can learn to cope with outer stimulation by dismissing it from your attention rather than feeling overwhelmed by it.

Interval Mindfulness™ also breaks traditional mindfulness and meditation up into doable, digestible, and smaller bits, and the more bits you can do, the better! In the workouts, we focus on the act of shifting (gears) and with more consistent training, you can handle your distractions in a better way. You'll never get rid of them completely and that's a fact, so the next best thing is to learn how to master, ignore, or maneuver around them. I want to train you to navigate chaotic environments so calmly, that you'll feel powerful when you encounter a distraction and you'll feel like you have a choice to accept, indulge, or simply ignore it. As you already know, any great choice you make depends on how strong your willpower is, so essentially: these workouts will be training you to strengthen the willpower that is already present in you.

Another thing that makes Innerval™ training so unique is that, unlike many other techniques, it works directly on your nerves stimulating your stress and relaxation responses. As you now know, your relaxation response should normally be in control most of the time, but most people have their stress response in control almost all of the time causing negative mental, physical, and emotional outcomes. Regular practice of Innerval™ training brings the activity of the two responses into a better balance by calming down your overactive stress response faster.

It may be a new, non-traditional, and hard concept to follow at first, but my Innervals™ are designed to be like completing a quick reset, jump-start, and deep cleansing of your mind, body, and nerves. It's not easy, it's training, and we know that training is never easy, but it's always worth it once you start seeing the little wins of your progress. You will see wins like being able to relax faster, calmer, managing stress better, and being more focused in a sea of distraction, endless information, and stimulation. If you want it easy though, you can keep taking pills and stay on the elliptical of symptom management.

There are several shorter Interval Mindfulness™ Innervals™ and combo workouts throughout this book. However, to access them in one place and do longer and more expansive inner workouts becoming a true Inner Athlete, you can access my Interval Mindfulness™ On-Demand video library at http://mariogodiva.com The maximum results of Interval Mindfulness™ will be reached when you can do follow-a-long video inner workouts, just like you would do for traditional interval training workouts.

FRUSTRATION INNERVAL™ COMBO. (3 minutes)

1. FULL-BODY TENSE INNERVAL™ // 30 seconds.

Think of a time when you became so frustrated and couldn't do anything about it. Then make fists, tense every muscle in your body, and open your mouth and start breathing as fast as you can (like hyperventilating.) Do this for 30 seconds or 60 times if you don't have a timer. At the end intentionally relax all of your muscles and slow down your breathing.

2. CORE BREATHING INNERVAL™ // 30 seconds.

Take long, slow, and deep inhales and take longer, slower, and deeper exhales for 30 seconds or 3 cycles (1 inhale/exhale) of breath if you don't have a timer. As you inhale for 3 seconds your core goes out, and as you exhale for 6 seconds your core goes in.

3. Repeat 2 times

STIMULATION. The motor cortex, phrenic nerves, vagus nerves, and posterior thoracic nerves.

8 //

INTERVAL TRAINING REIMAGINED

Interval training is the father and mindfulness is the mother of Interval Mindfulness™. Together they use short intervals of intentional breathing, micro-movements, nerve stimulation, and self-reflection to counteract the effects of anxiety and stress, paving the way for a calmer, happier, and more focused you. Interval Mindfulness™ believes in the value of approaching short intervals of mindfulness and meditation, with intensity, sharpness, and an all-out effort, and in order to do this, you need to be 100% committed, focused on the now, and be judgment-free.

How are mindfulness and interval training similar? They aren't really; they're opposites. Interval training or HIIT is the intensity, intervals, and efficiency, while mindfulness becomes your inner volume button. Using Interval Mindfulness™ and its Innervals™, you can quickly turn outer life down, while staying ready to instantly turn it up when it becomes necessary. Your inner perspective is your capacity for internal validation. It's something that can be trained and just like any muscle you have in your body, if you don't use it, you lose it. When you focus, strengthen, and develop your inner perspective, you get to fully understand your personal power, can dilute distractions, lose the need to control or manipulate others, and the need to seek approval from anyone.

Interval Mindfulness™ isn't meditation, but it trains you to be mindful in short, controlled, and micro intervals. It creates a digestible, relatable, and sustainable container to help you try it and stay with it. Anyone who tells you that they meditate most likely means they tried 3 minutes of a free 10-minute meditation and then moved on to something else. You could argue that Interval Mindfulness™ is replicating the environment and method in most of the scientific studies of mindfulness. Interval Mindfulness™ and its Innervals™ are basically giving you baby steps into mindfulness, meditation, and other relaxation practices.

It's like taking too many free samples from the grocery store (pre-COVID-19). It focuses on training you to handle the unpredictable right now, in a fraction of the time.

If you can focus on the now, judgment-free, you are being mindful. Your life will rapidly pass you by if you're busy, distracted, and not focused on what really matters to you. Whenever you take a mindful Innerval™, you're retreating to your inner perspective instead of the immediacy of your outer world. When you strengthen your mindfulness muscle, it supports (lifts up) many attitudes that lead to a satisfying life. When you're mindfully strong, you can easily marinate in life's pleasures, as they happen, moment to moment, have a higher capacity to handle challenging situations, and become more fully engaged in the world around you. You spend less time worrying about self-esteem and success and become better able to connect deeply and authentically with others. If you're not worrying about the future or regretting the past, life will feel pretty good!

Psychotherapists and many in the medical community have (belatedly) turned to mindfulness meditation as an important treatment for substance abuse, eating disorders, depression, and anxiety. Some experts think mindfulness helps people accept traumatic experiences, no matter how painful, rather than react to them with avoidance or hopelessness.[94] In addition, researchers have found that mindfulness techniques help improve your physical health, such as treating heart disease, lowering blood pressure, reducing chronic pain, improving sleep quality, relieving stress, and alleviating stomach and digestive issues.[95]

The pairing of interval training and mindfulness may seem odd to most, but it's important that you're able to effortlessly shift into the present moment. Why? Because the past and future don't exist. Most people create their own suffering by focusing too much on the past and using it to predict doom and gloom in the future. Your ability to hit "pause" on your ruminating thoughts lies in the present. This is how my Innervals™ will help train you to be present. You must be present to complete each short Innerval™ and they change every thirty to sixty seconds. If you can master being present for thirty to sixty seconds you'll be able to master being present for longer periods.

The current status quo is to train your mindfulness muscle linearly with a practice of mindfulness or meditation over a single, long, and sustained period. Your life on the other hand, is full of short intervals of information, stimulation, and distraction so this reality then begs the question: is the status quo really the best we can do? With my micro method, you'll be training yourself to control your emotional shifts that come in short intervals, instead of feeling like they are constantly out of your control.

Essentially, Interval Mindfulness™ is not only helping you manage your emotional energy and relax faster, but it's also training your focus so you can be more "focus fit" and less distracted by the daily assaults of information, stimulation, and distraction from your environment. During the various Innervals™, you will try to attain a quality-focused state in the present moment as quickly as possible when the short interval starts, and then you will also practice holding your focus until the short interval ends.

This is not a religious, philosophical, or spiritual experience but it is a disruptive game-changer. It teaches you to adopt an active, intense, and non-traditional approach that strengthens your nerves and builds resilience, increasing your neuro-flexibility; which is how fast you can switch from your stress response to your relaxation response.[96]

You will sharpen your willpower which in turn hones your discipline; a skill that can be applied to just about every aspect of your life. Discipline gives you the freedom to consciously distinguish between the things you want and the things you don't want, but it requires the backbone of concentration. When you're facing difficult situations and new environments, your newfound concentration and willpower will help you achieve the inner stability that you'll need to make the choices that are best for you. Interval Mindfulness™ helps you cultivate a strong inner attitude to develop and strengthen an advanced level of self-control, without which you could be easily manipulated, distracted, and driven farther away from those big hopes, dreams, and needs.

This practice can also be an alternative choice for people who struggle with relaxation-induced anxiety as I have described earlier but it's not intended to completely replace practices such as yoga or meditation. The majority of people with this kind of relaxation-induced anxiety are also the ones who can benefit from a healthy balance of the traditional contemplative practices as well as the Interval Mindfulness™.

Interval Mindfulness™ and its various inner workouts may seem a little strange, weird, or uncomfortable at first, but it should be viewed as playful not stressful. I hope that you can approach this practice with curiosity, and not judge yourself for the discomfort you may feel at the beginning. We complete Innervals™ of micromovements/fidgeting, laughing, breathing, speaking, and other things for nerve stimulation that we would randomly, naturally, and intuitively do when we're going about our normal day's activities. Adults have forgotten what it's like to play, and Innervals™ help with that in a fun, active, and strategic way. Practice makes permanent, and with each new try, you'll experience short Innervals™ of immediate relief that only grow to bigger, brighter, and longer Innervals™ of relief from most of your anxiety, stress, and negativity.

INNERVAL™ SNAPSHOT SHEET

Interval Mindfulness™ and its Innervals™ have several elements that are fused together and made up of many diverse practices. To access the full On-Demand Video library of 100s of different Innervals™ and inner workouts, you can go http://mariogodiva.com

Interval Breathing Technique (IBT): Breathing is a necessity of life, but most people have trained themselves to breathe in a dysfunctional way, fueling their stress response and making safety, health, and happiness a constant uphill battle. Breath Innervals™ help you retrain your default breathing rhythm to one that's calming, balancing, and relaxing.

Motor Brain Activation (MBA): Walking, running, driving, and talking are things you do at all hours of the day without having to really think about them. Your movement, called motor control, is hands-down one of the most important things that your body can do. Your motor pathway, called the motor cortex, located in your brain, is responsible for your movement and is where your brain initiates and issues your movement orders. Motor Innervals™ focus on micro-movements that chronologically and intermittently stimulate your motor cortex. When your stress response is triggered it takes blood flow away from your brain. Stimulating your motor cortex helps to release stress hormones and push blood flow to your brain, actively reversing the physiological effects of stress.

Mini Meditation Method (3M): Meditation is very similar to sports. Different names, organizations, teams, players, strategies, and rules use competition to seek betterment, or what they call winning. The problem is most people don't want to even try the many different types, styles, and practices because of the long, static, and sustained nature of the practice. Interval Mindfulness™ and its Innervals™ use short intervals of different styles of meditation to make it relatable and enjoyable for people who otherwise wouldn't want to even try it in the first place.

Vagus Nerve Stimulation (VNS): When your stress response gets triggered, pouring the stress hormones, cortisol and adrenaline, throughout your body, your vagus nerve acts as the emergency brake by activating your relaxation response. People with a stronger relaxation response recover faster after exercise, stress, injury, or illness. There are invasive, conventional medical procedures that are used to stimulate your vagus nerve, however, Interval Mindfulness™ and its Innervals™ use non-invasive techniques that stimulate your vagus nerve differently.

Reflex Relaxation Stimulation (RRS): Many of the movements that occur in your body occur automatically. Your reflexes and automatic body functions are called involuntary or unconscious movements. These movements, which are essential for survival, are governed by your brain, nervous system, and spinal cord, the most primitive parts of your body, and no thinking is required. Interval Mindfulness™ and its Innervals™ stimulate you to reflexively relax by directing you to do short intervals of active, aggressive, and intense efforts of various activities.

Tactile (Touch) Visualization (TTV): Touch is your innate first language and a powerful communication channel that plays a central role in your emotional well-being, your sense of safety, and your self-perception. It helps you interact with your world with many sensations, including itch, vibration, temperature, and pressure. People use touch to develop bonds with one another and use it to gather info about their surroundings. Interval Mindfulness™ and its Innervals™ use different types of touch methods paired with visualization as a relaxation, therapeutic, and health-promoting tool.

Self-Generation Protocols: If you voluntarily undergo some type of manageable sweat, effort, and discomfort to get something, you will be happier and value it more than if it came to you easily. Self-generation is when you create, produce, or reproduce something without the help of an external source. Interval Mindfulness™and its Innervals™ use various protocols that train you to self-generate joy and small positive thoughts, which will eventually lead to the trained mindset of self-generating bigger hopes, dreams, and needs.

This isn't an exhaustive list but it gives you a snapshot of some of the Interval Mindfulness™ and Innerval™ DNA. There are also other ways in real life to practice mindfulness by focusing on your moment-to-moment sensations. You can choose any activity or moment to practice what is referred to as informal mindfulness. This is done by single-tasking (don't multitask), doing only one thing at a time with 100% of your attention. Eating, showering, walking, petting your dog, or touching a partner can be practicing mindfulness if you're totally paying attention to the present moment, judgment-free. Just slow down the process of what you're doing and try to involve all your senses. But for all the people who want to try a hot, new, and remixed version of mindfulness, HIIT up my method, literally.

The absolute hardest Innerval™ we have is the one below. Can you literally "do nothing" meaning having absolutely no thoughts for 60 seconds? Or just be in the space between your thoughts for 60 seconds? It's okay if you can't right now but stick with me and you'll be doing it in no time! When anxiety and stress are high in life, it's especially helpful to have someone guide us in consciously connecting to resilient and relaxed nerve states.

DO NOTHING INNERVAL (RESTING AWARENESS) // 60 seconds.

This Innerval™ lets your mind truly rest, anchors you to the present, and allows you to simply just be. Don't focus on anything and just do nothing. You're aiming for the space between your thoughts. Thoughts may enter your mind but let them slowly drift away in the background like clouds. You can focus on your breath, a safe place, ocean waves, or something to anchor you in the present that keeps your thoughts at bay.

STIMULATION: Vagus nerve

MICRO MINDFUL INNERVAL (MI, or "My Innerval™")

An entire day is a macro concept filled with micro shifts that we call "time." Time is yet another concept that we have created to measure light and day cycles. Time, just like the sun is the sun, is time, and you can't "manage" something that's always there. However, you can manage how you perceive what's always there and, in this case, that'll be managing how you see time. You have 24 hours, 1,440 minutes, or 86,400 seconds each day, and you can break this "macro" day into micro Innervals™ of time. Time is always shifting and never stops, but no one focuses on the shift. Everyone has the same 24-hour days, but it's the people who are the most distracted, delusional, and disconnected and unable to manage their micro shifts within a day, that feel like they are "losing" time.

People who are masters at using time wisely don't focus on time but focus on their ability to use time efficiently. The passage of time is simply a series of micro shifts, and these people are simply masters at micro shifting because they practice and focus on the micro shifts. Their focus is more inward, and less outward, as far as mastering the use of time is concerned.

No one really focuses on what happens between things. What happens between thoughts? What happens between shifting your car from park to drive? People like to focus more intensely on the destinations, never the journey itself, or the goal states. This is why so many inspirational "Focus on the journey" social media posts are tone-deaf and cause many people to eye roll. People have never been trained to focus on the journey. Many people don't pay attention to the shifts that happen to get you into those states of having achieved a goal or arrived at a destination but there's power in the shift! But it's those shifts that give people an opportunity to shift into neutrality or the space in between; doing, being, and thinking nothing. We are all capable of leaning into a neutral state, but to do that, we must lean into the actual shift. This isn't easy at first and will take practice.

It's only not easy because we live in a society where we are conditioned to always be doing "something" to be successful. Scientists, historians, and plenty of self-help gurus tell us that getting your daily routine right is the key to success. You can read online a host of articles about the morning routines and daily habits to add to your schedule of celebs, CEOs, and other successful people. And while research shows that some of these activities are good for you like gratitude practicing, journaling, and awe walks in nature. If you just cram every healthy habit out there imaginable into your daily routine, you likely won't get enough of it. Too much of anything is overkill. All this pressure to have the perfect routine to reach your goals, not realizing that when we are pressed, we are stressed; when establishing healthy habits sends us knee-deep into our stress response, it can get counterintuitive. Science is just as clear that you also need plenty of "doing nothing" in your routine. It's this "doing nothing" that helps to lift you out of a stressed state into a relaxed state. And by keeping ourselves busy at all times, we may be losing our ability to sit still because our brains are actually being rewired.[97] According to Sandi Mann, a psychologist at the University of Central Lancashire in Britain daydreaming "literally makes us more creative, better at problem-solving, better at coming up with creative ideas."[98] However, in order for that to happen, total idleness or doing nothing is required.

For some people, the idea of short intervals of "doing nothing" may seem radical or extreme. But it's only because they were never conditioned that this is okay. You can't "just be" if you've never learned or been told that it's okay to "just be" without judging yourself. I get it that life happens, time flies, and you get busy. But the easiest way to notice, plan, and use your time wisely is by taking a personal break from time itself. Alone time that insulates you from the world's dramas, pressures, stressors, and noise. This can mean relaxing, breathing, daydreaming, and reflecting on your memories or thoughts, while taking what I call a "MY Innerval™" or MI. It's basically a bougie (classy) way of saying personal time that is exclusively yours. Research shows that blocks of disconnected, quiet, and alone time have a powerful effect on our thinking, creativity, and well-being.[99]

We need to build more MIs into our schedules to allow for mental distancing, which gives us a little space from our problems. This allows us to consider another person's point of view or see things from multiple perspectives. Relaxing, breathing, and daydreaming switch on the default mode network, enabling our subconscious to find remote associations between ideas. If we don't create the time to get that inner space from our emotions and take a break from the world, then we won't have the option of more choices and inner resources for the issues we face daily.

How much time should you take? That's your call. As much time as you need to recenter, rebalance, and refresh. In a best-case scenario, you should be setting aside at least nine minutes a day, that's just one minute at a time nine times a day, but we know that our individual worlds are far from best-case scenarios. No one gets extra time, though, so it's up to you to drone out, look at your 24 hours holistically, and map them out specifically so they serve you well. It's always good to schedule MIs where you are doing nothing to help you optimize.

The most important thing about an MI is that this is YOUR time, hence why I like to say: "My Innerval™," not your partner's, boss's, kid's, family's, or friend's. They already monopolize most, or all, of your other micro minutes of the day so it's time to take some MI time away to take care of yourself and your thoughts or emotions. Remember, the first part of "self-care" is self, so do something for yourself and choose to take three MIs a day with no exceptions. As a matter of fact, taking an MI will help you appreciate your day a little more and serve as a little energy refresh for your day. It's also beneficial because, during that time, the only thing you are focusing on is the internal without any external influences, so you know that your thoughts are genuinely yours. Seriously though, how often do you pause, take a break, and reflect on your thoughts throughout your day? Just taking the time to pay attention to your thoughts for a couple of minutes is a huge step forward.

You are a unique, beautiful, and powerful human being and taking planned MIs helps you relax internally, rebalance, and reclaim your power from the intimidating, overwhelming, and ever-changing external world. You lean into your inner intelligence when you take an MI and you'll be surprised to note that it has a lot of things to share with you.

We live in a world where people, places, and activities are constantly fighting for your attention and hijacking your inner focus. Companies are in the business of getting us over-stimulated, manipulated, and converted without our conscious awareness and this is actively taking place at every corner you turn. If you don't have proper inner perspective training, you'll never be 100% sure that you are making decisions for yourself instead of making decisions with prompts from someone else, and this factor really matters if you plan to make real progress in personal development and when it comes to achieving your hopes, dreams, and needs. Are you making decisions for yourself in an explicit way? Are you making those decisions right now because of someone else? Is fear playing a role in your decisions?

When you take an MI to see what feelings, sensations, and information your inner intelligence is sharing with you, you're able to look at what's going on with you in the moment but on a deeper level. Over time, these micro mindful Innervals™ allow you to process your emotions, thoughts, and issues more effectively throughout the day, often without you even realizing that you're doing it. Three mindful Innervals™ a day for a time as short as 60 seconds can help you release stress, clear your mind, and process issues more efficiently.

An added benefit is that you can boost your creativity, energy, and productivity with mindful Innervals™. They immediately ground you, bring you back to the present moment, and keep your focus on the task at hand. A constant rebalancing or resettling such as this gives you a boost of mental focus, especially, on days that demand a great deal of focus for you to get work done. A good MI schedule that I've found effective and which helps me reduce stress, rebalance, and re-center my focus is taking one MI every three hours. Yes! I complete a mindful Innerval™ every three hours. You can set up daily notifications or alarms on your cell phone because if it isn't scheduled beforehand, it probably won't get done at all and if it does get done, it's done by accident; these accidental MIs may not exactly produce the desired effects.

I get up at six am every morning so I have alarms starting from nine am every three hours until nine pm when I start getting ready for bed. My MIs are super simple and last for about one to three minutes. To complete them, I can just pay attention to my breath, or complete one of my active Innervals™ for about three minutes.

It's completely okay if you miss some of your mindful Innervals™ when you have to be out with friends or the day is packed with activities. The point is to always meet yourself halfway on this mindful journey you're taking and just do the best that you can. To that end, you can either make up the missed mindful Innervals™ during the next session or just remind yourself to get better at being less distracted from doing them no matter how packed your day becomes. You don't even need to be at home or in a quiet space! You can quickly check in with your breath from your desk at work, or complete an Innveral in the restroom at a friend's place. They are so short and doable that you can take them with you anywhere, and they can even help you be more present in the outside world.

Your micro mindful Innervals™ makes practicing mindfulness a mini-habit, and mini-habits turn into macro-habits. It's a way to make acting on behaviors you want to establish approachable, minimal, and digestible. When you complete mindful Innervals™ throughout your day, you're more likely to continue them and fall into some sort of routine. You'll also spend more time being mindful of every other task or activity that you engage in within the day than if you were to do a longer meditation session once per day.

The bottom line is we avoid concepts surrounding rest, recovery, and regeneration in today's society because we feel like we simply can't achieve any of it. The truth remains that you owe it to yourself to start taking your rest, recovery, and regeneration seriously. At this moment, your life's frustrations may seem big, overwhelming, and with no possible resolutions in sight, but all it takes are the constant, short, and easy steps that slowly chip away at the bulk of the frustrations.

The crucial role of Interval Mindfulness™ lies in giving you the sequential steps right down to the finish line where you finally overcome some of your life's biggest frustrations and the whole time, you'll be laughing (lol! not because you're losing it!) but because laughing triggers your vagus nerve and is a huge part of the Innervals™ in the Interval Mindfulness™ practice. Take some time right now and think about this: are your days REALLY yours?

Remember that you can find all of the different Innervals™ and inner workouts in this book and so much more online via my On-Demand library at my website http://mariogodiva.com

MY INNERVAL™ // 3 – 9 MINUTES (MINIMUM)

This Innerval™ allows you to take a personal wellness break from the outer world to relax, breathe, and reflect on your memories or thoughts. What are you doing during this time? Whatever the f*ck you want as long as it's YOUR personal time spent on YOU. Not your partner, kids, friends, or co-workers, YOU!

STIMULATION: Vagus nerve

This may seem like a hard Innerval™ to do but think of it as a self-care Innerval™. Some suggestions include:

- Read poetry, songs, and books that inspire, motivate, and move you.
- Reflect and take a trip down memory lane and revisit happier, healthier, and exciting times by reading old letters, emails, or cards from friends, loved ones, and coworkers.
- Go for a walk in nature with your phone on airplane mode
- Listen to relaxing music and inspiring podcasts
- Stretch, foam roll, or trigger point release
- Clean and rearrange
- Take a long shower or bath

9 //

MINDFULNESS WORKS FOR SOME; DOESN'T WORK FOR MOST

I just spent the last two chapters focusing on the interval approach, and now I'm going to do a mini dive into the nuances of mindfulness. Mindfulness is one of the trendiest buzzwords today fueled by a growing body of research, an overwhelmed work culture, and a promise of relieving stress and calming the mind. However, nothing in life is all pro with no con, and the growing popularity of mindfulness meditation in media, apps, and online may have eclipsed some of the science. I think many people will agree that mindfulness works for some but doesn't work for most. It's important that I dive into the concept here for many reasons. First, this term has become overwhelmingly prevalent in health and wellness discourse. Additionally, my theory derives from mindfulness, of course, but also "disagrees" with it or differs from it in many ways. A good understanding of the typical mindfulness practices will better inform why my approach might be better for you and lead the way to rapid self-healing as opposed to frustration or failure.

According to the CDC (2017), upwards of 14% of American adults meditated at least once, and the number of meditators has tripled since 2012.[100] Pew Research Center's 2014 Religious Landscape Study found that 40% of Americans in nearly all religious groups, and those who have no religious affiliation at all, say that they meditate at least once a week. Interestingly, 5% of children in the US meditate because schools are offering mindfulness practices that include meditation as part of their curriculum. The rationale behind this is that meditation can help ease the anxiety, stress, and negativity, which many young people face in today's modern world. Of all the adults who practice meditation, 76% do it for general wellness, 60% for improving energy, and 50%

for focus or memory. 29% do it to combat anxiety, 21% to fight stress, and 17% to counter depression.[101]

Meditation has also been shown to improve anxiety levels 60% of the time and can effectively cut the wake time of insomniacs by half, reducing heart disease by 87%, and even shows a 73% reduction in post-traumatic stress disorder (PTSD) symptoms. It's estimated that 200 – 500 million people meditate worldwide.[102] There's no shortage of meditation brands, companies, and gurus who actively practice, promote the benefits, and tell you how good it is for you. But if meditation is so good for you, why are most people NOT doing it? What's going on with the 86% of adults in the US who don't even want to try meditation or mindfulness?

As mentioned earlier, the truth is, even for the people who want to try meditation, mindfulness, or relaxation practices; they simply can't do it because their nerves won't let them. How can you meditate if your body is in a state of emergency? 17-53% of adults experience relaxation-induced anxiety[103], and anytime they try to do a traditional type of mindfulness, meditation, or relaxation practice, they will always be doomed to fail, get frustrated, and probably never want to try again. It's like having insomnia and trying to force yourself to go to sleep when your body is wide awake! The more you try to sleep, the more frustrated you get at not being able to sleep. It's not fun, nor is it something that you would want to willingly do for fun, sports, or leisure.

Meditation also has this supreme goal of enlightenment that's been shrouded in mystery for centuries. It's believed that it's only accessible indirectly through years, decades, or even lifetimes of tedious meditation practice. With most of the world sleeping or in an unconscious state, we should be learning how to be conscious or awake NOW instead of doing practices that are designed to bring about a future moment of awakening. Do you agree?

What the world needs is a neutral micro method that's neither a religious, philosophical, or spiritual experience. Something that's accessible, requires no skill and is attractive to people of all ages, religions, and cultures. A micro method that has the grounded, common, and widespread goal of quickly reducing anxiety, stress, and negativity. A method that allows people to master their stress, adapt to adversity, and activate rapid self-healing. Interval Mindfulness™ is THAT experience.

For most of us, meditating means silently repeating a mantra or sacred word, or following our breath, or labeling our thoughts and feelings as they arise, or trying to quiet our mind. But Interval Mindfulness™and its Innervals™ are about something entirely different. It's not a practice we do now to prepare for a future moment of enlightenment. What if waking up didn't have to be a long, drawn-out process leading toward an ultimately unpredictable result? What if, instead of spending time doing traditional meditation, mindfulness practices, watching your breath, or repeating mantras in an attempt to prepare for enlightenment, you could engage in a daily, easy-to-follow, and sustainable practice that gave you direct access to mental clarity, energy, and inner peace?

The mindfulness-based stress reduction (MBSR) program, developed by Jon Kabat-Zinn, Ph.D., who was a student of a Buddhist monk and scholar Thich Nhat Hanh, is one of the original standardized programs for mindfulness meditation. He is highly credited with bringing mindfulness to the mainstream by showing that when you regularly practice mindfulness, it can bring positive changes in health, behaviors, and attitudes, in addition to enhancements in both mental and physical symptoms. Since then, other simplified and secular mindfulness meditation interventions have been increasingly incorporated into medical settings to treat stress, pain, insomnia, and other chronic health issues. What they all got wrong was the assumption that everyone can and should do mindfulness meditation. They took a traditionally Buddhist method, stripped it down, and introduced it to the world without really understanding how it affected most people, not just a select few people who have the discipline, consistency, and motivation to stick with it or who are in controlled environments like monasteries away from the modern world and civilization. In the stressful, modern, and unpredictable world we live in, people barely have the discipline, consistency, and motivation to pay their bills on time, let alone pick up and perfect a practice that will take them months and years to reap the benefits of.

When you look at how the mainstream views mindfulness meditation, it gives the impression that the results of mindfulness meditation are exclusively happiness, calm, and increased well-being. However, mindfulness meditation wasn't created specifically for those things, those are just side effects of consistent practice that can take months or years to achieve. To the average person, this can be pretty confusing when you're looking at all the mindfulness meditation media, apps, and classes and trying to find what works for you. Then when you start to look at all the different scientific studies, it gets even more confusing.

Part of the reason why people are confused is because mindfulness and meditation are used as broad umbrella terms. Both words can be used to describe a variety of techniques, mental states, and practices from a wide variety of secular and religious contexts. When someone says mindfulness or meditation, you have no idea what they're talking about, unless they explain the exact technique, focus, and goal (which most people don't). It's hard to know sometimes what types of meditation and mindfulness are involved. With the current umbrella terms in the research, a 1-month meditation retreat might be treated and labeled as the same as a 5-minute meditation from a popular phone app. But those are two very different experiences with two very different potential outcomes.

Now, am I saying that you shouldn't want to try or continue practicing mindfulness meditation? Of course not. What I am saying is that it's a good idea to approach mindfulness meditation from a balanced point of view and pay attention to the potential good and bad effects of it. I'm definitely pro mindfulness, hence this book's focus on it and my adaptation of it, but I also feel that all the popular, scholarly, and expert discussions of mindfulness meditation are a little biased and unbalanced. No one is talking about adverse effects or asking if some practices are good or bad for certain people over others. No one is talking about how hard it is to practice mindfulness meditation if you are frozen in your stress response. If you are in the middle of a crisis or emergency, the very last thing you are going to do is sit or lay down in a room in silence and be still. Stillness is a hybrid nerve state that is only attainable with a balanced and fully functioning nervous system. Underneath it all, mindfulness is about awareness, awareness leads to deep self-work that is painful to confront and most people want to bypass that (by default).

We've taken traditional Buddhist meditation practices without fully understanding them, dropped Buddhism, and applied those meditation systems to science, medicine, and well-being. Because of this, many people only associate mindfulness meditation with relaxation, calming, and stress relief or productivity, attention, and managing emotions. None of the authorities, companies, or teachers prepare you for the potential horror, trauma, or shock that results from watching your own thoughts. No one prepares you for the struggle and resistance you'll experience from even trying in the first place.

Mindfulness meditation isn't just about relaxation, calm, and peace: it opens up a space for you to watch what's going on in your mind. Once you're in that witnessing space, sh*t has the potential to really hit the fan. Old inner wounds like childhood trauma, resentment, and repressed emotions can surface and require extra support to process, accept, and manage. Mindfulness meditation can be helpful, but the negative and undesirable effects of mindfulness meditation are often ignored or swept under the rug. It's hard to be mindful when you're triggered into your stress response. Recovering from a stress response requires movement and energy, not silence, stillness, and immobility. Once you are truly anchored in your relaxation response, silence, stillness, and immobility are easier.

While the media portrays instant nirvana, rampant information and misinformation out there about mindfulness meditation have people thinking that if they try it out for a while, all of their problems will magically go away. When you think about traditional Buddhist meditation, which is where mindfulness originates from, the intention wasn't to make us happier. It was designed to radically change our perception of the world, change our sense of self, and detach from the outer world. For someone who hasn't really been self-aware, has experienced intense trauma, or doesn't know how to properly handle emotions, this tidal wave of awareness can be a lot to process at once.

Becoming mindful is a full transition to a different way of being: conscious and aware. It's not gimmicky and requires an energy, time, and focus investment.

It's a practiced skill set of zooming out and seeing the world in a different way that takes practice, patience, and openness to develop. There are many ways to do things but jumping headfirst into a sea of mindfulness meditation when you don't know how to swim is a recipe for drowning in more anxiety and stress. My method gives you a micro approach so that you can tiptoe into it and sample different styles to see what really works for you.

Some people may notice a massive sense of peace when they practice, others may find that they struggle with nagging distractions or catastrophic thinking. Even if you're struggling, it's not a problem because you can be mindful in the midst of frustration, doubt, and chaos just as you can in moments of joy, peace, and calm. This is one of the very reasons that Interval Mindfulness™ takes an active and shifting approach. It's training you to actively be mindful in the midst of tension, stress, and activity. You're using the stimulation energy to ambush anxiety instead of feeling like a prisoner to it.

FOCUSED INTENT

Despite the shadow side of mindfulness, mindfulness practice can help you regulate your emotions better and studies show that regular practice can reduce anxiety, combat stress, fight depression, and increase self-compassion.[104] Plus, it gives you a nice brain boost by improving your focus, memory, and making you less likely to be hijacked by distractions…

Like all things health-related, your mind needs to be trained. With up to 6,200 thoughts a day[105], things can get crazy, uncomfortable, and confusing if you don't have a strong, stable, and well-developed mind that's capable of performing optimally in any environment. Even many religions from around the world include some type of prayer or meditation technique that shifts your thoughts from the inner monkey mind to an awareness and appreciation of the moment. This generally instills a feeling of oneness and allows people to have a broader perspective about life in general.

Every expert has their opinion about the definition of mindfulness, but for me, mindfulness is simply awareness of the present moment via these simple words, or mantra if you will:

FOCUS. NOW. JUDGMENT-FREE.™

It sounds like an incredibly easy thing to do, but in a world where people are overworked, overwhelmed, over-stimulated, and view being busy like it's a better badge of honor, it's too hard for most of us to comprehend. We simply don't train for it. However, when you actively train your mind to be in the present moment, you get better at it and it helps you live life in a more meaningful, connected, and authentic way. Furthermore, when you proactively practice shifting into and out of mindful moments, you train yourself to become a master of state shifting. Can you imagine if you walked into a grocery store, bought the food you needed, and had a hard time leaving the store because you are so focused on being in the store (state)? The shift would be then: leaving the store. Just like that, life is a series of micro shifts into different brainwave states, but no one thinks to practice and train people how to shift. The focus is always on the desired state or outcome.

There's incredible power in knowing and feeling that if you aren't happy with your current nerve state, you can simply shift out of it. That you aren't broken, you're simply frozen in an undesirable nerve state that's hijacked your body, thoughts, and emotions. Just like if you're in a place where you don't want to be, you can simply leave. You're never truly stuck unless your mentality or a false belief has you feeling like you're stuck somewhere. You aren't doomed to your current frustrations, challenges, or negative emotions. When you become a master at shifting, you are able to access your safest, most regenerative, and most powerful self-healing nerve state. With that state comes additional inner perspective and resources to efficiently deal with outer anxiety, stress, and negativity. Your thoughts are only intense, fast, and aggressive because you're in your stress response. Your mind is only cluttered because of your preconditioned self, but anything that's conditioned can always be reconditioned; it's not easy, it's training.

Just like you can train your body and muscles to be physically fit, you can also train your mind to be "focus fit." Your focus fuels your future.

MINDFULNESS BENEFITS

By refocusing your mind on the present moment, you can:[106,107]

- Dilute distractions and capture a wandering mind.
- Increase productivity by proactively managing attention, focus, and concentration.
- Increase your well-being and reduce stress.
- Help redirect energy away from negative emotions, like restlessness, anxiety, craving, and depression.
- Better deal with challenges, frustrations, and setbacks by building inner resilience.
- Boost the immune system's ability to fight off illness.
- Calm the amygdala, which is responsible for the fight-or-flight response.
- Lower cortisol, a stress hormone, which increases blood pressure and blood sugar.
- Strengthen areas of the brain that sustain attention, which usually shrink as we age.

Mindfulness is the quality of being present, aware, and fully engaged in whatever you're doing now, judgment- and distraction-free, and being aware of your thoughts, feelings, and emotions without engaging them. You could practice mindfulness while eating, driving, or even walking. It's kind of like people-watching but instead of watching outer people you're keeping an eye on your inner people, and the inner people are your thoughts, feelings, sensations, and emotions.

To begin your exploration of this unique approach to ambush anxiety, master your stress, and release negativity, I want to invite you to temporarily set aside everything you've already learned about meditation and mindfulness. Not because I think what you've learned is wrong or that my approach is "better," but simply because my approach to interval-based mindfulness, meditation, and stress relief may have little or nothing in common with meditation or mindfulness as you've been practicing it.

The vehicle we use with Interval Mindfulness™ is short, rapid-fire, mindful intervals grouped together that I call "Innervals™." Most companies manipulate, trick, and distract people into buying their products and services and I'm trying to manipulate, trick, and distract people into mindfulness, meditation, and stress relief because some are too stubborn to want to do it on their own. #realtalk

Interval Mindfulness™ takes on mindfulness in a non-traditional way by doing a specific set of Innervals™ to train your mind to sustain your attention in the present moment. And although your mind and body benefit from Innervals™, we focus on your nerves, because without your nerves, your mind-body connection wouldn't exist. Your nerves help your mind and body to connect, communicate, and coordinate with each other. The more you strengthen your relaxation response while practicing, the faster you'll be able to relax, and the more you will begin to gain calm awareness of your inner emotions, thoughts, and feelings, as well as your own body. The first step to self-healing is always self-awareness. You can't correct what you don't see.

I'm not promising that when you try my method, you'll be instantly enlightened, find your purpose, heal your pain, and reach your dreams or anything else these "get rich quick" folks are trying to sell you. The only thing I'm promising you with Interval Mindfulness™ and its Innervals™ is a way to quickly reduce your current anxiety, stress, and negativity levels. This will help you efficiently shrink the roadblocks that are preventing you from accomplishing what you want to achieve. It will also help you defrost and get unstuck. Anything else that happens because your stress and anxiety levels are now lowered and under proper management, is a bonus!

SELF-LOVE 9 INNERVAL™ COMBO. (3 minutes)
1. SELF-LOVE 9 INNERVAL™ // 30 seconds.

Close your eyes; using the finger of your non-dominant hand, write three things (more than three words) that you love about yourself on your dominant hand. After you write all three things, start drawing a slow circle on your palm and see how long you can spend reliving and feeling the emotions of each thing.

2. CORE BREATHING INNERVAL™ // 30 seconds.

Take long, slow, and deep inhales and take longer, slower, and deeper exhales for 30 seconds or 3 cycles (1 inhale/exhale) of breath if you don't have a timer.

3. Repeat 2 times picking 3 new things that you love about yourself each time you go through the combo.

STIMULATION: Tactile stimulation; prefrontal cortex; visualization; dopamine and serotonin release.

10 //

PRECONDITIONED SELF & ADAPTING TO ADVERSITY

As a kid, I didn't start out as a fit male. I remember seeing a doctor for a physical when I was younger and being told that, according to a health chart, I was obese. Every member of my family was overweight, so I thought I had no choice but to be overweight because that's all we knew. We ate what our parents fed us, and whatever they served us for lunch in school. We listened to whatever the commercials said was good for us; we craved the big, bright, and mesmerizing foods the TV ads instructed us to crave.

We begged, pleaded, and implored our parents to buy us candy, sweets, and other instantly gratifying junk food. How were we supposed to know any better? We were poor kids with no conscious awareness or control over our food intake and the effect it could have on us. Even though I was the oldest of four kids, I didn't know any better either.

I was a chubby black kid as a child and as a teenager and I was often teased and bullied because of my weight. I was called Fatty and Marshmallow Puff (from the fictional series, *Ghostbusters*). Sometimes, people my age or a little older than I was at the time would yell, "Hey, Kool-Aid," representing the big Kool-Aid pitcher man on the packets and containers of the drink. At the time, I was mostly unaware of the impact of bullying on my psyche but as I grew older, I got to learn that bullying triggers your stress response, and when you've already experienced some measure of this in childhood, it can spell trouble for adulthood.

The bullying increased when we moved to a small town in southern Wisconsin near the Illinois border, but now it also had undertones of racism. When we first arrived in our new neighborhood, we got a chilly reception. We were teased, ridiculed, and bullied because we were overweight, and our skin was black. We rode the bus to and from school with the many nasty neighborhood kids. They were the most savage little f*ckers I'd ever met before moving to that neighborhood. For each time my siblings and I faced their taunts, it was like a scene from the movie Mean Girls, but in our case, the bullies were these mean hillbilly girls and boys.

We were called the N-word, Burnt Back Toast, Tar Baby, and other racial slurs more times than we cared to keep up with and we were called these names by the "white bread with mayo" neighborhood kids, as we began to describe them after some time. We'd never before experienced racism, white nationalism (racism rebranded), or whatever new name it goes by these days. Luckily, we were pretty sassy! When someone yelled out, "Hey, Burnt Piece of Black Toast," we'd clap back with, "You're a piece of stale white bread, and that's worse." Somehow, we were able to figure (almost instinctively) that although they were trying to put us down, they were just boring and basic, like a Hanes T-shirt, repeatedly saying the words "like" and "OMG" in the same sentence.

Living miles from any gas stations or grocery stores, when we went grocery shopping, we had to shop for a week or two. To that end, every shopping trip was like the apocalypse was coming and we had to "stock up." My mother was creative with getting extra money to buy endless amounts of food. She was a master of reselling too: she bought cheap items from the Salvation Army store, fixed them up, and then held garage sales with the revamped items. She also got the clever idea to start running a neighborhood candy store and so we'd go to Sam's Club (a membership bulk store like Costco), and load up on all the bulk candy, sweets, and junk food that we could find, then repackage and sell them in small bags to the neighborhood kids. When you walked in through our back door, you would see a beautiful display of candy, snacks, treats, and other edible delights: a rainbow of colors. Our housing subdivision was full of kids, and once word spread that there was a candy store in the hood, our candy store became LIT (popular).

Sugar, in our case, turned out to be a pacifier for emotional wounds and a powerful drug—the great equalizer. The same kids who taunted us and called us the N-word suddenly wanted to be our best friends because we had VIP access to all the candy in the neighborhood. Reese's, Gobstoppers, Sour Punch Straws,

Snickers, Tootsie Rolls, Milky Ways, Pop Rocks, Fun Dips Airheads; you name it, we had it. We were even dubbed the Candy Family by the people that lived in the neighborhood and we soon expanded our service offerings, adding chips, soda pop, and other delicious delights that we knew kids loved.

Like the Dakota pipeline, we had a sugar pipeline, with more sugar flowing through than you would find in the many treats at a Disney theme park. Soon enough, we began receiving one apology after another, invite after invite for sleepovers and parties, and the same kids that once taunted us now stood up for us, whenever someone at school tried to bully us. It was the most surreal and amazing encounter we'd ever had with the popular phrase about "tables turning." We proceeded with running our LIT neighborhood candy shop side hustle and loved every bit of the experience.

Since we always had a handy supply of candy and junk food from our candy shop, it meant that we also ate our products; yep! We got high on our own supply. I still get weak when I see Reese's Peanut Butter Cups, but I try to stay strong! In this instance, sugar changed our lives for the better by acting as an equalizer in the rift between us and the neighborhood kids. My endless consumption and cramming of sugars and carbs while growing up, however, did nothing but set me up for crazy cravings in my adult life.

Mindful Self-Reflection Innerval™

Biased behavior such as my siblings and I witnessed at the hands of the neighborhood kids can be conscious or unconscious but is most definitely inherited and becomes situational for most of us. When were three different times you experienced conscious or unconscious bias from someone else? Or can you identify if you have ever expressed conscious or unconscious bias towards someone else? How does this reflect your life today? What are you actively doing to be mindful of any conscious or unconscious bias tendencies that you may have?

_____

_____

_____

MOMMY'S MEDICAL MURDER

My father's name was George and although I never feel comfortable talking about my father, I know it's important to put down the impact his absence had in my life, so I can maintain as holistic a view of my life's path as possible. I didn't know so much about my father because he neglected and abandoned me, my siblings and my mother. When you experience abandonment at such a young age, the trauma of that can sometimes create abandonment and attachment issues in adulthood. I certainly had no shortage of those types of issues. I didn't grow up liking my father at all. I actually hated and resented him.

He was a stereotypical black male and what I'd describe as a deadbeat. He never had a real job, was a troublemaker, and was always in and out of jail for odd crimes and defaults. At the time, I also didn't understand the gravity and depth of systemic racism present in the criminal justice system. My father left my mother and showed no desire to remain the slightest bit relevant in the lives of my sisters and me. As I grew more conscious of the way society is structured and how fathers and mothers played joint roles in helping raise a child, I was hurt to find that my father was not really in the picture. No one likes to feel unwanted by one of their birth parents and I was no exception. I had no idea, however, the toll that harboring anger, resentment, and unforgiving thoughts and emotions towards my father would have on my mental, physical, and emotional health in the future.

The only good thing my father taught me is the kind of adult man to not be, and maybe that is something after all. I learned firsthand how I shouldn't behave as a Black male in America. I vowed to be the complete opposite of my father as he was never a real man in my eyes and I couldn't idealize or look up to him to learn anything worthwhile. The only person he ever cared about was himself and this character trait was deeply ingrained in him to a fault. I was the opposite and deeply devoted myself to other people. I cared about my mother and sisters more than I cared about myself. That was one of my big inner wounds. Seeing my father be as selfish as he was, drove me to the opposite extreme: caring for my mom and sisters more than I cared for myself. A consistent self-betrayal that would carry well into my adult years.

My father died of a rare type of cancer when I was 12 and honestly it wasn't that much of a loss, since I had already lost him at a younger age from all the times he was absent from my life. I was intelligent, resilient, and strong, and believed I didn't need a father; I was my own father and I could be a better father to my younger sisters than my father ever was. It was a role I knew nothing about but one which I autonomously stepped into, especially when my mother got sick.

Holding on to anger and resentment is like burning your own house down. I spent years hating my father. That hate was like drinking poison and hoping that he would get sick. It wasn't until I truly forgave him that I finally felt free. Forgiveness didn't make him right but forgiveness set me personally free, lightened my anxiety and stress levels, and unleashed energy that I never knew I had before. Forgiveness unfroze me. Forgiveness allowed me to convert my resentment into growth. I now know and honor that my experiences with having an absent father truly shaped me into the responsible adult that I am today, and I wouldn't have it any other way.

My mother Monica on the other hand was my "everything"—she was more a best friend than a mother (in the traditional sense of the word and role), and I was her first-born son, the only boy she ever bore. Monica was intelligent, funny, engaging, and disruptive, and she would cut you defensively just as fast as she'd smile at you and gather you into her arms (after giving you an intense rebuke for any irresponsible behavior). I like to think that I get a lot of my emotional maturity and inner strength from my mother because those traits that I outlined above, also really describe me to a tee.

She had a resilient, strong, and beautiful spirit. She also had a wig-and-weave obsession; yep! For the most part, we never knew who we were going to wake up to, some days she'd come out of the house looking like Beyoncé with a straight weave, and other days she'd be looking like Patti Labelle with a signature wig with the bangs in front.

My mother was also epileptic and had grand mal seizures*—the worst kind. I'll never forget the first time I saw her have an episode of the seizures. I was seven years old and we were at a Walgreens drug store. She simply started shaking violently and fell to the ground. I screamed at the top of my lungs and my screams made other people around me scream as well. There was so much chaos right in front of me in the space of a few minutes but for some reason, my 7-year old brain absorbed the shock I felt and it immediately dissipated, allowing me to quickly spring into action. I called 9-1-1 and tried to help her in any way I could, along with the help of the other customers that had now come to aid the situation as well as watch what was transpiring and as an ambulance crew arrived, my mother was taken in and we sped off to the hospital.

Once we got to the hospital and she had regained consciousness, the first thing she did was scold me because we were poor and didn't have insurance, and the last thing we needed was an ambulance bill. Her response tore me to pieces and if her words had been announced to a crowd with a public address system, I would never again be able to look anyone in the eyes; that was how much pain and shame I felt about the situation that we were in as a family.

She hid her epilepsy from us for as long as she did, because she could tame the episodes with medicine, but from that day forward I started learning as much as I could about seizures and epilepsy so that I could help her whenever she suffered one. Seeing as we could not afford ambulance bills, I felt that it was crucial that I understood her seizures deeply, even though she constantly denied my reality of what I experienced.

One of the most misunderstood or overlooked types of trauma is when a parent denies a child's reality. My mother shrugged the seizure incident off as no big deal and instructed us to not really address or talk about it again, even after knowing that they could happen at any moment. My mother was in denial regarding her illness and in turn forced us into denial. Experiencing and having seizures is so emotionally overwhelming that instead of facing it, she simply created a narrative around it to help her cope. And just like that, she was constantly telling us that what we felt, saw, or heard was not valid.

This inner wound caused me to seek out the 'familiar' in adulthood. I would unwittingly get into relationships that mirror this dynamic and seek out narcissists and other unhealthy friends, work, and romantic relationships where people would constantly deny my reality. My reality was denied for so long that I developed a strong duality-based mindset to cope. Things were dramatically either right or wrong, bad or good, or all or nothing. I became my thoughts, opinions, and emotions because there was a time when my thoughts, feelings, and emotions were invalid. I would strongly invalidate the thoughts, opinions, and experiences of everyone around me to feel safe in my rigid headspace. This continued to happen until my big wake-up call.

Having to drop out of college at 19 to take care of me, my mother had an even harder time keeping jobs because of her disability, she would try to conceal it at her workplace but sooner or later, she would have a seizure and get fired. In those early years, I took on the role of son, and big brother, father, and caretaker intermittently, interchangeably, and all these roles remained interconnected as I grew older and took on more responsibility.

When she had a seizure, I'd put something in her mouth that was soft so she wouldn't bite her tongue. Once the convulsions stopped, she'd be a bit disoriented, temporarily forgetting where she was for about 5 to 10 minutes. In her disoriented state, I'd keep asking her questions to get her thinking which would in turn help revive her faster and shake off the temporary confusion. I'd talk and look into her eyes and for the most part, she wouldn't recognize me and was sometimes even scared of me. It was always painful to watch and endure these moments, but I loved my mother and I would've done it a million times over again.

THE LAST SEIZURE

I was 16 years old and in the 11th grade. I became a popular kid in high school; I was a jock who played football, ran track, and was also in choir and did musicals. Our high school and the activities that we engaged in at school were basically like the scenes from the TV show, Glee. We were good at EVERYTHING!

Due to my popularity in school, I was always busy. Track practice, football practice, choir rehearsals, school clubs—I'd leave home at 7 a.m. and get home at 9 p.m. What I didn't realize was that all the sports, singing, dancing, and other activities that were keeping me busy were actually a distraction to keep me from facing, digesting, and processing the emotional traumas, tragedies, and tribulations I was experiencing in my life on various levels.

On January 12, 1999, there was a massive snowstorm. We were let out from school early at 1 p.m., and this was not a very welcoming turn of events for me. I didn't want to go home and stay in because of the snow, but I also thought it presented a good chance to catch up on a video game I'd been playing. Even though I'd become more fit and active, I still loved video games from all those years when I was chubby and with no acquaintances to play with. I loved video games because they shielded me from my immediate surroundings, distracted me from my inner problems, and the issues from the outside world. They would instantly turn off my monkey mind. My personal form of escapism. At the time, the video game was Final Fantasy 7, a role-playing game I had become entranced, engaged, and entwined in, playing it religiously whenever I was home.

As soon as I came home, my mother had a seizure. This was no big deal, I thought, because I had experienced it many times, and so I stayed with her until it ended, and she was coherent again (as I always did). About 3 hours later, after my sisters were home, my mother had another seizure. She'd never had more than one seizure in a day, ever. I stayed with her through the second seizure and she told me she felt okay when I asked with some growing concern, even though she'd had two seizures. I felt that something was wrong or off, but she said she felt alright, so I didn't want to press her on it. Again, my reality was being denied. My inner knowing said that she wasn't fine, but I chose to ignore it.

Once she fell asleep, I went back downstairs to pick up from where I left off in my game. I checked on her one more time before I fell asleep myself and she looked fine and was sleeping soundly. At about 3 a.m., I was woken up by my sister, Myeshia. "Something is wrong with Mommy," she said. I quickly left the couch and raced upstairs to see her lying still on the bathroom floor. Her foot was lodged into the door of the bathroom under a towel and it looked like she had slipped and fallen in the middle of another seizure. This was the third one within a short space of time from the last one.

I called 9-1-1 and once the paramedics came, they added more fuel to an already traumatic fire. Three white paramedics, disrespectful with their words, kept making comments about my mommy's weight and acted as if it was an inconvenience to lift her lifeless body off the bathroom floor, put her on a stretcher, and bring her down to an ambulance. She was pronounced dead on arrival at our home and the cause of death was pronounced as "seizure disorder." That's it? Yes, she had a seizure disorder—it is called epilepsy but she died slipping and falling while having the third seizure in a day from medication pushed on her by a doctor who cared more about drug concession profits, kickbacks, and incentives than human life. This experience did nothing but sow resentment in me for the way everything was handled from the moment the paramedics arrived with the ambulance until she was pronounced dead. I blamed myself for her death and I always wondered how different the situation would've been if I had called 9-1-1 when my gut told me to—when the second seizure came.

I was 16, my mother was dead, and I had to bear ridicule from the very paramedics ("Heroes") that were supposed to provide aid and support just because we were Black and poor, but can we ever really know why people are so disrespectful (even in those kinds of circumstances)? As I would learn later on, the prescription drugs my mother was taking at the time, Neurontin (Gabapentin) could also induce seizures even though it's prescribed as a common "anti-epilepsy medicine." Yes, I know what you're probably thinking and frankly, I couldn't understand either why a drug with such an adverse effect, could and can still be prescribed for conditions as serious as grand mal seizures.

RIP (rest in power) Mommy—I'll love you always and forever.

Mindful Self-Reflection Innerval™

It took me over 10 years to forgive myself for my mother's death. What are three things you need to forgive yourself for right now?

_____

_____

_____

11 //

YOUR INNER MUSCLES

You may be unaware whenever you get frozen in a stress or shutdown response, however, the easiest way to defrost is to start to become aware. You become more aware when you practice things that strengthen your awareness, like Interval Mindfulness™. Thawing begins as you consciously sharpen some of your most underrated skills. There are many skills that are useful and necessary in your daily life and, depending on what part of life you are in, these skills can differ from person to person. Skills are the expertise or talent needed in order to do a job, sport, hobby, or task. They are what make you confident and independent in life and are essential for success. You aren't born with skills, they are learned, practiced, and strengthened. Certain skills may be more or less relevant to you depending on your life circumstances, culture, beliefs, age, geographic location, etc.

Life skills vary by culture and age, but they are the capacity for adaptive, positive, and healthy behaviors to deal effectively with the challenges, demands, and uncertainty of daily life: healthy coping if you must. They are real-life strategies, behavior changes, and awareness that promote mental well-being, healthy social relationships, and a positive outlook. People with strong life skills are typically older and mature, less likely to be reactive, and more aware of their surroundings and themselves. Personal skills are the essential life skills we require in order to maintain a healthy mind, body, and soul. However, they are like muscles, and with motivation, training, and consistency, all skills can not only be learned, but practiced, strengthened, and improved.

Out of all the skills that you could possibly possess, the most important life skill is the ability and willingness to learn. Learning is more than a formal education. Learning can (and should), be a lifelong process that enhances our understanding of the world and improves the quality of our life. By learning new skills, we increase our understanding of the world around us and equip ourselves with the tools we need to live a more productive and fulfilling life, finding balanced ways to cope with the challenges that life, inevitably, throws at us.

UNICEF, UNESCO, and WHO list the core life skill strategies and techniques as:[108]

- Problem-solving
- Decision-making
- Critical thinking
- Effective communication skills
- Assertiveness
- Creative thinking
- Interpersonal relationship skills
- Self-awareness building skills
- Empathy
- Coping with stress
- Managing emotions
- Resilience

Self-awareness, self-esteem, and self-confidence are central to assessing your strengths and weaknesses. This helps you distinguish between opportunities and threats and strengthens your social awareness of the concerns of your family, friends, and the world. With a strong set of life skills, you can make informed decisions when a problem arises.

INNERVAL™ TRAINING

There are a certain set of life skills that you didn't learn in school but that have everything to do with your happiness, success, and well-being. I call them your "Inner Muscles" and have divided them into primary and secondary inner muscles. "Innerval™ Training" your inner muscles, allows you to consciously micro observe your mental, physical, and emotional state. With this observation comes power because you become aware of your mindless routines, habits, and behavior and can make the decision to implement changes.

Developing your inner muscles can help you work in alignment with your values, find purpose in your life when you have no idea what you want to do, and help you get unstuck so you can live life on your terms. Strong inner muscles help you find the courage to be yourself, empower you to do the things you authentically want to do and transform aspects of your life to work aligned with your desired terms. Strong gains in self-worth, self-discipline, and self-esteem are gained with consistent practice. The best part about strengthening your inner muscles is that they give you the ability to transform multiple aspects of your life simultaneously without even having to think about it.

When it comes to training, do you fully understand what's happening every single time you do an exercise? Do you know what's happening every single time you do a squat? Thoughts are triggered, nerves, hormones, signals, feedback loops, blood flow, oxygen, muscles, ligaments, tendons, top-down, bottom-up, reflex, etc. A squat is a very simple movement in theory, but very complex actions accompany it subconsciously. When it comes to training and exercise, you don't really need to know exactly how everything works for it to be effective. There are tons of science and experts that do that. You just need to stay motivated, show up, and keep doing it! The more consistent you are, the more you start to notice measurable results that I call big and little "wins."

Interval Mindfulness™ works the same way. It's Innerval™ training for your inner muscles and we strengthen them by using the power of neuroplasticity, which you will read about next. Strong inner muscles are your first line of defense when it comes to uncontrollable anxiety, stress, and negativity and shrinking the obstacles preventing you from reaching your hopes, dreams, and needs. So, you don't need to understand exactly how each Innerval™ is functioning when you're doing it. Just know that as you complete more and more Innervals™, you will be strengthening your inner muscles. Most of us have very different habits, behaviors, and thoughts today than we did 20 years ago. As you know from reading the above chapters, this shift is neuroplasticity at work. Your brain and nervous system aren't fixed or immovable structures; they can be changed by trauma and by neural exercises. "Plastic," as an adjective, just means easily shaped or molded. All brains have plasticity, some more than others.

According to Dr. Celeste Campbell, a neuropsychologist in the Polytrauma Program at the Washington, DC Veterans Administration Medical Center, "neuroplasticity refers to the brain's ability to adapt. It refers to the physiological changes in the brain that happen as the result of our interactions with our environment. From the time the brain begins to develop in utero until the day we die, the connections among the cells in our brains reorganize in response to our changing needs. This dynamic process allows us to learn from and adapt to different experiences".[109] Our brains have the capacity to change as we experience, learn, and adapt by creating and reinforcing new neural pathways. These neural pathways are what I refer to as inner muscles and neuroplasticity is the 'muscle building' function of the brain. It happens daily but can also be stimulated and encouraged. Since the brain is pivotal to all we think and do, by harnessing neuroplasticity we can improve everything we do and think.

If you teach your brain to do something new and repeat that action, it will do the new thing instead. But it's also a double-edged sword; neural patterns are hard to break. This function of your nervous system was developed so that you could do things you have to do every day without thinking about them. Going to the bathroom, brushing your teeth, driving, etc. In order to break destructive habits reinforcing our traumas, we need to do some training. By stimulating, encouraging, and training neuroplasticity, you help your brain to alter its pathways, strengthen certain areas, and remain flexible in its interpretation of events. A brain with strong neuroplasticity can:

➤ Think more clearly and calmly.

➤ Learn new skills easily.

➤ Manage emotional reactivity better.

➤ Create new healthy habits.

➤ Expand its ability to focus.

➤ Let go of habits that no longer serve them.

There are four main ways your brain can change itself physically:

1.   New Synapses: When you learn new things and have new experiences, your brain creates new connections between neurons. A synapse is what holds those connections together.

2.   Strengthened Synapses: When you are creating and reinforcing a habit, the synapses that connect those neurons, making the desired behavior easy and available, grow stronger.

3.   Weakened Synapses: When you are trying to break a habit, the synapses that connect those neurons, making the undesirable behavior easy to repeat, grow weaker through nonuse.

4.   Neurogenesis: This is when new neurons are created because of positive experiences, exercise, lowered stress, and other stimulating experiences.

Learning is a great way to stimulate neuroplasticity, but not all learning is created equal. When we learn, we form new nerve pathways in the brain and with each lesson comes the potential to connect new neurons and change our brain's default mode of operating. Learning facts, names, or other novel information doesn't really take advantage of neuroplasticity in the brain. However, extended learning such as playing a musical instrument, learning a new language, or learning another complex skill, reinforces new pathways over and over again, telling our brain to keep them and strengthen them. This intentional type of learning is what will help you rewire your brain. How much we can leverage the near-magical capabilities of our brain, all depends on how invested we are in promoting neuroplasticity and how we go about life.

I'm sure you've heard many "gurus" and self-help people talk about a growth mindset. A growth mindset is a mindset that one's abilities can improve with determination. Neuroplasticity mirrors this because it's the brain's ability to adapt and develop beyond the usual developmental period of childhood. A person with a growth mindset believes that they can improve at something through sustained effort. Ironically, this is also what neuroplasticity tells us. Environments that contain novelty and challenges help promote neuroplasticity and can spur growth after the "critical learning period" of early childhood and young adulthood.[110–112]

According to positivepsychology.com, here are some other ways to boost, enhance, or stimulate neuroplasticity:[110]

• Non-dominant hand exercises can form new neural pathways and strengthen the connectivity between neurons. This is why many self-reflection Innervals™ contain non-dominant handwriting.

• Intermittent fasting increases synaptic adaptation, promotes neuron growth, improves overall cognitive function, and decreases the risk of neurodegenerative disease.

• Traveling exposes your brain to novel stimuli and new environments, opening up new pathways and activity in the brain.

• Memory training and brain games can enhance connectivity in the prefrontal parietal network and prevent some age-related memory loss.

• Learning a musical instrument may increase connectivity between brain regions and help form new neural networks.

• Reading fiction increases and enhances connectivity in the brain.

• Expanding your vocabulary activates the visual and auditory processes as well as memory processing.

• Creating artwork enhances the connectivity of the brain at rest (the "default mode network" or DMN), which can boost introspection, memory, empathy, attention, and focus.

• Dancing reduces the risk of Alzheimer's and increases neural connectivity.

• Sleeping encourages learning retention through the growth of the dendritic spines that act as connections between neurons and help transfer information across cells.

Non-dominant handwriting is a part of a lot of Innervals™, so here's a quick note about it. There's an "unfamiliarity" theme in strengthening the nervous system and encouraging neural flexibility. Forcing your brain to perform familiar tasks with an unfamiliar tool (your non-dominant hand) can increase neuroplasticity by building up strength and dexterity where it wasn't before. Normally when you use the dominant hand it engages the opposite hemisphere of your brain to the hand that you're using; writing with your left hand engages the right side of your brain. Using the non-dominant hand engages both hemispheres and studies have shown that encouraging yourself to perform tasks with your non-dominant hand helps advance your brain in spatial memory, spatial cognition, and memory-guided motor control. This means new neurons are growing, synaptic connections are strengthening, and neuroplasticity is advancing.

Another great thing about neuroplasticity is that it means that emotions such as happiness, compassion, and joy can be cultivated in the same way that a person can learn through repetition. It can be trained, practiced, and rehearsed until you get good at it! Once you're good at it, your mind will activate these rehearsed pathways throughout the day, making you happier and more compassionate even when you're not practicing. Because your brain loves novelty, curiosity, and efficiency, Interval Mindfulness™ puts a variety of short intervals of meditation and mindfulness practices in different Innervals™. Because of the variety and short intervals, your brain naturally wants to come back for more.

The number one problem that Interval Mindfulness™ mediates, is the one that arises with people who want to try and change and experience resistance. Whenever someone tries to do traditional mindfulness, meditation, or relaxation practices they often struggle because their mind is resisting. This is especially true if it's a massive change from the non-stop, busy, and on-the-go lifestyle they normally lead. While neuroplasticity has amazing benefits and potential for all, it realistically takes a lot of work to reinforce the appropriate neural pathways. This is why very few try it or consistently keep doing it. Nothing changes from doing something once in large quantities; change comes from what is done consistently, even in very small amounts, every day.

Your mind always favors familiarity and will protest when you try to change nerve connectivity. For this reason, it's important to take small blocks of time to do this type of work. This is the exact reason we have broken them down into short Innervals™, to set people up for establishing habits of doing daily inner work. If you do too much at once your brain will become fatigued quickly. Inner work and subconscious reprogramming will only work when your brain is in a rested and relaxed state. Most people are easily overwhelmed at the thought of watching their minds. By breaking this inner work into Innervals™, it allows people to slowly over time allow their brain to gain tolerance to these new activities and prevents them from going into stimulus overload. This is what sets them up for success! And because I'm more invested in your success than in your possible obstacles, here it is below, the simplified breakdown...

PRIMARY INNER MUSCLES

SELF-AWARENESS.

Self-awareness is your ability to inwardly and effortlessly control your attention. This is also your strength to observe your own mental, physical, and emotional state including your thoughts, habits, and behaviors.

SELF-DETERMINATION.

Self-determination is your inward realization that you have strength and control over your choices and life. Without outside influence, you can make decisions about how you want to think, feel, and behave and that will influence the outcome.

SELF-ACTION.

Self-action is your ability to take action that originates internally. Your inner call to action for new ways of thinking, feeling, and behaving.

These three primary muscles are independent but interrelated. You can't build awareness unless you learn how to inwardly control your attention. You can be aware of your thoughts, habits, and behaviors and not determine that you need to change or do something about them. Even if you do determine that you need to make changes, you won't get anywhere unless you are strong enough to take action on what you determine is the best for you.

Some of your secondary inner muscles that I won't cover as deeply, but that will come along with this practice, are: Resilience. Focus. Habits. Concentration. Assertiveness. Creativity. Willpower. Confidence. Motivation. Presence.

Are you inwardly controlling your attention or does your attention shift from outer and environmental cues? Your mind and its many functions are your most valuable assets. Energy flows where your attention goes, and your attention is a series of micro-investments. Are you getting good daily returns on your micro-investments? Probably not if you're letting your outer world direct your inner well-being. What's going on in your mind can make you feel grateful or miserable, successful or stuck, and energetic or drained.

Your mind triggers your anxiety, stress, and negativity and it's also the very thing that can quickly relieve them. The quality of your mind determines the quality of your life, and most people have a poor quality of life because they don't focus on their mental fitness. Yet, our mind can be molded, stretched, and shaped the same way people do with the body, but most people think of their mental fitness as an afterthought if even at all. The easiest way to change your mind is to change your nerve state.

I shared with you in the previous chapter, the series of beliefs and circumstances that created the earliest version of my preconditioned self, most people aren't aware of their preconditioned self and the fact that they're thinking the same thoughts, telling the same stories, and feeling the same feelings over and over again. So go on and write it down, find the triggers and beliefs that made your preconditioned self. We have the power to choose to act differently but without the awareness or mental fitness, we are reinforcing old, negative, and unhealthy patterns. Patterns are set up by our brain for survival and to conserve energy. Because we're so focused on survival and energy conservation, our attention selectively focuses on experiences that are pleasant, threatening, or different. The physical threats of our past have been replaced mostly with mental worries and hurt. Our mind naturally wanders because most of those worries and hurts happen in the realms of the past and the future.

There's SO MUCH emphasis on moving the body and physical fitness, yet many people wonder why they're having uncontrollable anxiety, stress, and negativity as well as other mental frustrations. We are inundated with sports, workouts, yoga, calisthenics, and more. These are all great because movement is great for the body and the body is designed to move. The problem is that people get so focused on the physical that they neglect the mental or emotional, or just assume focusing on the physical will naturally strengthen the mental and in turn their emotions. It does to a point, but you're only getting half the benefits of well-being by focusing just on outer workouts. But don't forget, your mind is also a muscle and it must be worked primarily and independently.

If you're just working your upper body and assuming that your lower body will get stronger as well, what do you think will happen? Just ask all those weightlifting bros out there that regularly skip leg day! Movement, exercising, and lifting may help to temporarily relieve our anxiety, stress, and negativity, but it's just a bodily band-aid. If we don't correct the problem at its source within the mind, we spend a lifetime internally bleeding, with inner and outer band-aids, and behind our challenges instead of in front of them.

SELF-AWARENESS. SELF-DETERMINATION. SELF-ACTION.

Attention is one of the most expensive and underestimated tools that can help you master all three skills (primary muscles). Most people take it for granted, have a very passive attitude towards it, and assume they have no control over it. Everything outside of you like people, technology, and your environment, as well as everything inside of you like your thoughts, emotions, and memories, are all auditioning for your attention.

Your attention is the fuel of your mind, and what you pay attention to will grow, expand, and self-generate. Likewise, what you take your attention away from will weaken, shrink, and evaporate. Every time you hit the gas and pay persistent attention to a thought, you are planting, reinforcing, and growing it, allowing it to consume you. Mastering your attention will make you the master of your mind, mastering your mind will make you the master of your anxiety and stress. What you think will always determine how you feel, what you do, and ultimately the type of life you will live.

...and how do you master anything? By consciously training it.

Another key muscle of your mind is your awareness. Awareness is one of the greatest skills that you can develop, but no one really trains it. Have you ever simply watched your thoughts, emotions, and behaviors judgment-free? Awareness is your ability to be in touch with what you're feeling in the moment and what's happening around you. Do I feel anxious or calm? Am I focused or fearful? Am I practicing habits that are bringing me closer to my hopes, dreams, and needs or further away from them? Awareness is a gift because it gives you the ability to choose. Ultimately, choosing is what gives us freedom and it's one of our greatest privileges.

Awareness is the super muscle that allows you to become aware of your external triggers and allows you to calmly respond instead of reflexively reacting. You become able to better intervene on negative, stressful, and limiting thoughts, actions, and habits and can quickly stop them at their tracks. Strengthening your self-observation skills is one of the proven benefits of meditation, mindfulness, yoga, and many other contemplative practices.

Building your self-awareness stimulates your prefrontal cortex, the planning part of your brain that regulates self-control, willpower, decision-making, and imagination. It's also the most powerful way to strengthen your insula and anterior cingulate (brain areas that are required for processing self-love, empathy, fairness, as well as pain, love, addiction, and craving). This area of your brain must be strong, for obvious reasons, unless you are happy being a hermit in a cave, awaiting the next snowstorm to go chop your next set of wood and call it a day.

Without a strong self-awareness muscle, you wouldn't even be aware of when your thoughts, emotions, and behaviors are working against your hopes, dreams, and needs instead of with them. The sooner that you can become aware of your thoughts, emotions, habits, and behaviors, the sooner you can self-determine what's working for you and what's not. Your strengthening of awareness leads to empowerment and the building of choices. When you're in the throngs of life or mounting anxiety, stress, and negativity, it's hard to realize that sometimes you have more choices than what's being presented.

Building your self-determination muscle means that you, with no or minimal outer input, decide how you want to think, feel, and behave. Self-reflection helps you self-determine what's right for you moment to moment. The first two primary inner muscles would be nothing without the third and final muscle, self-action. Anything you want to achieve in life requires a strong, flexible, and sustained focus. Slow and steady wins the race. The people who want instant gratification, fast results, and quick fixes mostly end up worse than they started in addition to wasting precious time. Just ask the 90% of dieters who regain more weight than they lost, 70% of lottery winners who lose their winnings within three years, and entrepreneurs that we never hear about that launch businesses and then fail.

Getting unfrozen requires you to consciously strengthen the above inner muscles. Ambushing anxiety, stress, and negativity and trying to reach your hopes, needs, and dreams require strong, flexible, and sustained focus over time. When you need to create new nerve pathways for how you want to think, feel, and act it takes time, training, and consistency just like training any muscle. You'll only get maximal results by Innerval™ Training regularly and that's why we eliminate most of the barriers, frustrations, and time constraints associated with consistency.

Mindful Self-Reflection Innerval™

You just learned about your primary inner muscles and how they intimately influence your attention. On a scale of 0 (weak) – 10 (strong), how strong are your primary inner muscles right now?

SELF-AWARENESS. Your ability to inwardly and effortlessly control your attention. Where are you on a scale of 0 – 10?

SELF-DETERMINATION. Your inward realization that you have strength and control over your life and choices. Where are you on a scale of 0 – 10?

SELF-ACTION. Your ability to take action that originates internally. Where are you on a scale of 0 – 10?

12 //

SUICIDAL CITY (BOTTLED GRIEF)

My mother's funeral was Saturday, January 16, 1999...I was 16 years old.

Thoughts of the best ways, reasons, and times to kill myself floated through my head like clouds would float through the sky. They were quiet, yet intense thoughts (in the background), always there, and moving very slowly. I gathered up the courage to try and do the unthinkable many times but as soon as these thoughts came up, I would think of how many people would be at my funeral if I did go through with killing myself, just as I once stood by my mother's grave on that fateful Saturday, bereft of all hope.

I am by nature a very selfless person, and that thought alone was enough energy to instantly sideline my daily road trips to a place I called "suicidal" city. Each time I gathered the courage, I would climb in my car, put my seatbelt on, safety first (right, perhaps, I wanted to be safely dead), and get on the road to suicide and then someone (like family, a close friend, teacher, or loved one) would jump in the middle of the street waving their arms to catch my attention and cause me to swerve off the road and into a side lane or ditch. Like the theme of the movie, Groundhog Day, this kind of behavior would be on a continuous loop and occurrence for a long time. I went on reliving the same thoughts and inclinations towards suicide every day during those first few months after my mommy's passing, but I never worked up the nerve to follow through with selfish suicide. The people that surrounded me simply watched me closely, which is why I'm still here, capable of sharing my experiences with you now. Some of my good friends at the time that disrupted my many attempts include Eric, Danielle, Matt, Paul, Pero, and Tiffany. I appreciate you all more than you know, and I'm thankful for your efforts.

Despite the overwhelming depression, grief, and sadness that I felt from losing my mother so early, I had to go on, if not for myself, then for my sisters, who were even younger than I was. I quickly realized that I had to delay my grieving, rise up to be the man of the house and be strong for my younger sisters. They looked up to me and I was the only father figure they knew. I believed that they had to see me handle this like an adult. The adult way that I chose was to hide my grief and "man up", a decision that wasn't the best for me in the long run. Growing up having my reality denied, I naturally became really good at doing it myself. This would be the first time that I would get frozen in my shutdown response.

In another area of my life, I was a popular 11th grader and that also meant that I couldn't be depressed or grieve in public. I was the person with all the energy. Everyone loved me. I would lift people's spirits and moods just by talking to them. I couldn't be depressed or bring anyone's moods down as a result of my low moods. So I went on to fake it months after my mom passed on—fake it till you make it, right? Well, I was a good faker and my shutdown response (autopilot mode) is very convincing; you'd hardly know if I didn't explicitly tell you.

Autopilot is also known as your shutdown response or down-and-depressed nerve state. When our nervous system experiences dysregulation due to trauma, we cope because the present moment doesn't feel safe. A dissociation where our mental awareness turns inward or even disappears entirely when overwhelming danger presents itself causing a withdrawal of consciousness from the body. We are not in the "here and now", and we may feel as if we're having an out-of-body experience (OBE). An OBE, or the shutdown response, feels as if you are watching what's going on from a great distance or above yourself. Normally this should be a temporary nerve state shift. However, because I was frozen in my shutdown response, that's where I stayed for months, years, and decades. I was physically there, mentally checked out, and functioning autonomously. We learn to begin dissociation in childhood when life feels too big to cope and there's no parent or caregiver to nurture, guide, or emotionally support us. I don't have a lot of memories from childhood because when we are chronically disassociated, we can't form memories, it's our mind's way of protecting us from the painful overwhelm we are feeling. Sigmund Freud was the first to connect childhood trauma with memory loss, or repressed memories.[113] This idea began to gather steam in the 1990s when a number of therapists suggested a link between unexplained mental health symptoms and forgotten childhood trauma.[114]

Losing my mother was the catalyst for my foray into fitness and becoming more active in the fitness industry. In my personal fitness workout sessions, the powerful surge of endorphins from all the lifting and exercise helped me cope with the grief, anger, and resentment of her death. You never stop grieving over the loss of a loved one, (especially a sudden and unexpected loss) and I know this deeply for I can still feel tiny sensations of grief every now and again, at the thought of not having my mom by my side. We just learn how to manage, work through, and cope with that grief over time as I have found from my experience.

I can tell you that there's no better feeling than a big endorphin rush from working out and I soon became addicted to "feeling good." People process trauma differently but what we all have in common is seeking something outside to be a self-soother: drugs, video games, porn, self-harm, and so forth. Maybe the image I had to sustain in front of others kept me sane. My ego saved me, because turning emo and gaining an eating disorder would have gone against the outside reassurance, I needed the most at that time, which was popularity, and people that relied on me. Plus, my nature was to be very active in high school, I couldn't ever sit still, I was always moving, even more than before, and always with a smile on my face.

During my workouts, I would convert all of my emotional energy into something more manageable or bearable by lifting heavy weights, exercising, football, track practice, and yes, choir, madrigals, and musicals (all the activities that are good for vagus nerve stimulation). I didn't know it at the time, but my nerves (literally, every fiber that existed inside my body) were carrying me through my emotional struggles. I was in therapy full-time by using all of those workouts and activities as outlets and as a personal treatment plan, which got me through the challenging times I had witnessed. Now I'm not recommending these types of things as a replacement for seeking help if you truly need it, whether that be with a (preferably holistic) psychologist, psychiatrist, or other mental health professional. These are the things that positively helped me cope with challenging times in those specific moments. They may work for some people and not for others. In my head at the time, this was better than drug use, abuse, and medications. But please try to stay away from medications if at all possible. Once you're on that medication train, it's hard to get off without crashing and burning.

My very unhealthy family gene pool puts me at high risk for a lot of illnesses—high blood pressure, cancer, diabetes, epilepsy, heart disease, just to name a few. After the loss of my mother, I lost my aunt and my grandfather and this was only the beginning as I would lose even more immediate family members, one after the other, to chronic diseases. Fitness was my therapy to cope with my losses all the time, but deep down, I also hoped that my newfound shift to fitness would help me outmaneuver any and all of those chronic diseases that I thought were slowly coming for me down the line since I was already genetically predisposed to them. These thoughts drove me into an endless marathon, trying to outrun what I call a "chronic disease bloodline."

THANKSGIVING TRAGEDY

When it came time to decide where I wanted to go to college, I wasn't sure what I wanted to do with my life. It hurt me deeply that I had no mom to talk my options over with. The one thing I knew in my heart that I really loved to do was to perform and each time I thought about my mommy sitting in the audience, it felt right. I could even see her smile. I opted for the University of Wisconsin-Stevens Point because they were nationally recognized for their musical theatre program, and that's what I wanted to study.

I stayed back in our small town, but my sisters went to live with my grandma Bernice in Memphis, Tennessee. Grandma Bernice, the second most important woman in my life, was a recovered alcoholic. She'd only had two daughters: my mother and my aunt. She'd lost my mother and not long after that, she lost my aunt to chronic heart disease. The gripping grief caused her to relapse, and she became an alcoholic again, while also picking back up smoking cigarettes. At the time, I had no idea that she had relapsed after my aunt's passing as I was off at college, trying to focus on becoming a musical theatre star.

Every year, even when my mommy was still alive, we had a tradition of going down to Memphis to visit Grandma Bernice to spend Thanksgiving with her. College was stressful and I was really looking forward to traveling down to Memphis from the UW for Thanksgiving. I left early on Wednesday morning, November 24, 2003. Memphis is about 750 miles away—an 11-hour drive and on my way, I blasted soundtracks to my favorite musicals, like Rent, Lion King, and Children of Eden, and envisioned the lemon tarts I would have for Thanksgiving dancing in front of me. Grandma Bernice made the best lemon tarts in the world.

Suddenly, my phone rang and quickly pulled me out of my daydream. The caller turned out to be some distant cousin who I'd never heard of before. "There's been a fire," she said. "Your grandma didn't make it out. She's gone..."

I was going at about 80 miles an hour on 1-94 and as that call and the news came through, I found myself swerving in and out of the lane as tears filled my eyes and everything became one big blur. I couldn't see through my tears, couldn't even hear from the roar of blood pumping in my ears. "What?! Say that again." For a moment, I thought I had heard her wrong. This could not be happening. My blood pressure went so high that all I could hear was a roar in my ears. "Huh?" At that moment I had thought I lost my Grandma Bernice, sisters, and basically everything. If I crashed, if I died, I didn't care at that moment. I then started thinking about how much fun I had around my grandmother and the last time I saw her. How I loved her cooking and I was obsessed with her lemon tarts. This short interval of a moment served as a "nightlight" or safety anchor to briefly bring me out of my hysteria and back into the present moment, where I was swerving in and out of lanes on I-94 at 80 miles per hour. My nightlight gave me enough relief that I finally pulled over to the side of the interstate, was able to calm down a little and have access to more inner resources and choices to deal with my current situation. On the side of the road, I hit the redial button on my phone and called my cousin back. "What about my sisters?" I asked. "They weren't at the house with your grandma. She needed a little break from them for the weekend, so she let them stay at their...your...cousin's house; they're fine, Mario."

When I got to Memphis 3 hours later, I saw the structure of a burned-out house, which was at the exact address my grandma had just moved to. I got out of my car and walked to the front door of the house. The inside of the house was charred, black, and full of debris. The smell of smoke filled the cool November air and tears poured down my face once again. I stood still for a minute and felt a mixture of cool and warm energy come over me in what seemed like my grandma's spirit.

I dropped down to my hands and knees on the porch and just bawled. "I'm so sorry, Grandma!" I apologized again and again to my grandma for not being able to be there to save her. If I'd only left sooner, I thought, I might've been able to save her. But I cried and cried, feeling so alone, so hurt, so guilty, and so sad. There would be no fancy Thanksgiving dinner, no lemon tarts, and no big arms to hug me and welcome me "home" from college.

Later on, I was told that there'd been an electrical malfunction that caused the fire. My grandma was actually trying to get out, but the smoke inhalation overpowered her before she could make it to the front door. As my grandmother was a smoker, I couldn't help but wonder what the case would've been if she hadn't damaged her lungs in that way; maybe she would have managed to get out in time before the smoke inhalation could completely inhibit her movement.

Once again, not wanting to digest, process, or touch my overwhelming emotions, I neurocepted into my shutdown response. I began to pile anger, grief, sadness, depression, and racing thoughts, which built bricks in my inner emotional closet. Who wants to embrace sadness? Who wants to face grief? Who wants to be exposed to so much tragedy so early on in their lives, before they've had the chance to develop shock absorbers? I can tell you; no one wants that, and I was no exception.

I kept experiencing more countless tragedies, losing one immediate family member after the other, to preventable chronic diseases, like diabetes and heart disease. Regardless of how happy I may have seemed in school, I was still dealing with grief discreetly and intensely. I continually sought out ways to handle all the emotional pain I felt and during that time, developing a love for all things sci-fi, comics, and anything supernatural, and I think it was because I was always yearning for an escape from the realities of my own life.

Life can be full of hardships and we are confronted by way more reality than many of us can process or stomach sometimes. Although it's nice to take a step back from reality and get lost in the fantasies of our minds, we have too many ways to ignore, dismiss, and reject our sometimes harsh realities. According to LifeHacker "Escapism is the tendency to seek distraction and relief from unpleasant realities, especially seeking entertainment or engaging in fantasy. It allows a momentary reprieve from your circumstances, giving you a chance to recharge your batteries before you jump back into the fray."[115] We scroll on social media, read books about wizards, hobbits, and faraway lands, and explore virtual worlds with powerful avatars.

Escapism has many forms. It can be the TV or movies you love, the music you listen to or even daydreaming. Escapism is completely normal until they become unchecked. Some of the more extreme forms of escapism are things that put your health or well-being at risk, things you wouldn't normally do and may regret later like substance abuse, or gambling. Escapism isn't necessarily a bad thing, but it can be unhealthy depending on what forms you are doing, how much of them you are doing, and if you're doing it for the long term. It may help you cope in the short term, but things will always degrade over time, or you'll get desensitized and require a higher intensity or riskier ways to escape. At some point, the escapee will have to face what they are avoiding because some things don't simply just blow over. People engaging in escapist behavior generally aren't thinking about how it will affect their lives long term because feeling better now is the only thing that matters. At the end of the day, we need a healthy amount of fantasy, daydreaming, and escaping into fake godlike security and freedom, cathartic theatrical outrage, and righteous indignation.

Speaking of avoiding, as a child, and even as a young adult, I was always avoidant when it came to negative emotions. I didn't understand that emotions carry a form of energy and the intensity of them only grows when you try to automatically avoid, hide, or run from them. Not only that, repressed, suppressed, and held-in emotional energy buries itself deep into your trillions of cells, making them heavier and having to work harder than they actually should. Like walking around with a 50lb heavy backpack, it takes a massive amount of energy to hold onto undigested, unprocessed, and untouched emotions. Your body also is naturally drawn to unresolved things. The more and more you try to avoid, the more and more your body tries to fight to get a resolution.

I reflexively reacted and one moment I didn't care if I lived or died and welcomed crashing my car. Then, all of a sudden, I focused on a night light, a micro-moment of safety that I would try to focus on for at least 30 seconds. I thought about hysterically laughing out loud with my grandmother and eating about 10 of her lemon tarts in one sitting. I invited this night light in and briefly allowed it to overtake me. This brief night light-triggered my ability to think rationally in a dark place for a split second, ultimately leading me to choose to carry on living. One short night light interval of safety anchored me into the present and allowed me to understand that I had more choices. That night light saved my life because at that moment, I was able to shift into my relaxation response nerve state and adopt a more proactive approach to my emotional reaction. Think of how many times it could possibly save yours and help you make better decisions for big emotional struggles and shifts or for smaller and non-life-threatening situations? I was able to constantly transcend my current experience of being overwhelmed, and all it took was a short night light interval to set my mind on the best path. Imagine what would happen with conscious and consistent practice?

Certain smells, sounds, places, and people, etc can trigger or activate a shift into a different nerve state. Triggers are quick and most commonly associated with shifting you into a stress response. Night lights are designed to help shift you into a relaxation response. How do you feel when you are truly seen, heard, and validated? How does it feel to receive unconditional love? What does it feel like to have your needs met? Who makes you feel safe? Who makes you feel warm and genuinely loved? Where do you feel safe? When was a time in your life when you were the happiest? The answers to these questions and more can serve as potential nightlights for you.

Night lights are short intervals (30 seconds) that are meant to invoke safety, anchors that help bring us back into our relaxation response when we feel overwhelmed with anxiety, stress, and negativity. You really need to be present and aware in these moments because how they make you feel when you experience life can be very subtle and nuanced. Look for moments in your life when you truly felt at peace, safe, loved, or enough. Night lights can help calm your stress response nerve state and bring you back to self-regulation or balance. When you regularly bring attention to these short safety intervals, you create momentum to shift you out of your stress response and back into your relaxation response. Sometimes you need to cycle through several night lights to make that positive nerve state shift. I have a core six set of night lights that I revisit time and time again. What are your core six?

Mindful Self-Reflection Innerval™

You saw that it took a short night light interval to change my thinking and get my focus on the right path that ultimately saved my life. I want you to think about your nightlights. Try to have a core six that you can always go to when you're drowning in your stress response.

1. What people, places, or things make you feel safe and connected?

2. What feelings, smells, or sensations make you feel safe and warm?

3. What does your nightlight feel like? What sensations or emotions does it bring up?

_____

_____

_____

"RUN, LOST BOY"

I was forced into adulthood as a kid. I wasn't a boy anymore and so I had to become a quick learner. I learned how to do everything I needed to do for myself because there was no other way around it. As soon as I got back to school, it was right back to business as usual. Everyone asked me how I was doing and told me they were sorry for my loss and once again, I hid any overt signs of grief and assured them that I was doing fine.

Trying to attempt to get out of my shutdown response, I tried everything I could imagine to keep triggering my stress response. However, instead of fighting, I chose running. I basically became a Black Forrest Gump. Self-betrayal was my BFF. If I said that I was fine enough times, I could actually be fine—following the power of repetition, or so I thought. This approach works if you have the energy resources to sustain it, but most people run out of energy resources trying to push past emotional struggles in this way, leaving them tired and wired constantly.

I was a musical theatre and dance major in college, so my schedule was always jam-packed—regular school classes, dance classes, vocal lessons, acting classes, studying, reading plays, and so much more. It felt good getting back to my school routine and having to be focused on something so that I could automatically avoid my grief as usual. I kept myself busy, was always on the run, and never stayed in one place for too long. Committing to anything was so scary to me and I really didn't know what a commitment would demand from me so I preferred to avoid it as often as I could. The only things that had been permanent in my life were my sisters and I felt that the relationships I had with them were enough for me (as far as commitments go). Subconsciously, I also figured that if I remained in constant motion, no more traumas could catch up with me.

So, run I did; Run, run, run...

Being a master (or so I thought) at operating from being frozen in either my stress or shutdown responses, I had built the constant habit of always repressing, suppressing, and auto avoiding my sadness, grief, and depression. One day, I woke up and I was incredibly tired. My eyes opened and I was trying to move but couldn't. In fact, I could barely speak, but I managed to call out to my roommate, Craig. I loved Craig, 5-foot, 10 inches, 160-pound, beautiful all-American white guy, who loved to go hunting. His nickname for me was "Jigga". Kind of a microaggression but his intent was to be endearing so I let him get away with it.

He took one look at me and called 9-1-1. This was the first time I had ever gotten sick to the point of going to an emergency room in an ambulance. I was always active and healthy, thanks to my regimen of dance and other exercises. I was diagnosed with strep* and mono* and had to remain in the hospital for two weeks. Being frozen had literally froze my *ss! The first thing I thought was this: all the years of witnessing deaths, family drama, and depressions, coupled with my frozen stress and shutdown responses has finally come full circle, in the form of two chronic infections at the same f*cking time. Good job, bro!

My body's energy was telling me to slow the TF down before I killed myself. Not really telling me, but crippling my mind, collapsing my body, and crazily crushing my energy to prevent me from doing anything productive, anything at all. Your body always keeps the receipts, and your body always wins, that's for sure! Most people often view themselves as a dictatorship or a one-way dysfunctional relationship. Their mind wants something to happen and so they command their body to follow suit with no regard to what their body really wants and needs.

Your body will try to whisper to you, talk with you, reason with you, and even try to adapt somewhat, but if you stay super-stubborn and constantly ignore your body's inner whispers, it will always find a way to hijack your attention with dramatic, paralyzing, and ear-piercing outer screams. When your body has to hijack your attention for any reason, it's never a good thing; and it's too little too late.

For two weeks, I had no choice but to lie in a hospital bed, recover, and finally grieve for my losses to some extent. To a person who has always strived to be busy and moving, two weeks lying still and bed-ridden seemed like an eternity and a torturous eternity at that, but my mind, body, and nerves were demanding it, and so that's what it had to be.

Mindful Self-Reflection Innerval™

Constantly leaving my emotions undigested, unprocessed, and untouched played a huge role in my double whammy of chronic infections. Have you ever had a major health issue? Reflecting on that issue, are you able to connect it to an unprocessed emotion or unresolved trauma?

_____

_____

_____

Side Note: Depression is very real; it will wear you out as days become gloomier. You will naturally isolate because only other depressed people can empathize with your pain if it's beyond other people's acceptable time frames for grieving. We all grieve differently, if you are considering self-harm or leaving this world, please reach out to the suicide hotline. National Suicide Prevention Lifeline 1-800-273-8255 suicidepreventionlifeline.org. I pulled myself out of it only because I'm stubborn, at the cost of getting ill. Perhaps it was a higher being or my mother from heaven but from my repeated trips to Suicidal City, dear aching soul: I see you, I hear you, and I feel you. Know that what you are feeling in this moment is temporary and you don't have to go through your pain alone. Lean into some type of support system that you feel is the best for you at this moment.

13 //

YOUR PRIMARY AND HYBRID NERVE STATES

In earlier chapters, I gave you a preview of the three primary nerve states. Now it's time for the deep dive as well as an introduction to the hybrid nerve states. You hear the most about your stress response, or fight-or-flight response because it's the fastest nerve state shift that does the most physical, mental, and emotional damage quickly. It's so trigger-happy that anything surprising, alarming, or unexpected can put it into action; mostly without you being conscious of it. Your relaxation response, on the other hand, takes longer to activate, and when it does, it generally goes away quickly, like a one-night stand. So, it takes way longer and more energy to relax than it does to fight or run; go figure! No wonder it seems like people are going crazy.

Your stress and relaxation responses are like opposing muscles that complement each other. For the most part, they are mutually exclusive, meaning they can't happen at the same time as they switch off between one or the other. Typically when one of them is strong and on, the other one is weaker or off (or its actions are extremely minimized). Like yin and yang, your stress and relaxation responses are necessary complements that keep your body in a state of homeostasis (balance). After sleeping all night and finally getting out of bed in the morning, you would experience a massive drop in blood pressure if your stress response didn't kick in, in order to balance your heart rate and get you moving. True balance is when both your relaxation and stress response muscles are strong, flexible, and responsive. Innervals™ help meet you where you are, no matter what your primary nerve state is, and help you take micro-moments of safety to help you take baby steps back to balance.

YOUR STRESS RESPONSE MUSCLE

When properly triggered, your body is capable of extraordinary things (all in the name of survival). Your stress response, originating from your sympathetic nervous system, is important to optimize your body for evasion and aggression.[116] It's activated to act in everyday life and when your mind or body "thinks" you're in immediate physical, mental, or emotional danger. If you shift into this nerve state, you are powered up to respond to threats with an almost superhuman effort. This fear-based movement tends to occur when you don't feel safe and is closely related to emotions of anxiety, anger, and fear. These root emotions can be the energy driver: in fighting for your life to overcome a threat or running for your life to avoid a dangerous situation.

Here are some of the changes your body goes through when your stress response is activated:

PHYSICAL

- Your pupils expand, allowing more light to enter your eyes, thus increasing vision.
- Your heartbeat speeds up.
- Your digestion comes to a screeching halt.
- Your glycogen (the storage form of carbs) is converted to glucose (carbs) and released into your blood; extra energy stores just in case you need them.
- You stop making spit and your mouth gets dry.
- Blood flows to your lungs and your bronchioles dilate, allowing for more oxygen exchange.
- Your muscles contract and spasm.
- Blood flows away from your skin.
- Blood flows to your muscles by as much as 1,200 percent.
- The response also stops you from pooping and peeing.

SOCIAL

- When you are in the "fight" part of your fight-or-flight stress response, you would be more confrontational with people and invade their space or privacy.
- You would have quicker and erratic movements, make aggressive eye contact with others, or avoid looking into the eyes of others.
- Your face would appear flat to others with wide eyes.
- Your voice would become short, fast, and monotone.
- When you are in the "flight" part of your fight-or-flight stress response, you would avoid people and situations or increase your distance between friends, family, and others.

PERCEPTION: The world feels threatening, dangerous, and out of control.

MENTAL: Concrete, evaluative, hyper-focused on the past or future.

EMOTIONAL: Feelings of anger, anxiety, danger, intensity, and tenseness.

PROS: You can move quickly, be aggressive, defensive, escape, or avoid.

CONS: You can't think clearly/critically, weigh options, be empathetic, or self-regulate/self-heal.

Critical functions like digestion, healing, and burning fat are put on hold so your body can be at its prime for fast, focused, and intense action. These changes maximize your ability to survive by ensuring that you have all you need for escape mechanisms for fighting infections and general wellbeing.

Your stress response isn't a bad thing, and your body needs it. It is somewhat engaged via hybrid nerve states during sports, friendly competitions, and even during sex. Being triggered into a stress response doesn't have to only be about physical violence, as you may have noticed in your body. It's anything that can be perceived as threatening, like sarcasm, negative comments, aggressive tone of voice, or verbal abuse. Aggression toward people and being passive-aggressive can stimulate your stress response, as much as holding onto what you don't like and not expressing how you feel. Unresolved trauma and other inner wounds constantly trigger your stress response. Emotions are energy, and when you don't express how you really feel, that energy has to be expressed somewhere else, normally somewhere in your body or mind: as anxiety.

Your stress response becomes overactive (frozen) in a number of diseases, according to a review in the journal Autonomic Neuroscience.[117] These include cardiovascular diseases[118] like heart disease[119], chronic heart failure, and hypertension. Beyond heart disease issues when your stress response is frozen it's also been associated with kidney disease[120], type II diabetes[121], obesity[122], metabolic syndrome[123], and even Parkinson's disease[124]. Being frozen in your stress response also underlies mental health conditions such as anxiety, depression, and chronic stress, an article in Forbes reported.[125] In short intervals, your stress response can be useful and grant an energizing boost of mental focus. If prolonged, however, the stress signals humming through your body wreak havoc. Besides maintaining a mental feeling of constant stress, the extra epinephrine and cortisol damage blood vessels, increase blood pressure, and promote a buildup of fat.[126]

So while your stress response serves an important purpose, you don't want to be frozen in it with it on all the time. In optimal health, your body should always return to baseline balance when the stressor, threat, or emergency goes away.[127] Ideally, you should only be in a stress-response state about 20% of the time daily. In today's modern society, however, people never leave it and get frozen in it. Being frozen in a stress response nerve state is the underlying issue for most chronic diseases.[128]

YOUR RELAXATION RESPONSE MUSCLE

The state that people need to be in most of the time surprisingly isn't really talked about a lot: your relaxation response, that originates from the ventral vagal side of your parasympathetic nervous system.[116] Your relaxation response optimizes the resources in your body for growth, healing, and restoration like the balance of bodily systems, hormone release, immune system[129], and digestive functioning. It takes longer to get into this state, yet it stimulates the more tranquil functions of your body, like lowering your heart rate[130], allowing you to take fuller breaths, and helps you to find calm, balance, and optimal health. Think of it as your "balance brake" or Zen state...

Here are some of the changes your body goes through when your relaxation response is activated:

PHYSICAL

- Digestive enzymes are released to help you digest your food.
- This dilates the blood vessels to your digestive tract, increasing blood flow.
- Your heartbeat slows down.
- Your muscles relax.
- Your pupils get smaller, allowing for close-up vision.
- You pee and poop more.
- Your mouth waters.
- You may get sexually aroused.
- Tears may flow.
- Your breathing constricts.

SOCIAL

- You can easily make gentle eye contact.
- You will feel more comfortable and safe around people.
- You can get closer to people physically and figuratively.
- You will have a wider range of facial expressions.
- You can hear human voices more accurately and tune out other noises.
- You have a wider range of posture and physical gestures.
- Vocal prosody: stress, pitch, intonation, pauses, volume, and pacing.

PERCEPTION: The world feels safe, peaceful, fun, interesting, and manageable.

MENTAL: Balanced thoughts, empathetic, curious, hopeful, and understanding.

EMOTIONAL: Feelings of calm, happiness, connection, joy, excitement, motivation, relaxation, awe, and hope.

PROS: Focus, plan, weigh options when making a decision, self-regulate and provide co-regulation, use play, and be self-reflective.

CONS: You can't move quickly, be aggressive, defensive, escape, or avoid.

Located between your spinal cord and your brain, your body's parasympathetic nervous system has two different branches and is organized to conserve energy, digest, and absorb. It does this by stimulating your body's relaxation response that promotes calm, rest, and repair. It also metabolizes your nutrients, helps with nutrient absorption, and takes protective measures, like curbing heat loss, slowing your heart rate, and reducing your energy.

Moving along longer pathways that are slower to activate, the primary job of your relaxation response is to control your body's homeostasis, or balance, of bodily functions. Just like Goldilocks, your relaxation response wants everything not too hot or cold, but just right: warm. It does this by resetting your body to a calm state, enhancing concentration, allowing your body to restore, repair, and relax after being triggered into excitement, stress response, or hyper-arousal.

Acting as a powerful balance brake, your relaxation response literally calms your nerves. It also relates to all the positive emotions that you experience, like love, joy, and satisfaction. When you feel safe, without feeling like you need to be on the defense, this makes your social interaction and engagement feel safe. It's crucial to your survival to cooperate socially with others whether you like to or not and it's your relaxation response that makes that possible.

Remember, the default state of every system in your body is balance or homeostasis. When your relaxation response is flexible, strong, and stable, you're actively social, calm, and feel good. You laugh, dance, play, or talk with friends and through it all, you feel safe. In fact, a healthy relaxation response allows you to connect to yourself and the world on deeper levels, and to empathize and bond with others. It helps you accurately read others' facial expressions to figure out whether they are safe to approach or not and also allows you to sense your gut feelings or inner intellect that inform you of safety and danger.

In optimal health, your relaxation response acts as the balance brake that gently suppresses the stress response unless it's truly needed.[131] Your relaxation response can also subtly immobilize you so you can hold still long enough to make love, bond, or snuggle with and care for babies, children, and pets – which is how the most vulnerable among us engage with protection: through connection with others.

The relaxation state's promotion of relaxation, rest, and regeneration is the precursor for optimal emotional, biological, and physical health, as well as loving relationships. Alternatively, when we shift into a stress response, we become egocentric and can't access our higher-order thinking. We abandon the realms of rational thought and conscious choice, and all our energy goes into defensive, instinctive, adaptive, and aggressive tendencies and behavior. This is why it's unwise to try to argue with or reason with someone who is having an emotional reaction to something, on the defense, or being triggered. Let them calm down first before engaging and try your best to compassionately disarm them.

FIGHT UPPER INNERVAL™ COMBO. (3 minutes)

1. PUNCH FORWARD INNERVAL™ 1 // 30 seconds.

Think of a time when you became so frustrated about something that you wanted to fight but couldn't. Then start fighting by punching forward (one fist at a time) as fast as you can. Do this for 30 seconds or 60 times if you don't have a timer.

2. CORE BREATHING INNERVAL™ // 30 seconds.

Take long, slow, and deep inhales and take longer, slower, and deeper exhales for 30 seconds or 3 cycles (1 inhale/exhale) of breath if you don't have a timer. As you inhale for 3 seconds your core goes out, and as you exhale for 6 seconds your core goes in.

3. Repeat 3 times

STIMULATION. The motor cortex, phrenic nerves, vagus nerves, and posterior thoracic nerves.

YOUR SHUTDOWN RESPONSE MUSCLE

This is the shutdown system of the dorsal vagal parasympathetic branch of the autonomic nervous system.[82] Whenever you face an overwhelming danger or imminent bodily harm, and your fight-or-flight measures are unlikely to succeed, your body shuts down its bodily processes to conserve its resources. This can look like temporarily losing consciousness, auto-pilot, or playing dead.[132] This nerve state is supposed to be temporary and something the body easily comes out of when they can move to safety. Some of the emotional reactions associated with this state are hopelessness, withdrawal, helplessness, and shutdown. If you've ever seen an animal on the side of the road that's hurt, it could be playing dead until it can get the energy to move to safety. When you're staring into the face of death, destruction, or fatal danger, your shutdown response is activated and can give way to shock, fainting, dissociation, or shutdown.[133] Your shutdown response is the oldest and most primitive nerve state response causing rapid shutdown, slow-down, disassociation, and other depressive behavior.

Here are some things that happen when your shutdown response is triggered:

PHYSICAL

- Your body slows down internal energy to death-like states.
- Your body stops movement at the cellular, mitochondrial, and other physiological system levels.
- Your body conserves energy by stopping all stress responses.
- Your survival becomes passive instead of active to wait out an overwhelming emergency.
- The immune system is suppressed and has decreased ability to fight bacterial, viral, and other infections.
- You have a harder time recovering from physical, mental, and emotional exertion.
- Blood pressure lowers.
- Gut wall lining weakens and sometimes develops into leaky gut syndrome.
- The body's ability to absorb nutrients decreases.
- Your body stores nutrients and fat.

SOCIAL

- You may experience numbness and disassociation.
- You will have a limited range of emotional expression.
- Disconnection from self and others can occur.
- You will make less eye contact.
- Movement will be inhibited.
- Your voice becomes more monotone and flatter.

PERCEPTION: The world feels overwhelming, uninteresting, demotivating, and pointless.

MENTAL: Thoughts become helpless, hopeless, gloomy, and apathetic.

EMOTIONAL: Feelings of hopelessness, tiredness, fogginess, numbness, aloneness, worthlessness, and disconnectedness.

PROS: You can conserve energy, temporarily numb discomfort, and ride things out until you can head to safety.

CONS: You lose motivation, energy, connection, and hope. You'll also become colder, disconnected, isolated, and lethargic.

Have you ever fainted at the sight of blood or of a needle? Or felt drilled to the ground unable to move during or after a scary or stressful event like hearing shots being fired, getting into a car accident, or witnessing something deeply disturbing? If you have, you've experienced firsthand what it's like to trigger your shutdown nerve state. Ever heard the expression that something scared the shit out of someone? That's because, if the shutdown response is activated, it can cause you to poop or pee suddenly because your body lets go of essential functions.

However, under threat, your shutdown response pulls its emergency brakes all the way up. Your shutdown response is not a conscious choice or some type of mind game during this threatening situation: it's rather an unconscious, unwitting, and undetectable nerve state that expresses as a last resort in situations where you feel helpless to address the threats, emergencies, or stressors because you believe they can't be overcome.

Your shutdown response can also flood your body with euphoria, numbness, or other feel-good hormones so that the pain of a physical assault, broken bone, or other emergency doesn't prevent you from engaging in fight-or-flight if you must. When your shutdown response is triggered, your body diverts energy from eating and digesting to selfishly conserving as many resources as possible to maximize survival. In the animal kingdom, giving up or sudden death can sometimes be lifesaving. By playing dead, you might avoid the attention of a predator or enemy. In many stories of mass shootings, you hear about people who survived because they played dead—this can happen either consciously or unconsciously. Although this may be good for the short-term, staying in this state for the long term becomes the problem.

If you're frozen in a shutdown response nerve state you could experience nausea, vomiting, and paranoia. You're in this autopilot state. You can complete tasks, think thoughts, daydream, and multi-task all without being fully conscious. You are not in the present and it could feel as if you're having an out-of-body experience. Often, during a traumatic event, you hear people say afterward that they don't remember what happened. That's because their brain was incapable of forming words or images about what had been going on, and they were reacting to their present situation from a more primitive part of the brain and nerves. This primitive part of the brain is sometimes referred to as the "lizard brain" and once it kicks in, it's like shifting into energy autopilot mode.

After a threat has passed and you are frozen in your shutdown response nerve state, you can have depressive feelings without being clinically diagnosed as having depression, just like you can have intense feelings of anxiety without being diagnosed with an anxiety disorder. People living with depression generally lose interest in the things that they once enjoyed, some may even think about (or attempt) suicide. Symptoms such as depression can be caused by the over-activation of your shutdown response. Living a life full of fear isn't truly living; it's paralyzing, literally. Your nerves can legitimately paralyze you completely!

HYBRID NERVE STATES

As you've learned, your nerve state is going to be either in a stress response, relaxation response, or shutdown response. These are the primary nerve states of the polyvagal theory by Dr. Stephen Porges. Your nerve state is going to be a reaction to the outer world, your inner world, and your perceptions of either or both. It does, however, get a little more complicated than that. Justin Sunseri LMFT, a licensed marriage and family therapist does a great job of making the polyvagal theory easy to understand, utilize, and digest.[134] He talks a lot about "mixed states", which in this book I will call hybrid states. Your primary nerve states can actually mix into hybrid states (like primary and secondary colors) and there appear to be different degrees of intensity for each. In essence, our nerve state isn't just how we behave, react, and feel, but also the filter that we experience the world through.

The narrative or stories that you tell yourself will be extremely different depending on what state you're in. Your state dictates your stories. Living in the relaxation response nerve state is more calm, soothing, connected, hopeful, and loving. In the stress response state life is more aggressive, stressful, anxious, and dangerous. And in the shutdown response state, life is very numb, empty, and disconnected. It's so important that we deep dive into each of the nerve states, primary and hybrid, because awareness becomes your power. The more you can recognize these states within yourself, the more control you will have over them. Essentially, if you don't know what response you are in, you can't take the appropriate steps to acknowledge or change it. With this understanding, you will have greater success on your Interval Mindfulness™ journey because you will be able to recognize and react to the various states. With that said, here are the three hybrid mixed states.

PLAY: Stress response + Relaxation response

FREEZE: Stress response + Shutdown response

STILLNESS: Relaxation response + Shutdown response

In order to access these hybrid nerve states easily where you shift in and out of them, your nervous system has to be balanced and regulated. Play is a hybrid nerve state that is shared, synchronous, in the same state and following the same rules. Face-to-face contact is an important aspect of ensuring that play remains safe, and play exercises the ability to self-regulate; to tap into the defensive states while staying in the safety state. We play a lot as children, but as adults, we seemingly have forgotten how much fun it is to play, how good it feels, and how rebalancing it can be.

Freeze is a hybrid nerve state that is being immobilized while being highly charged. Like if you were to push the brake and gas pedal at the same time. More commonly, someone may experience a freeze as a panic attack. During a panic attack, the body has a high level of stress response energy but immobilizes. The muscles are tense, breathing is shallow and thoughts of danger race, yet the body is paralyzed. Freeze energy may become frozen in the nervous system or the body. This is at the heart of PTSD, resulting in flashbacks, nightmares, being easily triggered, intense and prolonged distress, changes in thought and emotion, and increased isolation. That freeze energy is either chronically present or easily triggered into overwhelm, panic, or rage. A body in the freeze hybrid state has less access to the safety pathways. Building the strength of the relaxation response is important in allowing people to enter in and out of the freeze hybrid state and builds the person's resilience or tolerance to life's stressors.

Stillness is a hybrid nerve state that is being immobilized while feeling safe. The ability to be still while safe is important for basic life functioning like sleeping, sitting in silence, practicing self-reflection, and relaxing. People that are frozen in their stress response nerve state, may still experience feelings of danger. This is the main reason why a lot of traditional meditation, mindfulness, and relaxation practices don't work for people who are frozen in their stress response. Stillness doesn't feel safe if you're used to being on the go, busy, and operate primarily from your stress response. Your relaxation response isn't strong enough to anchor or help you settle into a calm stillness. When you're in a stress response, you're in emergency and survival mode with the fire alarms blaring. You need to be mobile, aggressive, and evasive. The last thing you want to do is sit in a chair or lay down and try to be silent while your brain is ruminating about all the things that are unsafe for you right now. If you're in the wild running from a tiger, the last thing you're going to do is hide behind a tree, calmly recite a mantra, and then go to sleep. You use the stress response energy inside of you to run or fight for your life until the threat passes. If the threat never passes like a pandemic, you get frozen.

How do you break this negative feedback loop of being frozen in a shutdown or stress response nerve state? You can strengthen, stabilize, and mobilize your relaxation response to kick in more often. Just like you have control over your stress response, you can also activate your relaxation response at will. Petting a dog or cat, getting a massage, foam rolling, or reading a book at night can stimulate your relaxation response. For others, yoga, meditation, or tai chi works just as well. Whatever you do, the point is to do something that makes you truly relaxed. This could be sports, social engagements, hobbies, or simply spending time laughing with good friends. Whatever you do, take note of your thoughts and feelings so that you can easily recreate that mental, emotional, and physical state for the times you come under stress. The specific Innervals™ of Interval Mindfulness™ are designed to strengthen your relaxation response so you're able to shift to balance faster and stay in balance longer.

FLIGHT FULL INNERVAL™ 1 COMBO. (3 minutes)
1. FLEE INNERVAL™ // 30 seconds.
Think of a time when you became so frustrated about something that you wanted to run but couldn't. Then start pumping your arms and running in place with high knees as fast as you can. Do this for 30 seconds or 60 steps if you don't have a timer.
2. CORE BREATHING INNERVAL™ // 30 seconds.
Take long, slow, and deep inhales and take longer, slower, and deeper exhales for 30 seconds or 3 cycles (1 inhale/exhale) of breath if you don't have a timer. As you inhale for 3 seconds your core goes out, and as you exhale for 6 seconds your core goes in.
3. Repeat 3 times
STIMULATION. The motor cortex, phrenic nerves, vagus nerves, and posterior thoracic nerves.

14 //

STRESS WEARS MANY OUTFITS

Overwhelming, overloading, and overcompensating stress is what freezes you and causes you to become frozen for long periods of time. This next section is important because it's vital that you understand all the different aspects of stress. One of the quickest ways that you can get instantly hijacked by your stress response is by experiencing inner and outer stress. Stress is adaptive, cumulative, and you can't master it unless you recognize the many different outfits it wears when it shows up in our lives. Just because you don't think you are stressed in your mind, doesn't mean that you aren't stressed in your body. Safety is felt in your body, not your mind. You master your stress by understanding all the different things to look for. Welcome to twenty-first-century America, where technology is supposed to make our lives easier. Now, don't get me wrong, it has in many ways, but what it ultimately has done is save us time on some types of chores so we can spend it on others, rather than enjoying consistent rest, relaxation, and regeneration. With that, we have the constant of STRESS...

I think it's crazy that we automate, outsource, and use technology to make things less stressful, only so that we can dive headfirst into other stressful situations and challenges. When you think about stress combined with the pandemic, an unhealthy political climate, and other major world events, the rise in senseless shootings, suicides, and chronic health issues begins to make sense. Now, add a layer of managing health issues, taking care of a loved one, looking for a job, having relationship issues, or raising a child. And now, for the icing on top, let's add the traffic jams, flight/train delays, work issues, and drama with friends, family, and loved ones.

Remember that our stress response helped our ancestors survive wildfires, animal attacks, floods, and conflicts with other humans. Nowadays, we are very rarely in an actual, physically threatening situation, but this response can still be triggered when you get an unexpected text, perceive a threat, or find yourself in a stressful situation. The stress reverberating through our body via our stress response is crucial in dire circumstances. But little of modern life truly requires a response of this magnitude. Most of the time, our stress responses are operating like the processor of a laptop, as a sort of background hum, keeping us anxious, hypervigilant, and on edge. When we train our relaxation response to turn that background hum off is when we can efficiently relax. This is why we must work harder on building new pathways to cope with changes that happen in our environment without intensifying real responses from our bodies. In today's stressful world we can no longer simply relax or turn "off" like a switch; we must train ourselves to relax so that we can effectively start to downshift so that it gets easier and we can naturally do it longer.

Like all things in your body, stress happens on a spectrum and it's all about balance. The balance of your stress levels and your inner resources are available to deal with your stress levels. Most people underestimate the amount of stress they are under and as a result fall into stress debt, default, or bankruptcy. Unlike financial institutions, stress doesn't send bill collectors or affect your credit, it sends diseases and negatively affects your life. Stress mastery happens when you're mindful of the dose, frequency, and load of your stress, just like in weight training. Trying to lift too much weight, too fast, and at one time will have you falling on your *ss in public and always have negative outcomes. After any and all stressful events, to counter your stress response, your relaxation response should kick in and your body should be able to easily, quickly, and calmly relax, in theory. Most of us, however, are frozen in our stress response and have a strong, dominant, and trigger-happy stress response, while the relaxation response lies weak, forgotten, and is rarely used. You can only rescue yourself from yourself, with a strong relaxation response muscle.

TYPES OF MODERN STRESS

Hans Selye was an Austrian-Canadian endocrinologist, who published more than 39 books and 1,700 articles, and is known today as the father of "stress research."[135] He defined the term stress as a "non-specific response of the body to any demand for change," as well as identified the hypothalamic-pituitary-adrenal (HPA) axis as the area of the brain that copes with stress. This traditional exploration of stress doesn't really cut it for modern times, however, because it does not take into account modern technology, the speed at which information travels, and the many cultural and political factors that I've mentioned. I will take Selye's basic definitions of stress, but will expand upon them using the information I have drawn from 20 years of clients, research, and personal experience. That said, I will list here my own version of some types of modern stress…

MICRO STRESS (HEALTHY). Also known as eustress, this type of stress is your body's instant reaction to a new, challenging, and uncomfortable situation, and everyone experiences it to one degree or another. Marriage, adventures, having a baby, winning something, new friends, or completing a big project are some examples of micro stress. It also has the common trait of providing a good endorphin high for anyone who experiences it.

Micro stress can be good for you; it keeps you energized, and its association with adrenaline can also be experienced if you're on a rollercoaster, skiing, surfing, or racing to meet a deadline. Once the micro stressor has passed, your body's systems should quickly return to normal.

H STRESS (HEALTHY). High, controlled, and short-term stress in balanced amounts can be fun and exciting and have positive effects on your body. I call this H STRESS (healthy) and it's also known as hormesis. H stress, like resistance training, cryotherapy, high-intensity exercise, infrared saunas, and sun exposure, aggressively challenge your body for a short, controlled, and low-dose period, triggering your body to later adapt, build resilience, get stronger, and increase your capacity to handle all other types of stress.

MANAGED STRESS (HEALTHY OR UNHEALTHY). This is a short-term type of stress that can be either positive or negative, depending on your perception, the load, frequency, and how you manage it with your available inner resources. Many people are depleted of their inner resources because of little to no rest, relaxation, and recovery. It is a recollection of stress that you encounter daily and have grown accustomed to: the stress associated with bills, jobs, kids, traffic jams, difficult people, or social conflicts. You may get anxious, irritable, or sad, or you can experience gut issues, migraines, and headaches. These discomforts stick around for a short time and normally disappear when your stress starts dissolving.

A-STRESS (UNHEALTHY when UNCHECKED). This is a self-imposed type of stress that's highly associated with "Type A" personalities. This self-inflicted stress is created by personalities whose core beliefs include an extraordinary competitive drive, impatience, aggressiveness, and a never-ending sense of urgency. Sometimes, this self-inoculated stress results from being reactive to hostility, deep-seated insecurity about performance, perfectionism, busyness, and overextending. If it goes unchecked, you'll be creating a life of relative or organized chaos.

N-STRESS (UNHEALTHY). This self-imposed stress is suffered by people with macro anxiety and worry, who are negative by default. This insidious, self-inflicted stress is associated with people who are negative binge thinkers and chronic complainers, and who always find a way to see the dark side of everything. They have incessant negative thoughts, always asking the "What if" questions to project negative outcomes, and always assume something awful is going to happen. Within their deeply fear-rooted reality, they start to imprison their own body too: demonstrating either chronic illness or hypochondria symptoms.

EVENT TRAUMA STRESS (UNHEALTHY). Also called acute stress disorder, this is an intense type of stress that often accompanies witnessing, experiencing, or being confronted with a traumatic event. These traumatic events can cause intense fear or horror, or make you feel helpless, and can last a few days, or be constant for up to a month. Some examples of traumas include abuse, sudden death, near-death experiences for you or a loved one, threat of serious injury to you or a loved one or becoming handicapped or dismembered.

CHILDHOOD TRAUMA STRESS (UNHEALTHY). Childhood trauma goes beyond a one-time traumatic event, assault, or extreme abuse. It's not the events themselves, it's the product of how those events and experiences are processed. A big traumatic experience for one person may not be a big traumatic experience for another, but when you're a small child, everything that happens to you seems big. How you process the traumatic event depends on how you've seen your parents process emotional events, emotional regulation, and any early-life habits. Childhood trauma includes lack of boundaries, unmet needs growing up, emotional neglect, not being seen/heard, having your reality denied, being told to hide certain emotions, having parents who can't regulate their emotions properly, and a variety of things that people (typically) don't view as trauma.

Many people associate childhood trauma with events, extreme abuse, and neglect. Many adults think nothing "big" happened in their childhood and unconsciously develop coping mechanisms that they need to help them survive. It's only when they get into adult life, after years and decades of conditioning those habits, that they realize how they no longer serve them in adulthood.

MACRO STRESS (UNHEALTHY). Also known as chronic stress or distress, this is a low-grade and long-term type of stress that's constant, intense, and never-ending, like an overwhelming career, a chronic health issue for you or a loved one, or a serious relationship or marriage gone sour. Or more recently known, a pandemic with no end in sight. Divorce, injury, negative feelings, or financial problems are negative life experiences that produce macro stress. It's a massive type of uncontrolled stress that your body thinks it can't handle, or ever effectively adapt to. Macro stress can also come from unresolved trauma experienced in early childhood. It quietly and unconsciously destroys your mind, body, and life, and causes dysfunction. It's the unwitting stress of war, poverty, dysfunctional families, abuse, trauma, racism, and violence. It gradually breaks the mental, emotional, and spiritual will of a person until they just completely give up all hope.

EMPATHETIC STRESS, aka MIRRORING. Have you ever cried while watching a movie or a touching TV commercial? What about experiencing a sense of excitement and joy when your favorite sports team wins a game? Whether in real life or via TV, phone, or online, when you see another person's behavior and emotions, your mirror nerves start to fire. Your mirror nerves reflect that person's experience as if the behavior were your own. This is what creates empathy and helps you enter their story. As you watch people having experiences, you feel like you're living that same experience. The daughter getting married is your daughter; the team winning the Super Bowl is your team. However, when you're stressed, your empathy is down and it's hard to show compassion or love toward others or even yourself. On the flip side, many people don't realize that stress is super-contagious. If you feel stressed and can't really figure out why, look at the people you engage with. Research shows that stress is highly contagious, not only regarding how you feel, but also in the way your body responds to it and it's all because of your mirror nerves.

BATTLE OF THE RESPONSES

Every time you're triggered into stress, there's a battle of your responses. When your body is under macro stress, it increases your stress-response tone; your stress response basically gets a six-pack, while your relaxation response becomes a limp noodle.

Your stress response should be balanced, not strong, because when it's strong, stubborn, and dominant (frozen), it puts your relaxation response on vacation and your body can't properly digest, relax, feel safe, or self-heal. One of the golden rules of nerves is that: if you don't use it, you lose it. Remember how I keep talking about being frozen in your stress response? Well, when you're able to have fun, play, laugh, and core breathe, you start to stimulate, strengthen, and tone your relaxation response. This raises the temperature allowing you to gently thaw out your nervous system which enhances the relaxation, safety, and self-healing processes of your body that can potentially trigger spontaneous healing. Interval Mindfulness™ and its Innervals™ are designed to help you strengthen your relaxation response muscle, defrost your nerves, and get these two responses closer to being balanced.

Your stress response is always fighting for dominance, and people tend to shift and (unwittingly) get frozen in their stress response as a dominant state. Truth is, you should be good at responding to the needs and demands of your ever-changing environment and also be good at switching off and relaxing. The question shouldn't be "how do I reduce stress" the question should be "how fast can I recover from any, and all stressors?" Those answers lie in the strength of your relaxation response. Most of the time, the state of your relaxation response should be dominant (60% or higher), so that you can relax, feel safe, and self-heal effectively from life's daily stressors.

JAW R/L MOTOR COMBO. (3 minutes)

1. JAW R/L MOTOR INNERVAL™ // 30 seconds.

Start moving your jaw from right to left as fast as you possibly can. Do this for 30 seconds or count to 30 if you don't have a timer.

2. CORE BREATHING INNERVAL™ // 30 seconds.

Take long, slow, and deep inhales and take longer, slower, and deeper exhales for 30 seconds or 3 times each if you don't have a timer. As you inhale for 3 seconds your core goes out, and as you exhale for 6 seconds your core goes in.

3. Repeat 2 times

STIMULATION. The phrenic nerves, vagus nerves, motor cortex (3), and posterior thoracic nerves.

REWARDS CLUB CARD: PATHWAY TO ADDICTION

You probably know this already, but if you don't, let's take the cat out of the bag: stressed people are a cash cow for a multitude of industries…

Are you stressed? How about social media, video games, gambling, food, sugar, salt, and other distractions to make you temporarily feel better for a few minutes?

Still stressed? Buy some clothes, electronics, novelty things you'll never use, and maybe go out for some fancy meals or drinks.

Really? You're still stressed? How about an expensive facial, massage, manicure/pedicure, gym membership, workout class, yoga, or come to our mindfulness retreat.

Simply put, if people weren't stressed, many businesses that serve as distractions, short-term remedies, and instant relief to stressors would be out of business. Your attempts to cope with stress fill their pockets with cash. Think about it!

Stress acts on the same pathways as your reward response and thus, alongside its expression, it triggers reward-seeking, obsessive, and addictive behavior. When you develop reward-seeking, obsessive, and addictive behaviors, it makes you less happy. Being less happy means lower levels of dopamine activated and with this, you'll have more intense cravings for your reward-seeking, obsessive, and addictive behavior, and even higher stress attached to it. It's a hamster wheel and your brain is the hamster. Over time, it will take a wider exposure to your reward-seeking, obsessive, and addictive behaviors, to reach an initial level of feeling euphoric, until the euphoria is no longer reachable, because frankly, how much larger can your exposure get?

Your reward response is a nerve circuit with a motivational role that tells you that completing certain actions like drinking water, eating, winning money, desserts, and sex are pleasurable. Hell yeah! Our reward response is what ensures that we thrive and keep reproducing by encouraging us to keep doing things that are pleasurable to us.

Addiction to drugs can hijack your reward response and these drugs stimulate euphoric feelings of their own, which is why it's so easy for people to become addicted to substances. At first, it's euphoria on demand, until it's not. Nerves in your ventral tegmental area (VTA) in your brain secrete dopamine, which controls your sensation of pleasure. Dopamine is released in your brain and makes you feel good when you do certain things in sync with survival, but having high levels of dopamine constantly flowing through your brain has been linked to substance abuse, food and alcohol binging, and drug abuse.[136]

Addiction to sex, smartphones, drugs, alcohol or any other form of addiction is a major stress signal that something deeper is going on with that person, but most people with these addictions never want to address what's really going on with them. The issue is that most people aren't being mindful about the quality and quantity of what they're consuming. This shouldn't be the case because even though you have this endless buffet of stimulation, information, and connection, your nerves should be shifting into rest, safety, and self-heal rhythms to balance out any over-consumption, and you should be able to know when to really slow things down.

Know that you have five times more fear-based nerve circuits in your brain than reward circuits, so by default, you already have a natural tendency to focus on what could hurt you, rather than what can help you, thus, being mindless in your consumption is only adding fuel to your negative fire.[137]

Social media on the other hand of modern addictions is actually "anti-social" media because it offers the illusion of connection without the actual benefits, kind of like random hookups. It's the people who spend the most time on social media who tend to be the most anxious, stressed, and depressed, and suffer from many health issues. Loneliness increases the stress hormone, cortisol (stress hormone), and you already know the damage that the constant presence of cortisol can do to a person's mind, body, emotions, and soul.[138] Instagram is a lot like gambling. People scroll endlessly and double-tap, constantly seeking gratification or "jackpot." It's like seek, seek, hit, seek, seek, hit; an endless loop that never stops. You cannot help but wonder at that constant chase which is a lot like a dog mindlessly chasing a car—if he caught it, what would he do?

When your reward response is activated, there's a decrease in present-moment anxiety and stress. And so it follows: when people are stressed, they're motivated to binge-eat satisfying snacks, fast food, and desserts, and this only raises the cravings. Why is this important? Ultimately because f*cking up your entire reward circuit or living like a hot mess by default, will grant you the benefits of a life filled with: chronic illness. You get it? You aren't supposed to live on edge with all your signals on, personal development is all about removing the layers of stressors, originated in trauma and living whole and fuller lives; you should feel like you're thriving instead of surviving!

INFLAMMATION INCINERATION

We just went through mostly outer stress, but most people don't realize the insidious, invisible, and inner stress that keeps them frozen in their stress response for long periods. I've talked about how getting frozen in your stress or shutdown response happens when there are danger cues in your inner and outer world. Outer world problems are the most relatable and recognized, but inner world problems are often invisible, insidious, and potentially more damaging. If your body is experiencing certain types of inflammation, especially over a long period, this can get you stuck in your stress response. Inflammation is an insidious inferno that sends out inner fire alarms that trigger your stress response. You get stuck in your stress response when you ignore your inner alarms and don't address the root cause of your inflammation incineration.

How often do you experience aches and pains? Do you have injuries, illnesses, or health challenges that you have been dealing with for a long time? Have you ever eaten something and felt bloated afterward? Have you just felt sick, had low energy, and did not know why? The root sources of your health challenges could be an undercover, slow-moving, and long-lasting internal fire of insidious inflammation. You are 'hot stuff, baby' but not in a good way.

You often hear people talk about inflammation regarding injuries or infections because when your body is infected or injured, your immune cells get the signal and produce inflammation factors called cytokines. Your friendly local cytokines round up other immune cells and escort them to the site of the infection, which causes the typical redness, soreness, and puffiness that you see. That red, swollen ankle is screaming, "Hey, look at me! I am hurt. Do something!"

If something toxic, harmful, or damaging affects a part of your body, there is a biological response to try to remove it. The body actually has its own bouncers, just without the cute and tight black T-shirt. Your immune system increases blood flow, dilates your blood vessels, and creates chemical messengers to respond to a perceived injury, infection, or threat. Inflammation is typically the first step to initiate your body's self-healing process (Hey, Brutus, get over here!) and without it, wounds, infections, and damage to your tissues would not heal. The signs and symptoms of inflammation may be annoying, inconvenient, and uncomfortable, but they show that your body is trying to self-heal.

Inflammation is a generalized term, can be quite incognito, and you will not really feel the true nature of its effect until it is too late; it expresses as a full-blown chronic disease. In fact, inflammation is one of the underlying conditions and the main contributor to most chronic diseases, dysfunction, and even death. Inflammation damages your body at the cellular level. Because of that, anything that depends on your cellular health and function comes to a screeching halt, with damaging effects to your entire body that can create and fuel chronic disease in many ways. This is why inflammation triggers a stress response. It's an inner stressor and often goes unnoticed as a small, contained fire burning in the background of your body.

What is heart disease? It is inflammation of your body's arteries. What is arthritis? It is inflammation of your joints. What is IBS and leaky gut? It is inflammation of your gut. I could go on and on, but hopefully you get the point. Prior to the manifestation of physical illness, and chronic disease, there is a long-term buildup of inflammation.

When you have a strong, balanced, and responsive nervous system, you can easily shift into your relaxation response. Shifting and staying in that nerve state helps naturally and dramatically to drop your inflammation levels. The first and most important step to taming your inflammation levels is listening to the sensations of your body, what I call inner whispers or self-feedback signals.

When you were born, certain defenses in your immune system were already in your body. This is called innate immunity and is different from adaptive immunity when your body learns to fight a specific infection after being prompted by a vaccine or actually infected. Your innate immunity consists of different boundaries that are your first line of defense, to keep harmful and damaging things out of your body like enzymes in your skin oils and tears, your cough reflex, mucus that traps microparticles and bacteria, and stomach acid. Inflammation is part of your innate immune responses. Think of it as a soldier on the front lines that has always been there to fight for you.

In an attempt at self-protection, your immune system will recognize pathogens, irritants, and injured cells, start your body's healing process, and use inflammation to protect you from injury, infections, diseases, and more. In this way, inflammation is helpful to you but it can also be harmful if it gets out of balance and runs away unchecked. No matter what health issues you are facing, once you reel in the underlying inflammation, it can be the number one strategy to overcome and even reverse a chronic health challenge. It could also be the thing that helps you get unfrozen.

Another important cause of inflammation is oxidative stress, and this can come up due to emotional stress, eating sh*tty foods, and electromagnetic pollution (cell phones, WiFi, etc), among other things. When your body is inflamed, your stress response is triggered, your immune system is weakened, and that can lead to autoimmune issues. Autoimmune issues keep the cycle going and just create more and more inflammation. To improve, prevent, or heal from an autoimmune condition it is necessary to reduce the inflammation in your body. Once you fully understand how these things influence your health, you will be empowered to take back control of your health.

Before you start freaking out, remember that inflammation is not always a bad thing; it's a vital part of your body's natural self-defense. When your body is sick, hurt, or triggered, your immune system (via your lymphatic system) races to the area with a squad of white blood cells and increases blood flow to make things better. In someone with optimal health, inflammation is a normal, effective, and required response. It is your immune system swooping in to remove harmful, malevolent, foreign invaders so that your body can optimally self-heal.

There are two main types of inflammation that I call micro and macro: one is friendly, and the other is really your enemy (or frenemy) because you do need it to some extent but it is an indication of larger issues at play. Micro inflammation is your body's innate defense against viruses, pathogens, and damaged cells that initiates quickly and allows your body to self-heal. Macro inflammation is whole-body, low-dose inflammation that can last for months, years, or even decades. It is pretty much the common root source of many chronic health issues and is linked in some way to almost every major health condition and disease.

It's not just one specific thing that causes inflammation in your body, it's a multitude of things like blood sugar issues, sleep deprivation, macro stress, environmental toxins, and inflammatory eating that can lead to macro inflammation. Your optimal health and well-being deeply depend on both understanding how micro and macro inflammation work, and proactively addressing the different factors. It's really macro inflammation that you have to be aware of. Research shows that an unchecked inflammation response is a precursor to chronic disease development.[139] Macro inflammation is the underlying cause of many degenerative diseases like diabetes, cancer, and heart disease. It can also make weight loss difficult and has been linked to obesity. Macro inflammation is linked to autoimmune issues and can also be caused by exposure to a low level of specific irritants like industrial chemicals, heavy metals, and GMOs over a long period.

According to a study published in the American Journal of Psychiatry, macro inflammation also plays a core role in depression.[140] Cathryn Lewis, the Professor of Genetic Epidemiology & Statistics at King's College London, and her colleagues showed in the largest study of its kind that reducing inflammation through diet, exercise, and other methods could potentially help people for whom antidepressants don't work. Researchers analyzed data from more than 86,000 people who participated in the UK Biobank project. They looked at information on mental health and a compound in the blood that signals inflammation, as well as lifestyle, behavior, physical health, and genetic links to specific diseases. They found that people with depression had higher levels of inflammation than those without depression, regardless of socioeconomic background, ill-health, or unhealthy habits.[141]

Unchecked inflammation freezes you and keeps you frozen. Of course, there are a lot of other things to consider, but nipping your macro inflammation in the bud helps your body easily exit your stress response and return to its full potential of self-healing where many health issues can easily be overcome. Your inflammation levels need to be carefully managed and strengthening your relaxation response is an easy way to do so. The more you train your relaxation response to be stronger, the better you will have your macro inflammation levels in check. Letting your macro inflammation response run unchecked will ultimately lead to tissue death, thickening, and scarring of your connective tissues. Damaged tissues can only heal with inflammation, but macro inflammation can lead to several chronic diseases as I've mentioned.

The problem is that chronic macro inflammation is hard to detect with conventional medical tests. It can be elusive and hide deep within some of your body's systems or tissues. Some diseases can be evasive and covert for so long (they are shady as hell) because they can only be detected with expensive, invasive, and crazy complicated tests. Your biology can be a bit of a hot mess, and most tests are not super reliable. Even the current tests that you can get from your doctor only display inflammation in "healthy ranges." Therefore, you will never know you have a problem with inflammation incineration until it is too late and some type of disease and or autoimmunity has reared its ugly head.

Inflammation's importance is directly related to the concepts I've discussed with you previously because it is a direct measure of your immunity. Your immune system is driven by sleep, nutrition, stress, and exercise, as well as your personality, attitude, and emotions. The higher functioning your immune system, the less likely it is that you will have macro inflammation.

Additionally, if you are often in your stress response, your body will keep triggering inflammation. This leads to being constantly stressed and constantly inflamed. In a healthy body and mind, the relaxation response also has anti-inflammatory properties and when you return to a relaxation state, the inflammation will also be appeased. But if the relaxation response is not strengthened, it becomes weak and is no longer able to calm inflammation, therefore leading to middle-aged and older individuals having autoimmune diseases more often. Additionally, if you don't access your relaxation response and spend most of your time in the stress response, autoimmune issues can express themselves in younger people.

While most people are fine with managing inflammation, I want to help you strengthen your relaxation response so that you can dramatically reduce it and lower your inflammation set point, so that it takes fewer inner triggers to set off an inflammatory response. You are empowered when you consistently practice Interval Mindfulness™ and its various Innervals™. Just these simple exercises will optimize all of these interconnected concepts of mind and body that I've presented so far.

IN A NUTSHELL

Managed stress can start out healthy if you have the inner resources to deal with it, but if you experience mini-crises constantly, live in a state of tension and unrelenting worry, and you get angry easily, this may be a sign that you're taking on too much in your life. Signs that you're coping with your stress in unhealthy ways include smoking, binge drinking, stress-eating, and staying in dysfunctional relationships. This is the type of stress that you tend to ignore or suppress because you think you're handling it well, but without active rest, relaxation, and resolution of this constant stress, you'll start to wear down your body, mind, immune system, and optimal health.

Macro stress is dangerous and increases a person's risk for autoimmune issues, digestive disorders, mental issues, heart disease, diabetes, and even weight gain or obesity. A lot of macro stress has to do with feeling out of control or helpless. Macro stress has been linked to heart disease in men who don't feel in control in their jobs[142], it will wear you down until a fatal or chronic breakdown occurs. Studies show that macro stress kills your brain cells[143], shrinks your brain[144], hurts your memory[145], and increases your risks of developing mental health issues[146,147]. Hello, nervous breakdown!

How well you age, your perception, and the overall quality of your life is determined by how well you can adapt to stress. On a great note, however, around 80% of your daily stressors can be converted to micro stress to build resilience and elevate your functioning by either training your nerves to boost resilience or changing how you think about your stressful situations or challenges. If you watch the TED talk by Health Psychologist Kelly McGonigal you'll see that she highlighted a huge piece of research at the University of Wisconsin-Madison that shocked many people.[148] The longitudinal research on 29,000 people over 8 years discovered that one's perception of stress impacts health significantly more than the stress itself. The research found that if you think stress is always bad for you, then your prediction will come true.[149] However, if you think stress is a good thing, something that can energize, challenge, and motivate you, then you're also right. People with a positive view of stress lived many years longer than those with a negative view of stress.

So what's your current view of your daily stress? If you're in a stress response nerve state, your view of stress will always be negative but if you're in your relaxation response, your view will be positive and you will feel like you can easily weather any and all stress. The key to mastering your stress is training yourself to be anchored in your relaxation response. And that's exactly what Interval Mindfulness™ and its various Innervals™ do in a very efficient way.

FACE MOTOR COMBO. (3 minutes)

1. FACE MOTOR INNERVAL™ // 30 seconds.

Make a happy face and hold for 3 seconds; then make a sad face and hold 3. Keep alternating happy and sad faces coupled with thoughts every 3 seconds; always end with a happy face before you start the next Innerval™. Do this for 30 seconds or do 10 face changes if you don't have a timer.

2. CORE BREATHING INNERVAL™ // 30 seconds.

Take long, slow, and deep inhales and take longer, slower, and deeper exhales for 30 seconds or 3 times each if you don't have a timer. As you inhale for 3 seconds your core goes out, and as you exhale for 6 seconds your core goes in.

3. Repeat 2 times

STIMULATION. The phrenic nerves, vagus nerves, motor cortex (5), and posterior thoracic nerves.

15 //

FITNESS RISE FORAY

Interval Mindfulness™ is a fitness-inspired micro method, so it's only fitting that I go into details of how I got into the fitness industry and how that ties into my story with illness. Getting really involved in the industry was never really my goal, as my initial desire growing up was to become an osteopathic physician (bone doctor). What actually happened was that I studied Musical Theatre and Dance. It turns out that this was just one of those happy detours we often take in life, like jumping in an Uber having no idea where it's headed, and the driver is using Apple maps to navigate. If you know, you know. The sometimes crazy or talkative driver you're paired with just takes you, fast and not always smooth, and before you know it, you've arrived at a destination and discovered a life you didn't know existed. Can you relate to that feeling? Are you currently doing what you believed you would do career-wise? Probably not.

My very first fitness job was at the UW's health and wellness centers. My college had student-run workout facilities and group fitness programs that were available to all students and I taught hip-hop dance alongside routine workouts. I would go on to create a college hip-hop dance party atmosphere (without the keg stands or weird black lights), where I'd scream and keep everyone moving to the music. No one knew what to make of me, but they liked my energy.

I was very high energy, and people really loved it and started to engage with me every Wednesday night at Berg's Gym. The Mario Hip-Hop Dance Show— I started with about 25 people in my very first class, and it only grew wildly, adding 15 more each new week. By the end of the first month of teaching classes, I had about 200 people coming in every week. Wednesday nights became LIT as word about the class spread fast: the big Black guy in the middle of Wisconsin teaching a hip-hop dance class on campus. There was nothing else going on around campus that was remotely similar to what I was doing; it was just a lot of fun, and it was also a legit workout. I danced my booty off, but also threw in plenty of athletic moves, like rhythmic squats, lunges, and pushups. Before I knew what was going on, the basketball, football, and track teams were making my class part of their cardio training and this new influx of people helped me max out at about 300 in class! Can you imagine how crazy that was?!

I danced on the bleachers while they followed me down on the court of this massive gym, and I moved around as much as I could (which was a lot, I might add). I was leading the most intense, inspiring, and invigorating dance moves humanly possible to the beats of Eminem, Outkast, and Britney (yes, Britney, don't judge!). I threw some pop music in there too. It was this way that my first theme in college emerged as "energy." I lived, inspired, and served energy 24/7, and everyone knew where they could go get some.

Self-Reflection Innerval™

Dance is one of my main outlets for relieving stress, expressing myself, and feeling good. What are the three different outlets for you? Why have you chosen them as your outlets? Are they healthy or unhealthy?

_____

_____

_____

BIG BOSS OF BOUNCE

In May 2006, I was at a fitness convention in Chicago, working a booth for a gym. Across from my booth was someone selling these crazy "bounce" shoes called Rebound Shoes. The top of the shoe looks like rollerblades, but the bottoms had this space-age oval-shaped springs that allow you to continuously jump and spring into the air: think pogo stick meets kicks. People also called them "moon shoes." They appeared gimmicky to me, especially at a first glance, but they absorbed up to 80% of the impact to your knees, hips, and joints, and with the high prevalence of exercise and running-related injuries, that was a serious non-gimmick (in my opinion).

The salesman tried to get me to demo a pair. I was scared to try them because I thought: hell yeah—I would fall, and they did look a little ridiculous. I put a pair on, however, and I walked around in them for a couple of minutes, with the help of salesman Phil, a 50-something Filipino, who weighed a buck 30 tops. When I started to get really comfortable, I took off for a run around the convention center and I can tell you that I felt almost superhuman as I strode out and hit full-speed. I ran everywhere and past everyone so fast I was sure I had caused a gust of wind in my trail. I felt like Forest Gump when he broke out of those nasty leg braces or how Usain Bolt would feel as he approached the finish line. The Rebound Shoes evoked instant energy. I fell in love with these magical shoes and bought them on the spot.

Phil instantly loved my energy and welcomed me aboard to be a member of his crew after our little networking session. Soon enough, I became part of the promo team and was trained in the old-school style of aerobics (which they said was the proper way to teach in the shoes), but I honestly wasn't thrilled with that approach. It felt stale and it just wasn't me. I was a natural dancer and I loved to move my body, and so I pioneered the very first Rebound Shoe workouts in the United States by dancing in them.

I went rogue and started shaking my *ss in crazy bouncing shoes. Everyone in Europe was doing the old-school aerobic-style training, but I was in Chicago, dancing my high-flying, bouncy *ss off in them. I created original choreographed routines and put them on YouTube, and some of the videos went viral. I thought Rebound Shoes were amazing, innovative, and going to be the next big fitness thing but unfortunately, most people didn't share my sentiments. Many of them had the same reaction to them that I had at first: this is a gimmick and a dangerous one at that.

Despite having a rough time getting people to try the Rebound Shoes, I continued having success with getting people to come to my classes, and as a result, I developed quite a large cult following. Employees from companies like Harpo, ABC, and the Chicago Tribune attended regularly, but other people still didn't take me so seriously. They laughed at me and my bouncy futuristic shoes and thought I was crazy. I was this big, high-energy Black man bouncing around like Tigger from The Winnie the Pooh Cartoon, in crazy jump shoes, sweating my ass off and screaming with joy, with the volume turned way up. Picture the happiest guy on a pogo stick you've ever seen... Yep! That's me.

For the people who had the courage to try them on for their routines, however, it changed their lives. Imagine having an injury and not being able to run outside anymore, and then I come along and show you that you can run and exercise at high intensity without reinjuring yourself? It was life-changing, literally. These shoes allowed for an efficient workout while providing low-impact on knees, joints, etc. with high intensity. I'm very social-media savvy, and back in the days before social media was ruined by everyone trying to monetize things, I started doing dance routines with these crazy Rebound Shoes, filming them, and then putting the videos up on YouTube. Soon enough, my convictions and efforts met the public eye recognition, despite the constant wave of detractors. In 2009, the Chicago Tribune named my workout class "Chicago's Best Workout." I was really flying high, literally and at that time, I had no idea that the power, gravity, and frequency of my energy would lead me to accomplish more than I could've ever imagined.

WINDY TO NEW YORK CITY

It was November of 2009, and I had started to make my mark in the fitness industry. After enjoying some minor success and attention in Chicago, I had my sights set on New York City, the City of Dreams. The gym where I had initially introduced my now popular fitness trend was going under and the company was pulling completely out of Chicago. If I was going to move to New York City on hopes and dreams, and have a job, the time to move was right then.

At the time, I had pioneered the workouts of Rebound Shoes and no one else in the country was using them for group fitness classes. I reached out to one of the corporate gym managers, Donna, but she didn't take me seriously at all and didn't think that my classes would be popular in New York City. Not taking no for an answer, I begged and pleaded with her to let me do just a one-month trial and I would personally pay to ship the shoes to New York City. They agreed to that compromise, and in December of 2009, I paid about $150 of my own money to ship out 20 pairs of crazy bounce shoes to New York City. When I finally arrived in New York City, I was set to start conducting the classes on a month's trial basis, starting in January 2010, and we decided to call the class a gimmicky name in line, with the other gimmicky names that the existing classes already had.

In December of 2009, before I had even taught a single class in New York City, I was contacted by the Today Show, Tyra (I F*CKING LOVE TYRA BANKS), and WPIX 11 News! They all wanted to know more about my unique fitness trend. I mean, who doesn't want to see a fit Black man jump around on stage, right? Naturally, I agreed to do interviews on all those shows, and needless to say, my one-month "trial" ended up being a permanently sold-out class at this box chain gym. I couldn't resist saying this but, I told you so, b*tches! Oh, you thought it wouldn't be popular in New York City? Well, I love proving people wrong. As a Black man, it's something you have to, unfortunately, do very often. After those interviews, I blasted into the fame stratosphere for pioneering this innovative fitness trend, and the media interviews, interest, and global attention started pouring in; the attention was both exciting and overwhelming.

I just wanted to make people happy so that I would in turn be happy, and so I accepted all the opportunities I was offered, worked hard, and never asked questions or questioned anyone's authority (at least I continued like this for the first couple of months). I had become an official fitness trend of 2010 and was being featured by many media sources and feeling like I definitely deserved it. I asked for a raise then and was denied. Imagine my shock. They said they'd given me a 10-dollar raise when I moved from Chicago and that I wouldn't qualify for a raise for another year. I was like, "Okay, but isn't the cost of living 10 times higher in NEW YORK CITY than it is in Chicago?"

Just to put things into a measurable perspective here, I was getting heavy national and local exposure for this corporate gym: a national box chain gym that would have gotten zero press without me. That media coverage was worth tens of thousands of dollars for them, yet I was only allowed to teach two classes a week (which were sold out) and made only 50 bucks an hour. To do the math so you can get it clearer, that's a hundred bucks a week. Do you know how much rent in the City costs? At that rate, I could barely afford to sleep on a park bench.

I had no contract or anything, because in the fitness industry, if you even think about trying to ask for some sort of contract, you will get laughed at and quickly shooed away, shunned, and made to feel like you are crazy for even thinking to ask for one. Again, the other influential factor is being a Black man in America, you must work 10 times as hard as mediocre White people and they'd still typically feel entitled to your time, energy, and focus. So I went along with the no-strings protocols until I started to feel a huge disparity between what I gave and what I was getting in return from the gym, sure I loved all of my students but I also needed to pay my rent.

You see, no one wants to sign contracts in the fitness world because they just want to steal ideas and pass them off as their own under their "brand." I learned this truth the hard way. Basically, this was the modern-day version of Twelve Years a Slave, one difference being that we are at least paid a little and sometimes offered questionable health benefits on the side. Being new on the scene, however, I didn't want to cause any drama or waves, so I just shut up and acted like a good little slave—I mean, employee. When they wanted me to tap-dance, I tap-danced. "Anything else for you, Massa?"

There I was, this fitness guy on TV, who everyone sees and knows, and I was barely making my park bench rent: crazy, isn't it? I trained a few clients on the side and subbed in other classes when I could, but my consistent weekly income was $100 a week. This was my welcome to NYC, the city of dreams, glorified grind, and hot mess hustle. WTF?

GRITTY GODIVA

Meanwhile, other opportunities outside of the gym flourished and I was approached by Austin, an old friend from Chicago, to train him on this reality TV show. Trying to be courteous, I emailed Donna (my "superior" at the gym) and her assistants to let them know that I was going to be on a reality TV show, and I would mention corporate gym and wear a corporate gym shirt if I could; it would be my personal courtesy, like the good little slave employee I was.

I got an email back that simply said, "UGH. I'm so over him," ...him, being me. This was from Kyra, the PR girl. How ironic, right? She had accidentally sent me this email. She'd intended to take me off the distribution list, but probably being a hot mess and trying to multitask or something, she accidentally took Lori off instead. Or maybe mercury was in retrograde. Awkward.

Wow, just wow. I'm looking at an email receipt from one of these shady corporate people saying that she's over me. Well, guess what? I've BEEN over you and this NEW YORK CITY glorified grind bullsh*t. I didn't respond right away—I gave it some time, so I was sure that I wouldn't get emotionally reactive. I'm emotional and can get emotionally reactive sometimes and since awareness for me is the first step to prevention, I took my time to process through most of the emotions I was feeling. When I did respond, I said, "Oh, this wasn't the response I was expecting from keeping you guys in the loop."

Kyra responded, "Oops, sent that email to the wrong person—have a great weekend!"

LOL! No sh*t Sherlock. The working relationship I had with them didn't last long after that and I didn't look back or second-guess myself at all. I sent a very gritty, emotional, electrifying, and rattling "farewell letter" to about 500 fitness instructors telling them that I was leaving, imploring them to stand up for their worth, and encouraging them to ask for a raise if they felt they deserved one. I try to be positive and lead with light, but sometimes light comes from burning down a f*cking bridge to make sure you never cross it again. I knew people who had been working for years in that place without raises and corporate gym management just didn't pay them any mind. In the farewell letter, I also included the inappropriate email that Kyra didn't mean to send to me. I thought it went well with the message I was sending to my instructor colleagues; the icing on a cake.

They still conduct the class without me to this day, acting as if they created it on their own, which is kind of funny, because with all the media I have done, everyone knows I pioneered and created the workouts for those shoes in the United States. That's the wonderful thing about being a creative person, you never stop creating, even when people are looking to steal your creations. Through my experience, I got to know that this sort of thing happens a lot in the fitness industry. People "borrow" your ideas, rebrand them, and pass them off as their own. That's why real, creative innovation has stalled across the board.

Self-Reflection Innerval™

The longer I stayed with that corporate gym the more anger, resentment, and frustration built inside of me. Leaving was the best thing for me, but I was scared to leave because I would essentially be venturing into the unknown. Can you name three instances where you were scared to venture into the unknown and you did it anyway? Has it worked out better than you expected?

_____

_____

_____

THE NEW YORK F*CKING TIMES

After the corporate gym exit, tensions were starting to rise between the Rebound Shoes company and me. I had helped make their product famous and they weren't paying me for it. They acted as if I was the lucky one for being able to sell and talk about their product to the media. That's some straight-up soap opera narcissistic sh*t. I enlisted the help of an attorney friend in communicating and trying to resolve my growing concerns with the shoe company. The founder also passed away around this time and his daughter took over the company and she had never worked a day in her life. Change surfaced from every corner with the only constant that I was yet again, getting screwed over.

Can you imagine not ever working a day in your life and then taking over a global company? It doesn't usually work out too well, and it didn't with this company either. Regardless, I had made their product explode into one of the hottest fitness trends on the planet, and they weren't paying me for it so I really wanted to be able to get to the source herself. The only money I was making was from selling the shoes and teaching classes, but the hundred or so other people who were also selling the shoes in the United States were making money off my promo work too, and not even working so hard at it.

I, on the other hand, would do appearances during workout sessions and classes in other countries, while it was always the distributor for that country who made the real money after I pitched the product to the media and public. I was a one-man show and didn't have a marketing or PR person, although I did have a wonderful friend, Deb, who worked for a PR firm, and she helped me when I was overwhelmed or made sure I didn't screw up a good opportunity. For the most part, though, all the media, press, and attention I received, came to me organically and through word of mouth and I handled the whole follow-up process myself where necessary.

On October 12, 2012, I got an email from Daniel Krieger, a reporter for the New York Times. He found me through searching current fitness trends. He'd heard about what I was doing and wanted to do a feature on me for his "Urban Athlete" column. He was writing about fresh, new, fun fitness ideas. Hey, that's me, right?! His email got me really excited—the New York F*cking Times, the most prestigious paper in the country! It felt as if I'd just been given an extra side of guac, no extra charge. People always dream of getting featured in the New York Times, but very few ever really do, especially in the fitness industry. Daniel and I had a 30-minute phone convo and discussed a variety of topics. He was curious about what I was doing, the benefits for different people that I was helping to exercise who normally couldn't because of injuries. He loved the idea, pitched it to his editor, and his editor green-lit the piece. The piece was published in print on November 29, 2012. Who's counting? Me! Come on! This was the NEW YORK F*CKING TIMES and I was ecstatic.

Words alone can't express the joy I felt for being featured. It was the ultimate validation of all my hard work, blood, sweat, and tears. It was also a big "F*ck-You" to everyone who had laughed in my face, didn't believe in me, or tried to exploit and take advantage of my work. With this newfound excitement, I emailed the Rebound Shoe head office with a digital link to the article. I'd just landed them one of the biggest media hits in the country and thought surely they were going to compensate, reward, or at the very least, thank me. I got nothing, zero; no response, at all. They did, however, post on their social media pages that they were featured in the New York Times and there was no mention or link to me in their post. Such SHADE! Wow, just wow. I had spent eight years being extremely loyal, had helped them amass millions of dollars in press and sales, and they were completely indifferent towards me and the strides I'd made in publicizing their product.

They didn't really care about me and only cared about the sales, free press, and attention I was getting them. It was then that I had a pretty devastating realization. I knew we were having challenges, but I assumed that they had some shred of human decency. Up until that point, I believed they had at least some type of moral compass or general regard for loyalty, work ethic, and excellence. Nope! That was the moment I felt a bazooka of betrayal shot directly into my heart. And so it began once more: another deadly descent to getting frozen in my shutdown response, triggered by stress-inducing feelings of betrayal, resentment, and depression.

Self-Reflection Innerval™

The major trigger to the challenge I would have with cancer started with this devastating betrayal. It was left undigested, unprocessed, and untouched. Name three times you've experienced a devastating betrayal. Did you digest, process, and touch those feelings? If not, why?

_____

_____

_____

16 //

YOUR BREATHING FUELS OR FIGHTS STRESS

What happened to me (life-threatening illness) can happen to you, or someone you know, especially if you stay fast asleep in a deeply dysfunctional, distracted, and delusional world of information, stimulation, and manipulation. On its head, the way I got sick is simple: I couldn't access my relaxation response and it was weak. Had it been stronger, that would've taken some of the weight of the daily stressors off my shoulders, reducing the pile in my Backpack of Stressors.

I'm sure you have worn or carried a backpack, duffel bag, or purse. We know that these things have a limit, and the heavier they are, the harder it is to carry them around. Imagine if you were carrying an inner backpack, duffel, or purse of stressors around every day, and every time your stress response was triggered you would put one item in your backpack, duffel, or purse weighing it down even more. Right before I started to get sick, here is a tally of the items I had in my Backpack of Stressors that were weighing me down daily; perhaps you can begin to visualize what I was really up against when it came to the way I handled stressors.

What a Backpack of Stressors looks like...

1. Bad Genetics. 20lbs.

2. Childhood Trauma. 20lbs.

3. Dominant Stress response. 20lbs.

4. Immune System repression. 20lbs.

5. Toxic Overload (from not detoxing properly). 20lbs.

6. Digestive issues. 20lbs.

7. Helper and over-extender preconditioned self. 20lbs.

8. Codependency preconditioned personality. 20lbs.

9. Achiever preconditioned self. 20lbs.

10. Sleep imbalances (getting 4 or 5 hours of sleep). 20lbs.

11. Constantly drinking coffee, caffeine, and stimulants. 20lbs.

12. Unhealthy emotional triggers (because of undigested trauma). 20lbs.

13. Daily life stressors (hustle and bustle of NYC). 20, well, 100lbs.

I'm missing a ton of other items that are also present in the daily Backpack of Stressors I used to carry around with me, but hopefully, you get the picture. I only weigh 200lbs, but there I was, carrying this Backpack of Stressors with me, weighing myself down with it until the point of chronic disease expression. My body was trying to adapt to my Backpack of Stressors load, but truth is, I simply had too many things in it and I was carrying them all at once. My body had run out of energy and adaptive resources to not only carry the additional load but also meet the essential demands that my mind, body, and nerves needed to navigate life. This is what paves the way for chronic health issues. Here's a little secret though: your stressors will always seem heavier when you are in your stress response, they will seem lighter and easier to manage when you're in your relaxation response, and they will literally crush you so that you can't move in your shutdown response. How well you manage your Backpack of Stressors depends on what nerve state you're in the most.

When you start to consistently Innerval™ train and stimulate your vagus nerve as much as you can, you'll start to increase your body's resiliency for handling stressors. That means even if you don't take anything out of your backpack, you'll get stronger and what's in your backpack will weigh you down less. Soon enough 100 lbs will feel like 20 lbs on your body because you have increased your resiliency, and that's a noticeable difference if you ask anyone who trains!

Self-Reflection Innerval™

What's in your Backpack of Stressors today? The more days you answer this, the more aware you become of the "baggage" that you're carrying around with you, literally.

_____

_____

_____

UNHEALTHY BREATHING

The first thing we do as we enter the world at birth is breathe. The word inspiration is referring to the way we relate to our breath and is derived from the Latin word inspire, which means to "breathe into." There are a lot of people who are unhealthy breathers, meaning they breathe shallowly and from the chest creating and sustaining a stressed state. Breathing provides the flow of life and a safe way to exit stressful responses effectively: breathe it out, they say! You can even see from some of the Innervals™ you've done in this book so far, that breathing is an essential element of my practice, and the ability to control breath is a valuable tool. This is why a deep dive into healthy and unhealthy breathing practices is so important. We need to bring it back to basics and ensure that something as simple as breathing is not holding you back from overcoming stress, anxiety, adversity, and health issues in your life. Breathing is such a basic, involuntary activity that most of the time you aren't conscious that it's happening. Unfortunately, this "lack of consciousness" is one of our biggest problems, causing widespread stress, anxiety, and many health issues. We take breathing for granted because it normally happens on autopilot, but without our respiratory system, our bodies wouldn't be able to get the vital oxygen it needs to survive and function from moment to moment.

Breathing also is one of the quickest ways to shift your nerve state. Shallow, fast, and mouth breathing triggers your stress response while long, slow, and deep core breathing activates your relaxation response.[150] Mounting research studies are showing that when you focus on and learn how to consciously regulate your breathing, it leads to lower levels of stress, improves your mood, and even improves your overall health, mainly because it strengthens your relaxation response and tone.[151,152] Occurring 12 to 20 times a minute for the average person, your breathing rhythm is a process that consists of "inhales" that bring in fresh oxygen and "exhales" that purge the body of carbon dioxide. Your breathing rhythm can be conscious at times, like when you're holding your breath, or unconscious, like when you're asleep.

Your breathing begins in your nose or mouth and as you inhale, your diaphragm contracts and the air whooshes down the back of your throat and into your windpipe and at this point, the inhaled air then divides into air passages called bronchial tubes. Happening alongside all this, your heart rate speeds up to signal your brain to increase blood flow to your lungs so that more of your blood can be oxygenated. For your lungs to function optimally, your airways need to be open when you breathe and free of blockages like mucus, swelling, or bad posture.

After your lungs absorb the oxygen, that blood exits your lungs and is shuttled to your heart, which then pumps it through your entire body, to provide oxygen for your organs, tissues, and cells. When your cells use oxygen for various functions, carbon dioxide (CO_2) is produced and absorbed in your blood, and then carried back to your lungs. Meanwhile, during this time, your heart rate slows to decrease the blood flow to your lungs and this discourages gas exchange so, while your lungs are still full of CO_2 air, your diaphragm relaxes and this pressure change in your lungs forces the air and CO_2 waste back up and out of your lungs through your nose and mouth again,

...and AHHHH. You've taken a full breath.

Most people think of breathing as taking in oxygen. Strangely enough, it's getting rid of the CO_2 that motivates your breathing for the most part, because the need for oxygen only drives your breathing when its levels fall below 50%. Too much CO_2 in your blood makes it acidic (acidosis), which can hurt your cellular function and this is why you need to get rid of it always. This may sound weird and counterintuitive, but the more you breathe, the less oxygen you get. If you're breathing too much like when you're panting, with superficial and shallow breathing, it can dramatically reduce the CO_2 levels in your blood, causing the receptors in your brain to adapt to the lowered levels and increases sensitivity. When your CO_2 sensitivity increases, this lowers your CO_2 tolerance and can make you feel breathless and triggers exhales more often.

When you keep that panting habit up over time, it tightens your blood vessels and stops your cells from getting the oxygen they need, and this can eventually lead to health issues, like weight gain, high blood pressure, fatigue, poor concentration, and even heart disease. When you breathe heavily and too much CO_2 is lost, it causes you to lose even MORE CO_2, which tightens your airways even more. In witnessing asthma attacks, most people (including the patient) think that taking bigger breaths through their mouth will help them get more oxygen and feel better, but really the complete opposite happens: the only way to break out of that cycle is to breathe less and through your nose.

Mouth breathing and over-breathing are associated with sleep apnea, snoring, and other sleep issues[153] that start to chip away at your health, all because you're not breathing properly. Your breath should always be quiet, gentle, and covert even when you're breathing properly.

MOUTH BREATHING (What not to do)

When your body is stressed, say during exercise, your breathing rhythm becomes faster, louder, and shallower, and this makes you more prone to breathing through your mouth and only with your upper lung area, which can prompt you to hyperventilate and shift into a stress response. Mouth breathing tricks your brain into thinking that CO_2 is leaving your body too fast and this triggers the production of mucus as your body tries to put the brakes on your breathing (especially the exhalation part). When this happens, your body is preventing the exhalation of too much CO_2 during mouth breathing and you may get a tight feeling in your chest or have trouble breathing. Your brain would essentially stop your diaphragm from expanding to limit the amount of CO_2 that you would lose, causing you to breathe superficially.

Breathing through your mouth creates and sustains stress and drives oxygen into the upper lobes of your lungs. The upper lobes have more stress-response receptors, which are activated when you breathe through your mouth. So, mouth breathing is a stressed breathing pattern that increases your stress response, has associations with negative emotions, and keeps you in a heightened state of stress.[154]

Are you a mouth breather? Is your life a hot mess? Do you see the connection now? Add to that your Backpack of Daily Stressors accumulating more and more triggers per day! Your breathing directly influences your heart rate, and even if you don't have heart issues now, you may develop them eventually. Mouth breathing and associated hyperventilation put fuel on the fire of high blood pressure, heart disease, asthma, and other health issues. When you breathe through your mouth, you over-breathe, and your lungs are overstimulated with oxygen, but your airways get dried and smaller, making it harder for oxygen to be absorbed in your lungs.

If you relate to this section and have identified that you are breathing incorrectly, the good news is there are things you can do to improve your breathing, and in turn, reduce your stress. The primary source of your breathing rhythm is the dome-shaped muscle under your lungs called your diaphragm. When you take a breath, 80% of the work is done by your diaphragm. Your diaphragm has its own nerve supply, can work involuntarily and voluntarily, and is the most important muscle that regulates your breathing. When your body is in a stressed, anxious, or stress-response state, it's easier to breathe with the accessory muscles (neck, chest, and shoulders) because it occurs automatically without you thinking about it. The problem is that this can easily confuse your body into thinking that you are in a stressed state. If you are stressed, have an injury or issue, or just have trouble breathing in general, your accessory muscles can help you breathe. The trouble is that accessory muscles are not meant to be used in normal breathing, and so, whatever the purpose of the accessory muscles working while breathing, your body will shift into and remain in a stress response. In other words, working on bettering your breathing will be a MAJOR stress reduction technique that you can easily implement daily to reduce your stressors once you take note of them and start rewiring them through Innervals™.

How can you work on bettering your breathing? By consciously breathing through your nose and practicing the various Breath Innervals™ that pair active breathing with passive core breathing. Here are some other ways to better your breathing:

- Engage in core breathing regularly. This is also called deep diaphragmatic breathing where you are consciously moving your diaphragm as you breathe. You have experienced this already in my Core Breathing Innerval™.

- Practice simple, slow, and deep breathing.
- "Count" your breaths. Count to 3, 6, or 9 as you inhale, and then again as you exhale.
- Watch your posture. Better posture will allow for better breathing.
- Stay hydrated. It's easier to breathe when you're properly hydrated.
- Laughing stimulates the vagus nerve which also helps to better your breathing.
- Stay active with different types of cardio movement to help your breathing and breathing capacity.
- Tape your mouth shut when you sleep. I literally do this. Don't use duct tape, but there are companies that make a specialized tape for your mouth when you sleep. Pro tip: Just search "mouth tape" on Amazon.

STRESS/RELAX INNERVAL COMBO. (3 minutes)

1. FAST MOUTH BREATH INNERVAL™ // 30 seconds.

Inhale and exhale through your mouth equally for as fast as you can. Do this for 30 seconds or 60 times if you don't have a timer.

2. CORE BREATHING INNERVAL™ // 30 seconds.

Take long, slow, and deep inhales and take longer, slower, and deeper exhales for 30 seconds or 3 cycles (1 inhale/exhale) of breath if you don't have a timer. As you inhale for 3 seconds your core goes out, and as you exhale for 6 seconds your core goes in.

3. Repeat 3 times

STIMULATION. The phrenic nerves, vagus nerves, and posterior thoracic nerves.

NOSE BREATHING (What you should be doing)

When you breathe in and out through your nose, it helps you take long, slow, and deep core breaths that stimulate your lower lung to pump more oxygen throughout your body. Nose breathing increases blood circulation and also forces you to slow down until a proper breathing rhythm is achieved, which is great for shrinking stress and tension and it also stops you from overdoing mouth breathing when you exercise.

Your nose is the only organ that's enabled to properly "prepare" the air you breathe. Your nose is home to more than 50 species of good and bad bacteria. If you skip your nose and breathe through your mouth, there's no stopping all the bad bacteria contained in the air that you breathe from reaching inside your body. The mucous membrane lining in your nose extends all the way down your throat to your lungs and germs get caught and die along the walls of that mucus membrane.

Your nose regulates many functions in your body. Your nose also has four layers of tissues and a four-stage filtration system:

- the hairs in your nose filter out the particles in the air
- the mucus secreted by the mucous membrane has an enzyme that kills viruses and bacteria
- your turbinate and sinuses warm and cool the air
- nitric oxide opens your airways and improves your lung function

Your lungs are super-sensitive and respond better to air that has gone through these four different filters in your nose, versus through your mouth. Wouldn't you rather drink filtered water than tap? I hope so!

Nose breathing drives oxygen more efficiently into your lower lung and all five lobes (upper and lower) of your lungs are used to breathe instead of just the upper lung. Your lower lung triggers more relaxation responses, comprising more repairing, and calming nerve receptors, which are activated during nose breathing. Deep core nose breathing engages all 12 ribs to act as levers that massage the heart and lungs, rather than acting as a cage that squeezes your heart and lungs. This kind of rib cage engagement also acts as a pump to pull lymph fluid from the lower part of your body up to your chest to enhance lymph flow and cellular detox. Full rib cage activation is also important for optimal flexibility in your head, neck, spine, and lower back.[155-156]

Have you ever huffed and puffed during exercise? This is because your body isn't efficiently removing CO_2. Breathing deeply into your lower lung also massages and exercises your diaphragm (the primary muscle of breathing), making it more efficient and easier to take longer, slower, and deeper breaths. If you breathe deeply during exercise, you will have a less-perceived exertion, meaning that exercise will seem easier than it really is, not to mention that you'll get shorter recovery times and better endurance than mouth breathing.

Nose breathing stimulates the production of more alpha brain waves[157], which are produced in meditative, calm, and relaxed states. So basically, always keep your mouth shut for breathing, even when you exhale. If you are working out or exercising so hard to the point where you must open your mouth, slow down and bring your exertion back to a point where you can just breathe through your nose. This will help you increase your endurance while exercising and will help you steer clear of all the pitfalls of mouth breathing. Even when you breathe through your nose, try to keep it lighter than you normally do, and always be mindful of your breathing when you're stressed, manually attempting to slow it down and bring it back through your nose.

SLOW DOWN INNERVAL COMBO. (3 minutes)
1. SLOW BREATH 1.1 NOSE INNERVAL™ // 30 seconds
Inhale through your nose slowly for 1 count or second and exhale through your nose for 1 count or second. 1 cycle (inhale/exhale) of breath is 2 seconds. Do this for 30 seconds or 15 times if you don't have a timer.
2. CORE BREATHING INNERVAL™ // 30 seconds.
Take long, slow, and deep inhales and take longer, slower, and deeper exhales for 30 seconds or 3 cycles. A cycle of breath is 1 inhale and exhale. As you inhale for 3 seconds your core goes out, and as you exhale for 6 seconds your core goes in.
3. Repeat 3 times.
STIMULATION. The phrenic nerves, vagus nerves, and posterior thoracic nerves.

17 //

DECISION MAKING WITH "INNER INTELLIGENCE"

To rapidly heal from stage four cancer in 50 days, I had to make a lot of fast, important, and controversial decisions. What helped me make many of those decisions was simply taking a mindful Innerval™ by myself to tune in to my breath. Breathing is one of the most underrated ways of improving your health and shifting into your relaxation response. It's that shift that allows you to make the best decisions from seeing more available options. When you don't focus on your breathing it can make you frozen in your stress response, narrow your choices, and delay your healing. You can't listen to what your body wants to tell you unless you're conscious of your breathing patterns. Every healing journey has its detours, and sometimes you need to make instinctive decisions about moving forward. Because these decisions are instinctive, you won't always know what the f*ck you are doing and that's okay.

If you are currently battling disease, whether acute, chronic, or terminal I urge you to take a mindful Innerval™ as you have been taking at various points while reading my story and be alone to think things through and just breathe. No family, friends, or loved ones should be present to influence you. It's your body; it's your life or your death. Your loved ones mean well, granted, but they can make matters worse by projecting their own fears, negativity, and insecurities on you, further ramping up your stress response. They also can't relate to what you're going through unless they are going through it as well or have gone through it themselves. Hearing about or knowing someone else who went through it doesn't really count.

Every single time you take a mindful Innerval™, you do a rep to strengthen the connection between your mind, body, and nerves and your inner intelligence.

No matter what kind of health issues you're currently going through, you need to know that the kind of healthcare you receive is always YOUR decision. Never let a doctor, specialist, or medical professional selectively suggest, riskily recommend, or proactively push you to take any treatment option that you don't feel comfortable with. At the very least, you should be able to take some time to really think about what's best for you and your loved ones because no one has the answer but YOU. Your BEST decisions will always come from a relaxed nerve state, not a defensive or depressive one.

INNER INTELLIGENCE: INITIATING FIRST CONTACT

Have you ever felt a big YES regarding something, while family, friends, loved ones, and coworkers thought you were out of your mind? I bet you have and right now, I can tell you that was your contact with your inner intelligence, a step closer to retrieving your authentic self.

How do you start trying to access your inner intelligence better and more frequently? You can start by talking to it, meeting it frequently in the present, and asking it questions. Yes, talking to yourself and getting an inner dialogue rolling is a great way to start that necessary relationship. There could be other ways, but there are four main inner intelligence pipelines that you can explore, and I have called them; inner insight, inner inflow, inner in-tune, and inner info. Some people will find that they're stronger in one of the four pipelines, but everyone can train their inner intelligence and play around with accessing new pipelines at every turn.

INNER INSIGHT (just seeing images)

This is an advanced level of inner intelligence in people who can "see" things that generally have a metaphorical meaning. An image of an earthquake could mean that you're experiencing some radical, unstable, and disrupting life changes, or an image of something flying in the wind could mean that you need to ground yourself more often. Interpretations of this infinite information will be different for everyone that discovers this pipeline as dominant in them. As you start to harness, hone, and help your inner intelligence grow, take note of any images, scenes, or objects that randomly pop into your head out of nowhere or things that consistently keep popping up repeatedly. Bridges can indicate transitions and so forth. You can look in a dream dictionary to see some common symbols, but dreams can only be understood in the larger context of the person's unfolding and self-discovery. You need to understand how these images relate to you.

INNER INFLOW (just knowing)

An intermediate-to-advanced level of inner intelligence, inner inflow is when your conscious brain gets an immediate "download" of information from your inner intelligence, often without understanding why. You suddenly have the answer to a question, instant idea, or confirmation of something you were mentally wrestling with. Ask your inner inflow out loud (by yourself, obviously) for the solution to a vexing problem. If there's resistance, go to sleep and ask for the answer to be there when you wake up. It may seem crazy, but when you ask questions out loud, it validates the question by bringing the energy from your mind to your body and nerves (into your conscious reality).

It may not be instantly or in the way that you envisioned it, but you will get it because your inner inflow is always listening, and you have now set your intention into motion. Look out for numerology, synchronicity, serendipity, and epiphanies as these are signs of your inner inflow at work. The more questions you ask yourself, the more your inner inflow will provide answers.

INNER IN-TUNE (just hearing voices)

Another intermediate-to-advanced level of inner intelligence, inner in-tune messages may sound as if someone is talking to you in your mind. I am not speaking about auditory hallucinations that can occur in schizophrenia and other disorders. This voice will not be sharp or torturous, it will typically be calm, soothing, and straight to the point. Sometimes, it's a single word or it can be phrases and sentences like "Don't fall for it, b*tch" or "Beware, this person is shady." Sometimes, they can be abstract, poetic, or cliché, such as "follow your heart."

The best way to increase your inner in-tune potential is to spend more time alone and without distractions. It's so difficult to do nothing, but if you don't give your mind space, you will never "hear" internally what it has to say. Even reading texts like mine, or other texts about inner instincts and intuition can get the energy flowing. I'm not promising that you are going to start hearing the "future," but at the very least, you can begin to tune in, and be able to listen for warnings when you may be headed in the wrong direction.

INNER INFO (just recognizing feelings)

A beginner level of inner intelligence, inner info is one of the most common inner-intelligence pipelines and comes to you in the form of feelings. Have you ever walked into a room and felt the energy? Have you ever felt something off about someone's energy? Reading, feeling, and shifting through the emotions of other people, trusting your gut, and reading the energy of an environment or object are the kinds of feelings that fall under inner info. The best way to hone your inner info energy is to write in a journal or take notes on your phone each time you have a strong urge or push from some inner info. Once you start to recognize which of these urges are real and consistent, you'll be able to receive more of them.

In following any of these pipelines, you must also be aware that sometimes, your old negative memory tapes, habits, ego, and preconditioning covertly resurface and wear a mask of inner intelligence to try to sabotage you. It's not inner guidance—it's an insidious incitement to something comfortable.

If you are fearful and focused on the worst-case scenario, the repetition of your thoughts combined with emotional energy that keeps re-creating your state of being conditions your body to become the mind of fear, this is also your greatest giveaway that you are acting predominantly on your ego and not on your inner intelligence. In those moments, ask yourself if fake fear is trying to stop your growth, or if you are really being protected by your inner intelligence? If you have a habit of taking mindful Innervals™, it's easier to distinguish between instant instincts that are fake fear and your inner intelligence moving you forward quickly. You must turn down your outer noise in order to turn up your inner intelligence.

In addition to retraining the ego from its fake fear moments, we also have the mind-body connection. I'll be going into this more later, but your emotions are the language of your body, your thoughts are the language of your brain, and your nerves are the translators of both. How you think, feel, and translate is what self-generates your state of being, a healthy or unhealthy one. Did I forget to mention that tapping into your inner intelligence will also help you determine for yourself the root cause of your own illnesses? That's right! It's that one superpower that you can train until you fully recover it, despite your ego wreaking havoc on you earlier in life.

Consistently practicing all the different Innerval™ workouts and reading up on your favorite intuitive role models can work "micro-miracles" to stay motivated to pursue higher versions of yourself and tap into higher realities than your current situation. Some of my role models are Dr. Joe Dispenza, Dr. Tara Swart, and Gabrielle Bernstein if you want to dig deeper. Stay with this process, and don't be discouraged, you'll get to an intermediate-or-advanced level of inner intelligence with time and patience. It's a journey, and never forget that journeys are not instant.

The best place to start is where your strongest signals come from, your gut. Whether you are aware of it or not, you constantly experience gut feelings that motivate you subconsciously. Commonly called intuition, it's an inner intelligence, holistic hunch, or investigative insight that is mostly subtle, and minimal. It is made up of the vital information that your biology already knows subconsciously, and it's trying to relay that info to you consciously at the present moment. More inner whispers. The effective relay of this vital info can be pretty hard when you're constantly living in the past or future with your thoughts. You can only ever access your inner intelligence when you're in the NOW when you're listening.

One way to view your inner intelligence is an instant, situational understanding of what's going on around you. Your inner intelligence can be a powerful, strong, and engaging presence providing a sometimes uncanny, unexplainable, and unconscious line of reasoning for your thoughts and the way they influence your life. Sometimes, you think you are crazy to trust it, and other times, you listen to it and dodge a bullet. Normally, the people who are the most successful at what they do actively use it, and leaders worth their salt lead with it, even though it's completely different from traditionally acceptable approaches to thinking, logic, or analysis.

Sometimes, you just know when you need to leave a job, cut off a friend, or break up with a partner, and this can be very useful when it comes to reducing your stressors as the answer to some of your daily problems may be to actually transition out of certain situations and into the new, unknown or deeper into a direction you had once abandoned, that suddenly becomes relevant again. Not all inner intelligence follows the same patterns or expressions. It's often downplayed by negative naysayers because of its association with gifted, psychic, or other supernatural notions. When its insight proves invaluable, these naysayers equate it to lucky guesswork, like winning the lottery.

Researchers who study the inner intelligence of the human body know it's a very real thing that comes from a deep-rooted level inside of you and tells you what you need to know a lot sooner than your conscious mind, which is often playing catch-up.[154] It can be in the form of physical, mental, emotional, and biological impulses which have been registered in different experiments and highlighted on various brainwave scans. In 2006 a paper, The Theory Of Unconscious Thought by Ap Dijksterhuis and his colleagues (University of Amsterdam,) they came to a similarly favorable view of intuition's value. The researchers tested what they called the "deliberation without attention".[155] The hypothesis was although conscious thought makes the most sense for simple decisions (for example, what type of clothes to put on), it can actually be detrimental when considering more complex matters, such as buying a car. More recently a team of researchers from the University of New South Wales has come up with a novel technique demonstrating just how much unconscious intuition can inform and improve our decision-making. Psychological scientists Galang Lufityanto, Chris Donkin, and Joel Pearson published their findings in Psychological Science.[154]

To measure intuition, the researchers designed an experiment in which participants were exposed to emotional images outside conscious awareness as they attempted to make accurate decisions. The results of the study demonstrate that even when people were unaware of the images, they were still able to use information from the images to make more confident and accurate decisions. "These data suggest that we can use unconscious information in our body or brain to help guide us through life, to enable better decisions, faster decisions, and be more confident in the decisions we make," Pearson says.[154] There's a scientific reason people tend to decide to go with their gut when making choices and decisions, but it's always wise to double-check your gut because sometimes it could be fake fear and old trained habits that are trying to sabotage you as well. Would you say that you know the difference?

HOW TRUSTING YOUR GUT WORKS

Scientific studies show that your gut has its own nervous system portion called the enteric nervous system (ENS) that has cross-talk between your regular nervous system and your brain. It's also called the gut-brain connection or the gut-brain axis. Your ENS is made up of two thin layers of a mesh-like network of more than 100 million neurons that are present in your digestive tract (gut) and this system contains more neurons than your spinal cord. The main role of your ENS is to control digestion, from the swallowing to the release of digestive enzymes that break down your food, to the control of blood flow that helps with nutrient absorption, to elimination of waste after digestion is complete.[158]

According to Dr. Micheal D. Gershon, a professor of pathology and cell biology at Columbia, your gut can act independently of your brain, and he coined the term "the second brain."[159,160] This system of neurons that are located in your gut is called your second brain for a reason; your gut and brain are interconnected through this system called the gut-brain axis and an extensive racetrack of hormones and chemicals that are constantly providing feedback about your stress levels, hunger levels, or any possible danger. The ENS also heavily influences your mood by regulating serotonin, a molecule messenger that is responsible for happiness. The feeling of butterflies (nervousness) in your stomach is a self-feedback part of your psychological stress responses and the feeling is mediated by this system. Instead of receiving most information from your brain as we typically believe is the way we respond to situations in our environment, up to 90% of these neurons are carrying information about the environment to your brain. That means that whatever happens around you, the gut gets the information first, and then relays it to your brain; a big reason you hear the phrase, "Trust your gut," a lot is because it carries real-time information.

While the second brain in your gut doesn't get involved in thought processes like political debates, ideological reflection, or complex problem solving, studies suggest that it does control behavior on its own.[161] Your gut can process, feel, and think just like your brain can, and can also act independently of your brain's executive functions. Your gut has the power to freeze your digestion, send a sharp pain to your conscious brain as a warning sign, and complete a variety of other self-feedback actions. Your gut is the only other system that can operate independently of your actual brain because technically (as far as being innervated with neurons go), it IS a brain. Inner intelligence decisions are not things you think through rationally, carefully, and thoroughly with reason; they come quickly out of the truest form of inner information; gut feelings.

When you feel pangs of anxiety or stress in your gut, it's basically your body telling you to stop whatever it is you're doing and just take a good step back. How often do you ignore those inner alerts? Can you even tell when your gut is sending them? Your gut can signal you to leave a stressful situation or remain in a situation that is good for you. Whenever you are making big decisions that can be potentially life-changing, it's always a good idea to go with your inner intelligence. When you have smaller and simpler problems to solve, you can use your more rational brain as it can easily give you the kind of solutions that will fit nicely with those problems.

As human beings with somewhat limited foresight, we are mostly focused on what we can see so much so that we don't really pay attention to what we can't see. How do you recognize a signal if you don't practice receiving and following that signal? You can learn how to access, harness, and develop your inner intelligence just like you would any other muscle in your body. Through training, you can hone and harmonize the power of your inner guide and learn to listen to your gut. Your inner intelligence has important and often life-saving information to relay to you, but you must be able to recognize it first in order to listen to it. Remember, just because you don't understand how something works doesn't mean that it doesn't work, right?

You were never told in school that you had an inner intelligence, let alone how to hear, practice, and strengthen it. Your inner intelligence is as natural as breathing and taps into the subtle and minimal forms of energy that exist outside of the main energy forms that you're aware of. As a result, you are constantly sending and receiving inner intelligence every single moment of your life, and you do it unconsciously, fluidly, and naturally as you breathe. It's shifting from your fear response (ego-based) to your inner intelligence (intuition-based).

So how do you learn to start trusting your gut? Here are a few ways you can start training today.

- Breathwork. The intentional manipulation of the breath can yield powerful insights very quickly. This is why Interval Mindfulness™ has a variety of Breath Innervals™ for you to practice to help instigate insights the more you practice.

- Your Dreams. When you're awake, your overthinking mind can override messages that you may get from your inner intelligence. However, when you're sleeping, your overthinking mind rests, and your inner intelligence can talk to you in your dreams. Grab a dream dictionary to help you try to decode them.

- Your senses. Start practicing and exploring as much as you can with all five of your senses. Things like closing your eyes and smelling an object or food is an example of stimulating your sense of smell. You could also use your hands to feel various textures, trees, and objects while you're on a walk. You can practice tuning in and out of noises and sounds around you with your eyes closed. Doing this will help raise sensitivity to your sixth sense.

- Test Your Hunches. Do you have a feeling that something is going to happen? Think your friend's new lover is bad news? If you have gut feelings about things that may happen in the future, write them down, track them, and see how often you were right. I would start with low-risk type things.

• Repetitive Movement. Cycle, run, walk, or dance. Repetitive physical actions can calm the thinking mind and open up your inner intelligence.

• Meditate. Messages from your inner intelligence tend to be quiet, so spending time in silence will help you hear and translate those messages. You can integrate traditional meditation with Interval Mindfulness™ by doing it at a different time on the same day or cycle doing it every other day.

• Nature. Being in nature away from technology and distractions can open up the kind of inner intelligence we need to survive and feel safe in our environments as hunters and gatherers.

• Practice Sensing. See what kind of information you can glean from observing people and feeling their energy or vibe before you talk to them or learn anything about them from other people.

• Read. You can read the following books to go deeper into intuition exploration. Try Sonia Choquette's *Trust Your Vibes*, Gabrielle Bernstein's *Super Attractor*, or Caroline Myss' *Sacred Contracts*.

Self-Reflection Innerval™

Listening to my inner intelligence helped me navigate uncertain parts of my healing journey. Can you think of three different times where you had gut feelings or followed your inner intelligence and it helped?

_____

_____

_____

18 //

INTIMIDATING INFLUENCES

Many fitness pros don't practice what they preach and can look like they don't follow their own advice most of the time. We've all seen CrossFit Trainers standing outside their gym chain-smoking and shot-gunning donuts, which is a little too much YOLO sentimentality in my opinion. Starting out, I prided myself on being one of those living inspirational fitness pros who always walked their talk and lived their message. I was the optimal picture of health: the real f*cking deal.

Living in NEW YORK CITY was a rude awakening for me. It's hard to not be overwhelmed by intimidating influences that are mostly unhealthy. Everyone is frozen in their stress response running around in a constant state of emergency and constantly digesting too much information, stimulation, and distraction, not to mention using alcohol, smoking, and recreational drugs to try and escape from or deal with their frozen emergency state of being. The New York State of Mind is truly the New York Nerve State of Stress. Pro survival, anti-thriving, unless you're in the 1%.

New York City, for the average person, is a city of survival, and you never feel truly "safe" in New York City because you're always worried about what you can and can't do, what you can and can't afford, or who you can or can't offend. Safety isn't just physical or having your basic needs met like food, water, and a safe home. It's emotional, psychological, and spiritual. When I say spiritual, I'm really talking about your personal belief system. When you truly feel safe in your environment you have your emotional and physical boundaries respected, your authentic self is accepted, and you feel close with your family, friends, and loved ones. In the line of work I'm in, those things are but a mere hindrance (useless matters). Your income is generated literally by what you do, the glorified grind, hot mess hustle, and busy badge are celebrated, as much as they aren't sustainable.

You hear it all the time: "Work hard, play hard." "Go big or go home." "Fit in or get left out." "Walk fast or get hit by a horse-drawn carriage." Okay, I made that last one up!

Authenticity is often buried deep below onion layers of preconditioned personality patterns. I used to think I was supposed to be one of those super-annoying healthy people who ate 100% clean all the time—chicken, broccoli, brown rice, quinoa, you name it! If it was healthy, I was eating it, and only that. I was a fitness guru at new heights in my career, so I had to practice what I was preaching. Everyone was looking at me, literally, and probably hoping to see me fail at something and I knew this.

The pressure to be popular, celebrated, and trusted, one of the in-crowd, in any industry, is very real, intense, and for me, it became a slippery slope. I went from having what could be considered a "perfect diet" to an imperfect dysfunctional diet, but hey I had tons of friends and when you eat unhealthily, it's okay as long as there are other people eating unhealthily with you, right?

Constantly busy and always on the move, I no longer had time to prepare my own meals. I found myself eating out, having lunch, dinner, and everything in-between, with friends or at events. What could go wrong? I thought. Chipotle is healthy, right? I mean, they serve guac and salads. I soon went from beating myself up over food choices to thinking that because I was fit and super-active, I could just eat what I wanted, and it didn't matter if it wasn't always the healthiest option. I was a fitness guru who looked good, why couldn't I eat whatever I wanted as long as I burned it off? I convinced myself it wouldn't affect me all that much.

I sweet-talked myself into a 180-degree shift from feelings of guilt, shame, and stress over my self-indulgent and lazy eating habits to just unapologetically eating whatever the f*ck I wanted. The refrigerator light became my beacon to heaven. I became a carb junkie, carboholic, mayor of gluten town, and sugar-obsessed freak. It felt good to lift the guilt with weights and workouts and I still looked good (even after months of binging on all of my cravings). Maybe, I thought, I really could have it all—being self-indulgent, eating unhealthy food, and still have a great body. Oh, and let's not forget to mention alcohol! My new nickname was Messy Mario, though I can't imagine why...

"Work hard, play hard!" is one of the most glorified mantras in the world, and I was thinking that going way high would counteract going way low, and vice versa. It's hard to turn down alcohol when you're being social and surrounded by so many play-hard "pushers." They'd had a rough, intense, and busy work week and now the weekend was here for them to release all their built-up tension. Wanting to fit in, instead of being viewed as some weird-shady-fitness-freak that doesn't drink, I would generally cave in and indulge in shots, shots, shots (also drinks, then shots) every weekend. Red Bull Vodka drinks and I had wings, yes I did!

Every weekend doesn't really sound like a lot when you are in the moment of said weekend and doing it with friends, loved ones, and coworkers. I would tell myself, "I'm not drinking during the week, so I'm not an alcoholic." Then it became, "Well, sometimes we should drink during the week for birthdays, work after-hours, special charity events, Taco Tuesdays, Messy Mondays, Hump Day Wednesdays, Thirsty Thursdays, F*ck it's Fridays, and holidays." I mean...I don't want people to think I'm a snob. But I still kept telling myself: "That's okay. I'm not an alcoholic if I'm drinking with other people. Alcoholics drink alone at home, right?" And so, the justifications and excuses that came out of my mouth were dripping with dishonesty, delusion, and rationalization.

The mind is a very powerful thing. I "thought" I was doing everything I should to stay in optimal health, but I was pretty much doing the exact opposite, and I found comfort and familiarity in my trained unhealthy behaviors. My body, mind, and nerves started to slowly, steadily, and covertly break down. I ignored all the inner whispers and warning signs that my body was trying to send to me and always made excuses for what I was feeling. What I didn't know, like so many people today, is that I was frozen in my stress response. A dominant fight-or-flight mode that had me either active or working out (fighting) or running from place to place (flying).

Before I formed a more holistic view, fitness to me was all about being active, exercising, and lifting. I slipped into overexercising to cope with my constant stress. Not realizing that I was just adding more tension to my body and more stress. Because who really wants to foam roll and stretch?!? "What's a rest day?" I would say. You rest when you're dead. Please run from anyone who says that now. I would do a workout or two every single day of the week lifting harder, faster, and stronger. I would try different training protocols and push my body to its limit constantly. I never took a rest day. It was just push, push, push, and pull, pull, pull. Sleep went from eight to seven to six to five to four hours a night progressively. But I always had tons of energy regardless of how I slept. You can do that in your 20s though.

Yoga is good for stimulating your vagus nerve and strengthening your relaxation response, but back then I would never have even dreamed of taking a yoga class. It was my good friend Tess, a fellow writer as well, who convinced me to try my first ever Kundalini yoga class, and even that was a struggle. I hated the thought of being still, especially for an hour and a half. Luckily there was a spontaneous movement that kept me from flying right out of there.

To fuel my fitness, I would just eat. Despite everything I learned and was preaching, I was doing everything to the extreme and out of context. Forced deprivation, labeling foods as "good" or "bad" and beating myself up over food choices when they were what I (or society) perceived as "bad." Why does food have a morality association anyway? Who started that whole thing? Why is food labeled as either good or bad? Isn't food just food? Better yet, isn't food technically fuel? Am I now a criminal because I pigged out on Ben and Jerry's and had 3 pieces of bodega pizza while drunk last night? Am I now a saint because I ate a salad and I frequent whole foods? These were the types of questions that I would have in my head as I was learning about food, exercise, and overall health.

From late 2013 to early 2014, I was on this dysfunctional, damaging, and disconnected rollercoaster ride. I didn't want to get off though, not yet. I loved the thrill of something new, exciting, and fun. I thought I knew what balance was, but I was focusing on balancing my behaviors and habits at opposite extremes. To counteract all of my binging, I started doing intermittent purging via all these extreme, crash, and fad diets. I had tried nearly every single diet. High-protein, low-carb, carb-cycling, no-carb, paleo, Mediterranean, high-fat, and intermittent fasting. If there was a diet out there, I tried it. I followed tons of uninformed plans, started eating fake diet foods, and would be starving myself regularly. I lived in the moment, and I was always satisfied with the quick and great results that I got from binging and purging. What I didn't realize was that my constant, dramatic, and extreme change in behavior was putting me on a path to inner health destruction. I may have looked great on the outside, but I had become a complete hot mess train wreck on the inside. I was keeping my calories way too low, depriving myself of real foods, and dragging my metabolism to a screeching halt. And you need your metabolism not only for burning fat, but for detoxing your body as I soon was to find out.

TAKE ANTIBIOTICS AND CALL ME IN 10 DAYS

Imagine that someone was playing for their life, frantically, nonstop on an African drum, and then add the sound of a jackhammer during a dentist's cavity drill—that was my heart rate of hell for four months straight, ferociously firing at a very casual "resting rate" of 160 beats per minute (bpm). The rate of my body's metabolism was fast and furious 24/7. Everyone dreams of a fast metabolism, but I assure you, it's not all that it's cracked up to be. My normal resting heart rate should've been around 55 bpm.

I went to the Duane Reade Minute clinic in Times Square because I thought low energy and a high heart rate weren't that big of a deal—just different or unusual. The Duane Reade Minute clinic is supposed to be this quick alternative to waiting in the ER of a hospital. With doctors on-site, you generally go there if you don't have life-threatening health issues. So, I filled out my forms and waited patiently to see the doctor. A nice-ish older white male in their mid-fifties asked me tons of questions like I was interviewing to be an intern at the clinic, including "Do you drink alcohol?" "Me? Nooooo!" Why do we lie to doctors about drinking alcohol? I felt like he would've judged me if I said yes and would've prescribed me to stay out of the club or something.

He concluded that I had some acute infection, probably sinus-related, according to the feedback I gave him of my body at the time. He prescribed Bactrim, a sulfa-antibiotic. I remember wondering at the time about the meaning of the word antibiotic; anti- means against, bio means life. Why are antibiotics, something that is "against life", always the first line of defense when a person is sick? Aren't we living?! Repeated use of antibiotics is also proven to destroy gut health.[162] I f*cking hate antibiotics, but at the time, I wanted to feel better ASAP so that I could work.

I took the Bactrim for about 10 days, and I wasn't feeling better. I started to actually feel worse and had even lower energy. I started to panic—WTF was happening to me? Thinking that the Minute Clinic doctor may have been a little shady because you don't know who the Duane Reade could be putting on their payroll, I decided to make an appointment with an ear, nose, and throat specialist.

What followed was that I went to see this specialist, and it was another nice-ish Indian man in his mid-fifties. After regular check-up protocol, he was taken aback by the speed of my heart. I was like "I know, right, are you jealous of my fast metabolism? I can eat whatever I want!" He didn't think it was funny, probably because he didn't have a sense of humor. He then went on to investigate what was going on inside my nose and throat cavities and wanted to do what's called a laryngoscopy. Uncomfortable as it was having a tube down my nose, I heaved a big sigh of relief when he finally finished. However, I soon found out that my right nostril was severely deviated to the right, and was all kinds of inflamed with red, and mucus-y particles in my throat.

You, reader, likely see the connection between the lifestyle I had been living, the concept of inflammation I broke down for you earlier, and the outcome the doctor presented. The first thing I thought, however, was: I could get a nose job and it would be legitimate. I thought, isn't that what people do? Get one and claim it was because they had a deviated septum? And I have one! I know! Not exactly what anyone would think at that moment, but hey! I was trying to distract myself from the discomfort I was feeling at that moment.

After all the laryngoscopy drama, what did the specialist do? He prescribed me a Z-pack and told me to check back in 10 days to see how I felt. After 10 days, I only got worse. I saw a few more doctors and more specialists. I was never really satisfied with what they thought was going on with me. I got a second, third, fourth, and fifth opinion and what did they all do? Antibiotics and check back in 10 days: at every turn. It was like I was in the antibiotics twilight zone, an antibiotic Armageddon, and a zombie antibiotic apocalypse that was slowly killing me. I knew someone had to get to the root cause of my heart rate that raced like hell, eventually, or so I thought...nonetheless, I kept living life on the fast lane, because it was what I knew. Naturally and unapologetically, it became my tattooed MO Modus Operandi.

DISASTROUS DENIALS

"SHUT THE HELL UP!"

My body and energy were knocking on the door, trying to talk to me, and I would never answer because I knew it was something I didn't want to hear, like a Jehovah's Witness trying to spread their good news or a Girl Scout selling overpriced cookies or some political activist spreading their propaganda. Typically, if I wasn't expecting someone to come knocking at home or to call, I don't answer because I don't want to be held hostage by some unexpected news or another person's drama.

I constantly denied the reality of what my body was trying to tell me. My body would even sometimes booty call me in the middle of the night. "Hey, G, U up?" And I'd respond, "Nah, body, I'm asleep. Not tonight." My body would send inner whispers to my DMs (direct messages) on Facebook/Instagram, and I would just delete the message without even reading it. When it came to the warning signals that I knew my body was sending me, I always retreated to pure avoidance and treating my body like it was a crazy f*cking ex. "We aren't getting back together, but I wish you the best!"

The thing is, that energy and those inner messages had to go somewhere, right? Each vertebra of our spinal cord is like a minicomputer station servicing through to the server: the brain. Our nervous system is the master communicator to all of our organs and our body is a master compensator depending on the signals of imbalance that it receives.

Many imbalances can be locked into the nervous system and inside the body that then become unacknowledged and consequently stored there. This storage is another factor that can keep us frozen in our stress response. Any trauma we go through in our lives whether it's an infection at the age of 2, falling off our bike at the age of 12, splitting up with our first love at 16, car accident at 21, or so forth, it gets stored in the body, the body stores that trauma. Your body always saves those trauma receipts. In addition, we all have genetic weak links from things we have inherited. Generational trauma and disease is a very real thing, why do you think a big medical question asks for what type of diseases are common in your family? For me it's my deviated septum, it's the first place my body is going tug at when I'm chronically out of balance. Having said that, it's important to not hold onto these references though, they're simply lessons your ancestors failed to learn, you can always break the cycle, and the cycle is broken with becoming aware and retraining yourself for health and wholeness. This happens by strengthening your relaxation response nerve state. How do you retrain yourself? With all the different Innervals™ you are encountering from my book, duh!

In the meantime, those trauma messages can be woken up again or triggered. A trigger can violently and unexpectedly give you a sharp emotional reaction as it jerks you into a deep stress response nerve state. This is why "trigger" is such a buzzword now, because people are constantly being triggered and finally starting to become aware that they need to start doing inner work, to get to the root of their triggers.

The problem is we don't work them out because our society has a widespread type of "emotional phobia". Most people weren't taught how to properly manage emotions growing up, nor to honor them for their messages. Because of this, the word "triggered" has a negative association. There's nothing bad or negative about triggers. Triggers are teachers, inner whispers, and a gateway to unresolved trauma. We've been trained from a young age to externalize things, so many adults don't know how to handle this foreign and strong inner information.

Triggers are unhealed inner wounds from the past that rise to the surface in the present. It's the mind, body, and nerve's attempt to release and heal. Being triggered creates an involuntary, emotional, and bodily reaction to an experience (that happened in your past). Your heart speeds up, you get sweaty palms, your stomach gets tight or you get annoyed by something someone said or did. Your chest gets tight, breathing becomes shallow, and your posture shifts because your nerves are protecting you by responding to a "perceived threat". Triggers yank you into your stress response nerve state and earlier I talked about how your nerve state dictates the stories you tell yourself. Whenever you feel triggered, the best thing to do is to activate your relaxation response so you can calm down and rationally look at and or analyze why you were triggered. Trying to figure out a trigger while you're in a defensive nerve state is counterproductive and will more than likely lead to frustration.

Everyone experiences triggers (in different degrees) daily and if you aren't conscious, you probably don't know that it's happening. However, you're more sensitive to triggers in the stress response nerve state. When you're experiencing a trigger, you're reacting to your past in the present moment. The trigger is actually a call to action that's trying to help you heal, a subtle (or sometimes not so subtle) inner whisper. When you're triggered, you're acting upon information stored in your subconscious mind, that gets "flared" let's say by an outside event (hence, the trigger). If you reflexively react without thinking about it, your inner wound will remain. You'll play the victim and seek to blame a person, situation, or external thing because you don't realize you're simply reacting to your past. Your emotional reaction to the trigger will never seem proportionate to what's going on in the moment because the trigger has nothing to do with the other person or what external thing caused it. It has everything to do with you and your inner environment. It's a call to heal any unresolved inner wounds from your past.

Instead of reacting, discharging, or shutting down, allow yourself to get curious about your triggers. Working through your triggers heals them. Start watching, self-reflecting, and getting curious about why you're being triggered in the first place. Be open and nonjudgmental about what triggers you, because observing your triggers is where your true inner power lies. The more conscious you are of your triggers, the more you widen your ability to choose different responses before just reacting to them. But remember, this self-reflection works the best when you're in a relaxed nerve state. Nervous breakdowns can oftentimes be the result of simply reacting to triggers and probably a lot (that have been compounded). With practice, training, and repetition, you can rewire the pathways of the brain enabling you the ability to respond rather than react. In order to heal your inner wounds, you have to create a new relationship with your triggers. It's not easy: it's training.

No matter how healthy you think you are, these memories that the body stores lay very deep in the nervous system and the subconscious. Most people aren't aware of these weak links that we have to our inner intelligence and our body. Your inner intelligence tries to let you know via different bodily signals. I call them inner whispers but there's a technical term for it: self-feedback. My body was trying to have "the self-feedback talk" with me, but I wasn't having it at all. Don't you avoid your boss when you know they have feedback for you? Just me? My body would call me up: "Yo, Mario, whatchu doin,' man? You know that sh*t ain't good for you!" My body would text, and I wouldn't respond, but I had my read receipts turned on, so my body knew I had read the message (even though I had chosen not to respond). Just because we read something doesn't mean we should respond on your time, relax neurotic b*tches and take a breath, or three.

I didn't want to face the root cause of my issues, I wanted to escape them in any way, shape, or form. That's one thing we don't really talk about in our hyper-modern world: the variety of outlets we can use to escape our reality at will. The same urge we have when mindlessly scrolling through social media is the same one our ancestors had when they dreamed of distant lands. Escapism is ancient, but modern forms of media, art, and music are created to help us escape our present reality and shift to another one. The book you're reading, museums, the music you listen to, social media, and TV/ movies are all avenues that allow you to escape.

My relentless urge for escapism fueled other distractions like drinking, recreational drugs, and other coping behaviors I'm not the proudest of. Even though exercising was my therapy for everything, I soon started to notice that I had little pockets of fat: pokey pudgy, little love handles, and some jiggly jelly. I freaked OUT! I'm a f*cking fitness guru. I don't get pudgy! What's happening to me? As I relentlessly ignored my self-feedback signals, my dysfunctional, damaging, and disconnected binges led to anxiety, depression, a slower metabolism, hormonal imbalance, sleep issues, digestive problems, and so much more. Rather than address these problems or inquire into the reason I was having them like a normal person probably would, I just skateboarded over them.

My own ego prevented me from listening, feeling, and having authentic conversations with my body about what was really going on and what it really needed. Although I was doing everything I knew to be healthy and active at the time, I was also missing the "whole" picture. I didn't realize how everything was so interconnected, interdependent, and intertwined with my nerves, and how the consistent imbalance of one area directly affected the stability of the other areas. I assumed that I was at my healthiest, simply because I ate healthily for the most part and worked out every day. When you don't really grasp life's complete physical, mental, and emotional picture, then fatigue, illness, and chronic health issues are some of the results you have to deal with.

I turned to caffeine, over-exercising, and alcohol to get me through my days and weekends. Sounds like a good time, right? At the time, I thought it was. What happened to me has probably happened to you and if it hasn't, let's be real, it f*cking will, because the modern world we live in is super demanding. If you are in this place right now, however, despite what you may think, it's not entirely your fault. I'm telling you that I ignored my body's inner whispers, triggers, and self-talk because I wasn't conscious of them. You could be having constant inner whispers, triggers, and self-talk right now too and be completely unaware because you aren't aware. Or you could be rationalizing or intellectualizing why you feel like crap. Cultivating self-awareness, via practicing different Innervals™, is extremely important because you can finally start to become aware of your inner whispers, triggers, and body's self-talk and chose to deal with them before they become a chronic health issue. Your body inner whispers before it outer screams. Innervals™ help you to see the whispers and give you a chance to course-correct before they become screams.

Self-Reflection Innerval™

My body was constantly trying to send me signs that trouble was on the horizon, but I chose to ignore them. Name three times your body has tried to send self-feedback signals to you. Did you listen and take action, or did you ignore them?

_____

_____

_____

19 //

YOUR EMOTIONAL CLOSET

Your emotions and nerve states are interconnected and affect one another interchangeably. This is why understanding your own emotions is so important, because they do influence your mind, your body, and the connection between them. As with most concepts I share with you, focusing on this singular aspect is one piece of an interconnected whole. Not only are your emotions influential to your innate survival mechanisms, but they're also the foundation for your connections with others. When you're in your relaxation response, emotions allow you to experience empathy, compassion and feel happiness and joy. However, when you're in your stress response, emotions make you feel anger, anxiety, resentment, intenseness, and defensiveness. They are the flavor, color, intrigue, and motivation to our relationship with the world and others. You can form bonds with family, friends, animals, and your environment all because of your emotions. It's how you authentically connect with the world around you. Without emotions, life would be boring and how we function would be even more limited.

Emotions are energy. You and your experience of life are filled with energy. It bewilders me how so many people don't understand that their emotions are a form of energy, and most importantly, that energy flows wherever your focus goes. The Latin derivative for the word emotion is "emovere," which means energy in motion. Emotions aren't good or bad, they are neutral sensations of inner information being relayed to you. These emotions only have meaning and become no longer neutral when your mind assigns a meaning to the emotion. Emotions begin to affect your mind and body more deeply when you integrate them into your sense of self, allow them to become a permanent story that you tell yourself about yourself. This is also the point at which they can affect those around you as you project your emotions onto your interactions with others.

Because emotion is a human experience, every language has created many words to describe our different feelings. When we put language or labels to emotions, it helps us feel like we have more control over them, even helps us turn down the not-so-fun emotions. From an emotional intelligence perspective, every feeling is an inner message with something important for you to understand. One way to get that insight is to find the best name for the feeling.

When we can identify our own emotions, it also allows us to be mindful of how these emotions affect others around us or how we are affected by them. Emotions are contagious and feelings spread between people like a virus in real life and on social media, even if we're not paying attention to emotions. Whether you're in a group or with just one other person, you can pick up both positive and negative emotions. Why? Because we are evolved social creatures. Humans have historically thrived and survived in groups. Because of that, we have a trained habit of picking up on each other's emotional states. If you see someone with fear on their face, you are more than likely to survive if you respond quickly (by your fear response being activated instantly). Besides fear, we're constantly picking up and sending emotional messages through a variety of nerve-related mechanisms like facial expressions, vocal tone, behavior, and posture.

Our emotions are a nonstop feedback system delivering information that drives decisions and behavior. They provide information about ourselves and others. Emotional literacy then is the ability to access and translate this information. Many danger or safety cues are picked up by neuroception that can instantly shift our nerve state.

However, our society doesn't value teaching about emotions or how to process them. Emotional intelligence, resistance, and resilience are some of the most underrated skills of life. Because most people are in the habit of being an emotion (I AM happy, I AM sad, etc) they become the emotion instead of letting the energy completely flow through them. They never learned how to properly work through them or feel them without becoming them. Emotions aren't a destination or an end state: they are temporary shifts or hits like waves.

In all honesty, very few adults know how to properly feel, process, and release emotions. Emotions however affect every single part of your body, organs, nervous system, and how your brain communicates. Emotions shift your body's physiology and release neurotransmitters or molecule messengers. The "fix" of these emotions and the chemical cocktail in the body, causes people to consistently self-sabotage by an emotional addiction when it comes to negative emotion. They're often aware of negative patterns and behavior but the preconditioned self's pull towards the emotion gets trained to be powerful.

Most people experience emotions in one of three ways:

➢ Feel emotion, then react to emotion.

➢ Feel emotion, then repress emotion.

➢ Feel emotion, then distract themselves from emotion.

Most people live in one predominant emotional state, this emotional state creates a mindset to back it up: either positive (aligned, motivated, grateful) or negative (disconnected, discouraged, confused). Those who have a predominantly negative emotional state (characterized by pessimism), are mostly oblivious to it. They wouldn't think that they were "negative" people even though they find themselves constantly stuck in the same cycles: the same drama, the same toxic relationships, the same misfortunes, the same breakdowns, etc. We think of addiction as external substances like drugs, alcohol, cellphones, and food, but no one really talks about inner addictions as a result of our inner pharmacy.

How can something so natural and inside of you be addicting? Ironically enough, the root of all addictions is internal, specifically in your body and brain. Addiction is a response to extreme relief or pleasure by regular use of, response to, or swallowing of some substance or behavior that relieves discomfort like stress, anxiety, or pain. When it comes to emotions, the response an addict has is to the flood of feelings.

Because of the neurotransmitters being released, emotions cause a powerful shift to your mental state. Even if the emotion brings you anxiety, drama, and stress or makes you feel out of control, you seek it out because it makes you feel safe: it's familiar. This is the basis of emotional addiction which can cause you to become frozen.

Most of the time, the addiction starts with the emotion you felt or repressed the most growing up and your preconditioned self recreates it repeatedly or keeps seeking it in scenarios that trigger it. Once you become addicted to a certain emotion, you'll end up in a cycle of finding your next emotional fix. Your mind will unwittingly create thoughts to trigger that emotion and you'll always be scanning your environment for it. When you continually indulge an emotion, your brain responds to this constant fix by firing nerves and making your nerve pathways stronger. In a sense, you start training this behavior and the expectation of this emotion. Soon enough, the reward center in your brain is rewired and your preconditioned self seeks out this emotion over and over again. People stuck in emotional addiction are actually seeking connection. They want to feel something based on what they learned to feel, through others.

Have you ever asked yourself, why do people stay in toxic relationships? Why do people let themselves keep getting taken advantage of? Why do people keep telling you stories of struggle, drama, or negativity? Well, in many cases it's because of emotional addiction (the fix of that specific emotion they now crave). Your brain has trained for it and it will continue to find it wherever it can. Emotional addiction holds many people hostage in a cycle where they unknowingly seek that emotion. Over time your body needs more and more of the chemical cocktails to feel and when you don't get them, you tend to feel bored or numb. Feeling becomes the primary focus even if feeling those emotions have negative outcomes.

What does emotional addiction look like?

➤ Being drawn to relationships that revolve around (repeatedly) feeling the emotion you're addicted to.

➤ Engaging in emotional roller coasters because you feel alive even if they are negative or destructive.

➤ Feeling bored or apathetic until you experience the addictive emotion.

➤ Retelling trauma or a story repeatedly for years to different people, reliving the moment in the present to get that high again.

➤ Seeking TV shows, movies, and songs with the emotion you're addicted to.

> ➢ Finding yourself in routine emotional cycles even, if you desperately want to get out of them (cycles of exploitation, being taken advantage of, ghosted, etc).

> ➢ Social media stalking to feel the emotion you've become addicted to (seeking lots of comfort groups online that celebrate what you're trying to validate).

> ➢ Re-reading texts, emails, and other conversations (obsessing over spilled milk and staying stuck on memory or regret lane).

Emotional addiction can also present itself in turning to things on the outside to make yourself feel better. Chronic depression is married to chronic consumerism. Why does shopping feel like "therapy"? When you buy new things for yourself, as you should every once in a while, you make yourself feel better but that's only superficial and only works temporarily if you should be unpacking repressed emotions that have filled up your mental space. Nonetheless, companies in the world that supposedly "make you feel better" with all their attractions and distractions, have a vested interest in making sure that your emotional energy is crippling and congested, because you will keep them flowing to the bank. That is, keeping you emotionally addicted to outlets for emotional addiction (stuff, movies, gossip, entertainment, social media, etc). When you begin to cultivate more awareness of your own emotions, you will be better able to discern what you are doing because you enjoy it and what you are doing to repress or dismiss an emotion.

If you weren't raised with emotional intelligence, resistance, and resilience like most people, you must teach yourself. Start to watch your emotions and create space between you, your emotions, and your thoughts by practicing mindfulness and that's where many of my Innervals™ will help. Ultimately, you break out of emotional addiction by cultivating self-awareness, becoming conscious of your emotions, and training your brain to view them (instead of being them). You must start to shine a light on how you speak, think, and behave. You must understand what you're feeling (try to identify the emotion at the very least) and what triggered that feeling (and the origin of the reaction, what really upset you?). At the end of the day, beyond all of this complex jargon, all you need to remember is that: cultivating self-awareness is your path to self-healing.

The Innervals™ in Interval Mindfulness™ give you a variety of exercises to help you easily do the inner work needed to reconnect to yourself and reframe every life experience as an opportunity for growth. Your brain can be trained, and new nerve pathways can be formed with practice, intention, and patience. The Innervals™ give you a quick break from the outer world and help create space between you and your emotional responses. This helps you learn from what you're feeling (because it's important information) because you have activated your relaxation response and lifted out of your stress response. They also help you get the mind quiet, flexible, and open, rather than fearful, rigid, and reactive. You'll start to feel empowered and no longer feel trapped in emotional reactivity or emotional avoidance. If you ever feel yourself having an unexpected emotional reaction, the best thing you can do is try to lift yourself out of your stress response state.

SORTING OUT EMOTIONS

EMOTIONAL REPRESSION

re·pressed. /rə ˈprest/

restrained, inhibited, or oppressed.

History, movies, and media have shown us countless times, over and over again, people and things that are oppressed, restrained, or hidden: always overcome adversity. The truth is, secrets are never kept buried, what's in darkness always comes to the light, and tyrannized people will always overthrow a tyrant (normally). Even the law of Karma (cause and effect), reminds us that what goes around comes around. Even though we know this, many people still automatically repress their emotions, without understanding the consequences of this practice.

Scientists estimate that your body can have nearly thirty-seven trillion cells.[163] Those cells create and are powered by energy and they're always in flux, never stagnant. They constantly reset, renew, and regenerate, making you stronger or weaker, functional or dysfunctional, high energy or low energy. Your skin cells change every thirty days, red blood cells are regenerated every four months, and the cells in your gut can renew in less than a week. 330 billion cells are replaced in your body and almost four million cells are created every second.[164] Every thought that you have is an energy form and is making your cells stronger or weaker according to the nature of the energy.

Who is the mastermind behind all these energy conversions and energy flow through your cells? Your nerves. What happens when your nerves hold onto things against the natural way the body handles things? Imbalance, Infection, illness, and disease. In order to assess your level of repression or even emotional baggage, I want you to picture your emotional energy as a closet that has limited space. Your emotional closet gets filled up with unnecessary baggage: when you're clinging to your paralyzing past or when focused on your future. Think about it! Do you have SPACE in your emotional closet for more love, joy, and happiness? You won't have that space if you have massive amounts of unprocessed emotional energy which takes up a lot of space, crowding out your ability to be present.

One of the emotions that takes up the most space in people's emotional closets is resentment. You will experience great peace of mind, great physical and emotional health simply by retraining yourself to release the lack of forgiveness that results in resentment. Typically, you store (and pay rent for) the energy of emotions and thoughts that, for whatever reason, you're unable to deal with at the time and you continue to store this until you're ready to let go of them. Dealing with emotional energy in this way is not natural: it's counterintuitive and goes against your inner intelligence by holding onto anger, resentment, bitterness, and grudges. You must understand that your subconscious mind doesn't hold on to anything—it just flows. Your subconscious cares the most about survival and efficiency. It's costly, not efficient, to hold on to emotions.

Repressed anger energy draws more anger, and angry people attract more angry people and situations because they are alike, and the emotional addiction cycle continues, now with the reinforcement of patterns and of others. What kind of emotional energy do you want to store or attract to yourself? Your nerves will follow your lead and attract more of the same kinds of energy that you want. Pain in your neck? Stiffness in your back? Aches in your joints? These things don't just magically occur—they are energy suppression, expression, and progression, made possible by the work of your nerves.

Anxiety and chronic stress are the by-products of anger, fear, sadness, or aggression. They're produced by a frozen stress response and what's worse is: these repressed emotions become addictive for people. You may not be conscious of it, but over time, the addiction to those repressed emotions starts to connect people, places, and problems in your life. You can start to become aware by assessing those people, places, and problems in order to rationalize an addiction to emotions, which you may not be even aware of, all because they've been locked away in your emotional closet and therefore deeply affected your body as well.

If you hate your life, you start to get addicted to the life that you hate, and the fact that you hate the life you're living. This addiction makes it hard to change anything about your life because what happens when you start to break away from an addiction? Withdrawals, and in this case, it's the emotional withdrawals that you will experience that make it hard to change your behavior. You must embrace, face, and fully release every single emotion, whether you think it's good or bad. Feel the hell out of your f*cking feelings! Emotions aren't good or bad, they are sensations of information.

How do you begin releasing pent-up emotion from your closet? The first active stance is conflict resolution: call that person and clear the air, it doesn't matter if it's been a few days or a few years, clear your own path and personal history from miscommunications, grudges, and misunderstandings. Or if you would rather not talk to that person at all, write a letter or email to them of everything you would want to say and delete it after you have finished. Make sure you don't mistakenly send it though. That might get awkward. Also before you try and clear the air, please make sure you're calm and in your relaxation response state. You must connect before you attempt to correct. How will you know? Do one of my active Innervals™ if you're having doubts. Discern when a situation that still provokes you an emotional reaction, calls for building a bridge (mending) or burning a bridge (closure). Check with your internal intelligence to see what line of action is more appropriate to put the matter to rest.

A more personal approach (when unable to initiate conflict resolution) is to make a Forgiveness List and write down all the shady people who have done you wrong and forgive them individually. Say it out loud and check them off the list, one by one. Start from childhood and search your memory for people that have caused you pain you may have forgotten about: your mom, dad, siblings, family members, bullies, kids at school, and friends. Put them on the list, and then send them some love—your haters are, after all, your biggest fans.

Self-Reflection Innerval™

Create a "Forgiveness List" (or "F List") below; I like to always start with myself. For each line write the name of the person you want to forgive and what you're forgiving them for. Ex. John Doe: I forgive you for your hurtful and insensitive comments that triggered me into getting upset. If someone really pissed you off, make sure you're using some well-orchestrated F-bombs or other profanity. Nobody will see this but you, so the aim is to release as much of the damaging resentment as possible. Three people is the minimum but aim for six or nine people total.

1. ....

2. ....

3. ....

Don't forget to do the opposite as well: ask for forgiveness, reconcile, or make amends with anyone about things you said or did that may have also hurt them. Don't make excuses for what you did—just be humble and ask for forgiveness. That's all it needs to be. The weight will be lifted off your shoulders, whether they respond positively and forgive you or not. If you are sincere, asking for forgiveness can also be the initial step to healing a broken relationship. This not only benefits the relationship, but will also benefit you, as it opens space in your emotional closet.

These emotions we store affect all systems of the body. Sometimes they express physically (like posture) but they are mostly unseen. Hidden away from therapists, medical doctors, our partners, and our friends, they drive our behaviors and keep us locked in unconscious habit patterns, stored in our cells and nervous system (they can be positive or negative). The emotions that are more negative in nature like anger, resentment, grief, and so on, can be the root cause of many disorders. Stored emotions affect the nervous system, make us frozen, and weaken the immune system. Just as environmental factors contribute to inflammation, so do our own unprocessed emotions and inner wounds. We can (and should) address nutrition, sleep, and lifestyle, but until we do the inner work resolving the emotional (mind-body) component, we can't heal. Part of this inner work includes strengthening your relaxation response.

Healing the emotional body is about feeling, and then releasing emotions. Trauma isn't a fleeting experience; it's branded in our subconscious. It's something we can self-heal in order to free ourselves from the past and create a brighter future. That's why I believe forgiveness is so powerful. Forgiveness transforms these stored emotions into new energy that allows us to create our life experience, instead of being slaves to our emotional past. You don't start to notice your thoughts, habits, and behaviors unless you're doing the inner work and cultivating awareness. All of my Innervals™ are here to help you do just that!

RIDING THE WAVES

We feel emotions to help us pay attention, and to focus our attention. Even though they might be confusing, emotions are part of us, so we might as well learn to use them more efficiently. Emotions are absorbed in the body in about six seconds. From the time each burst of emotional chemicals is created in the hypothalamus, to the time they are completely broken down and absorbed, about six seconds go by. If you're feeling emotions for longer than six seconds you are, at some capacity, choosing to recreate and refuel those feelings.

People talk a lot about "releasing" emotions without really explaining how to release them. One way to release them is to embrace and face them head-on, and it's only after this point that you will naturally release them because you have physically felt them. You can do this by laughing, crying, growling, screaming, and engaging in more things that trigger an unconventional stress hormone release.

Think of your body as your home. In general, you keep your home clean, or at least you know you're supposed to. You clean the dishes after you use them, you take out the trash, you recycle (or at least you're supposed to), you wipe stuff down and clean sh*t out. Can you imagine if you didn't do that regularly? How all that messy crap would build up in your house?

You shouldn't wait until you get cancer or any other chronic disease to realize how connected everything is. You don't need to get cancer to realize that you should take out your emotional trash routinely and that you should take actionable steps to reach optimal health. Every seven years or so, you become a completely different person because of all the changes that your body and cells go through. Can you imagine seven years of never cleaning or throwing away garbage from your home? Seven years of wearing the same dirty clothes that never got washed, seven years of never cleaning your room, kitchen, or bathroom? I can't imagine that either.

Your emotional breakdowns are energy breakthroughs, in which you're finally digesting, processing, and touching emotional energy in your emotional closet (even if you're now doing it under some duress). Embrace your anger or fear with a hug, look your anger or fear in the eye, and then release that hug and walk the other way. It's funny to me, the people who are always afraid of getting "hurt." I like to always say, "This won't be the first time you get hurt, nor will it be the last time."

Why not focus on how you handle getting hurt, instead of trying not to get hurt by running away from your emotions and feelings? Or why not focus on the emotional strength you gain after getting hurt and healing properly? Letting yourself feel a variety of emotions is like training. The more familiar you are with certain emotions, the easier it is for you to fully experience, embrace, and then release them. You learn how to manage sadness by embracing, facing, and releasing moments when you are truly sad. You learn how to be genuinely happy by embracing, facing, and releasing happiness. Your emotions are sensations of information that come in moments, and moments are temporary. See, one moment is long gone already.

It's a fine line to walk because you should try to feel your emotions fully, but then you should also have the tools to release that emotion after you've allowed yourself to examine it. Doing both of those things is not easy. If you experience a negative emotion that becomes too overwhelming and overpowering, the next best thing you can do after fully feeling it is trying to convert it to something else. You are essentially converting that emotion's energy into something useful and productive. To convert means to change from one form to another. If sadness is overwhelming you and keeping you down for an extended amount of time, try to convert it by actively doing things that make you happy, joyful, optimistic, and grateful. The worst thing you can do when you are overwhelmed with emotional energy is nothing. Rather than avoid or suppress intense and overwhelming negative emotions, I also sometimes like to give myself a timed interval of fully feeling negative emotions (3, 6, or 9 minutes) and after that time has passed, I do things to convert it like writing, walking, running, biking, or exercising. The idea is to control the conversion of emotional energy inside of you, to an activity outside of you before it converts uncontrollably to imbalance, infection, illness, and disease. But it's also important to fully acknowledge, experience, and process that emotion before moving the energy elsewhere.

Will you always be happy? Absolutely not—it's crazy to think you'll ALWAYS be happy. However, your default state of being should be happy. You are born happy (once you get over the shock of leaving the womb). The more you can self-generate moments of happiness, the easier it will be to shift back to a happy place when you are anxious, stressed, or feel yourself going down a negative rabbit hole. You must actively and routinely train yourself to be in a dominant state of happiness. It's not easy; it's training.

It's worth noting that negative emotional energy like sadness, anger, fear, and guilt isn't bad by itself because it gives us feedback about our surroundings, experiences, and environment. Clinging to negative emotions past the six seconds point for natural release, however, is unhealthy for your mind, body, and nerves.

Once you embrace and loosen the crippling congestion of untouched emotional energy, you'll gain the power, passion, and purpose to live a lighter life, without your old emotional energy hiding in the closet and crowding you out of your present.

The power and essence of your emotions is that they allow you to respond innately, and it's all about maintaining a balanced response. The healthy part of emotions is that they make you connect at the deepest and most heartfelt levels of yourself. On the other hand, overwhelming emotions can lead people unwittingly to avoidance, problems, ignoring clear consequences, and adaptive learning. When you start to see your emotions instead of reacting to them or allowing yourself to become that emotion, you'll be shocked at how often your emotions shift in one day. Emotional energy flows through you all day and changes like waves in the ocean. When you start seeing how often it changes, you'll understand that you don't need to react or be every emotion you feel. Energy flows because it comes and goes. You can't control when you will die, but you can heal yourself and bring yourself out of a painful (grief-infused death) and at least leave this world at ease, with no regrets, having found peace, balance, joy, and forgiveness.

Self-Reflection Innerval™

I talked about how things from your past could be causing crippling congestion in your present. What are three areas of your mind, body, or nerves that are congested? How do you think each area became that way?

_____

_____

_____

20 //

DANCING AT DEATH ISRAEL

MISDIAGNOSIS, MISSTEPS, AND MALPRACTICE

I started my deadly downturn in January 2014, and following super-high dose strengths of Bactrim, it turned out that I was allergic to sulfa, the main ingredient in Bactrim. The complications of this allergy then led to anemia, and a slow, steady, and sharp deterioration of my immunity (and every other crucial element of my health). The one thing that ALL the doctors, specialists, and other medical professionals knew was that whatever was wrong with me, antibiotics, aka the holy trinity of the medical industry, would not only cure it but was worth the other potential risks.

Can you imagine that your car broke down, and the mechanic never once looked under the hood, but said, "I know what's going to fix your car, NEW TIRES!" Well, that's exactly what I feel that some doctors did with my case. It was the same old story: They had no idea what I had, how I got it, and how long I would have it for, but they knew antibiotics would solve it—without a shred of doubt. No matter the doctor I saw, I was always met with instant-gratification Western medicine methods that ruined my gut flora and didn't address the root cause, but rather, brought about an allergic reaction and painful deterioration of my entire health altogether.

The funny thing is that they'll ask you if you have any questions and then get shady and short and shoo you right out of the door when you do, so they can get to their next patient. I completely understand that doctors are human just like you and me, and capable of making mistakes, like all humans. However, unlike you (I'm assuming that you are not a doctor), a simple oops, uh-oh, or miscalculation could mean sudden death for someone, and before this, you'd have already signed 100+ HIPPA, consent, and release of liability forms that leave them off the hook, claiming that they're not at fault for any complications. After enduring over 20 different medical errors, the only thing I had a right to do was complain. Does that seem right to you? Not to me.

It might be shocking that I went through 23 doctors in such a short period of time, but when you're a Black man in America, you're deprioritized in the healthcare system. People tend to not listen or take you seriously, or want to invest in your situation further than throwing some antibiotics at you. This is just my observation from personal experience. I feel like if I was an all-American White male, they would have rolled out the red carpet, given me VIP service, and probably found the cancer at its first stage instead of constant misdiagnosis that led it to progress to its fourth stage. At that time, it didn't occur to me that my body was capable of healing itself because I was preconditioned to put my blind faith in doctors and medicine and overall, not question authority.

It took a little bit of retraining, but it soon became increasingly clear that I had to become my own advocate and do my own due diligence to help figure out what was really going on. I was quickly labeled the "difficult patient" because I was asking a lot of questions. Simple questions like "Why are you giving me this drug?" "What are the side effects?" "What are other potential options that you are not recommending?" "Do you have any Black friends?" Nothing too unreasonable, or so I thought. I asked questions that questioned the authority of every doctor, specialist, and medical professional, and their decisions about what to do and how to move forward. Why? Because they weren't listening to me or taking me seriously. Ironically, that was really the only way to force them to engage with me more. But why shouldn't I (or you) ask questions? I'm sorry if my questions are too forward but this is, after all, my life we're talking about. Little Note: If you're ever sick or in a situation where you're in a hospital, ASK F*CKING QUESTIONS! Ask a hundred questions if you need to.

I don't want to paint all my doctors in a negative light, as some of them were wonderful, while others were part Dr. House/part Darth Vader. Overall, they were doctors, blinded by the perspective of the standard approach of conventional Western medicine, to just about every ailment they come across. With the exception of maybe three doctors, I never really felt like any of them were really looking out for ME or had my own best interest in mind. The appointments, questions, diagnoses, and tests felt autonomous, routine, and disconnected...

My fever shot up to 104 degrees consistently. Even though I was incredibly sick, I pushed past the pain I felt at every turn and kept training clients and teaching classes at a corporate gym in NY. In my head, I wasn't that sick—I was just moving a little slower than I would've liked to. I reached a point where I couldn't take the stairs, walking even 10 stairs would wipe me out for about 15 or 20 minutes and I would have to sit down and catch my breath.

After repeatedly signing my life away and releasing them of any liability for my death, disfigurement, and disability whatsoever, I became entrenched in this vicious cycle of "guessing the germ therapy" and following the archaic standards of care of conventional Western medicine. This approach would work for some people, if they guess right the first, second, or even third time but by the twentieth time, the giddy guessing game is no longer a fun game, method, or plan of action for the pissed-off patient (in constant devastating duress). They sure had A LOT of goddam guesses though, and my health wasn't getting any better. My Uber driver has more answers about the things that go on around him, but these guys somehow don't know about something that's within their area of expertise?

Self-Reflection Innerval™

Before I got the real diagnosis, I went four months misdiagnosed and trapped on what I call the Elliptical of Symptom Management. I kept completing boring movements, staring at a screen, and going nowhere else fast. Name three times you've climbed on this Elliptical of Symptom Management but knew something deeper was wrong (even though the doctors were convinced otherwise).

_____

_____

_____

DEATH ISRAEL HOSPITAL

I got severely frustrated that no highly trained doctor or skilled ENT specialist could tell me what was going on with me so I went to see an allergist, thinking maybe I had a severe reaction and they could point me in the right direction to help me counteract this reaction. Dr. Heather was nice, warm, and encouraging, the first doctor out of 20 or so that I felt genuinely cared about me (like actually cared if I lived or died).

Dr. Heather was concerned with how sick I looked. She maintained an unshakable air of positivity, motivation, and encouragement as far as figuring things out went. When she took my temperature, things got intense: it was 104°F, and I was sporting a resting heart rate of 160 bpm. She was mortified and ordered me to go to the ER immediately. She actually wanted to call an ambulance, but I refused. The nearest hospital was Beth Israel, now nicknamed Death Israel because of the reported cases of patients dying for unknown reasons, allegedly from massive medical errors. I was hesitant but she called the hospital to let them know my condition and to have them let me in right away.

I was as excited to go to Death Israel as I would be if I was going to a haunted Kansas (or Charlottesville) cornfield as a lone Black man. In my head, I wasn't that sick and I wasn't going back to the ER. Somehow, taking stairs, sitting down every 10 to 15 minutes to catch my breath was, ahem, normal to a "healthy 32-year-old," who was a fitness guru.

Death Israel looked like a hot mess from the outside with the massive ongoing construction projects all around the hospital complex. Once inside the ER triage, it quickly morphed from a hospital to a scene from the movie, Resident Evil 3. Patients looked like zombies, but instead of acting crazy and eating people, they were lazing about, waiting to be screened. Picture zombies who moved to Florida to retire and you'd have some idea about the way it was looking at the time. There were about a hundred zombies in the waiting room, waiting to be pre-screened to determine if they were sick enough to be admitted into the ER. It was like a nightclub, but the opposite; the worse you looked the easier it would be to get in.

Luckily for me, my allergist had called me in and they were expecting me, or so I thought. I approached the triage window and there was this white woman, mid-30s, with brown hair at the window. I told her that my allergist had called me in to be seen right away because of my fever, fatigue, and high heartbeat. She looked at me like I was crazy and told me that doctors can't call patients in and told me that I had to wait. I insisted that she did and asked if she could double-check, but she shut me down. Annoyed, low on energy, and really having no choice, I sat down and waited with the rest of the zombies. As I sat there, I saw this older white lady, blonde hair, maybe around 50 walk up to the counter I had just left and ask to be seen. The lady answered a few questions and like magic, she was whisked in to be seen immediately. She literally had a light cough. I'm dead serious.

As soon as I saw this I was deeply triggered and became completely enraged. I'm an intelligent Black man who works in fitness and health. Almost daily people are condescending towards me, show ill feelings toward me, or are just plain disrespectful to me because of my race. Growing up in Wisconsin has helped me become resilient to racism and its many subsidiaries. It still hurts, just hurts less and less the more I experience it. Race isn't always the first thing that pops into my head when things like this happen, but it has to always be a factor considered when things don't add up or seem right. Or maybe people are simply scared of me. Regardless of me intentionally smiling and laughing to feel safe and disarm people. People sometimes lock their car doors when I'm walking by, women clench their purses sometimes when I'm in an elevator with them, or people will cross the street when I'm walking towards them. On the flip side, many people randomly ask me if I'm "the guy on TV that kicks and punches (Billy Blanks)." It is what it is.

I'm not righteous about being Black, however; it's my reality. I live in a country whose systems were built on White supremacy. I have to accept and intentionally navigate that fundamental fact. As a Black man you can do one of two things when you experience racism, ignore it and subsequently repress it, or snap and become the "angry Black man" that people stereotypically think you will be. For once, I did the latter. I f*cking snapped. I was at the lowest point of my life: feverish, fatigued, overcome with sickness, and I was told to wait in this state while they just let a White lady in with a light cough. On one hand, I'm a well-mannered Wisconsin guy who is polite, and would of course let a woman go before me, especially an older woman. I'm a mama's boy for life. On the other hand, I was in a sick, delusional state, frozen in my stress response, and in a deteriorating state. So, I lost my mind for a hot second. "I'm a f*cking fitness guru and I'm calling the NY Times, Maury, ABC, and NBC, and the NY Post to tell them what you just did! How DARE you!?! This is DISCRIMINATION!" Why I said I would call Maury I have no idea. I name-dropped media outlets profusely and literally went crazy on that triage attendant! She wasn't ready for or expecting that. She knew exactly what she did, and I called her out on it hardcore style. Sometimes though, you need to do a good snap on a b*tch to let them know about your boundaries. NY'ers are intense, loud, and can go calm to nuclear in half a second. I calmed down and sat back down, looking frantically at my phone like I was going to call someone. I wasn't. haha. Five names later, I was magically called into the triage. Hmm…And this would be the start of my hellish experience at Death Israel Hospital. It couldn't possibly get worse than this, or could it?

F*CK YOUR FOOD

"You're hiding my f*cking food?!?" I screamed at about four indifferent nurses who were sitting behind a hospital floor reception desk, because they were literally hiding my food from me, and if you know me, hiding food is the worst thing you can do to me. #nomnomnom It had already been three days at Death Israel hospital and they still didn't know what was wrong with me.

That didn't stop them from making me an instant cash cow running every single test on me known to man, to try and find out: MRIs, constant blood work, CT Scan, X-ray, biopsies. You name it, they tested me with it. Patients who are undergoing surgery, medical procedures, and a variety of other medical tests, are often asked to "fast" prior to the treatment or procedure. This is apparently supposed to help doctors get accurate results and establish a solid baseline to inform future tests and procedures that may be needed down the road.

With each test and procedure that they did on me, came a forced fast via an NPO order. NPO means "nothing by mouth." And it can typically be anywhere from six to eight hours before a hospital test or procedure, and sometimes it's even longer. When you are used to eating a lot under duress, this seems like torture. Eating was the only thing that I could control in that moment of my experience. You only get three chances at eating in a hospital: breakfast, lunch, and dinner. And when you have a medical test or procedure scheduled, you are missing one and sometimes two of those chances to eat, and three if you are having a really bad day.

I was in so much discomfort, delusion, and disarray that I literally thought they were trying to purposely kill me by not allowing me to eat. Food is comfort and the easiest and quickest way that we can self-soothe ourselves, and if you have trained your hunger hormones to always expect food, it's traumatizing when you are forced not to have it. Another strange thing to think about is why, at a medical facility, the food is so sh*tty and unhealthy!

I would always ask to see my chart, and they would never let me see it; they always said that I would get a record of my chart and tests and that they couldn't show them to me. I remember one time I was wheeled to a room for a procedure and my chart was in this binder in the back of my hospital bed. I was waiting so I reached for it and started reading and flipping through it. All of a sudden "SNATCH," and a nurse literally snatched the chart out of my hands while I was reading it. WTF?!? B*tch stole my chart. I was the "difficult patient." This is what they called me among other things in their shady notes on my medical records (I covertly peaked at them all the time). The next time you're a patient in the hospital, ask to see your chart and see what they do or say. I'm still mystified as to why our own records are kept secret from us. Or maybe it's just a Black thing.

The food issue eventually led to my breaking point. It happened on my third day when I missed breakfast because I was waiting for a test that never happened, and then I missed lunch. The prospect of missing dinner was the FINAL straw for me, I thought they were trying to kill me! I had to use what little energy I had left to confront them and demand to eat, because I had been already waiting over 12 hours. "I'm not taking that f*cking test," I exclaimed. As I did, I looked down to see a tray of food with a piece of paper with my name written on it. They were f*cking hiding my food from me! It seemed all too inhumane to hide a patient's food just because I was waiting to get a test. It wasn't my fault that I couldn't take the test, it was theirs. I thought I was going to die without having food every few hours, especially because I was so sick. Boy was I so wrong. Wronger than middle-aged dads are about crocs (who still wears them tho?) Little did I know, those nurses unknowingly planted the first seed of something that I would later discover to be healing: fasting for optimal health.

Fasting has been used for religious and health reasons for thousands of years. It's as simple as consciously not eating for a specific period of time, and instead choosing nothing or minimal calorie drinks like water, coffee, and herbal teas. Countless studies show various benefits of fasting[165], and my preferred way of fasting is intermittent fasting. Every night that you go to sleep, your body goes into a "fasting" state to reduce energy, regenerate, and recharge for the following day. This is where the term "breakfast" comes from. It means to "break" your overnight "fast." Your body takes an energy break. And it should because it works overdrive daily fueling your body, mind, and all your biological functions day in and day out. Like day and night, and yin to the yang, when you are eating and not eating is all about balance. Certain processes for proper digestion need to occur during the times when you are not eating.

People who practice IF eat less frequently, feel hungry less often, and are fuller when they do eat. By eating fewer meals, you are taking in fewer calories, and by restricting calories, you're forcing the body to look elsewhere than your gut for energy. This was just my approach and one IF practice of many. Typically you would be eating the same amount of calories you would normally in a day, but just within a shorter feeding window. This causes mild metabolic stress, encourages cellular repair, and your body utilizes stored overfat directly as fuel first. Our digestion uses a massive amount of energy to function. Our bodies have an energy capacity, we don't have limitless energy. The energy has to always be converted from somewhere. The less energy we use for digestion, the more energy we have for healing and repairing our bodies. Fasting also is a powerful way to train your nerves by stimulating your vagus nerve and increasing your vagal tone. It doesn't work for everyone, but due to all of these positive benefits in line with my philosophy, I highly recommend trying it out. Please note though, fasting IS NOT starving yourself. There is a difference and you should probably get a coach or other professional to help you understand the difference between the two.

If you have never tried fasting before, getting started is simple and easy for most people. It's one of the pillars I used to help me rapidly self-heal and it's the foundation of my health coaching clients because it's the most powerful way to trigger your body into self-regulating internally. From everything from flushing fat, to a cognitive boost, to helping heal chronic health issues, intermittent fasting has several applications. There are a variety of intermittent fasting protocols, and based on extensive research, my 50-day complete remission recovery, my post-cancer treatment recovery, and 1000s of my clients, I have developed a very effective, efficient, and easy-to-follow "Feed focused" approach in my EMPOWERED HEALTH COACHING program with specific guidelines tailored to athletes, fitness enthusiasts, resistance strength trainers, and the beginner. You can find more info about it at http://mariogodiva.com

Regardless of the unplanned fasting experience, I left Death Israel sicker, weaker, and in more pain than when I was admitted. How does that happen? Seven days of what seemed like hundreds of tests with zero results, different blood tests, X-rays, CT scans, and MRIs on almost every part of my anatomy and they still didn't know what was wrong. I was the ultimate VIP cash cow and they wasted no time putting me through the wringer. A chest MRI showed a dark haze over my lungs plus several nodules. I asked what those ominous markings were and if they were common in people. They responded, "No, the dark haze is common, and nodules are mostly benign. We're looking for an acute infection."

The medical opinion I received after the chest X-ray just didn't feel right to me. My gut and body were trying to send me inner intelligence again, and I completely ignored them in favor of the opinions that the doctors were throwing at me, but I did have a feeling then that something wasn't right. As it turned out, the haze they found at the time was the first stage of high-grade cancer and if the doctors checked or investigated further, it could've been caught and treated in its first stage, well, before it progressed to stage 4, leaving me with only a week's worth of life. At the time, they didn't think it could be cancer because they'd become so obsessed with finding out what the acute infection was. They just obsessed about the type of infection and what antibiotics would possibly cure it, without asking about the secret source, or root cause of the infection.

The hospital lost my blood samples several times, treating me like a blood gas station (how does a hospital lose blood and test samples?). I was even quarantined, and they told my roommate it was because I might have Ebola (a HIPAA violation, itself!). Can you imagine being in a hospital right when that whole Ebola scare happened? I was quarantined against my will with urgency and no questions asked. "It's a Black man, it must be Ebola!" I thought they were trying to kill me. I believed that I was surely going to die and that they wouldn't do anything about it. In fact, they were moving my demise along quicker!

I had a consistently high fever with my temperature remaining almost permanently at 104 degrees and only lowering temporarily a few hours after taking Tylenol or ibuprofen. Nevertheless, I'd be sitting very calmly, relaxed, sometimes even smiling and looking at me, you'd wonder how I could have a high fever, yet just feel so unaffected by it all? The truth is I was anything but unaffected! I was in such constant pain, mental shock, and agonizing duress but when you spend months in this state, you just learn to cope with your body adjusting to that state of insane distress and sometimes, you finish off the coping with a smile. I was extremely frozen in my stress response nerve state. Our bodies are highly adaptable, and my chronic adaptation from all those years and the present situation was bordering on malevolence. My mind, body, and nerves had negatively adapted to my new frozen state to keep up with my symptoms, states of sickness, and chronic stress but I came to terms with the fact that it could only tolerate being frozen in emergency mode for so long, with the flight of my life gradually descending to an imminent and fatal crash.

What other choice did I have than to simply deny that I was that sick in the first place? My oxygen level was so low that I constantly walked on the edge of suffocation. Often, I had to be hooked up to oxygen to breathe and to get oxygen flowing through my body. My thoughts of denial were willing me to live, but healing wasn't happening because I was frozen in my stress response and my mind, body, and nerves were disconnected, divorced, and divided from each other.

NECK/HEAD CR SLOW MOTOR COMBO. (3 minutes)

1. NECK/HEAD CR SLOW MOTOR INNERVAL™ // 30 seconds.

Move your neck and head in a circle going right as slow as you possibly can. Do this for 30 seconds or count to 30 if you don't have a timer. Relax your neck and head back to neutral before you start the next Innerval™.

2. CORE BREATHING INNERVAL™ // 30 seconds.

Take long, slow, and deep inhales and take longer, slower, and deeper exhales for 30 seconds or 3 times each if you don't have a timer. As you inhale for 3 seconds your core goes out, and as you exhale for 6 seconds your core goes in.

3. Repeat 2 times

STIMULATION. The phrenic nerves, vagus nerves, motor cortex (18), and posterior thoracic nerves.

21 //

THE DEADLY DIAGNOSIS

There's one doctor I considered a "shero" ("female hero") and that was the sinus specialist I saw after the ER episode. When I finally mustered the strength to see another doctor again (and this took a while after my ER experience), my "23rd opinion" for my new "dying state" was from a sinus doctor who was extremely concerned and advised that I agree to be readmitted into the hospital. Here we go with the hospital again, hell to the no! "Dr. Shero" hooked me up to an oxygen tank because my oxygen levels were extremely low and I could barely walk. She left to get another doctor's supporting opinion to have me readmitted, because I just wasn't buying any of it. Seconds later, a wave of panic came over me. "What if she was going to get the police to force me back to the hospital?"

She comforted me when she came back though, assuring me that I wouldn't have to go back to the hospital if I didn't want to but only as long as I made one promise: that I wouldn't be a hero. If I felt deathly ill at all, I'd have to get readmitted. She knew I was stubborn, and this was a way to reach a compromise and so I agreed. I agreed to work with her to figure out not only what was wrong with me, but why. I did this because she was really keen on getting to the root cause. She was only the second doctor that seemed interested in that.

She fixed me up with a portable oxygen tank to take home and called me on my cell phone to see if I'd returned safely. No doctor had EVER called me on my cellphone to check up on me before. Seeing her was the most pleasant doctor experience I'd ever had in my entire life. What a breath of fresh air! She was hopeful, oozed kindness, and went out of her way to try and figure out what was wrong with me, and why. Most importantly, she assured me I would get better and all I needed to do was to hang on. So I did. It felt like I was hanging on by a thread, but I stayed strong, thanks to her compassion and dedicated patient care.

Many people might experience one or two bad doctors but after 20 horrifying doctor experiences, it only took one with the kindness, compassion, and warmth she had to get me on the path to find out what was wrong, to correctly diagnose my malaise, and to slowly regain normal bits of my life.

Self-Reflection Innerval™

We're hardwired to focus on the negative experiences. During my whole experience, I did have some pleasant experiences with doctors who were truly concerned about my well-being and were genuinely trying to help me get better. Can you think of a situation that was largely negative, and now try to pull out three positive things that occurred within it?

_____

_____

_____

LIVER THE SIZE OF TEXAS

Things were going pretty well at some point, and when I say pretty well, I mean I felt that I was still dying but dying slower. I started eating healthier and juicing so that my body could absorb the nutrients. I was taking supplements like probiotics, vitamin d, fish oil, zinc, silver, and magnesium. I was staying plenty hydrated and stopped taking the awful antibiotics that were killing me. In the grand scheme of things, I felt pretty "good," considering I was still under great distress after four long months going around and around the medical merry-go-round.

My 23rd-opinion doctor was one of the main reasons I chose to go to the hospital on one pivotal night. Had I not gone to the hospital, I may not have made it through the night. The first night before going into the hospital, I just thought I was experiencing inflammation that was going to resolve itself soon. The second night, I felt the pain kick in and noticed that I hadn't been able to go to the bathroom in three days. The third night, I attempted to get some more sleep again, all to no avail, and I later figured that my liver must've grown to the size of Texas (and this was without needing to run any tests). It turned out that I was actually in septic shock. My liver had shut down, all of my organs started to fail, and I started to drown from the inside out from a back-up of all of my bodily fluids. I looked like *The Nutty Professor* (a comedy film with Eddie Murphy). Sepsis is a full-body inflammatory response to an infection in the blood. It can lead to septic shock which may cause respiratory or heart failure, stroke, failure of other organs, and death.[166]

As I lay there in pain, I convulsed, cried, and contemplated. I feverishly flipped and flopped, until finally, I heard her voice and warning resonate so loudly within me that I couldn't even think about ignoring it: "Don't be a hero, Mario." It was the voice of my 23rd-opinion doctor, Dr. Shero, echoing in my head, almost like it was haunting me.

With that, I finally decided to commit to going to the hospital, despite the post-traumatic stress I had from Death Israel, from my first trip there. I packed a medium-size luggage bag and loaded it with essentials as if I was going on vacation, but this would turn out to be a "staycation" at a resort where residents had to wear hideous hospital gowns and eat nasty food. The good news was I had now become a pro at going to the hospital and knew exactly what I needed. I brought some extra food because I knew they were going to starve me again when I had to undergo tests. I slowly put on some comfortable sweat clothes and then called 9-1-1. "Hi Operator, my name is Mario Godiva. My stomach is really swollen, and I feel really sick. I'm not sure what's wrong, but I think I need an ambulance to take me to the hospital."

I became entranced by the high-pitched beeps, machine swooshes, and other unrecognizable noises as they played a symphony while I lay in my ICU bed. After a dozen (or so) doctors and nurses attended to me, three doctors walked back into my room and gave me my first grim prognosis. And before you even start to think that I was finally getting proper treatment, there was actually one main doctor and the rest were interns, residents, or minions, however you want to classify them. The main female doctor said, "Mr. Godiva, your liver has shut down and your body is holding onto all of its fluids internally, and you are in septic shock. We could try to drain the excess fluid, but that would risk puncturing or rupturing a vital organ. Or we can give you a high dose of our most powerful antibiotic, but that would damage your liver even further."

For me, the choice was between risk A and risk B?

I remember wondering at that moment if this was the season finale of The Mario Show? I took a few moments and really absorbed the new piece of information. I started to do a few core breaths to help me activate my relaxation response if I could. They worked and I was surprisingly calm and felt pretty indifferent about it. After a couple of moments of processing it, I asked, "Is there anything I can do or eat to help my liver function again?" The main female doctor and her two minion's collective response was a strong "NO." Just like that, no. No hope, no way out, and no better place than what we're offering you right now.

Their collective "No" hit me deep in my gut and shifted me right into my shutdown response. For a moment, I did what most people would probably do and just accepted what the doctors told me. It's their profession, their living, their area of expertise. How could I possibly question them? They are the experts in my situation. So there they stood, three Grim Reapers in scrubs, delivering the news that there was no hope for me.

As I watched them nervously fidget under my stare, I could tell how uncomfortable they were with giving me the news. For me, it simply felt like a category-5 hurricane was hitting my entire body. The room became one giant blur as tears gushed from my eyes. In crept my shutdown response stories of hopelessness, helplessness, and giving up. I convulsed like I was having a seizure from sobbing so hard. My heart ached, my soul shook, and my mouth tasted both bitter and salty from rising bile and falling tears. I could smell the sterile stench of the hideous hospital gowns I was wearing, and the sheets of my bed mixed with my tears and mucus. I'd become so bloated that I had to wear two or three hospital gowns to cover my girth. I decided that there was no hope, and I was just readying myself to die. I'd lived a great life and accomplished many things and I wasn't scared of death. I was the oldest living member of my entire family and most importantly, I had known death since it started taking away older members of my family; death and I were frenemies.

As I thought about all of my family deaths and especially my mother's, I started to experience a deep trigger and hyper-emotional reaction in my body. I shifted from my shutdown response to my stress response. I told them that I needed a moment to process this and asked if they could come back. I knew I couldn't make the best decision in this hysterical state, so I gave myself time to fully feel my feelings. I cried, convulsed, and conceded. After a couple of minutes, I decided to take a mindful Innerval™. I did active Innervals™ that met me in my stress response and then helped me shift back into my relaxation response. Of course, at the time, I didn't know that I was doing an Innveral™, but these experiences are the fundamental ones that aided me in creating this practice. I understood that it was impossible to just relax, and I had to literally incrementally train myself to relax. I knew that taking a short break to do some core breathing, self-reflection, and focusing on my nightlights would help me calm my nerves and enable me to make a better decision, regardless of how hard it is to do at the moment. I've been talking a lot about Innervals™ and you have been doing many of them (hopefully) throughout this book. I think it's important to clearly define what exactly an Innerval™ is and why I think active and mindful Innervals™ are so important in life.

The root of Innerval™ is to "innerve."

Innerve:

1.   To give nervous energy or power to:

2.   To give increased energy, force, strength, or courage to:

3.   INVIGORATE, STIMULATE, ANIMATE

Innervals™ are a way to encourage mindfulness and help you activate your relaxation response in an active way, a healthy distraction. Instead of being passive, the Innervals™ are supposed to be proactive. You proactively put energy into motion with a thought-provoking question, insight, or self-reflection. Or you can stimulate your nerves with action, vocalization, meditation, or breathwork. I was always active, on the go, and a go-getter, who never wanted to sit still. I hadn't ever had the luxury of exploring therapy, meditation, or mindfulness by going to classes, workshops, or fancy retreats. I was dying in a hospital bed and I had to make the meaning of mindfulness my own; I had to make it work for me at a time of extreme duress. I had to actively work to direct my thoughts away from anxiety, stress, hopelessness, and self-harm. All it took was one short mindful Innerval™ of me getting outside of my circumstance to activate my relaxation response...

FOCUS. NOW. JUDGMENT-FREE.

At that moment, I had to rebrand, reframe, and reimagine mindfulness for myself by creating a unique brand essence at that moment. Every time I took a mindful Innerval™, the following inner monologue would generally ensue:

FOCUS. NOW. JUDGMENT-FREE.

FOCUS. Where is your focus? Is it just on one thing?

- NOW. Where are your thoughts right now? The past and future don't f*cking exist in this moment, literally.
- JUDGMENT-FREE. Are you Judge Judy or John? If not, stop f*cking judging yourself and others!
- MAKE A MINDFUL DECISION. NOW.

This is the essence of exactly what mindfulness is: focusing on the now, judgment-free. In that moment, I wanted to make the destination of mindfulness and the act of being mindful more accessible to myself in a simple enough manner. I also knew that if I took more of an active approach to activating my relaxation response, I would get there faster and more often.

This new "Innerval™ mindset" triggered a deep, defiant, and dramatic activation of my relaxation response that allowed me to make the best decisions, which ultimately saved my life and healed me in record time. With the toxins overflowing inside of me, and with my other organs failing, I was dying as fast as a fish on a hot sidewalk. But after my hot mess tear-soaked nervous breakdown, I realized that the doctors' "no" made me take a short mindful Innerval™, which lifted me to relaxation and allowed me to make a conscious, informed, and better decision. Their "no" motivated me the same way that all the "NOs" I'd ever heard had motivated me in the past to prove them wrong.

I was so overwhelmed by pain and despair at that moment, I could hardly notice that this mindful Innerval™ triggered a beam of inner drive that seemed miles away. I barely saw it, but I started to focus on it, like it was a distant lighthouse and I was on a storm-tossed sea, searching for a light to guide me. Eventually, I started concentrating on it as hard as I could. What started as a small mindful Innerval™ of drive, slowly but steadily grew. As it grew, I also felt resilience and defiance spread and grow—they spread fast as if they were under a fast-forward time-lapse, getting faster, higher, and louder, until I eventually declared, "F*ck these doctors, I'm going to figure this out myself!"

GOOGLE, HELP ME REBOOT MY LIVER!

The next thing I knew, I was cozied up to Google, trying to figure out how to restart my liver. I Googled things like "liver shut down," "how to restart liver," "dog that's also an accountant" (lol! I had to laugh too), and "help detox the liver," etc. I was Googling for my life, trying to figure out how to do something—anything at all.

My doctors were focused on what was happening to my body while I was focused on what was happening to my mind, and I had completely forgotten what connected the two—my nerves. The sole reason that your mind and body connect, communicate and coordinate is because of your nerves. When your nerves aren't talking, nothing gets done, as in nothing at all. How come no one really talks about that? Nerves are so important, namely your vagus nerve, which is the most important nerve in your body—it runs down your neck, through your chest, and to your colon. It's in charge of reining in your runaway stress response by triggering your relaxation response, which lowers your heart rate and induces calm.

For four months, my body was under chronic stress and unable to heal itself, not only from my frozen stress response, but also from the antibiotic assault that nuked my good gut bacteria repeatedly causing nutrient imbalances, autoimmune issues, and gave me a leaky gut. Desperation had slowly crept in and I was willing to try it all. I really had nothing better to do. I was dying in a hospital bed. I also didn't feel right about what the doctors were telling me about how I couldn't use food or any other alternative besides antibiotics or a medical procedure to get better.

The life-saving Google research I conducted from my hospital bed brought me to a variety of methods and soon I was on the phone with several friends having them bring me certain foods and drinks: lemons, probiotics, juices, supplements, broccoli, organic coffee enemas, you name it! Sometimes, they had to "smuggle" them in, like a drug dealer, because the doctors didn't want me to take certain foods, drinks, or supplements while I was in the ICU. They always told me that these "extras" would interfere with the medications and tests that I was taking. Shout out to my surrogate Jewish mother, Abby, for smuggling in a lot of stuff I needed! It was like the Underground Railroad, but this time, the destination was the hospital, and we were smuggling food instead of slaves. I then started to eat, drink, and take everything I could theorize would work.

The first and most ugly remedy was an organic coffee enema. As horrible as it sounds, there was an overwhelming cache of sources and firsthand accounts of it working brilliantly. It turns out coffee enemas powerfully stimulate your vagus nerve. I was in septic shock dying in a hospital and desperation was my BFF at the moment, so I was eager to try it out.

The way to do it properly is to have an enema bag and organic coffee and have it seep into you, holding it for about 15 or 20 minutes, and then empty it out. I had no time for acting proper or anything of that sort. I had two Fleet enema boxes, organic coffee from Whole Foods, and a prayer to Jesus, Buddha, or whatever higher being was available at the time. I had to pull what White people call a "Macgyver" and what Black people call a "ghetto." I emptied out the enema solution, refilled it with organic coffee and water, and then proceeded to squeeze it up to my "you know where." Is this rock bottom? Squeezing coffee into my booty? I sure hope this is as far as rock bottom goes! As I mentioned, coffee enemas are an extremely powerful way to stimulate your vagus nerve (relaxation response). So when I say my nerves saved my *ss, I really mean that literally, figuratively, and everything in between!

Nothing really happened right away, but that night, I went to the bathroom (number two), for the first time in almost two weeks. It felt like an exorcism. I think I also did see Jesus for a second. I was happy and proud of myself for many reasons, mostly because I had figured this out on my own. There WAS some activity that I could do and some food I could eat to get my liver started again, and it had to do with activating my relaxation response in some way or form. After a day or so, my liver started working again, slowly but surely. As more hope built inside of me from the results I was getting, my energy only grew stronger. I updated my near-death experience scorecard: Fitness Guru 1:0 to Doctors with Little or No Nutrition Experience. Thank you, nerves, for saving my life.

DIAGNOSIS DAY

30 tests later, the main doctor decided to do a liver biopsy to find out why my liver had gotten so big. Why wait so long though? I'm exaggerating about the 30 tests, it was more like 15 tests, but still why does it take so long to do a liver biopsy when your liver is shut down, you are in septic shock, and you are quickly deteriorating on a hard, sterile, and basic ICU bed? You would think all liver options would be the FIRST options explored and not the last. I also wasn't too thrilled with them sticking a giant *ss needle into me to take a piece of my liver out and test it, but I agreed. And yes, it is just as awful as it sounds.

I finally received a liver biopsy, and of course, there were complications. This would be my 13th medical error. It took them three different stabs to finally get in and get a piece of my liver. Three. F*cking. Stabs. Into my liver. You guys may think I'm joking, but they were trying to kill my *ss by medical error. No question. On April 7, 2014, after a long, suspenseful, and many "Why the f*ck is this taking so long?" moments, seven days after the liver biopsy, they discovered that I was in the fourth stage of a rare and aggressive (high-grade) cancer. But seriously why does it take seven days for a liver biopsy to come back when you are in the ICU? Aren't you somewhat a VIP when you're in the ICU because you're basically a step away from death? Another example of me being deprioritized as a Black patient. I could have easily died in the seven days it took to get those results. What type of cancer? It was a rare type of cancer, but it doesn't really matter what type of cancer because cancer is cancer. The type of cancer isn't the focus, the type basically just means where it is located. The focus should be on me and my expeditious healing of cancer. Cancer doesn't befall its victims through magic, but through lifestyle. You are empowered when you're focusing on YOU, not a disease that tries to corrupt you. Why would I focus on cancer instead of my ability to heal from cancer?

The prospect that I had cancer had come up before from only one of the doctors (of the 23 I consulted), but it was ruled out after I received a bone marrow biopsy and it came up inconclusive. This was medical error number nine with three stabs to try and successfully get a sample. Do you know how painful it is to be stabbed in your bone just once, let alone three times? I had a needle shoved into my bones three times basically for no reason. While I was in Death Israel, I did point out the strangeness of the haze that appeared in my lungs and the several nodules (the first stage of this rare cancer) in my chest MRI but was told that it wasn't an issue.

I navigated healthcare hell (the second book I write will be named this) and what I experienced was more than an epic fail of our healthcare system and Western medicine in general and this is without even going deeper into the blatant racial disparity of the American healthcare system. I often joked, second-guessed, and actually believed some doctors were trying to kill me because I was Black. Or maybe I was low on the patient priority list or something? Regardless of the reason, it makes no sense at all why I was treated that way. Does it look that way to you, reader? It certainly felt that way for the most part. They took my temperature, listened to my heart and breathing, ran blood tests, and asked me about my symptoms, and when they started the interviews and questionnaires about my past, lifestyle, and travel, it was for the mere purpose of doctors "guessing" what type of acute infection or germ I had. It was a case of doctor choreography with recurring antibiotic party favors. NOT ONCE WAS THERE ANY MENTION OF THE ROOT CAUSE, NOR UNDERLYING PRECONDITIONS FOR MY SYMPTOMS.

The nodules and a haze in my lungs spread and quickly infected four different areas of my body with billions and billions of rare-type cancer cells. These cancer cells hijacked my liver, causing it to quickly morph to about five times its normal size. How could 23 doctors, specialists, and medical professionals miss that I had a rare form of cancer for four f*cking months? Because they wanted to miss it. What do you think would have happened had I not been my own healthcare advocate, as intensely as I was? I would have died, no question.

Knowing I had cancer, however, meant I could FINALLY treat the secret source of my physical, mental, emotional, and spiritual duress! It felt like getting closure months after the end of a long, intense, and f*cked up relationship. My honeymoon period of finding out what I had, ended very abruptly after my cancer diagnosis. Not only was I challenged with cancer, but it was also a life-threatening, rare, aggressive form of cancer that had progressed to its fourth stage or the final chapter. It was basically an evil mutant of cancers that had quickly wreaked havoc on all of my body's internal systems.

My body had been wasting away while trying its best to counteract the influx of the very unwelcome "guests." It also looked as if I was dying in an ugly hospital gown (two hospital gowns actually). Yet the only echoing thought I can really recall was OMG! I have a rare form of cancer. I'm a f*cking fitness guru, and I have a f*cking rare cancer. WTF?! How can I have a rare form of cancer? You may remember that earlier I told you that my father died from a rare illness, and it turns out it was the same thing that I had. But I still couldn't wrap my mind around the possibility. My father wasn't fit; he wasn't a fitness guru like I was.

Self-Reflection Innerval™

Although I was excited to finally get a diagnosis, I soon accepted that the rare cancer diagnosis wasn't the secret source of my initial symptoms. Cancer was the third stage of the progression; the chronic imbalance had been the second stage of progression, and the first, secret source was my deviated septum combined with over a decade of undigested, unprocessed, and untouched emotional energy.

Sinus infections, postnasal drip, and pneumonia expressed themselves in my lungs and were the first stage of the rare cancer. Conventional doctors could never trace it there, but functional doctors would have been able to. Think about your top three current inner whispers that are being expressed as imbalances. What do you think the secret source of each inner whisper is?

_____

_____

_____

22 //

YOU ARE THE F*CKING CURE

Trigger alert This chapter may be triggering to some people. If you feel triggered or defensive reading this chapter or any part of this book, I challenge you to dig deeper and try to understand why. Triggers are teachers and are a feedback map showing you what and where you need to be healed.

"We're searching for the cure", "Please help us find the cure", "It will take a lot more money, but we will eventually find a cure" "We will search for a cure until our last dying breath, support our mission!" The way that some doctors, scientists, and most notably charitable organizations talk, you would think that they are on this massive, epic, and *Lord Of The Rings* style journey to find various magical, mythical, and mysterious cures for cancer as well as a multitude of other health ailments. But instead of it being a trilogy, it's infinity. Their collective thirst for various superficial cures is unquenchable, unusual, and unreasonable. They pretend that everyone is born without a fully functional, adaptable, and repairable immune system and needs about 30+ different drugs, protocols, and medical procedures for every single disease known to man. I call these "superficial cures." Superficial means existing or occurring at the surface; and that seems appropriate because these solutions do not dig into the root cause, they remain on the surface. And although you can be born with certain immunity deficiencies, the good news is that we are largely in control of our immune health. There are so many natural and easy ways to balance your immune system and take control of your health. Spoiler alert: It doesn't happen overnight.

I must admit though, it's kind of a brilliant strategy. Fundraisers take in donations finding a cure, normally exploiting sick people's personal stories of illness and loss to emotionally guilt people into giving them money. Then the benefactors of this pity money have plenty of play money to experiment, test, and run scientific studies that lead not to a cure but to more drugs and products that can be put on the market to sell. You know, like you would do for any typical investment or business venture known to man, but it's much more fun to invest money that's not yours! I'll agree to that. Once they find a suitable superficial cure, they try to patent and protect it, and make a ridiculous amount of profit off of their patented or protected superficial cure. Now don't get me wrong, many legitimate charities use donations to find treatments, superficial cures, and medical advancements. Some even support patients and families which I think is a great thing. However, there also are bogus charities that exploit your generosity to line their own pockets. The FTC made a complaint about four cancer charities and there are surely many more that we don't even know about.[167] Although a massive amount of research and resources have come out of the medical field that keeps people alive way longer today than ever before, one must ask why a multi-trillion dollar industry feels the need to ask for money for heart-tugging causes where they maximize profit by patenting and protecting what their funded research yields. So be careful where and who you donate to. I always like to see what percentage of money and where it is going in any organization that I donate to.

There's also just one fundamental problem with all of these superficial cures out there. A cure is not as tangible as these companies make it sound. It will not be a pill or a shot that supposedly "cures cancer." A cure is not a destination that you arrive at, park, and then stay there for the rest of your life. A cure is not a product, protocol, or procedure. A cure isn't a finish line. A cure is never permanent or an endpoint. If anything, being cured should be a starting point. You're starting back at optimal balance when you're on the other side of sickness. Are you not? Every single time you get sick, self-heal, and then become healthy again, you technically are "curing" yourself every single time that happens. But you are doing that, no one is doing that for you. No one is "saving" you every single time you are sick. You save you.

A cure is a concept, a delusion, and it's utter bullsh*t. You can't be "cured" because you literally are the authentic CURE. Y-O-U! Curing your health issues happens from the inside, not the outside. Not only that, but these manufactured superficial cures are also temporary because if you're still engaging in an unhealthy lifestyle, have unresolved issues, chronic stress, or holding any other imbalances in your body you'll get sick again, and often it's worse the second time. At the end of the day, the question shouldn't be "How do we kill this disease that's inside of you?" it should be "What happened to you that allowed this disease to become a part of you?" Illness is the ultimate self-betrayal. Not only do you first have to forgive yourself for this betrayal, but you must also then accept, investigate, and understand how that self-betrayal happened in the first place.

Whatever went or is going wrong in your body because of YOU, can ALWAYS be corrected by YOU. It's really that simple, and if anyone tells you otherwise, it's because they want your f*cking money. The keyword is YOU. Infection, illness, and disease thrive when you put your focus on it. You give it power by giving it attention. What you should be doing is giving yourself power so that you can self-heal. You start doing this by practicing ways to activate your relaxation response like using my various Innervals™. You are more powerful than you know, but conventional doctors don't want you to know that. They routinely instill micro amounts of fake fear in you to make you think, feel, and reflexively come back to them for your own self-care. Why can't you just daily, weekly, monthly, and consistently give yourself your own self-care and never go to a doctor unless it's some type of emergency?

Why is it that we only notice when things are different? Why do we wait until things go wrong to take action? Why do we default to being reactive and not default to being proactive when it comes to our own health? How you look, move, feel, and heal is always determined by your lifestyle, behavior, and daily, macro, and micro choices. You have the power to proactively make your body run at optimal efficiency. It's when you are reactive instead of proactive, that sh*t hits the fan. Your body's default state is to remain in balance, homeostasis, at all times. It takes a lot of stubbornness, avoidance, and ignorance for you to get chronically sick. Before chronic infection, illness, and disease, is acute infection, illness, and disease. Before acute infection, illness, and disease are consistent, congesting, and crippling whole-body inflammation or localized somewhere in your body. And before that, your body sends you inner whispers or symptoms of imbalance. That's why we need to tune into that very first phase of inner whispers so that we can proactively listen and make changes in our life.

Just because your body can do something doesn't mean that you should be making it do it for no reason. Do you think your body wants to always be battling infections, illnesses, and diseases? No; your body wants balance. It wants you to prevent infections, illnesses, and diseases first, and then help it stay at optimal health so it can quickly, efficiently, and robustly use its energy to resolve any physical, mental, biological, or emotional issues that come up. When you look past all the fancy names, the areas, the stages, the duration, the cure rates, the infectability, and all the other pathology jargon that Western medicine has trained us to focus on, infection, illness, and disease is nothing more than an inner communication breakdown. Wouldn't you rather talk to your loved ones (including your "self") and resolve any miscommunications, issues, or breakdowns first, before resorting to poisoning, poking, or killing them to resolve the issue? Conversations are helpful; violent confrontations are harmful.

My doctors were focused on pathology while I was more focused on activating my own self-healing ability. Chemo, radiation, surgery, and drugs may be designed to kill an infection or cancer cells, but your body doesn't need them to survive. You're not going to get sick and die if you NEVER have chemo, radiation, and surgery in your life. What were people doing for 100s of years before those medical practices? They were created in the first place (by man), to kill things. So, it would make sense that they are more than likely to kill (eventually if not accidently) you over anything else because they are not natural, and you are injecting them directly into your blood. Obviously if you have no choice and things look dire, you should use those methods. However, if you discover you have cancer and it's not growing wildly or dramatically disrupting your quality of life, I much prefer the "Watch and Wait" approach, major lifestyle changes, and trying a few natural methods first. Just because you discover cancer doesn't mean it's growing or getting worse. It could just be chilling, literally. Waiting for the right fuel (alcohol, sugar, gluten, toxins, lack of movement) for it to grow.

On the flipside, micronutrients like vitamins, minerals, and some herbs are what your body REQUIRES to survive. When you are deficient in vitamins, minerals, and nutrients, your immune system is weakened and you get sick. Not only does your body need micronutrients like vitamins, minerals, and herbs to survive and function optimally, they are specifically designed to strengthen your immune system so that it can neutralize, negate, and nix any foreign invaders and keep you at optimal health. So, wouldn't this make complete common sense to focus on enhancing and using what your body needs to survive first before resorting to other harmful, chemical, and lethal methods of disease destruction? And, isn't it proven that those who focus on these things already are far less likely to encounter these health issues?

Your first line of defense for everything is your immune system. Western medicine has it a little backward; it's not JUST about pathology, pills, medical machines, and medical protocols, procedures, and practices, it's about unlocking YOUR (keyword YOU) natural, innate, and powerful self-healing ability. Activating your authentic cure potential. With the right lifestyle, behavior, patterns, food, thoughts, healthy habits, and inner environment, you have the potential to become the authentic cure of almost anything. Whenever you get sick, the first thing you need to do is step back, take a few core breaths, and really analyze all the internal, external, emotional, and biochemical reasons why you think you are sick. You become sick for a reason, it was not magic, luck, or random. You didn't win the sick Mega Millions.

Alternative healers and eastern medicine practices share a very common belief. They see cancer, sickness, illness, and disease as something that your body can fight off as long as your mind, body, and spirit are in a balanced, functional, and optimal state. Alternative healers and eastern medicine practices are focused on strengthening the patients' mind, body, and spirit system as much as possible. Energy work, herbs, vitamins, micronutrients, all with the focus of supercharging your inner environment so that cancer, sickness, illness, and disease can't thrive.

These are two treatment styles (focused on disease—conventional medicine/focused on self-healing—holistic) rooted in two very different belief systems or mental models. Remember, you are what you have been trained to believe, so I don't blame you if this sounds a bit out there. You were trained to trust doctors and go to Western medicine as your first line of defense for every health issue. Western medicine today tends to view cancer (as well as many other diseases) as a hostile invader that the body can't fight off when actually, it's part of your body, just a corrupted part of your body that has changed due to illness. Why would you want to kill off a part of your own body? Battle cancer? Why would you jump to being so violent with yourself? Wouldn't you want to try and do a little self-interview or conflict resolution first? Maybe at least have a brief talk with yourself before you decide to pick the nuclear option?

Because of this default trained belief of cancer, cancer doctors default to chemo, radiation, or surgery to remove the cancer. What about before cancer? How come doctors aren't more focused on what happens before you get cancer or in the early stages of cancer? There is no incentive for the medical industry to teach doctors to catch cancer early and best practices for early treatment through holistic lifestyle changes, though. The best incentive is catching it later when you actually think about it, because that is when the medical industry can make money. That's capitalism in healthcare at its finest. It's not the fault of the individual doctors, either, and we shouldn't shoot the messenger. The medical industry as a whole needs large structural changes surrounding how they acknowledge and treat disease, including options that are not Western medicine. In America, the medical industry being for-profit contributes deeply to this conflict. Health is a public issue and should be a public service that is never incentivized by profit, but by what is truly the best route for the individual. I believe that change would revolutionize the way that patients are treated and how they gain access to that treatment. It's time to stop tiptoeing and tap dancing around the bullsh*t. Someone has to scream foul, and it might as well be a big Black man that they deprioritized, minimized, and unwittingly tried to kill.

YOUR INSPIRING IMMUNE SYSTEM

Why do I say that you are the f*cking cure? Because you have an immune system, and it's only when the performance of your immune system is compromised that you face illness. You are continually exposed to pathogens, bacteria, toxins, etc that are swallowed, inhaled, put on your skin, and find their way to your mucous membranes. Whether or not they lead to disease or not is decided by the integrity of your body's defense mechanisms, or your immune system.[168]

You were born with an innovative, intricate, and insightful self-healing mechanism that detoxes harmful substances, attacks foreign invaders, and escorts them out of your body.[169] It protects you every day, and when it's running properly, you don't even notice it. Your immune system is an interactive network of organs, tissues, proteins, cells, and the biochemicals they secrete. They communicate, illuminate, and eliminate foreign substances together as a team, and defend your body against hazardous pathogens like viruses, bacteria, chemicals, parasites, and other bad stuff. They also fight against your body's own cells that have been corrupted and changed due to an illness.

Your immune system's main job is to protect your body against outside invaders to keep you healthy.[170] It does this by recognizing and mobilizing against antigens, which are the parts of foreign bacteria, viruses, or other invading substances that trigger an immune response. When an intruder enters your body, your immune system springs into action. When an antigen is found in your body your immune system will create antibodies to mark the foreign invader for your body to destroy. Antibodies are like your immune system's health scouts. They find antigens, stick to them like a key into a lock, and identify for your immune system the type so that it can be destroyed. When an antigen tries to enter your body, your immune system is triggered, and chemical signals are sent to spring all the different parts of your immune system into action.

In order for your body's natural defenses to run smoothly, your immune system must be able to differentiate between "self" and "non-self" cells, substances, and other things in your body. "Self" substances are proteins on the surface of our own cells that our body has learned to identify as "self." However, when your body mistakenly identifies its own body as "non-self" and fights it, this is when we get an autoimmune reaction. "Non-self" substances are called antigens and include proteins on the surfaces of fungi, bacteria, and viruses. Your immune system cells detect the presence of antigens and work to defend themselves.

Just like all things in your body, the key to a healthy immune system is balance.[172] If your immune system is over-reactive, it can be overly dramatic to every threat. This can lead to inner whispers of allergies, asthma, eczema, multiple food sensitivities, or even autoimmune conditions or cancer. Autoimmune diseases can be triggered by an overactive immune system that is out of balance. For example, when the immune system attacks the body's joints, the result is rheumatoid arthritis. On the flip side, if your immune system is under-reactive, it can expose your body to increased vulnerability to infections and disease. Many things can weaken your immune system, including inner/outer toxins, viruses, and physical or emotional stress. Underactive immunity or overactive immunity can be equally harmful to you, increasing your risk of developing infections and other health issues.[172]

The amazing thing about your immune system is that it's constantly adapting and learning so that your body can fight against bacteria or viruses that change over time. There are two major parts to your immunity defense.

- The first is called innate immunity and it's something that all babies are born with. It's a general defense against pathogens and launches a universal attack on any type of foreign invader.

- The second is adaptive immunity, and it's a learned defense that is acquired over a lifetime. It targets very specific pathogens that your body has already had contact with. It's the reason why we only get some illnesses like chickenpox only once. As you engage with different antigens, your immune system can remember them and fight them more effectively the next time you're exposed.

The two major parts of your immune system complement each other in any reaction to a pathogen or harmful substance. Your immune system uses your energy each time it has to respond, reduce, and remove foreign objects. Have you ever noticed that you are tired when you start to come down with something or get sick? The bigger the invaders and the more areas they are in, the more energy your immune system has to use to neutralize those threats. When there is no threat and your immune system has to respond, it wastes energy. When it's functioning optimally, it strikes down bacteria, illness, and disease-causing microorganisms easily, efficiently, and effectively. This is why people say that you should rest when you feel sick, because creating excess energy while your body is trying to internally heal will slow, stop, and strip the potential of your healing.

According to research from the National Institute of Health, underactivity of your immune system can result in severe infections and tumors of immunodeficiency, while overactivity results in allergic and autoimmune diseases.[168] When your immune system can't do its job, sh*t can hit the fan for you internally, holistically, and energetically. Allergies, sensitives, or asthma make your immune system respond to things that aren't really a threat, leading to wasted energy. Because your immune system is so massive and complex, it requires a number of different components working together and sometimes there can be miscommunication, misfires, and misinformation. Both adaptive and innate immunity uses white blood cells, which are like your body's security guards, constantly scanning and looking for issues. There are different types of white blood cells, but they all collectively help your body fight off infection, and when they aren't working properly, it can leave you vulnerable to illness.

If your white blood cells overreact to antigens, for example, it can cause dangerous levels of macro inflammation inside your body and lead to chronic health conditions like allergies. Immune deficiency diseases are when one or more parts of your immune system are missing. You probably panic when your iPhone goes missing (or you can't remember where you left it), imagine if a part of your immune system went missing? Sometimes your immune system can create autoimmune issues, which is when your immune system attacks your body's own healthy cells and tissues by mistake. (There are more than 100 types of autoimmune diseases, including Type 1 diabetes, rheumatoid arthritis, multiple sclerosis, and Crohn's disease.) In other cases, you may have a weak immune system because you're growing older and your white blood cell production drops.

Your lifestyle has a MASSIVE effect on how well your immune system is working. Unhealthy eating patterns can weaken your immune system.[173] Whether we digest, process, and assimilate the nutrients from our food is also monumental to immunity. Just because you're eating food, doesn't mean your body is able to properly digest that food, break it down into micro molecules, and assimilate it so that your body can actually use the vitamins and nutrients. Digestion is a complicated process and the vitamins and nutrients that we put into our body plays a massive role in keeping our immune system strong. Eating a lot of processed food can increase the number of harmful gut bacteria and reduce the number of helpful bacteria.[174] This leads to gut imbalance and leaky gut, which is a weakening of the gut wall barrier that allows toxins, pathogens, and undigested food to leak out of the gut and into our bloodstream. This leads to a system-wide immune dysfunction.

As you know from earlier chapters, the gut is more important than we give it credit for. 70 to 80% of your immune system is in your gut.[5] It's the mix of helpful bacteria inside of your gut that helps regulate your immune function by preventing it from overreacting or underreacting to antigens. It's your immune system's front line of defense because your body knows that most of the things that you are going to be exposed to that will be harmful will come to your gut first.

YOUR IMMUNE SYSTEM SUPPRESSION

A well-functioning immune system is critical for survival, but when it's not functioning properly, you're more vulnerable to infections and disease. I'm sure you've heard the word "immunocompromised" a lot lately because of the fact that those who are immunocompromised from other conditions are more likely to contract and have a severe case of COVID-19. Immunocompromised means that the body's immune defenses are weakened, suppressed, and don't function properly. When immune function is compromised, we are at a greater risk of facing serious infections and illnesses. The vulnerability to infection and illness depends on each person's degree of immunosuppression, which can vary greatly from person to person. It's possible to have partial or full suppression of the immune system.

Some people are more vulnerable to infections because of their weakened immunity, while others have severe reactions to infections and are at risk of life-threatening circumstances. This all depends on how much of the immunity is suppressed. Immunodeficiency disorders can be primary or secondary. Primary immunodeficiencies are inherited immune disorders that result from genetic mutations. There are over 300 types of primary deficiencies, but they are considered rare. Although people are born with these types of immunodeficiency, some aren't clinically diagnosed until later in life. Secondary immunodeficiencies are more common and result from disease, poor eating habits, environmental factors, and certain drug therapies. As you can probably surmise, I am speaking mostly about the secondary immunodeficiencies that can be shifted through lifestyle changes.

Your immune system wants to be powerful, but many factors can either support, sideline, or suppress your immune system. Just like anything, it can get overworked, overwhelmed, and overdo it to the point of chronic dysfunction. Hypothetically speaking, your immune system can neutralize about 100,000 toxins a day. In other words, there is a limit and a threshold to the amount of toxins your immune system is physically capable of holding back. If you are eating, breathing, and touching over a million toxins, bacteria, and other harmful pathogens, your immune system simply can't keep up. It's powerful, but not that f*cking powerful. It needs a break just like every other system in your body. You could take all the antibiotics, medications, magic potions, superficial cures, and other treatments in the world, but if you don't have a strong immune system, nothing else will matter, PERIOD. All those things are aiding and abetting your immune system because for some reason it's supremely suppressed.

Even though you're born with and have a natural ability to protect yourself, most people chronically deprive themselves of their body's innate healing processes due to their lifestyle, what they eat/drink, and what they think. When you have to go to a doctor's office or hospital, it's too late. What you eat, do, and think directly affects how you self-heal, literally. Every thought you have can be felt by every single cell in your body via molecule messengers or neurotransmitters. Your lifestyle, behavior, and daily choices either support or suppress your immune system.

Dr. Dale Bredesen is at UCLA and runs the Alzheimer's research center, the Buck Institute. In November of 2014, Dr. Bredesen published his trial in which he completely reversed Alzheimer's in 9 of 10 people at UCLA. Yes, it took five years, but he was able to completely arrest and reverse this dangerous disease that we are all so scared of. He has over 100 documented card-carrying Alzheimer's patients and he has completely reversed their symptoms.[176] How did he do it? A series of protocols in the form of a checklist with 37 items. Most of those things on his checklist are holistic and lifestyle strategies. We never hear "reverse" in the conventional world because the goal is to "manage". Alzheimer's is a major chronic health issue that is proven to be reversible by Dr. Dale Bredesen. So imagine how many other chronic health issues are reversible that we couldn't have imagined previously? I would venture to say that most of them are.

Western medicine ideology has trained us from birth that we can take a pill and feel better. In turn, people eat sh*tty food, stress themselves out to the max, binge drink, and run their bodies down to the ground because they know they can take a pill and feel better if they get sick. What people are slowly starting to realize, is those little pills add up. Antibiotics wipe out your good gut bacteria, and this makes it easier to get sicker down the road plus get digestive, mental, and emotional issues. Before chronic disease is acute disease, and before acute disease, is the incubation and buildup of disease. Antibiotics are just a veneer and instant gratification fix to symptoms with a long-term underlying cause. Wouldn't you rather figure out the source, root, and underlying cause of your symptoms so that they don't come back?

What inspires you to live a life with optimal health is your immune system. There is no magic pill, drug, or vitamin. It's your lifestyle that sets you on a path to a certain chronic disease. It's often a long path, and your immune system will do its best to send you warnings via self-feedback. Are you breathing toxins from pollution? Is mold in your house? Are you eating processed foods? Are you binge drinking alcohol? Are you abusing drugs? The point is, it's not just one thing that suppresses your immune system, it's the synergy of MANY things, and it takes a synergy response to counter it.

Here are some things that weaken your immune system:

- Aging
- Chemotherapy
- Chronic diseases, including diabetes, hepatitis, and kidney disease
- Certain medications, including corticosteroids
- Antibiotic use
- Poor eating habits
- Eating too much grain, refined sugar, and processed foods
- Poor digestion and malabsorption of nutrients
- Micronutrient imbalance
- Sedentary lifestyle
- Obesity
- Pregnancy
- Lack of sun exposure
- Smoking
- Alcohol and binge drinking
- Isolation and loneliness
- Chronic stress
- Poor sleep habits
- Not enough sun; vitamin D deficiency
- Toxin overload: prescription drugs, pesticides, herbicides, GMOs, hormones in meat, dairy, soy, table salt, artificial sweeteners, etc
- EMF, radioactive elements, and other harmful electromagnetic frequencies

I get it, we live in a very f*cking modern world that makes it seem almost impossible to avoid any and all of these things, but you can limit first before you completely eliminate them. Toggle the bandwidth so that these things are coming into your body at a smaller rate. Less of something bad will be better than more of something bad every time. Make sense?

You hear a lot of people talk about boosting your immune system and there are a lot of remedies that will do just that. However, a constant state of stimulation isn't really ideal. For example, over stimulated immune cells, like T-cells, may enhance the pathology associated with inflammatory bowel disease or other inflammatory conditions.[177] On the flip side, we don't want to simply suppress an overactive immune system. The focus should really be on immune modulation with natural products not boosting or suppressing it. This helps to bring the immune system back in balance to help us self-heal. One of the most important aspects of self-healing is balancing a volatile immune system that can present as overactive or underactive at the flip of a coin. Your body and its complex systems give a f*ck about one thing: balance. The more you give it what it genuinely craves, the healthier you'll be, and the longer you'll live. It's really that simple. In the next two chapters, I'll go over how you can start to rebalance your immune system energy.

LEGS/KNEES MOTOR COMBO. (3 minutes)

1. LEGS/KNEES INNERVAL™ // 30 seconds.

Move your legs and knees releasing any tension, tightness, or stress. Do this for 30 seconds or count to 30 if you don't have a timer. Relax your legs and knees back to neutral before you start the next Innerval™.

2. CORE BREATHING INNERVAL™ // 30 seconds.

Take long, slow, and deep inhales and take longer, slower, and deeper exhales for 30 seconds or 3 times each if you don't have a timer. As you inhale for 3 seconds your core goes out, and as you exhale for 6 seconds your core goes in.

3. Repeat 2 times

STIMULATION. The phrenic nerves, vagus nerves, motor cortex (21), and posterior thoracic nerves.

23 //

TO DIE OR NOT TO DIE?

My drives to "suicidal" city didn't end with the grief that overwhelmed me after the death of my family members. At the point of my diagnosis, I was grieving for myself, for the first time in my life...

One doctor came into my room (a dorky-looking white guy with glasses, brown hair, nothing against dorks) and gave me the second grim prognosis I would receive on this journey. He insisted that if I didn't start chemotherapy immediately, I wouldn't last through the week because of the state I was in. He also warned me of chemo's efficacy: a 17% cure rate over five years. Blah, blah, blah. He added that there could also be other complications, including death. He recommended a "palliative" treatment protocol that would at least help ease the burden on my internal bodily systems and slow the progression of the disease so that I could live longer than a week.

I could tell that he was very uncomfortable telling me all of this sad news. Who wants to tell someone that they're going to die? He gave me his recommendation and asked what I wanted to do from that point. I told him that I needed time to really process this and that I would get back to him when I had reached a decision. He pressured me a little harder, reiterating that there wasn't a lot of time left and that I would need to get started right away.

After he left, I was dragged down into my shutdown response, and I literally lost it. My heart was violently aching, my soul relentlessly shaking, and my resilience fatally breaking. Once again, I decided I was done. "F*ck this!" I said. This isn't the way life should be lived. I fell down again into a deep well of despair full of the thick and dark water of hopelessness. I reached the point a second time where I felt death was slowly, silently, and soothingly creeping up on me, disguised as well-needed sleep. I was mentally, physically, and emotionally tired. I felt so low that I could feel death get intimately close to me. It felt as though death was gently caressing me, hugging me, and comforting me, telling me that everything would be okay as long as I just let go and went to sleep. All of my pain would go away, all of my frustration would disappear, and eternal happiness was just a permanent slumber away. Everlasting sleep was wooing me, trying to win me over. It creatively flirted with me, slyly cat-called me, and waited intensely for my response. It was the complete opposite of aggression: it was so sensual, warm, and inviting, like a good snuggle, one of those snuggles where you just want to hold on to a person tightly all day and never let them go. But did I really want to snuggle with death?

I was so overwhelmed with emotional energy, and I had no idea how I was going to overcome the feeling. All that I felt I could do was to silently surrender to my final slumber, and surrender I did, as Master Yoda once said. I felt myself slowly let go and gently fall asleep. I knew this wouldn't be any normal sleep, it would be my final sleep. As I dozed off, I was telling my body "It's okay, you can stop fighting now. We can finally be at peace." Peace in any way, shape, or form had been virtually unrecognizable for quite some time and maybe this was finally it.

That time in my life felt like a fall from grace. I've seen people with cancer who go through chemo, radiation, and surgery. Most of those people's lives are never the same, plus the cancer normally comes back. All of these preconditioned negative scenarios were playing in my head and I used these sad stories to justify giving up, letting myself die without getting on to any treatment procedures. I figured I had a slight chance of making it through chemical chemo and who knows how the rest of my life would be? You hear and see the stories of people post-cancer treatment but only if they're lucky to make it through. How could I know if I would be one of the lucky ones to make it? I started to fight my everlasting sleep, and knew I had to do something to safely anchor me in the present away from my dangerous, depressive, and shutdown thoughts.

When you have ADD like me, you really can only be mindful for short periods of time. Wait, what? So again, I took another mindful Innerval™. FOCUS. NOW. JUDGMENT-FREE. When we don't know what to do, we do nothing. I resisted doing nothing and pulled out my iPhone again. Really, it's probably my iPhone that saved my life because it was the only way I was able to check in with people, research, and learn all the questions that I had to ask my doctors, specialists, and medical professionals. I opened Evernote (I f*cking love Evernote!) and started to type out something I call a "G-list." This was a list of things that were going well in my life, things that I was grateful for, and things that I wanted to be alive to continue experiencing because they made me feel good.

I had to make a final decision there and then, give up and die quickly, or fight and live on mysteriously. Admittedly, it was a very small list. Nonetheless, I said the contents of the list out loud three times and I read it to myself about a hundred times. I memorized it and I really thought about each and every thing that was on my list. I became obsessed with it because it was literally the only thing that I was holding onto, besides my phone. I even started writing it on my dominant hand and arm using my non-dominant hand. Using your non-dominant hand to write strengthens the neural connections in your brain and grows new ones. Both sides of your brain are also activated which allows you to think differently and access more creativity, feelings, gut instinct, and inner wisdom. That list was the only nightlight in my sea of darkness, despair, and death. But as my thoughts were in this free fall, I felt a sharp shift of a second wind fight come on. My list nightlight helped me climb out of my shutdown response into my stress response, where I was motivated to fight again. After what seemed like an eternity, I made an out-loud proclamation that "I WILL WIN, AND CANCER WILL LOSE!" I said it three times.

I always take three big breaths and say words or phrases out loud. Why? The first time I say it for my mind, the second time I say it for my body, and the third time I say it for my nerves. A trinity of enforcement if you will. We can be stubborn and sometimes it takes at least three times to get something to sink in. Am I right? Whenever you want to self-generate anything, and I'll go over the protocol in more detail later in the book, just say things three times with three breaths. Of course, I said it in my thoughts sometimes, but when I said it aloud, I heard it, I felt it, I imprinted it into my mind, body, and nerves, and I truly experienced it. Not only that, this practice stimulates your relaxation response with intentional vocal speech. It became real for me then when I said it out loud. It also reinforced it in every single cell of my body. After I proclaimed it, I received a rush of exciting energy, and with this newfound energy, I felt a little fire light up inside of me again, and I was quickly motivated to prove these doctors wrong, once again.

For my nerves, it was also the first step to training, rehearsing, and practicing my intended positive outcome. When it comes to healing, what you expect to be is not always what is to be. My healing wasn't instant when I affirmed it to myself, because no healing is ever instant. You have to understand that healing is a process and although I experienced an accelerated process afterward, it was still a journey, nonetheless.

I would think, write, and say this affirmation at least three times a day. It was my mantra, theme, and essence. Every day I was training, rehearsing, and practicing my desired positive outcome until it got stronger and stronger. At first, I didn't believe in the words 100% of the time, but that didn't matter, I just faked it until I made it. That's when my epiphany hit. Why not take the rare cancer diagnosis on with chemical chemotherapy and also naturally at the same time? Why don't I attack this disease holistically? I knew if I wanted to beat cancer and never have to face it again, I had to do the inner work to uncover how I was able to let cancer progress in the first place.

This is why I'm now a holistic health coach in addition to working in fitness. Before I was just focused on fitness and not really on other elements of health. I didn't realize that they were all interconnected, and didn't realize that focusing on other elements of my health would actually improve my fitness, too. At that time, I had no idea what holistic truly meant, I just figured it was worth a shot since it helped me get my liver moving when nothing else would work. If chemical chemo and natural methods of cancer treatment are both highly chance-based, wouldn't it be common sense to combine chemo and a holistic approach to increase my chances of effectively treating it?

I'm not a doctor, but a f*cking fitness guru, and this seemed like common sense 101 to me, even though my doctors were strongly pushing only the aggressive chemical chemo protocol. A big negative of chemical chemo is that it's toxic and can cause complications. My rationale was that when my body gets toxic from the chemical chemo, why not do all that I could do to help and support my body to detox from the chemical chemo? Isn't there a way to boost and recharge my immune system to help with the fight against rare cancer as well? Looking for the answers to all of these questions, and more, left me again mentally, emotionally, and physically fatigued.

Make no mistake—had I willed myself to die, I would have died, many times. All it took was a short series of mindful Innervals™ amid chaos to lift me from my stress response and stressed way of thinking. Once I activated my relaxation response, I realized that I could muster the will to live and fight instead. My nerve state story told me that I could get through this: they were like "Godiva, you got this!" They made me instantly feel like I had a choice, I could choose to die and give up granted, but I could also choose to live and get through this. It didn't tell me what to do—it told me that I had a choice and that was a powerful feeling. The mindful Innerval™ I took acted as a buffer, allowing me to quickly realize that I did indeed have a choice, even though I couldn't see how right away.

As soon as I agreed to chemical chemo, I had those liability release forms in my hands faster than you can say "chemo commission" and I had to sign that they wouldn't be liable for anything that went wrong, including death. Wow! This is the world that we live in: I'm dying and I finally agree to chemical chemo, and I have to sign a liability waiver form on my deathbed, literally. Doctors, specialists, and medical professionals (and hospitals) of Western medicine really give zero f*cks about the health, harmony, and happiness of their patients. Signing those forms gives them a free pass to do whatever the f*ck they want. I already experienced that firsthand by having over 20 different medical errors inflicted on me. We are still supposed to "trust you" after you just made us sign a form saying that you aren't at fault if we die—a pre-op prenup? This was especially ridiculous to me as a Black man that was routinely deprioritized by most of my doctors.

Fun, but not-so-fun Fact: Cancer doctors have a legitimate financial incentive for prescribing certain chemical chemo regimens over others because of the higher reimbursement rates they receive—this is commonly known as drug concession profits. In layman's terms, they make MORE money prescribing chemical chemo than any other manufactured medication. Oncologists are some of the best-paid doctors in the world, collectively making hundreds of millions of dollars by selling drugs to patients, but not going to jail for it. And I'm not talking about weed, molly, and edibles either. Several General Account Office reports state that some doctors, specifically oncologists who specialize in the treatment of cancer, get a massive discount (up to 86 percent) on certain chemical chemo drugs. Hospitals and private practices buy the chemical chemo drugs themselves directly from the manufacturer, often at a discount for buying them in bulk and then up-sell to give them to their patients intravenously.[178]

I believe doctors don't want people to die, however, I do think they are trained to be indifferent to the deaths of their patients; especially the minority patients that are often deprioritized like I was. This indifference, in my opinion, can fuel ignorance. Nonetheless, make no mistake—I was absolutely going to refuse to sign those papers and several times I flip-flopped on it. They knew I would die quickly if I refused, but they didn't really tell me that with their mouth. They did, however, unknowingly communicate it with their eyes, body language, and overall demeanor toward me. From the second that I was brought into the hospital ICU, every single doctor, nurse, specialist, and medical professional was very non-committal to me. No cuddles or brunch after a hookup type of non-committal.

Maybe if any doctor was able to diagnose me sooner, I would have tried to fight it off completely naturally, but my liver, lymph nodes, groin, and lungs were being invaded by billions of cancer cells that were running amuck of their appearance, function, and longevity. The cancer cells were metabolizing at lightning speed, keeping my heart rate sky-high at 160 beats per minute no matter what I did. Even when my body was at rest, my heart was racing like I was running a never-ending Olympic marathon. Not the kind of fast metabolism you would want, trust me.

Self-Reflection Innerval™

On two separate occasions, you saw that I took a mindful interval, created a "G-List", and that was enough to quickly shift my thinking from wanting to die to wanting to fight for my life. Write three things that you are grateful for below. After each thought, also write WHY you are grateful for it.

1. ....

2. ....

3. ....

24 //

MY DOCTORS STABBED ME IN THE BACK, LITERALLY

Medical errors and preventable harm are all too common in western medicine. But no one really talks about it. According to a study in the British Medical Journal, roughly one in 20 patients is impacted by preventable medical errors.[179] What's more, about 12% of preventable patient harm results in "prolonged, permanent disability" or even death. Researchers estimate that 9.5% of all annual U.S. deaths are the result of medical error, making medical error the third leading cause of death in the country.[180] The largest share of this preventable harm was related to medication and other treatments. Here is one of the over 20 medical errors that I encountered during my experience.

As if the aggressive chemical chemo inception infusion wasn't enough, I was also told that I had to do a lumbar punch (also called a spinal tap) as a prophylactic "just in case" the rare cancer was to spread to my brain and spine. Feeling fearful of getting brain cancer, because most people would when a cancer doctor tells you this, I agreed to this series of exponentially worse procedures. Although they called it a lumbar punch, probably because it felt like someone was repeatedly punching you hard in the spine, I had never done a spinal tap before and I had no idea what to expect. I initially refused but was told by my doctor that the cancer could very well be on its way up to my brain. Once it reached my brain apparently it was then game over, you don't pass go, and you don't collect $500.

I agreed, but I wasn't thrilled about it at all. Who wants to get stabbed in the back by a giant needle? Definitely not me, I hate f*cking needles. I have always had a fear of needles from a young age. Also clowns, I hate clowns, I'm terrified of them. I was chased by a killer clown when I was younger, but that's another story altogether. The first time I ever had stitches was when I was 10 years old. I had slipped and landed right into a corner of a wall. Ouch. I had to get stitches in my eye. It took about 10 (not exaggerating) doctors, nurses, and my mother to literally restrain me while I was getting stitches. I was NOT having it. So you can imagine how I felt as I was wheeled to the radiology department operation room and being switched from the commuter hospital bed to the radiology table so they could set me up. They told me they would take out five milliliters of my spinal fluid to test for cancer and then inject five milliliters of chemical chemo into my spine as a prophylactic. They needed to puncture my spine with a big needle, and then infuse my spine with terribly toxic chemicals. Sounds like a good time right? It wasn't.

As I waited for them to puncture, I felt this deep and intense pain stab me in the back. I wasn't even remotely ready. I screamed unexpectedly and then started crying. It was a sharp pain, but then it seemed to fade away. I thought all was well and that they were done. Boy was I wrong. They missed the spot. You're kidding me, right? You missed the spot? I stared blankly in disbelief as they told me they had to stab me again. What could I do? Lumbar punch part deux I guess. They stabbed me a second time. Equally as painful, I knew what to expect so I didn't scream or cry the second time. I tried my best to stay strong and not be this big Black man that's scared of a mouse (or a needle). They missed, again.

By this time, I was more than super annoyed. "You have to WHAT?!?" I exclaimed. They calmed me down and again I had to brace for this sharp stab in the back. They always say a third time's a charm, I figured I had just one more left and I would finally be free. I braced, and all of a sudden, a third sharp pain to my back, this time harder and for longer as if the needle was literally in me and they were digging around trying to find my spine. I again let out a big scream. A bigger and longer scream than before to match the pain, and then proceeded to start to uncontrollably cry again. So much for being strong I thought.

Thinking it was finally all over, there was a long awkward pause. WTF? Why are they being silent all of a sudden? What happened, what went wrong??? They. F*cking. MISSED. AGAIN! For the third time. Who are these people? Interns?!? This time, I went Emily Rose exorcism on them. I was pissed! "How the f*ck do you miss stabbing a back three times in a row?!?" I screamed! "F*ck you!" "I hate you!" "I'm suing you!". Profanities poured out of my mouth, tears tore down my eyes, and defiance dived from deep within me. "F*ck you, I'm not doing this again. Take me back to my room." I wailed. Yep, I lost it, and I'm not proud of this behavior. This went on for a good ten minutes. They were trying to convince me to try one last time, that I really needed this, and I was not having any of it.

Finally, after fifteen minutes I agreed to let the head doctor try again. Apparently, the person who tried before was an intern, resident, or whatever. Whatever the case, it was their first spinal tap. I'm dying, literally, and you let a person do their FIRST spinal tap on me? I can't make this sh*t up! When you are on the edge of death, the last thing you want is an intern (sorry interns) doing something to you that they have never done before (especially since you have just signed your life away, literally). I was livid. Am I crazy or is this a legitimate thought that a person should have? Thankfully, the fourth time was the charm. They successfully penetrated my spine (I can't believe I just said that) and were able to withdraw five milliliters of my spinal fluid and infuse the five milliliters of chemical chemo into my spine. However, the four attempts resulted in four holes in my spine. At least I'm still alive I thought, but it's hard to call this living.

RIGHT REALITY

Initially, I was supposed to do six of these lumbar punches to coincide with my six different chemical chemo infusions, however, I was not having it. I was traumatized, tired, and terrified all at the same time. I called up the head doctor and their team to my room, and I laid into them about how I was treated. I was rightfully upset and was taking it out on them. After all, they were the people who were doing this to me in the first place. My best interest was not to be stabbed four times for an extra procedure that I was doing "just in case." Why was I doing this procedure in the first place? More chemo directly in my spine just in case? How about direct toxic exposure to my spine and brain?!? Does that not do anything?

Profanities poured, more tears tore, and I quickly quivered while recounting my horrible experience and yelling at them that the procedure was botched. "You botched my back!" I screamed at one point. "Mr. Godiva, the procedure wasn't botched, it was simply unsuccessful. We're sorry for your inconvenience." I was told by the head doctor. "Unsuccessful"? What? It was the ultimate gaslight. My perspective was that I was unfairly abused, and the procedure was botched, and their perspective was that it was "simply unsuccessful." So, what happens when they accidentally kill someone or cause death by infection? Is that still an inconvenience? Is that still unsuccessful? Were they just sending them off to their new life? This moment shook me deeply.

Anytime you walk into a room, space, or environment, you instantly experience a personal subjective reality. When I was brought into the operating room for the spinal tap procedure, even though it was the same room, the doctors, nurses, and I all perceived it differently. The same tools, table, and machines were there, but our attention would be drawn to different things. Our cultivated, trained, and predisposed focus, that was influenced by our trained beliefs. As soon as I was wheeled in, I was looking at the table and any needles that were possibly going into me; as soon as the doctors walked in, they immediately looked for my chart, supplies, and where they were going to prep for the procedure.

If 20 different people walked into that radiology operating room, there would be 20 different interpretations of that room, and they would all perceive 20 different subjective realities. None of those realities would be totally wrong, but none of those realities would be the whole truth either. Your personal reality is a never-ending environment of reality subjectivity. Doctors, specialists, and medical professionals are highly intelligent, but they don't know it all nor can they perceive it all. Their medical mental model of thinking is flawed because it's the only mental model they have been trained to know. Anything that differs from what they know to be true is quickly shooed, shamed, and shunned, with no questions asked. Default cynicism, pessimism, and objections to anything that differs from their deeply trained, heavily ingrained, and hard rooted beliefs.

We all have a lens of subjective reality that is created by our own life's experiences, lessons, and challenges, and this in turn shapes our life's personal experiences. You are what you have been trained to believe, and you perceive what you have been trained to believe. Just like I am what I have been trained to believe, and I perceive what I have been trained to believe. The only thing that changes your subjective reality from mine is what you focus on. What's your personal focus?

Doctors, specialists, and medical professionals are focused on pathology, prescription drugs, medical machines, and medical protocols, procedures, and practices. I was just focused on why I wasn't feeling well, what happened to my body, and what I could do to help my body holistically heal. We had two different subjective realities to my health challenges and healing from the start. Their focus on pathology, manufactured medications, medical machines, and medical protocols, procedures, and practices failed me, hurt me, traumatized me, and almost killed me. My unwavering focus on my body as a whole, recharging my immune system, radically changing my lifestyle, reducing stress, and other "self" focused strategies saved my life, empowered me, and allowed me to go from stage four of a rare cancer to complete remission in 50 days.

Not only that, there is a long and dark history of the use of Black Americans as unwilling research subjects and that's one of the biggest reasons why there is a deep distrust among many Black Americans and the US Healthcare system.[181] From 1932 to 1972, the U.S. Public Health Service (PHS) conducted a cruel experiment on Black men who suffered from syphilis. The PHS did not administer any treatment, which led to hundreds of men dying awful deaths.[182] This wasn't a one-time incident, there's a lot more to that history. Today there continues to be systemic medical racism in the U.S. I can't say for sure, but I definitely wonder if they chose me for the interns to experiment on because of their preconceived notions, whether they even realized that they were devaluing my life.

I had no choice but to focus on myself and become my own healthcare advocate. No one was going to save my Black *ss, literally. Because I focused on me, myself, and my body's innate self-healing abilities, I was able to heal myself in record time. The quickest way to change your life is to change your focus. My unwavering focus on my whole self (all the parts), created more powerful self-healing. What do you think would have happened had I just focused on pathology, prescription drugs, medical machines, and medical protocols, procedures, and practices like my doctors (especially since I'm not a doctor)? I wouldn't be here today. Period. I don't have the level of expertise that doctors, specialists, and medical professionals have when it comes to pathology, prescription drugs, medical machines, and medical protocols, procedures, and practices, however, I do have the expertise when it comes to all aspects of me, myself, and my body's innate self-healing potential. Just like YOU are the expert of your whole self, it's your f*cking body. So why wouldn't you want to learn more about how you can better empower your entire SELF? Well, I'm going to make it a little easier for you to get EMPOWERED in the next section.

EYEBROWS FAST MOTOR COMBO. (3 minutes)

1. EYEBROWS FAST MOTOR INNERVAL™ // 30 seconds.

With your eyes closed move your eyebrows up and down as fast as you possibly can. Do this for 30 seconds or count to 30 if you don't have a timer. Relax your eyebrows back to neutral before you start the next Innerval™.

2. CORE BREATHING INNERVAL™ // 30 seconds.

Take long, slow, and deep inhales and take longer, slower, and deeper exhales for 30 seconds or 3 times each if you don't have a timer. Each inhale should be around 3 seconds and each exhale should be around 6 seconds. As you breathe in, your core goes out, as you breathe out, your core goes in.

3. Repeat 2 times

STIMULATION. The phrenic nerves, vagus nerves, motor cortex (8), and posterior thoracic nerves.

25 //

REBALANCE YOUR IMMUNITY ENERGY

Awareness leads to empowerment, and what better way to start the journey toward awareness than with an activity you do daily: eating. As I've mentioned a number of times, the systems that influence our health and wellness are so deeply interconnected, and what you put into your body is one element that is very much within your control. The standard american diet (SAD) is pretty sad indeed. The mainstream way of eating is high in processed carbs and foods, which elevates your blood sugar levels even more and harms your gut health, and high in refined veggie oils (includes deep-fried foods) that are loaded with toxins that create, percolate, and exacerbate disease.

Have you ever asked a conventional doctor, specialist, or medical professional about nutrition? It's so funny sometimes. When you want to learn about nutrition and what types of nutrients that you need to help you when you are sick, let's say you google and search for nutrition. You see all these sites come up about nutrition from the government, Harvard, and other medical institutions that include guidelines and text about why nutrition is so important for you. They say you should have this many servings of grains, and that many servings of fruit. If all of these doctors, specialists, and health professionals think nutrition is so important, why then do they get shady when you are sick in their office? They all of a sudden get amnesia about nutrition, avoid talking about it, or if they do talk about it, it's often not the most important aspect of their diagnosis or recommendations.

In addition, you'll remember my earlier comments about hospital food. Why do hospitals who harbor people who are sick, and are supposed to help them get well, give them food that technically makes them sicker? Do they just not give a f*ck? Are they that cash-strapped that they can't serve whole, healthy, and organic food to sick patients? Or anything loaded with antioxidants and anti-inflammatory effects? Antioxidants are molecules that play a massive role in preventing chronic health issues like cancer, heart disease, and diabetes by defending your cells against oxidative stress, or inflammation. Aren't hospitals supposed to heal? How do you heal eating chemicals, gluten, GMOs, antibiotics, and pesticides? All things that are known to cause inflammation in your body. Asking for a friend. Does anyone else think that is so messed up or is it just me?!?

This was literally an exchange between one of my doctors and I:

Me: "What kind of nutrition should I have to help make myself feel better?"

Doctor: "Nutri who?"

Me: "Nutrition."

Doctor: "What type of drug is that?"

Me: "It's not a drug, human nutrition."

Doctor: "Nutri what? Oh…just good nutrition."

*Long awkward pause

What in the flying f*ck is "good nutrition"? And if I'm sick, in duress, and trusting you with my life, why are you being ambiguous, nonchalant, and shady about something that is supposed to be "so important" according to medical professions everywhere? Conventional doctors with little or no nutrition training beyond their university textbook tend to tell you that nutrition is not important when it comes to a serious diagnosis. They will even steer you away from vitamins, nutrients, and other herbal supplements because they instill the fear in you that those items will interfere with their traditional medical treatments. Yes, they will interfere, as I learned firsthand, in a good f*cking way.

Another key to having good immunity is rebalancing your energy, and that happens primarily through what you eat, digest, and absorb. In a perfect world, we should be getting all of our vitamins and nutrients from the food we're eating. Unfortunately, this isn't Westworld, and we don't really live in an environment where that's possible. Not only that, but most people today have done damage way beyond speedy repair. It will take a bit more than whole foods and a good diet to be able to self-heal. Some people are so damaged that they need higher doses of nutrients like orthomolecular medicine or a nutritional medicine-based approach to self-healing in order to be able to correct some of those nutrient deficiencies.

You hear a lot of people talking about "boosting" your immune system but you technically can't give your immunity a super boost in one or two days. Even if you are doing some of the eating and lifestyle changes that I recommend below, it's going to take a while for those to kick in. For me, it was 50 days for me to see the direct result, for you if you're going through a challenging health issue right now, who knows. But your healing will ALWAYS be faster the more layers of recommendations that you can do at once because of the power of synergy. It's extremely important to note that even though it took me 50 days to see a massive result, I did see little "wins" every week or every other week along the way that reinforced that I was on the right self-healing track. All of my daily micro-decisions built up to a macro self-healing effect.

When trying to support and rebalance your immune system, it's important to understand that you don't need to boost it, you need to balance or modulate it. It's when your immune system is unbalanced either way, that things get uncomfortable for you. If your immunity is trigger happy and fires too much, that's autoimmunity and chronic inflammation, if it's underactive, sluggish, or suppressed, that leads to chronic health issues. There's also the issue of your immune system still going strong after you resolve a health issue that can lead to more health issues or even death.

Called a "cytokine storm", when infection first happens, many different cells and immune cells produce pro-inflammatory cytokines to help activate the body's innate immune cells to eradicate foreign invaders. This process is normally pretty efficient, but sometimes your immune system can overreact causing an uncontrolled, pro-inflammatory response that can harm your body's healthy tissues. Fighting bacteria, viruses, and other pathogens requires a fine-tuned immune system. Immunity energy that can launch a powerful attack when an infection is first detected and knows when to pull back once the bacteria, virus, or pathogen is resolved. Well-balanced immunity energy is the true ultimate goal so that your immune system knows when to properly push or pull. One of the easiest, actionable, and most powerful ways to do that is through nutrition.

Taking vitamins, herbs, and minerals helps give your immune system the tools it needs to efficiently clear your body of a variety of toxins like pesticides, chemicals, heavy metals, bacteria, viruses, and parasites. Many of them also have powerful antioxidant, antimicrobial, and anti-inflammatory effects. Our modern-day technology has replaced simple germs and bacteria with chemically engineered pesticides, heavy metals, and antibiotic-resistant bacteria. These corrupting, complex, and crazy chemicals send mixed messages to your body causing imbalances that lead to chronic health issues. You always start outbalanced. Like Resident Evil 3 or any other zombie apocalypse scenario, your trillions of cells start healthy, alive, and vibrant, until one pissy pathogen, b*tchy bacteria, or violent virus bites them and then corrupts them into a zombie. And then they keep biting healthy cells until you have a shit load of zombie cells, an inner zombie apocalypse, and BOOM...chronic disease.

People have gotten so lazy, passive, and reckless when it comes to taking care of their mind, body, and emotional health. People push hard, pull hard, and play harder running their bodies down and think they can just take a magic pill, potion, or procedure to feel better again. It's not entirely their fault though, as this is something that has been instilled in us from a young age and wildly perpetuated by Western medicine. High blood pressure? Let's take a pill instead of reducing stress and getting more sleep. Back, knee, and joint pain? Let's pop some Advil and painkillers instead of getting more active and limiting the time spent seated.

Supplements can be great, but by themselves, they are not enough. When you are sick and have a nutrient deficiency, they can help you quickly regain your immune system balance and optimal health, but they are not magic pellets that you should only depend on. They do make up for the vital vitamins, minerals, and nutrients that are lacking in today's food supply and help you delicately detox from our very modern world. Even though the right supplements provide synergy support to the healing functions of your body, supplements will be sh*tty if you aren't willing to make the actual changes to your lifestyle and eating experience.

They are called "supplements" for a reason; they are meant to supplement and support an already healthy eating experience and fill in small gaps for optimal nutrition. You can't keep smoking just because you are drinking Kombucha. WTF?!?

Your daily eating experience alone isn't enough to rebalance your immunity energy, you need supplements, and the power lies in your gut balance. Just because you change the food that you eat DOESN'T mean that your body is absorbing that food's nutrients. If your gut is a hot mess and unbalanced, you're going to have a hard time absorbing, processing, and assimilating anything you put in your body. That includes food and supplements. You must first work to repair, restore, and reseal your gut. Some people have deep nutritional deficiencies and that's where supplements come in to help you balance out and replenish those deficiencies. The quickest way to boost your body's immunity energy is to restore your gut balance. 70% of your immune system is in your gut, and in order to give your body the energy it needs for balanced immunity, you need to be mindful of the things you're eating. Probiotics, prebiotics, and pectin are part of my FOOD ENERGY IMMUNITY protocol, but you still need to do more. That's just one of really three main ways to restore gut immunity. The second way is that you need to also be conscious that you aren't damaging your gut by chronic stress, eating sh*tty foods, and drinking alcohol.

I am very pro-supplements as a supportive tool on your journey, but supplementation will only truly be effective when combined with an equally effective approach to food. Meaning you should be eating whole, mostly organic, and healing foods daily and not just relying on getting everything you need from supplements. There are many things you can do that either strengthen, support, and sharpen your immune system or shock, sour, and suppress it. If you think about rebalancing your immune system energy from a multipronged, multidimensional, and multifaceted approach, you will efficiently recharge, refresh, and regenerate it to optimal function keeping you away from illness, disease, and wasting. Supplementation is simply one of those many prongs that can help you get back to balance quicker. Imagine being so healthy that you never or rarely get sick? Is that such a crazy pipe dream? It's actually easily attainable, but it takes consistent training and work. To help you get on your way to that new reality, here are a few helpful supplementations and food strategies you may begin to implement.

GODIVA'S FOOD IMMUNITY TRINITY

1. PROBIOTICS
2. PREBIOTICS
3. PECTIN

There are a lot of foods that you should be eating to help rebalance your immune system, but I think these three categories are the most important.

PROBIOTICS. Probiotics are helpful bacteria that aid in digestion, boost the detoxification of your colon, and support your immune system. Because leaky gut is a major cause of food sensitivities, autoimmune disease, and immune imbalance or a weakened immune system, it's important to consume probiotic foods and supplements. The more that you can eat of these the better because when you eat fermented foods, especially veggies when they ferment, they produce colonies of helpful bacteria. When you eat them as veggies, you colonize and inoculate your gut with trillions of helpful bacteria of hundreds of different types of species. Taking high-potency probiotic supplements is definitely helpful, but they can never really create the colonies that you need alone. You have to actually eat fermented veggies to re-inoculate your gut with helpful bacteria.

Kefir / Water Kefir / Coconut Kefir / Kombucha / Sauerkraut / Pickles / Pickled Vegetables / Miso / Tempeh / Beet Kvass / Nato / Kimchi / Raw cheese / Dairy or Non-Dairy Yogurt / Sourdough Bread / Lassi

PREBIOTICS. Prebiotics are non-digestible fiber compounds that are degraded by gut bacteria, and they are the most under-rated and lacking thing in what people eat daily. They feed the probiotics and just like other high-fiber foods, prebiotic compounds pass through the upper part of the GI tract. Once they pass through the small intestine, they reach the colon, where they're fermented by gut bacteria.

Banana / Chicory Root / Dandelion Greens / Jerusalem Artichoke / Garlic / Onions / Leeks / Asparagus / Barley / Oats / Apples / Konjac Root / Cocoa / Burdock Root / Flax Seeds / Yacon Root / Jicama Root / Wheat Bran / Seaweed

PECTIN. Pectin is a carb that's extracted from fruits, vegetables, and seeds. The main use is as a gelling agent, thickening agent, and stabilizer in food. Pectin is important because it helps heal the tears in your gut wall lining, also known as leaky gut.[183] It's also antibacterial and it helps feed the probiotics in your gut.[184] Pectin in apples increases IAP which is good for you.[183] Intestinal alkaline phosphatase (IAP) has an important role in gut mucosal defense. Research has asserted that dietary IAP may have an effect in improving inflammatory gut diseases.[185]

Lemons / Pears / Plums / Guavas / Quince / Peaches / Apples / Oranges / Grapefruit / Apricots / Carrots / Tomatoes / Peas / All Berries / Grapes / Cherries

Beyond these three important items, here are some other elements of nutrition, supplementation, and lifestyle that I swear by to help balance your immune system:

YOUR EATING EXPERIENCE

I don't like to use the word "diet" because I feel like it has an automatic conscious and unconscious negative association. It can be a downright traumatizing experience for people to constantly see and think about a "diet". I reframe it and prefer calling it an "eating experience", because that is exactly what eating is, an experience that can have a healthy or unhealthy outcome depending on what you are consistently putting into your body. With many of my clients who are battling chronic health issues, I give them this simple analogy. You are on fire, literally, a California wildfire of inflammation inside your entire body. Every single thing you put into your mouth is either feeding or containing that wildfire. One of the big reasons that some people have a weak or suppressed immune system is because they are triggering it every single time they eat or drink. Imagine a fire alarm going off every single time you eat or drink. That would probably get annoying to you real fast so think about how your body feels? Your immunity energy shouldn't be attacking your food.

Remixing your eating experience doesn't need to be difficult. All you need to do is make a few easy swaps to what you eat currently, add in some immune-balancing foods, and you will notice a massive benefit. Many foods give you an assortment of specific nutrients that promote immune system health while also allowing you to eat a variety of essential nutrients in your daily eating experience. So many people get so perplexed about what they should and shouldn't be eating. While I agree that it can get a little nuanced depending on what your own specific needs are, you can't go wrong if you follow my very simple rule of thumb.

The more sh*t that is in your food, the more sh*t your body has to go through trying to digest, absorb, and detox that sh*t.

It's like trying to pick a fight with every single stranger you meet on the street. Why would you do that? Unless you love drama, and many people do (no judgment), why would you want to put your body through unnecessary drama every single time you eat or drink? Then have the audacity to think that you can always abuse, push, gaslight, and run your body down with no consequences whatsoever. Your body always keeps the receipts. Please start doing it a favor and being more mindful of what you eat. You won't be young and be able to bounce back from your unhealthy lifestyle forever. I say that with love and compassion.

So, what should you eat to rebalance your immunity energy? Generally, your eating experience should be full of foods that are whole, anti-inflammatory, and nutrient-dense. Clean protein like grass-fed beef, wild-caught fish, and free-range poultry. Healthy fats like avocado, coconut oil, and grass-fed butter. Organic greens like spinach, chard, and other veggies. Low glycemic fruits like lemon, berries, and lime. Fermented foods like sauerkraut, kimchi, and kombucha. Medicinal mushrooms like turkey tail, reishi, and cordyceps.

Here's a more detailed list for adults and kids. Yes, I love alliteration if you haven't already noticed.

GODIVA'S IMMUNITY ENERGY FOOD LIST

FOODS TO EAT DAILY >>

POWER PROTEINS: Wild-Caught Fish / Grass-Fed beef / Eggs / Free-Range poultry / Legumes / Greek Yogurt (Full-fat) / Almonds / Oats / Cottage Cheese / Lentils / Quinoa

FIXING FATS: Grass-fed butter / MCT Oil / Coconut Oil / Ghee / Extra Virgin Olive Oil / High-lignan Flaxseed Oil / Avocados / Dark Chocolate (70% cacao) / Fatty Fish (Salmon, Sardines, Trout, Mackerel, Herring, and Fresh (Not Canned) Tuna / Olives / Brazil Nuts / Walnuts / Macadamia Nuts / Edamame

SUPER SEEDS: Chia Seeds / Flax Seeds / Sunflower Seeds / Seed Butters / Pumpkin Seeds

VIBRANT VEGGIES: Bell Peppers / Broccoli / Pumpkin / Brussels Sprouts / Spinach / Tomatoes / Chard / Kale / Cauliflower / Beetroot / Artichoke / Cabbage / Bok Choy / Cucumber / Celery / Carrots / Lettuce (All types) / Leafy or Herb Greens / Onions / Zuchinni

FOCUS FRUITS: Lemon / Lime / Watermelon / Strawberries / Oranges / Cherries / Plums / Blackberries / Blueberries / Grapes / Nectarines / Kiwi / Raspberries / Pineapple / Papaya

COLOR CARBS: Whole Grains or Gluten-Free Grains / Sweet Potatoes / Quinoa / Barley / Brown Rice / Oats / Buckwheat / Farro / Couscous / Chickpeas / Kidney Beans / Bananas / Apples / Grapefruit / Amaranth / Millet / Butternut and Acorn Squash / Red Potatoes / Rice Crackers

SPECIAL SPICES: Garlic / Ginger / Black Pepper / Cinnamon / Cayenne Pepper / Mustard / Turmeric / Cloves / Coriander / Dill / Cumin / Fennel / Bay Leaves / Thyme / Oregano / Cilantro / Parsley

BALANCED BEVERAGES: Water (Filtered or Alkaline) / Organic Lemon Water / Electrolyte Water / Green Tea / Kombucha / Cran-Water /

Apple Cider Vinegar / Almond Milk / Organic Coffee / Coconut Water / Kefir / Cold Pressed Juices / Ginger, Chamomile, and Peppermint Tea

CASUAL CONDIMENTS: Pink Himalayan Salt / Bone Broth or Regular Broth / Coconut Aminos / Balsamic Vinegar

While it's super important to eat a variety of foods that support healthy immunity energy, it's just as important to limit eating certain foods that tend to throw your immunity energy off balance. I like to say limit because avoiding these foods at all times is nearly impossible. If you think you have the willpower to avoid these foods all the time, I will be the first person to tell you that you are f*cking delusional. I would rather you focus on adhering to these recommendations a majority of the time instead of all the time. I want balance, longevity, and sustainability, not bingeing, purging, and other willpower-based extremes. This will not only set you up for success, but you won't fall into a shame or guilt rabbit hole if you do end up consuming these foods. Because you will, especially if alcohol is involved.

Earlier I was talking about sh*t in your food, well below is all the sh*t that literally stresses your body out biologically every single time you eat it. In general, you should limit processed meat that's loaded with antibiotics, hormones, and other chemicals. Limit foods that are refined, last forever, are high in added sugar, and are heavily processed. I view heavily processed as more than nine ingredients, but the lower the ingredients the better. Also limit foods with preservatives, additives, artificial colors, and sweeteners.

The following foods trigger inflammation[186], aka create an internal wildfire in your body.

FOODS TO LIMIT (0 - 3 TIMES A WEEK) >>

RADICALLY REFINED: Gluten / Pasta / White Bread / Chips / Tortillas / Crackers / Bagels / Waffles / Pastries / Breakfast Cereals / Pizza / White Rice / Soda / Fruit Juice

PAINFULLY PROCESSED: Fast Food / Fried Foods / Anything with more than nine ingredients / Convenient Meals / Baked Goods / Trans fats (Partially hydrogenated oils) / Food additives and preservatives / Highly processed vegetable and seed oils

TOXIC LAND & SEA: Conventionally raised meat and dairy / Salami / Bacon / Lunch Meats / Beef Jerky / Bologna / Farm raised fish and seafood

DRAINING DRINKS: Alcohol (Any amount) / Energy Drinks / Sports Drinks / Soda / Sweet Tea / Fruit Juice

SYNTHETIC SUGAR: High-Fructose Corn Syrup (HFCS) / Corn Sweetener / Agave Nectar / Table Sugar / Molasses / Sucrose / Dextrose / Honey / Fruit Juice Concentrate / Aspartame / Sucralose

GODIVA'S IMMUNE-BALANCING FOODS

Now I'm going to get into some different foods and supplements that can help rebalance your immunity energy. Please understand that a single supplement or food can't prevent or "cure" disease but feeding your body specific foods can help give your immunity energy the tools it needs to keep your immunity strong and increase your resilience to infections and diseases. Visiting your local grocery store can be a simple way to help prevent infections, colds, the flu, and help keep your inflammation in check.

CITRUS FRUITS. This is number one on the list because not only do I love them, I think we all collectively love them. We put lemon and lime wedges in basically everything! Citrus fruits have a treasure trove of many human health benefits. One of the biggest benefits is that they are high in vitamin C, but they also have good amounts of minerals and vitamins that your body needs to properly function like magnesium, potassium, and B vitamins.[187] Citrus fruits are rich in over 60 varieties of plant compounds like carotenoids, flavonoids, and essential oils that have a variety of health benefits including antioxidant and anti-inflammatory effects.[188] With the many options of citrus fruits to choose from, it's pretty painless to add citrus fruits to pretty much any meal during your day.

Limes (Key, Persian, Kaffir) / Lemons (Meyer, Eureka, Rough) / Oranges (Valencia, Navel, Blood Orange, Cara Cara) / Grapefruit (Ruby Red, White, Oro Blanco) / Mandarins (Satsuma, Clementine, Tangor, Tangelo) / Citron / Yuzu / Pomelos / Tangerines / Kumquat / Sudachi

VITAMIN C. Because humans aren't able to produce or store our own supply of vitamin C, we need it daily for optimal health. The recommended daily amount (RDA) of vitamin C is 90mg for men and 75 mg for women.[189] We must get it from outside sources like supplements or from food It's a good practice to eat foods that are high in vitamin C, and in addition to citrus fruits, many foods are high in vitamin C and have powerful antioxidant and anti-inflammatory properties.

Getting enough Vitamin C (with Zinc) can help shorten or reduce the symptoms of respiratory illnesses like bronchitis and the common cold.[190] As a powerful antioxidant, vitamin C also acts as an antihistamine to control inflammation responses to allergies, colds, and the flu. Your white blood cells need vitamin C to fight and defend against foreign invaders in your body and vitamin c regulates inflammation responses to damaged tissues.

Bell Peppers (Red, Orange, Yellow) / Broccoli / Kale / Kiwi / Kakadu Plums / Acerola Cherries / Rose Hips / Chili Peppers / Guavas / Thyme / Parsley / Mustard Spinach / Brussel Sprouts / Lychees / American Persimmons / Papayas / Strawberries / Snow Peas / Tomatoes / Camu Camu

BETA CAROTENE. In addition to vitamin C, another powerful category of antioxidants are called carotenoids and over 600 of them have been identified in different foods.[191] The most important provitamin A carotenoid is beta-carotene. Beta-carotene has been shown to increase immune cell activity and numbers, lower inflammation, combat oxidative stress, and enhance immune functions that fight cancer in healthy people.[192]

Sweet Potatoes / Carrot / Spinach / Kale / Pumpkin / Collard Greens / Turnip Greens / Winter Squash / Mango / Cantaloupe / Apricot / Dandelion Greens / Papaya / Watermelon / Zucchini / Apples

GINGER. When many people get sick, they turn to ginger because of its powerful antioxidant and anti-inflammatory activity. Ginger has been used in Ayurvedic medicine since the beginning of time to cleanse the lymphatic system, treat inflammation issues, and help rebalance the immune system. Some studies have shown that ginger has antimicrobial potential, which can help treat infectious diseases.[193] Ginger also helps improve digestion, reduce inflammation, helps with nausea, and reduces chronic pain.[194] Ginger may also help to lower your cholesterol.[195]

GARLIC & ONIONS. Used in almost every type of cuisine in many cultures around the world, garlic and onions are close family members with pretty similar health benefits. They promote immune health and are anti-inflammatory. Our ancestors recognized their power in fighting infections and helping with healing. Garlic's main immune balancing property comes from a high-dose amount of allicin, a sulfur-containing compound.[196] Garlic has also been shown lower blood pressure and slow the hardening of arteries.[197] They are extremely versatile, easy to use, and can be added to soups, salads, dressings, and a variety of main course dishes.

GREEN TEA. A simple way to strengthen your immune system is by drinking high-quality green tea daily. Green tea possesses a variety of bioactive healthy compounds like polyphenols, which have been shown to fight cancer and reduce inflammation.[198] Green tea also is a great source of L-theanine, an amino acid that helps beef up the immune function of your T cells.[199] Green tea is also packed with a massive number of powerful antioxidants with immune balancing properties like flavonoids and epigallocatechin (EGCG). Being one of the most powerful compounds in green tea, EGCG has been shown in various studies to increase immune function.[200] According to research, the health benefits of green tea for a wide variety of ailments, including different types of cancer, heart disease, and liver disease, were reported.[201]

MEDICINAL MUSHROOMS. Yes, I'm telling you to go shrooming, kind of. Medicinal mushrooms have become all the rage lately and many are called superfoods for their amazing health benefits. But mushrooms have been used in Eastern medicine for thousands of years. The benefits of medicinal mushrooms are massive and include brain-boosting, cancer, and inflammation-fighting, and being high in antioxidants. The easiest way to use them is in powder form. You can add them to your morning coffee, salad, or afternoon smoothie.

Each mushroom has its own specific health benefits and is unique, but here is a rundown of the top six medicinal mushrooms. Sometimes called "Nature's Xanax", Reishi promotes healing and is one of the most popular mushrooms for improving your immune health, fighting cancer cells, and supporting your mood.[202] Thanks to a compound called triterpene, reishi has this calming effect and ability to promote better sleep, ease depression, and reduce anxiety from these mood-boosting compounds.[203]

Lion's Mane is packed with antioxidants, great for immunity, and promotes mental clarity by combating brain fog. Lion's mane is unique in that it helps to boost brain health by promoting the production of myelin (fatty insulation around nerve fibers) and nerve growth factor (NGF).[204] It's also been shown to increase concentration, reduce anxiety, and improve cognition.[205]

Chaga mushrooms are antioxidant superheroes that reduce inflammation and fight free radicals by combating oxidative stress.[206] It's also been shown to lower your "bad" cholesterol, or low-density lipoprotein (LDL).[207] Shiitake mushrooms are loaded with cardioprotective compounds.[208,209]

With a compound called polysaccharide-K (PSK) that can enhance the immune system, Turkey tail is a mushroom antioxidant powerhouse that is the raining champ of cancer-fighting mushrooms. Turkey tail has been shown to fight leukemia, improve the survival of people with certain cancers, and help to improve the immune system of people who are undergoing chemotherapy cancer treatment.

Before grabbing a pre-workout or that extra cup of coffee, consider letting Cordyceps mushrooms give you a little energy boost. Cordyceps can help improve blood flow and help the body use oxygen more efficiently. In addition to helping with athletic and exercise performance, it's also been shown to help with recovery.

TURMERIC. Another powerful superfood that helps to strengthen your immunity energy is turmeric. With its very distinct bright yellow color, this bitter spice has been a go-to for years to treat a variety of inflammation-based health issues. What makes turmeric so unique, powerful, and immune balancing is its high concentration of curcumin, a phyto-derivative that has potent healing properties.[210] Derived from the root of the turmeric plant *Curcuma longa*, curcumin has been long been praised as a beneficial anti-inflammatory and antioxidant against a wide variety of diseases and is one the most well-researched therapeutic ingredients that comes from all-natural sources. Curcumin also has antiviral activity and its immune-balancing properties can be helpful for people who are battling chronic stress.[211]

BONE BROTH. Full of vitamins, minerals, and collagen that can give a massive boost to your immunity energy, bone broth is a nutritious, powerful, and delicious liquid that is great for your digestion, joints, and overall immune health. It's made by brewing the connective tissues of chicken, cow, and sometimes fish. The amino acids and collagen in bone broth promote the health of your gut by reducing inflammation, supporting the integrity of your gut wall lining, and sealing the small openings in your gut wall lining; also known as leaky gut syndrome. Since 70% of your immune system is in your gut, gut health plays a massive role in how your immune system functions. Be careful with the type of bone broth you are using and make sure it's appropriate for your blood type. (i.e. chicken bone broth is helpful for some and harmful for others.)

APPLE CIDER VINEGAR (ACV). Apple cider vinegar is one of the most popular home remedies out there. Created via a two-step process from the unstrained juice of fermented crushed apples, there seems to be a use for it for literally everything! This superfood is super versatile and can be used as a natural cleaning product, a beauty product, or inside and outside of your body to enhance your health. People have been using ACV for hundreds of years in medicine, cooking, and cleaning. ACV has antioxidant and antimicrobial properties, has probiotic benefits, and is high in vitamin C and vitamin E. ACV has also been shown to enhance immune health and help with colds and congestion.

Because vinegar has been used traditionally for cleaning, disinfecting, treating nail fungus, and other infections, many people are claiming that it is a cure-all for many different health issues. There's some truth to that because research shows that ACV can help to kill off bacteria and other pesky pathogens. The main active compound in ACV is acetic acid (the main ingredient in white vinegar), and this is what gives ACV its strong flavor and sour smell. Researchers believe that most of ACV's health benefits come from acetic acid. Unfiltered and organic ACV also has a substance called "mother" that is made up of probiotics, enzymes, and proteins that give it this very murky look. Add a tablespoon of ACV to your water in the morning for a nice immune balancing boost and it's great in the morning for people who struggle with acid reflux as well. Mix 2 - 3 tablespoons of organic manuka or raw honey, 1 part ACV, and 5 - 6 parts water for congestion or colds.

EXTRA VIRGIN OLIVE OIL (EVOO). Extracted from olives, the fruit of the olive tree, extra virgin olive oil is primarily used throughout the Mediterranean and is a major part of the Mediterranean diet. It's loaded with powerful antioxidants and is a hit in the US for dipping, cooking, and dressings. The antioxidants in extra virgin olive oil are biologically active, anti-inflammatory, and may reduce the risk of chronic health issues.[212] Extra virgin olive oil has many nutrients that could kill or slow down bacteria that are harmful and many studies show that it has a positive effect on insulin sensitivity and blood sugar.[213-214]

Oleocanthal is the main antioxidant responsible for extra virgin olive oil's anti-inflammatory effect, similar to ibuprofen.[215] The primary fatty acid in olive oil is a monounsaturated fat called oleic acid and makes up roughly 70% of the oil content.[216] Because monounsaturated fats are super resistant to high heat, olive oil is an extremely healthy oil to use for cooking. Olive oil is great raw or can be a wonderful addition to any sauce or salad dressing. It's also great to pour over entree meals of beef, chicken, or fish. One of my favorite ways to consume it is by adding Himalayan salt to it and dipping gluten-free bread into it.

GODIVA'S IMMUNE-BALANCING SUPPLEMENTS & HERBS

Vitamin D. Sometimes the easiest way to help rebalance your immunity energy is by addressing nutritional deficiencies, and vitamin D is the most common one. Vitamin D may be called a vitamin, but it's actually a hormone that promotes the absorption of calcium in the body. It also helps boost up our natural T helper cells that work to hold back inflammation and balance the immune response so that it's more effective. Unfortunately, it's not very naturally occurring in foods besides oily fish. Most people get this vitamin by spending time in the sunshine, after which our bodies are able to produce the vitamin on their own. However, these days a large amount of the population is vitamin D deficient[217], so supplementation is often recommended. Vitamin D can modulate your innate and adaptive immune responses and a vitamin D deficiency is associated with increased autoimmunity.[218] Because vitamin D is a fat-soluble vitamin, I recommend taking this supplement with a meal that contains healthy fats or a fish oil supplement so your body can appropriately absorb and utilize the vitamin.[219]

ZINC. Another common micronutrient deficiency is zinc. Zinc is an essential trace element which means your body can't make it on its own and you must get it through what you eat or through supplements. You probably hear about zinc a lot during cold and flu season, but this powerful mineral is essential to your immunity and overall health. Zinc should be consumed in small amounts every day because it provides many health benefits.

Zinc is like a powerful sidekick for your immune system, performs over a hundred important functions in your body, and zinc supplements are often used as an over-the-counter remedy for fighting colds and other illnesses. It has been shown to reduce cold-related symptoms and shorten the duration of the common cold. Zinc is also great for stabilizing an under or overactive immune system.[36] It acts like a powerful anti-inflammatory that can have therapeutic effects for chronic health issues like heart disease or cancer. Some foods that are naturally high in zinc include lamb, grass-fed dairy, salmon, spinach, and pumpkin seeds, hemp seeds, chickpeas, lentils, yogurt, and kefir. Zinc also acts as an antioxidant in the body and fights free-radical damage. This helps to slow down the aging process.[220] Zinc deficiency can lead to a host of chronic health issues like hormonal imbalance, digestive problems, and chronic fatigue. If you aren't getting enough zinc every day, you might experience getting sick frequently, struggle with focus, always feel tired, or have a hard time healing wounds.

According to the National Institutes of Health, "Severe zinc deficiency depresses immune function, and even mild to moderate degrees of zinc deficiency can impair [immune cell] activity."[221] Zinc helps the body return back to balance after an immune response, so it's an important mineral for your immunity energy.

ECHINACEA. Used for centuries by indigenous people to treat a variety of health issues, echinacea is a popular supplement that is used to treat the common cold and flu all around the world. It's loaded with antioxidants and is also used to treat inflammation, pain, migraines, and a wide variety of other health problems. Several studies have shown that echinacea can help you recover faster from illness and may help your immune system fight off viruses, bacteria, and other pathogens.[222] In a meta-analysis of 14 studies it was found that taking echinacea may lower the risk of developing colds by more than 50% and shorten the duration of colds by one and a half days.[223]

Also called purple coneflower, echinacea is the name of a group of nine species from the daisy family. Out of the nine, only three *Echinacea pallida, Echinacea purpurea,* and *Echinacea angustifolia* are used in supplements.[224] Many studies link echinacea to improved immunity, lower blood sugar levels, and many other immune balancing benefits. Research also shows that one of echinacea's benefits is its effect when it is used on a variety of recurring infections. Many of the chemical properties in echinacea make it a powerful immune system stimulant. There's also research that some compounds in echinacea lower feelings of anxiety. Some of the powerful active compounds that make echinacea unique are phenolic acids, alkamides, caffeic acid, and a lot more. Antioxidants are molecules that help defend your cells against oxidative stress, a state that has been linked to chronic diseases, such as diabetes, heart disease, and many others.

In another study, adults with osteoarthritis found that taking an echinacea supplement dramatically reduces chronic pain, swelling, and inflammation. The interesting thing was that these people didn't respond well to conventional non-steroidal inflammatory drugs (NSAIDS) but found the echinacea supplement super helpful.[225]

ELDERBERRY. Elderberry is one of the most commonly used medicinal plants in the world. The Sambucus tree is a variety of flowering shrub species that belong to the *Adoxaceae* family, and these plants create bunches of small dark black, blue, and purple berries called elderberries. Native to North America and Europe, *the Sambucas nigra* is the most common type and many parts of the elderberry tree have been used for cooking and medicinal purposes all throughout history.[226] The bark has been used as a laxative, diuretic, and to trigger vomiting and the flowers and leaves have been used for inflammation, pain relief, swelling, and to trigger sweating.[226]

Elderberries contain strong antioxidants like phenolic acids, flavanols, and anthocyanins, and are high in vitamin C and dietary fiber.[227] Elderberries have a tart flavor and are generally used in sauces, jellies, jams, wines, and pies. Commercially they are sold in products like syrups, gummies, lozenges, teas, and supplements. Elderberry has a wide variety of health benefits that include fighting allergies, colds, the flu, and inflammation. Many studies show that elderberry is a powerful immune system modulator, helps treat the symptoms of the common cold and flu, and helps reduce the duration of the common cold and flu.[228] A 2018 research review also showed that elderberry helped to relieve cough, runny nose, and nasal congestion: all symptoms of an upper respiratory infection.

GINSENG. A staple in traditional Chinese medicine for hundreds of years, out of the many types of ginseng, Asian ginseng (*Panax ginseng*) and American ginseng (*Panax quinquefolius*) are the most popular.[229] Ginseng can strengthen the immune system, has powerful anti-inflammatory and antioxidant properties, and gintonin and ginsenosides are the two major compounds that provide the health benefits.[230] Ginseng helps improve your immune system efficiency by regulating each type of immune cell.[231] The roots, stems, and leaves have been used in a variety of ways to stabilize immune balance and improve resistance to infection or illnesses. Ginseng also has antimicrobial properties that help defend against viral and bacterial infections. Ginseng is also shown to help improve mood, memory, and behavior. Ginseng has also been shown to help to reduce the risk of cancer and may help improve patients who are undergoing chemo, reducing side effects and increasing the effectiveness of some of the treatment options. Finally, a review of over 155 studies shows that ginseng supplements help reduce fatigue and enhance physical activity.

BETA GLUCAN. Beta Glucan compounds are one of the most powerful immune balancers on this entire list. It's a naturally occurring soluble fiber that's strongly linked to enhancing heart health, lowering cholesterol levels, slowing cancer growth, and protecting again pathogens. Beta glucans are made up of multiple sugars joined together called polysaccharides, that can be found in oats, medicinal mushrooms (maitake, shiitake, reishi), yeasts, fermented foods, seaweed, and some algae. They can also be found in baker's yeast, whole grains, barley, wheat, and bran. Polysaccharides are biologically active, each source has it is own unique shape and health benefits, and the most studied source is 1,3-D Beta Glucan. Because beta glucans don't occur naturally in the human body and can't be synthesized by the body, they need to be eaten as foods or supplements.

Beta glucans are called a "biological response modifier" which allows them to attach to white blood cells and improve their immunity coordination. Studies have also shown that they have an extraordinary ability to prepare immune cells and stimulate natural killer (NK cells), macrophages, T cells, and cytokines interleukin 1 and 2 into action to help them precisely coordinate their attack on their different targets. From a 2008 article published in Mutation Research/Reviews in Mutation Research, beta glucan polysaccharides "stimulate the immune system… and thereby have a beneficial effect in fighting infections (bacterial, viral, fungal, and parasitic). Beta glucans also exhibit hypocholesterolemic and anticoagulant properties [and] have been demonstrated to be anti-cytotoxic, antimutagenic, and anti-tumorogenic, making them promising candidates as pharmacological promoters of health." Basically, they are saying it's a powerful multipronged choice for immune balancing.

OMEGA 3 FATTY ACIDS. Found in fatty fish, walnuts, flax seeds, and fish oil supplements, omega-3s are a family of essential fatty acids that have major health roles in your body and deliver a host of health benefits. Our body can't produce them on its own so you must get them from eating food or supplementation. Omega-3s have been shown to fight inflammation, improve cognition, and offer protection against heart disease.[232]

ASTRAGALUS ROOT. Astragalus is a plant in the legumes and bean family that's native to Asia with over 2,000 species. The two that are mainly used in supplements, *Astragalus membranaceus* and *Astragalus mongholicus,* are thought to prolong life and have been used for a variety of health issues like heart disease, diabetes, common cold, fatigue, and allergies.[233] It's really the root that has many active plant compounds that help strengthen immunity, reduce inflammation, and provide other powerful benefits. The root of astragulus is made into many different supplements, powders, teas, and liquid extracts. Astragalus root has been used in Chinese medicine for thousands of years as an adaptogen, and it's been shown to have many amazing health benefits like anti-aging, immune-boosting, and anti-inflammatory properties. Some studies show that astragalus can increase your body's white blood cells count, which helps defend against illness and inflammation. Researchers from this study also concluded that astragalus helps rebalance the immune system, protects from cancers, and reduces gut inflammation.

GLUTATHIONE. Called the mother of all antioxidants and found in every cell of the body, glutathione is a potent antioxidant made up of three amino acids; glycine, glutamine, and cysteine.[234] Glutathione is a powerful detox agent produced naturally in the body and has been shown to improve insulin sensitivity It also helps to control inflammation and regulate other antioxidants in the body like vitamin C. It's been shown to treat autism, increase fat metabolism, prevent cancer, and have powerful anti-aging properties. Glutathione also strengthens your T cells which in turn helps you fight off viruses, bacteria, parasites, and other harmful pathogens better.

Autoimmune diseases cause chronic inflammation that can increase oxidative stress, a precursor of chronic health issues. High levels of oxidative stress in your body are a precursor to a variety of chronic health issues like cancer, diabetes, IBS, and rheumatoid arthritis. Glutathione tampers down the impact of oxidative stress which can help reduce chronic diseases.[235]

The production of glutathione declines with age and also as a result of stress, environmental toxins, and poor nutrition. Glutathione is in some foods, but pasteurization and cooking can shrink those levels a lot. The highest amounts can be found in very rare or raw meat, unpasteurized milk and dairy products, and freshly picked veggies and fruits like avocado and asparagus. Foods that are high in sulfur can also help boost glutathione production in the body naturally because it has sulfur molecules. These include broccoli, brussels sprouts, bok choy, garlic, onions, eggs, nuts, legumes, chicken, fish, milk thistle, whey, guso seaweed, and flaxseed.[236] You can also increase your glutathione levels orally, intravenously, topically, or as an inhalant. Some supplements that help to activate natural glutathione production in the body are milk thistle, superoxide dismutase, and N-acetyl cysteine. Eating healthier foods, reducing your exposure to toxins, and getting enough sleep all help to keep your glutathione levels high.

GODIVA'S LIFESTYLE IMMUNE-BALANCING HABITS

Earlier I mentioned some things that suppress your immune system. Before I take a deep dive into the lifestyle things that you can do to balance your immunity energy, it's important to first understand the common things that cause immune imbalance. Many factors like exposure to toxins, sleep deprivation, vitamin deficiencies, and chronic stress can all harm your immune system.

MORE MOVEMENT. You should be moving a lot daily, but don't get crazy. Overtraining, prolonged intense exercise, or not exercising at all can make your immune system imbalanced.[237] However, regular moderate exercise can actually give it a little boost. Research shows that even one session of moderate exercise can boost the effectiveness of vaccines in people with a compromised immune system.[238] So imagine what it does for people with a healthy immune system? Studies also show that regular moderate exercise helps your immune cells regenerate regularly and reduces inflammation.[239]

It doesn't matter how or where you do it, but consistent intentional movement daily and weekly is very important to your immunity energy balance. Not only that, but the intentional movement also improves your heart health, lung function, mood, and energy levels while helping you build strength, muscle, and reducing inflammation. Aim for a variety of intentional movements like walking, biking, dance, or running, as well as strength and resistance training like weightlifting, body-weight exercises, yoga, high-intensity interval training (HIIT), and Pilates. 10,000 to 15,000 steps is a good goal to aim for and doing any type of intentional movement for 20 to 30 minutes a day. It doesn't have to be just exercise, a short walk will do, gardening, some light stretching, or dance like a crazy person to one of your favorite songs like no one is watching.

STRESS MASTERY. There's a reason that most people get sick during the more stressful parts of their lives. Your stress levels can make or break immunity. A mountain of studies suggests that lowering your anxiety and stress levels is the key to optimal immune health. One of the big reasons that I became sick was because I let my anxiety and stress levels runaway unchecked. That's why one of the main goals of this book is to help you master your stress; because unchecked anxiety and stress are devastating to you mentally, physically, emotionally, and biologically. Long-term stress causes an imbalance in immune cell functioning as well as promotes inflammation.[240] It can even suppress the immune response in children.[241]

Mental stress activates the body's immune cells and too much stress can overstimulate these innate immune cells and take away energy from other components of immunity that target viruses.[242] Research shows that negative mood states and chronic stress are associated with a higher vulnerability to infectious disease. Our antiviral immune responses lower when we are swimming in chronic stress, especially for a long time. According to research, even when you get a flu vaccine, people with higher stress levels have a reduced antibody response, meaning that it is not as effective. It can be very challenging in our modern, fast-paced, and hustle culture society, but mastering your stress levels is a requirement for optimal health and healing. Things that can help you manage stress more effectively include creating boundaries, removing yourself from stressful situations, minimizing contact with stressful people, exercise, journaling, traditional mindfulness and meditation, yoga, other mindfulness practices, and most importantly, my method Interval Mindfulness™.

SLEEP RHYTHM. We all know how important it is to have a regular and consistent sleep routine. Sleep and immunity are intimately linked and getting enough quality sleep is essential to your immune health and overall well-being. Your body needs time to rest, repair, and regenerate to function at its best, and not getting enough or quality sleep consistently disrupts the normal cycle of regeneration, increases the stress response in your body, and is linked to a higher susceptibility to sickness.[243] Not getting enough sleep at night or poor-quality sleep can also cause unchecked activation of innate immune cells and lower antiviral activity as well.[244] Getting enough rest, which is on average 7 - 9 hours of sleep every night, strengthens immunity, and if you have ever been sick before you know that you may sleep more to help your immune system fight whatever illness you're experiencing.[245]

If you're getting less than 7 hours of sleep consistently, this will increase inflammation, chronic stress, and immune imbalance in your body.[246] If you're having a challenging time sleeping at night, try to limit screen time (cell phone, laptop, TV) for an hour before bed. The blue light that is emitted from these screens can disrupt your circadian rhythm and cause your body to "think" it's the afternoon instead of the evening. Having your room cool and as dark as possible will also help. Avoid caffeine within eight hours of sleeping, don't eat within three hours of sleeping, and get at least 30 minutes of sun exposure during the day. Also, a dark room, earplugs, mouth tape, a sleep mask, and going to be around the same time every night may work. This all may sound a bit dramatic, but it's better than not sleeping well every night and being that person that is ALWAYS sick, stressed, and overly caffeinated.

LIMIT ALCOHOL. For most people, this is going to be the first thing they ignore on this list. Alcohol has a tight grip on many people consciously and unconsciously and the way that society has normalized consuming it for weekdays, weekends, events, and celebrations isn't really helping. I don't know who needs to hear this, but you don't need a glass of wine every night before you go to sleep. You also don't need to get white/black girl/guy wasted and blacked out on the weekends, and call it "fun". You are capable of being social and around loved ones, friends, and co-workers without the presence of a drug. I used to be a hot mess, Messy Mario they called me. So, while I am no longer a hot mess on the weekends and now only drink on special occasions, I understand and can relate to people who tend to do just that.

The reality and uncomfortable truth is that alcohol hurts your immune system and is one of the worst things that you can put into your body, period. Don't believe me? Here is a statement straight from the World Health Organization (WHO) in April 2020 in response to the massive surge of global alcohol sales during the pandemic:

"Alcohol consumption is associated with a range of communicable and noncommunicable diseases and mental health disorders, which can make a person more vulnerable to COVID-19. In particular, alcohol compromises the body's immune system and increases the risk of adverse health outcomes."[247]

Alcohol is an internal distraction for your body, and the second you drink it, your body puts many of its other functions on hold like fat burning while it tries to get the alcohol out of your body.[248] Alcohol makes it harder for your immune system to mobilize and defend against damaging germs by default. Alcohol disrupts every single system in your body, ruins your gut health, and makes you more susceptible to harmful bacteria, viruses, and pathogens. Because people like to shoot the messenger while ignoring the message, here's another quote about alcohol and immunity from Dr. E. Jennifer Edelman, a Yale Medicine addiction specialist.

"Alcohol has diverse adverse effects throughout the body, including on all cells of the immune system, that lead to increased risk of serious infections."[249]

Not only does drinking alcohol make it harder for your body to do other functions, like defending against diseases, alcohol also damages the fine hairs and immune cells in your lungs that must clear your airway of pathogens. This means that viruses and other harmful particles can easily slip in and create havoc in your body. When your body can't resolve a pathogen, an infection can ensue and progress to something more severe, even death. Alcohol triggers whole-body inflammation and slaughters healthy gut bacteria the gut and intestines that manage immune health. This increases the risk of infection and harms overall health. Research shows that drinking alcohol leads to serious lung diseases and pulmonary diseases like pneumonia.

Even if you have just one sip of alcohol, your body will prioritize breaking down the alcohol and getting it out of your body. Alcohol is a toxin, and your body doesn't store alcohol like carbs or fats. As soon as it's in your body it must get sent straight to your liver so it can get metabolized. Alcohol also messes up your sleep quality and as you saw earlier, the less sleep you get the higher the risk is that you will get sick. And according to the Mayo Clinic, a lack of sleep can also affect how long it takes for a person to recover if they do get sick. Before you start wondering how much alcohol you can drink to get away with not having the negative immune health effects, research shows that even smaller amounts of alcohol can have a negative effect on immunity. Sorry. I'm not going to suggest or tell you what to do when it comes to alcohol, you're a grown *ss adult. However, if you're currently battling a chronic health issue and you're on fire, drinking gasoline alcohol every day or weekend probably isn't going to get you to reduce or reverse that chronic health issue anytime soon. Alcohol isn't going extinct anytime soon and will for sure be there waiting for you (with open arms) once you heal or reach your goals.

HIGH SUGAR. Sugar is in everything and everyone absolutely LOVES sugar! Eating a lot of sugar or refined carbs may feel good at first, but the long-term effects can be very bad for your immune health. If your daily eating experience is full of sugary foods and carby, you're probably experiencing weakened immunity. Eating too much sugar weakens your immune system, feeds harmful bacteria like candida, feeds parasites in your body, leads to the development of abnormal bodily tissues, and may lead to cancer. Eating too much sugar contributes to being overweight and obese, which puts you at a higher risk for a multitude of chronic health issues.[250] Too much sugar depletes many of the powerful immune-balancing nutrients on this list like vitamin c, glutathione, and zinc.

In particular with vitamin C, your white blood cells need vitamin C to perform certain immune system functions. Glucose and vitamin C have a similar chemical makeup, and both rely on insulin and its signaling to get into the body's cells. Glucose is prioritized by your cells, so the more sugar that is in your body, the less your body's cells can use vitamin C. This explains why eating too much sugar and refined carbs weaken immunity. So, if you're eating too much sugar and refined carbs, you would have to be taking even more immune-balancing things to reach optimal function. Reducing your sugar and refined carb intake can help with weight loss, lower inflammation, and reduce your risk of getting chronic health issues like cancer, heart disease, and type 2 diabetes.

HYDRATION HYGIENE. 75% of Americans are chronically dehydrated.[251] Most of your body is water and your life started in water, so it should make sense that proper hydration is important for your immune and overall health. Most people don't drink enough water or simply forget to drink more water. These same people then chronically consume coffee, sugar, caffeine, and alcohol not realizing that all these things are further dehydrating them. Your body must take water from other parts of your body when you're massively dehydrated. This can lead to chronic pain, headaches, allergies, and a variety of other health problems.

Hydration hygiene is super important for your health, but what kind of water you're drinking also matters. Tap water can be incredibly toxic to your body and has a high amount of toxins like fluoride, heavy metals, chlorine, and arsenic. All of these toxins increase the toxic load on the body and make your immune system work harder to remove them. Exposure to toxins like arsenic and lead can result in the imbalance of different parts of the immune system. The best way to get high-quality water is to have a filtration system at home, filter, or use spring water. Glass bottles or stainless-steel bottles are better to use over plastic bottles because sometimes the plastic can leech into the water. Your body needs minerals and clean water to properly conduct electrical signals, and those signals are how your body and brain communicate and how your cells function. When the water you drink is toxic, this process can be inhibited and negatively impact other processes in your body. Aim to be drinking more than half of your body weight in ounces of water a day.

GRAND GRATITUDE. Gratitude doesn't come from the mind, it comes from the heart. One of the easiest ways to help keep your anxiety and stress levels down is to train a positive mindset and practice gratitude. Gratitude can increase oxytocin, dopamine, and serotonin, your feel-good hormones, and lead to a lower risk of depression. Studies also show that a consistent gratitude practice can lower your blood pressure, make you more resilient against stressors, and reduce inflammation. They also show that Grateful people are more likely to have healthier habits like eating healthy, exercising, and avoiding unhealthy habits like smoking or drinking.[252]

Practicing regularly is the best way to engage gratitude but you also need to figure out what works for you. Keeping a gratitude journal, doing gratitude Innervals™, or just stopping a few times during your day to be thankful for different things will help lower your stress and protect your immunity. Writing thank-you notes or emails, making gratitude calls, or reaching out to people to let them know you see, hear, and appreciate them. Also being intentional about engaging in positive, supportive, or uplifting activities like playing with your kids or pets, listening to music, watching a comedy, connecting with good friends, or reading one of your favorite books. Do what you feel works for you. What makes you truly happy? What brings you unlimited joy? Do more of those things that do and less of the things that don't. If you're struggling with sustaining a positive mindset you could seek help from a support group, therapist, or health/life coach. Or you know, me.

THUMBS FAST MOTOR COMBO. (3 minutes)

1. THUMBS FAST MOTOR INNERVAL™ // 30 seconds.

Move both of your thumbs as fast as you possibly can. Do this for 30 seconds or count to 30 if you don't have a timer. Relax your thumbs back to neutral before you start the next Innerval™.

2. CORE BREATHING INNERVAL™ // 30 seconds.

Take long, slow, and deep inhales and take longer, slower, and deeper exhales for 30 seconds or 3 times each if you don't have a timer. As you inhale for 3 seconds your core goes out, and as you exhale for 6 seconds your core goes in.

3. Repeat 2 times

STIMULATION. The phrenic nerves, vagus nerves, motor cortex (9), and posterior thoracic nerves.

26 //

MY DISASTROUS DISCHARGE

Two days after my chemical chemo infusion and botched spinal tap, my stomach had finally started to return to its normal size. I no longer looked like I was pregnant with triplets. To me, this was an amazing success. I didn't really look "good" yet, though. I had only gone from severely bloated with a liver the size of Texas, to completely flushed and looking like a cast member of The Walking Dead. Even my smile was scary. Anyone who looked at me would immediately know something was very wrong with me. Since I had responded well to the first round of chemical chemo, the doctors were quick to put me on the full aggressive protocol and then discharge me. "Wham, bam, thank you, ma'am, and bring on the chemo commission! Who's buying the first round of drinks tonight?"

They were pleased with themselves for finally figuring out what was wrong with me. For me, though, this was also a moment of great happiness and joy. I had been under duress, shock, and turmoil for four months straight, and this was the first time I felt almost normal again, almost. If you call normal a hundred pounds lighter than my average weight. Every single muscle in my body was atrophied or weakened. I could barely walk, but at least I didn't need to depend on oxygen to breathe or have to live in an ICU anymore. Hallelujah! As I walked out of the hospital doors after my three-week hospital stint, I felt the warm rays of sunshine on my face. I was finally free, and it was exhilarating! That excitement was short-lived as the reality of what I went through and anxiety slowly hijacked me.

Being fit, active, and having big muscles most of my life, I was used to getting a lot of attention. I was also very present and attentive, so people noticed me right away. Many uncomfortable eye-locks happened when I and someone else—even strangers—looked at each other. I'm not going to lie, I f*cking loved it! I worked hard to look good, and it feels good when others seem to appreciate and admire that hard work. In restaurants, at the gym, no matter where I went, people noticed me. My new reality hit me the minute I left the hospital: I quickly realized that no one noticed me or made eye contact at all. People actually looked right through me, over me, or bumped into me, like I wasn't even there. I felt I had visually disappeared, and for the first time in my life, I knew what homeless people must feel. Invisible. Not worthy of a second look. I felt like a ghost too, dead on the inside from the insidious infusion of the chemical chemo. I remember this day vividly because I thought it was a good idea to take a photo and put it on social media. Like no one would notice that I was half my size! I still hadn't publicly opened up about what I was going through.

What happened to me? It seemed the real me—Mario—had disappeared down some medical rabbit hole. They had extended my life longer than a week but had killed my spirit. What kind of f*cking tradeoff is that? The events of the past five months were still very surreal to me. It seemed like one long dream that had happened so fast. It felt like I was completely fine just the other day when in reality, I was very sick for a very long time. I was walking, talking, and physically there, but I wasn't REALLY there. I was frozen in my shutdown response, a deeply disassociated and autonomous state of being that I often shifted into throughout all my life's traumas, in order to temporarily deal with them. No matter what I did, I couldn't help but feel this visceral state of anxious unease.

I was dealing with the deadly diagnosis privately and no one knew except a few close friends. I didn't want anyone to know that I was sick with cancer; I couldn't believe it and was downright embarrassed by it. How could I get cancer? I shuddered in shame as I tried to stomach this new reality for me. Even though I shared it with a few friends, I still felt incredibly lonely and isolated, like I was hiding from the world. I had just been all over TV, talk shows, and newspapers as the hottest fitness trend, and now I was depressed, dysfunctional, and dead inside. Struggling to find the will to keep living and wondering if I made a mistake.

MESSY MEMORIAL DAY WEEKEND

I was released right before the Memorial Day weekend of 2014. I was instructed that if anything went wrong, I should immediately go to the ER, because I could die. Okay, great. If I get a fever or anything goes wrong, I'm dead. I had a chemical chemo pump and had to administer a shot to myself to keep my white blood cell count high. UGH, I f*cking hate needles! Can you imagine hating needles and then being trusted to inject yourself with a needle? Talk about facing your fears! It's one thing to have a stranger stab you while you don't look or brace, but it's a whole new level when you actually have to stick yourself with a needle and make sure you do it properly! What if I missed the vein? The doctors missed my spine three times, and they are allegedly professionals! Apparently, this was life or death though. I had zero immune system function left and I would be injecting white blood cells just so my body could retain some basic immunity.

The first day wasn't too terrible but I also couldn't do much. I tried to defy the fact that I was undergoing chemical chemo treatment and live as normal of a life as I could. Working in the fitness industry, you have to physically work to make an income. And who wants to take fitness advice from someone who is obviously very sick. So, I had been financially setback for the past four months by being in and out of the hospital. And worker's comp, temporary disability, and medical leave for companies (who will remain nameless) is total BS. I think I was paid maybe 5% of my total income after filling out a hundred different forms. It's like, "Oh, you aren't valuable unless you are physically doing something for us. Here are some pennies while you get well to work again for us. Never mind your years of loyal and wonderful service. Next?"

Shaun, one of my good friends at the time, had lost his father to the same rare cancer and was one of my super supportive friends; he helped get me through that challenging time. At the time, it didn't really dawn on me how triggering it could have been for him to help me. He allowed me to crash with him while I recovered and got back on my feet. He was gone for Memorial Day weekend, so it was just me in his place the entire weekend. Shaun lived around 38th Street and 9th Avenue, in the Hell's Kitchen neighborhood. I tried my best to act like things were normal, and I was able to get around somewhat, but I had to move slowly. All of my clothes were extra baggy because I'd lost so much weight, and my staple outfit was dark gray sweatpants and a light gray hoodie: I called it my illness uniform. I tried to grab food from a grocery store nearby, but when my cart was about half full, I started getting nauseous, shaking, and fell to the floor with a massive migraine. People rushed to me to make sure that I was okay. "I'm fine, I'm just a little sick." So embarrassing.

They helped me up and pulled me to the corner of the store where I could sit and recover. Once I was able to get up again, I quickly paid for the groceries and they offered to deliver them to me where I was staying. I hobbled back to Shaun's place and fell to the floor again, shaking and crying. Frozen in my shutdown response, I started to tell myself hopeless stories. This was not AT ALL the life that I wanted to live. I really thought I could do this, but then I started having second thoughts. Anxiety swallowed me whole and my ego started playing narratives in my mind. What if I don't make it? What if the cancer comes back? How will I make a living if I'm sick for a long time? So many negative thoughts ruminating in my mind pouring gasoline on my fire of anxiety.

The massive migraine wasn't a single occurrence, and I noticed that every single time I stood up, I would get this massive migraine. I could feel the veins on the side of my head throbbing like they were about to burst. It felt like my head was boiling a pot of water with the cover on it creating massive pressure. Imagine the worst headache you've ever had in your life, times a hundred; I'm not exaggerating. They were headaches from hell. It was awful, crippling even. They were so bad that I thought about taking my own life, for the 1000th time. All I could do was lay down and crouch in the fetal position until they subsided. It wouldn't come right away but when it did, it was like an ocean wave hitting me and knocking me over. I spent most of the day laying down, so I didn't have to endure that massive migraine that I knew was coming. This made my first experience out of the hospital pure hell. After a day or two of this torture, I called the hospital to tell them about the headaches. What was their response? "Come into the ER so we can check things out."

Go to the ER on a holiday weekend? You have got to be kidding me? They had instilled in me a major fear that if I didn't go to the hospital if I had a fever or felt anything wrong, I would die. After everything I had been through and knowing how hospitals work, the last thing I was going to do was go to the ER, especially on a holiday weekend. I would rather die, and I was ready to. And then it hit me: What if this was what my life was going to be? Massive migraines, nasty nausea, pulsing pain, and stripping struggle? Afraid to go to the hospital; afraid not to. Was this how I want to live the rest of my life? F*ck no! I took a mindful Innerval™ to focus on my breathing and help me calm down. It was short-lived, but it helped greatly at that moment. When you're experiencing a deep freeze in your stress or shutdown response, sometimes it takes more effort to climb out of them back into your relaxation response, but an Innerval™ can be helpful as the first step.

The massive migraines were so incredibly intense that I couldn't even think, all I could do was cry. Back in came the darkness, misery, and despair. I slowly started my deadly descent into a deep, dark, and deadly depression. I took another mindful Innerval™ for nine minutes to just breathe and be in the present. That one helped me activate my relaxation response and slowly brought me back to my senses where I started to Google for my life again. I looked up "Severe Brain Migraine." After a couple of creative searches, I finally figured out what was going on with me. I was getting the migraines because there were four holes in my spine from the botched spinal tap, lackluster lumbar punch, or whatever the f*ck you want to call it. When they do the procedure successfully the first time (like they are supposed to), there is only one hole so it's not so bad and heals fast. But I had four holes in my back. Your brain and spine are in a sac, and holes allow pressure from the sac to escape. Whenever I would stand up, the pressure would leak out of the sac, and voilà! Mario gets a massive migraine from the pressure drop. A massive migraine that made me break down, cry, and want to just die, all because of a medical error. Once I figured this all out on my own, I simply bought tons of Neosporin and bandages and applied pressure to all of the holes in my back to keep the pressure from leaking and hoped this MacGyver/ghetto technique would work. It did. Another win for GOOGLE! I was able to stand up with no massive migraine in about a day or two. Had I not taken a short mindful Innerval™ at that moment, I wouldn't have been able to look past the overwhelming moments full of pain to make a better and more conscious decision.

I can only imagine what would have happened if I had actually gone to the ER, on a holiday weekend, with all those crazies. I probably would have died, for real. Or maybe they would have figured, "Hey, this Black guy knows nothing. And we need more practice punching holes in spinal columns!" I could have come out looking like dark Swiss cheese, only with a massive migraine.

EYEBROWS FAST MOTOR COMBO. (3 minutes)

1. EYEBROWS FAST MOTOR INNERVAL™ // 30 seconds.

With your eyes closed move your eyebrows up and down as fast as you possibly can. Do this for 30 seconds or count to 30 if you don't have a timer. Relax your eyebrows back to neutral before you start the next Innerval™.

2. CORE BREATHING INNERVAL™ // 30 seconds.

Take long, slow, and deep inhales and take longer, slower, and deeper exhales for 30 seconds or 3 times each if you don't have a timer. Each inhale should be around 3 seconds and each exhale should be around 6 seconds. As you breathe in, your core goes out, as you breathe out, your core goes in.

3. Repeat 2 times

STIMULATION. The phrenic nerves, vagus nerves, motor cortex (8), and posterior thoracic nerves.

27 //

CO-REGULATE BEFORE YOU MEDICATE

Once I was finally on my feet enough to be in my own place, I found a new apartment in Harlem. I used to live in Hell's Kitchen, on 9th avenue and 55th st, right by the Alvin Ailey dance company. 9th avenue is one of the busier main streets in NYC and I didn't want to be seen by people, let alone anyone that I knew. Harlem was a great retreat because I didn't know anyone there and it could be a truly fresh start. My roommate Aerial was amazing, and he had this cute one-year-old Shih Tzu named Pema. At first, Pema hated me, ferociously barked at me nonstop, and chased me. I think she was used to being the b*tch of the house, protecting her owner. I'm definitely a dog person, but I didn't really like her at first. One day she actually bit me, so I decided to change my approach. Instead of yelling at her, I bought treats, and when she barked at me, I dangled the treats and made her sit and shut up to get one. She loved her treats, so it worked. We became great friends, started co-regulating, and she would even come into my room and cuddle with me. Whenever I was feeling down in my shutdown response or anxious in my stress response, Pema would give me a little boost up to my relaxation response. Pema definitely helped me cope with my cancer recovery, when she wasn't being a little diva Shih Tzu b*tch. Why is it always the small dogs that are super feisty?

I had been dealing with my cancer diagnosis privately because I was extremely ashamed. It was my biggest and darkest secret that unwittingly reinforced my shutdown and stress response states. I want to give a shout-out to some close friends who truly helped me out through this tough time. It was your beautiful actions during my time of deep duress, that helped lift me (literally) out of frozen stress and shutdown states. My friend Kayla and her parents Bambie and Pete. Kayla is my ride-or-die friend and client who visited me several times in the hospital. Abby, my Jewish surrogate mother, friend, and client that would sneak in all the foods, supplements, and other goodies that I wasn't supposed to have while I was in the ICU. My friend Deb, visited me in the hospital and helped to support me with things that I needed when I was at the hospital. My friend Drew, who came to visit and also brought me an iPhone charger to the hospital. Google couldn't have saved my life if I didn't have a phone charger! My friend Shauna, who was with me the night before my demise started and was always super supportive during my whole ordeal. My friend and client Steve, who supported me, helped me fundraise, and allowed me to get some comic-relief (literally my first stand-up show). My friend and broski Chris, who really supported me in training a positive mindset about my situation as I was literally training him. There are so many others who came to visit and support me, and I have no memories or only vague memories of a lot of my traumatic experiences. So, if I missed you, I'm sorry and I truly appreciate that you showed up for me in my darkest hour.

Despite the support of a few close friends, I continued to feel like a failure; a fitness guru getting cancer? Ridiculous! At the time I couldn't fully explain it to myself or let alone explain it to others. It's so much easier to blame others for your health problems, but does blaming make you any healthier? No. Deliberate action towards improving your health makes you healthier. Nonetheless, I kept searching for explanations, excuses, and anything that was outside of myself to blame for my cancer. Maybe it was this, or maybe it was that. Maybe I was drinking too much, or could it have been the weed? Maybe I shouldn't have done cocaine, or maybe I should have never taken ecstasy. I was convinced there had to be just one reason, cause, and root. Maybe it was genetics. I lost my father to cancer, mother to epilepsy, and scores of other immediate family members to heart disease, stroke, and diabetes, so maybe this was supposed to happen to me. Generational trauma or some sort of curse.

I found myself initially agreeing with my doctors: My cancer must have been by chance and partly genetic. Like playing the Mega Millions lottery. One person in every million gets cancer, according to my doctors. They told me it's just "one of those things that happens to people" and it's really hard to pinpoint who, why, or when. They basically acted like I bought a cancer lotto ticket and unfortunately hit the jackpot. Of course, it was their financial jackpot, not mine. After some time playing the role of victim, and actively training to spend more time in my relaxation response, I shook myself and realized that this was definitely 500% my fault. Who was I kidding, trying to blame someone or something else for my daily, macro, and micro choices?

I am not a victim, nor are most of the people who experience cancer. Even if children get it, it's not necessarily their fault, but some fault does rest with the parent's biology that is passed down and the decisions they make in life after they conceive. This is not to be harsh or place explicit blame on anyone, because obviously a lot of factors come into play, but science is pretty consistent and clear about risk factors that lead to chronic health issues. It was their daily, macro, and micro choices that led to that situation. But people would rather retreat under the cover of denial than take responsibility for their actions, myself included. You can't knowingly indulge in multiple unhealthy lifestyle factors and expect to not have a challenging health outcome. I know that health can be so confusing because we have so much access to information. No carbs, yes carbs, no cardio only lifting, no lifting only cardio, keto is good, carbs are good, juice cleanses, focus on micronutrients, focus on macros only, etc. But deep down, your body already knows what's healthy and unhealthy for you; the true question is whether or not you are listening? Your body whispers before it screams. You should do what is good for you, actively make an effort to live a healthy lifestyle and stop engaging in what you know are unhealthy habits. If you are listening to your mind and body, it will guide you. It can seem easy to hide under the cover of ignorance, but even that has consequences. You can't be internally on fire, continually drink gasoline with your daily, macro, and micro choices, and expect not to eventually become a raging California wildfire.

I eventually took full responsibility for the lifestyle that was killing me. This wasn't an instant one-and-done thing. This happened gradually by practicing my various Innervals™ and training to get into my relaxation response. I was able to become aware of my past conditioning, actions, and patterns by training my nerves and practicing different Innervals™, which helped me cultivate stronger self-awareness allowing me to watch my own thoughts and patterns. You can't correct what you can't see. I would still be thinking that I was a victim today had I not taken proactive action. My stress load and daily stressors were killing me. The garbage, processed, and toxic food I was eating was killing me. Binge drinking every weekend and during the week was killing me. Holding on to anger, resentment, and grief was killing me. Recreational drug use every weekend to avoid and escape my inner pain was killing me. Not listening to my body's inner whispers was killing me. There wasn't just one single thing that caused cancer to express, it was the synergy of unhealthy, unbalanced, and uncontrollable hazardous habits that were killing me, that led to cancer expressing.

I had clung to the illusion that I was healthy simply because I worked out every day and was a fitness guru. Overtraining creates physical stress, so using stress to combat stress may seem like a brilliant idea, but without proper recovery, you're just compounding stress and making it collectively worse. Boy was I wrong. Nothing like cancer to give you a big *ss wake-up call. Once I took full responsibility for my situation like an adult, I was also able to heal myself in record time. I transformed my mentality from victim to victor, simply by training my nerves. My daily macro and micro choices had allowed me to get to that point, so it made sense to me that my daily macro and micro choices would help me arrest, regress, and holistically heal. According to the National Institutes of Health, 5 to 10% of cancers are genetic and the rest are caused by what you eat, how you live your life, and your inner and outer environment.[253] Cancer was living, breathing, and thriving inside of me because of no one else but me. No one was holding a gun to my head and saying, "Run yourself down until you have cancer."

What you aren't told by doctors, specialists, and medical professionals is that cancer is completely natural, normal, and nominal in everyone. If you are reading this book right now, chances are, you have precancerous or cancer cells in you right now. Yep, and that's okay. As long as your immune system isn't suppressed or compromised, it will take care of those cancer cells. I have hopefully provided you with the tools in this book so far to recognize if your immune functions are compromised or not.

Everyone gets cancer cells in their life, and the difference between people who get diagnosed with cancer and those who don't is the state of their different immune systems. Cancer cells are like a small fire, little embers of energy that your immune system has to stamp out. When your immune system is busy doing other stuff or suppressed, those little energy embers grow and spread. What happens when you pour gasoline on embers? A F*CKING FIRE! What's the gasoline? Your daily, macro, and micro choices. Eating unhealthy food is gasoline. Being overwhelmed with stress is gasoline. Eating processed foods, GMOs, and other artificial crap is gasoline. Holding on to suppressed emotions, trauma, and unresolved issues is gallons of gasoline. Anger, sadness, grief, and other negative emotions are gasoline. Inhaling environmental pollutants is gasoline. Drinking alcohol is gasoline. I really could go on and on but hopefully you get the point.

Your daily macro and micro choices create either a negative or positive inner environment. Cancer is the same way. When some of the trillions of your cells become injured, they usually repair themselves or die, but sometimes they will mutate to survive, because who wants to die, even a cancer cell? Those cancer cells are like, "Please, eat some Cheetos and have a beer. I want to live my best life!"

Every single cell in your body is programmed to die at some point, it could be days, weeks, or even months, but they are predisposed to a timely death. When cells start to get cancerous, they start dividing relentlessly and then lose their auto self-destruct program. They go rogue and try to hijack as many normal cells as possible. Safety in numbers. Sometimes tumor cells can leave the tumor and form in other parts of your body. A tumor isn't detected in Western medicine until it reaches one milliliter in size and has amassed 100,000 to a million cancer cells. Why do you think that is? Why do Western medicine methods of detecting cancer only register when it's that advanced and already spreading? We can hear ET signals from different galaxies, maintain and have an international space station, and clone animals (and people too, I'm sure), but for some reason, we can "only" detect cancer when it becomes a problem? Smells like bullsh*t to me.

We don't go to school at Hogwarts, and as I've said, cancer isn't magic. By the time it expresses itself, it's likely been brewing in you for weeks, months, or years, as well as many other infections, illnesses, and diseases. "Early detection" by Western medicine standards is metastatic (spreading) and too late, and it would be silly to think it's not on purpose, especially since we have capitalism rooted in our healthcare that always puts profits over people. Everything in this world is created with intention, and if you don't question everything you will fall for anything. Through minimal information, misinformation, and malevolent medicine, the healthcare industry keeps you in limbo between sick and dying. The best-case scenario for them is to have you frequently get sick so that you become a VIP repeat customer who is taking their product (prescription pills) for life. They don't want you at optimal health; there's no money in that. But the fantastic news I want to share is that when it comes to infections, illnesses, and chronic diseases, if your biology can create it, your immune system can heal it. You just need the right physical, mental, emotional, and biochemical inner environment balance and support.

COREGULATION

While going through the cancer challenge, I became frozen in my shutdown response; I was extremely withdrawn, isolated, and yet again reached a deep and dark depression. I thought I could just do treatment and bounce back like I wasn't dying from cancer. I'm not kidding. I slipped in and out of denial; maybe you can relate. When you are going through chemical chemo treatment, you have good days and bad. The good days mean there is no pain or nausea. The bad days mean that's all you know.

I was given pills for nausea, pain, and antibiotics to prevent infections, but I hated taking them. It felt like a weakness to me. But nausea and pain broke me. Days and nights of shaking and crying commenced until I finally caved and took the pain and nausea meds. This was not the way that I wanted to live my life. Google had been my BFF and savior throughout my entire experience, and I was going to call on her one last time. Ready to give the hell up, I searched "How to die from an overdose." I was never scared of death. I've lost almost all of my family to death and I have snuggled with death several times. Why does death always lure you in when you are feeling tired, helpless, and weak? But these were only my thoughts coming from being in my shutdown response. They weren't the thoughts of fighting to live that I would have when I was in my stress response or thoughts of optimism and hope that I would have when I was in my relaxation response. I was deep in my shutdown response, despondent, and there death was again, calling, wooing, and sweetly singing me to my everlasting sleep.

I found all the information I needed to do the unthinkable, and then prepared myself mentally. I was taking tons of f*cking pills anyway, my organs were already faltering from the high toxicity of chemical chemo, and it wouldn't take much for me to die. Just a gentle push from my BFF, Google. My inner intelligence told me to publicly announce what I was going through. After all, for the four months leading up to my cancer diagnosis, I was posting on social media about being sick and all the malevolent medical malpractice, missteps, and medical errors I had experienced. I figured people should at least know what happened and why I died. It was the perfect way for me to just give up and take my final bows. "Hasta la vista, baby." Mario out.

I announced on Facebook and Instagram that I had finally figured out the source, root, and cause of my deteriorating health, rare cancer, and that I was given a week to live. I also proclaimed that I was taking an integrative approach and vowed, "I will win, and cancer will lose." It technically wasn't a lie because I did say that and believe that initially when I was in my relaxation response, I just flip-flopped on my commitment depending on what nerve state I was in. Like when friends commit to something and then bail on you last minute. I was channeling that shady friend who always bails. Whenever I was rooted in my relaxation response, I was calm, peaceful, and optimistic. If I was triggered into my stress response, I was fearful, worrisome, and pessimistic. And whenever I fell all the way down to my shutdown response, I was depressed, disassociated, and hopeless. My goal was to constantly train my nerves so that I could stay anchored in my relaxation response as much as possible. But when you're in the midst of a cancer challenge full of pain, uncertainty, and struggle, it's challenging to do that on your own. I knew deep down that I needed help, otherwise, I wasn't going to make it.

I had mixed feelings as to whether or not I should post publicly about it. Part of me still didn't want so many people to know because I was still riddled with guilt and ashamed that I was competing with cancer. But when I finally did muster up the courage as more of a farewell post than anything, something crazy happened. I received SO MUCH. Love. And support! I was overcome with overwhelm from how so many people cared. It was so powerful that it lifted my spirits as well as my nerve state massively. I had endured doctor after doctor who seemingly didn't give AF if I lived or died constantly deprioritizing me. Even when I was diagnosed, I felt zero comfort or support from the medical community. I was offered pamphlets, not hugs or encouragement as I was hysterically crying over the diagnosis. "You have cancer and a week to live. You need to do chemical chemo ASAP. Also, here are some pamphlets if you need social support. There are many cancer groups."

I was so scared to announce publicly what I was going through because I thought that I was going to be judged, shamed, and shooed by family, friends, loved ones, and fans, but it was the complete opposite. Friends, family, strangers, fans, and more, sent me unconditional love. The texts poured in, the emails came crashing into my inbox, the direct messages overflowed; people were calling, sending cards, sending money, and sending get-well gifts. I didn't know what to do with it all. I was so wonderfully overwhelmed with good feelings that it seemed for the first time I was frozen in my relaxation response, which is basically impossible in this day and age unless you're a monk. I was powerfully uplifted from the surge of healing hormones every time someone reached out to check on me and send their love and support. It was like a bright stage spotlight that would be shined in my dark cave of despair. The ultimate nightlight. The massive anchor that I desperately needed to keep me in my self-healing state and on my rapid healing journey, came in the form of social support and co-regulation. Now having said that the social support needs to be supportive, not negative. Having someone overly worried, anxious, and projecting their own fears, insecurities, and negativity on you will have the opposite effect. It will dysregulate you to being frozen in your stress response, where self-healing can't happen. People either co-regulate you or dysregulate you, there's no neutral exchange.

Co-regulation is one of the three pillars of the polyvagal theory coined by Dr. Stephen Porges. He explains that before language, mammals used their voice to indicate if they were dangerous or safe to come close to. Dogs still growl when they want to appear threatening or do a high-pitched bark to alert them of potential danger. Co-regulation happens between mammals (dogs and cats included) and it's a social and supportive interaction that helps to regulate our bodies, optimize our inner resources, and positively shift our nerve state.

For example, if your friend is emotional or upset over something, and you offer to cheer them up by talking with them on the phone or spending some quality time with them, you are co-regulating with them. They are in a more stressed or shutdown response nerve state, you are anchored in your relaxation response, and you are helping to lift their spirits and move them into a relaxation response state. Once they are back in that state, they will have an easier time self-regulating. This can backfire if the person you're trying to co-regulate with doesn't have a strong relaxation response or isn't safely anchored in it. It can lead to dysregulation, the opposite of co-regulation, in the form of reliance on others to access the relaxation response. The most common form of this is codependency when a person can't regulate themselves and constantly relies on co-regulation from another. On the other hand, when you're interacting with someone negative, nasty, and a drain, or someone who may be stressed, defensive, or frozen in their stress response, they are dysregulating you. This is why it's so important to surround yourself with the right people while you're on this journey toward your healthiest life.

When we're anchored in our relaxation response, we are compassionate, empathetic, and can connect with others. We can also use this nerve state to help others who are in stress or shutdown states to activate their relaxation response in co-regulation. Think of co-regulation as a way to gently disarm someone who is defensive, stressed, or hypervigilant. We use this system to make eye contact, authentically smile at one another, coo to a baby, talk to our animals, and sing lullabies. Our inner world determines many of our aspects, including our vulnerabilities. There's an overall contradiction in that people who seem to be really great at self-regulating themselves. They can do so because they have had more chances to properly coregulate with others. Their nervous system in a sense cultivates resilience by their history of "nerve training."

What exactly is self-regulation? To pause or think before reacting or to easily control your emotions, thoughts, and behavior to reach long-term goals, that's what it means to self-regulate. To be able to cheer yourself up after being disappointed or being able to fully express yourself authentically in line with your personal values. All humans need to be coregulated and the experience of coregulation, especially earlier in life, helps a person to self-regulate when they can't co-regulate. When you aren't co-regulated in early life (unmet needs, childhood trauma, attachment trauma, etc), your inner capacity to self-regulate is dramatically ruined and your behavior can be extremely disruptive. An adult with weak and untrained self-regulation skills may lack self-confidence, self-esteem, and self-awareness. Not only that, but they also may have trouble handling stress, anxiety, and frustration. This could be expressed as anger or anxiety, and in more severe cases, may be diagnosed as a mental health issue. We all need to feel safe in the arms of another appropriate mammal, although some people co-regulate more effectively with their pets than with their spouses.

Some service or emotional support animals have a purpose beyond performing tasks. They help people co-regulate. If you are a pet (mammals) owner, you know exactly how they feel because they show it all over their bodies and with their faces. Don't you love your pet like it was one of your own children? When they feel happy and safe, they instantly get closer to you and cuddle. They become more energetic, playful, and look you in the eye. Their eyes, ears, and tails all express how safe they feel. Our nervous system picks up their safety cues and this causes activation of safety within us.

The co-regulation from a dog, cat, or other mammalian pet is just like from another human. It's spontaneous. When we're in our relaxation response or state of safety, we instantaneously give cues of safety to those around us. It's not a conscious, planned thing; it's just something that mammals do passively for each other. How does it feel when your pet passes away or you lose them? Terrible, right? It's because of the lost love, social support, and co-regulation. If you can purposefully surround yourself with safe humans and pets, you're going to increase the number of safety cues coming your way. Safe friends, safe family, safe coworkers, and even safe pets. Co-regulation is passive, but you can increase those passive cues and chances for neuroceptions of safety.

I think what we truly crave besides balance, is safety, and co-regulation is our fundamental approach to experience and feel safe. Safety is our relaxation response nerve state that allows us to feel calm, connected, and conscious. Our body is always speaking to us and in its own language. Even though our language has assigned meaning to our different bodily reactions, we can't always be sure what we assume is happening is 100% accurate. What our body needs is to be co-regulated, and we can't do it on our own. Safety leads to closeness and touch, and closeness may have been adaptive for survival. Self-regulation is built upon co-regulation. Some of the self-regulation skills we hope kids have first come from co-regulation at home and with peers. When it comes to successful co-regulation, we have to have at least one safe person that is anchored in their relaxation response and can tolerate being triggered and shifting back and forth to different nerve states. Someone who isn't frozen in a nerve state and remains flexible in them. This can be trained, and this is why I created Innervals™ to help you do just that.

I am by default a giver and I often give when I don't have anything to give in the first place. Chronically giving past the point of full depletion. I habitually help, give, and overextend myself to the point of infection, illness, and disease. Committing suicide is one of the most selfish things that a person can do. Now that I had this outpouring of support and social love, how could I possibly kill myself? There would be so many people at my funeral. I couldn't bring myself to do it anymore. Something in me changed internally after being so powerfully co-regulated. It was an instant reset, simply from the love and social support that I received. And so, I began chronicling my journey on social media, set up a PayPal account where people could donate to help me with expenses, and I documented every single day of my cancer journey with family, friends, fans, and strangers all cheering me on and sending me unconditional love. A massive pipeline of authentic co-regulation. It all made SUCH a difference!

STAY STRONG

Until it touches your life, cancer is a remote fear that you hope you or your loved ones never get. You see it on TV, ads, the Internet, but it never becomes REAL for you until you or someone you know is struggling with it. Cancer can also be an awkward thing. What do you say to someone who has cancer? Do you give them hope? Do you say some cheesy inspirational quote? Technically you shouldn't really "say" anything. People process health issues differently. You should ask if they need anything or tell them that they are in your thoughts. They need to be co-regulated and supported. They don't need to be reminded that they have cancer or talk about the details of it. They also don't need you to project your worries or fear of their potential outcome. It's not about how you feel, it's about how they feel. And they can only self-heal if they are feeling supported, loved, and co-regulated. They also don't need to hear your advice. It's always great to share resources that you think will be helpful, but only when you are asked. People battling cancer are already so overwhelmed as it is. Some people want to say something and be encouraging and don't know what to say or how to help someone going through their cancer challenge. I'll tell you what worked for me. Out of everything that people said to me, what resonated most with me were two words: STAY STRONG.

So simple, yet so powerfully effective. Every time someone would say those two words to me, I would feel a surge of motivational energy shoot through my entire body that invigorated, motivated, and captivated each of my trillions of cells. It instantaneously made me feel better. Strong is what I had always been and would be again. I would reassure myself of it and practice it until it was true. When I was depressed, down, and feeling defeated, their words were like a crutch, a ray of hope shining in my dark tunnel of despair. The love and social support that you have the power to give through words or actions is multidimensional, multifunctional, and multidirectional. Send your love to people you know who are sick. I like to say, "I'm sending you well wishes for a speedy recovery" or "I'm sending you healing energy." You want it to be supportive, uplifting, and mood-boosting. The worst thing you could do is ask "How are you?" How the f*ck do you think a person is that is being challenged by cancer? Probably not that great. You want whatever you say or send to lift them to their relaxation response so that they can heal faster. It will help them get better by clearing out any energy blocks, congestion, or imbalances and helps them shift back to a better balance.

I didn't realize it at the time, but it turns out receiving love and social support from others has been shown to really benefit people who are sick.[254] A few studies have shown that people with more social connections live a lot longer than those with fewer social connections[255] and have lower cancer rates.[256] Love and social support are so health-enhancing, that it's been shown to be more beneficial than exercising, nutrition, or not drinking or smoking. Isn't that crazy? Close communities that relax and do regular activities together generally live longer, even if they have an unhealthy lifestyle.

Specifically, with cancer, having a strong social support system has been shown to lengthen survival time by an average of 25% and reduce the risk of dying by 70%. Love and strong social support in life are what matters most, regardless of if you are sick or not. Strong social support is two close friends, thirty acquaintances, or one life partner. From the scientific perspective, what has been found by researchers analyzing MRIs, blood tests, and saliva is that receiving love and social support produces an increase in holistic healing hormones like dopamine, serotonin, and other endorphins. So, it makes sense why sending love and social support is healing. Send love and make sure you allow yourself to also receive your own self-love. Forgive yourself, you're doing the best that you can in life with your given circumstances and limited inner and outer resources.

Even though I received a big outpouring of support, it hurt me that a few of my so-called "good friends" never reached out, visited me, or said anything about what happened to me at all. New York is chock full of fake friends, friends with benefits, or friends who can do something for you or get you in somewhere. You can be in a room surrounded by hundreds of people and still feel so alone. I did that all the time in NYC. I was popular, was always invited to different events and parties, but most of those people weren't really my friends. They loved my energy and liked me being around. To some, I was their personal jester that loved when I entertained them with my thunderous laugh and antics. I was their light that filled their dark, dank, and deep void. I was their super co-regulator, and slowly it was killing me. I'm a super empath, highly sensitive to energy. Empaths attract nasty narcissists; it's the most common dysfunctional social relationship there is, whether it be family, friends, or lovers. A narcissist is someone with an inflated sense of importance, a deep need for excessive attention and admiration, and possesses a lack of empathy for others. Something tells me that someone popped into your head as you read that description.

HUMAN HARMONY

How much love do you have in your life? Who supports you? How are your personal social relationships? Do you unconditionally love or feel loved? Human harmony requires us to be social beings; it's programmed into our DNA. At conception, a fetus needs the mother as a host to survive, grow, and thrive. From the second we come into this world, we instinctively depend on another human being to co-regulate us and this is the case for the rest of our lives.[257] But that social bond goes deeper than just functionally taking care of someone.[258]

As you've learned from the previous sections, social support is literally scientifically proven to help in cases of infection, illness, or disease. These studies also show that the love from family, friends, significant others, and even pets, helps your body in a more complex, connected, and complimentary way. Giving love and receiving love helps your body heal, which is why we do it automatically. This may also, to some extent, explain the often touted "power of prayer." When people are praying for you, it means they care. That care translates to a boost for your natural immune system.

Loneliness can be a covert killer while love and social support can be an immunity booster. Loneliness increases your cortisol (stress) levels and suppresses your immune system.[138] In addition to social support and receiving (and giving) love, physical contact is incredibly important to holistic health healing. Cuddling, snuggling, and hugging with family, friends, loved ones, or pets releases a surge of healing hormones like oxytocin (the cuddle hormone) that help your body heal in many ways.[259] You normally do this instinctually around people that you are comfortable with, but giving someone a massage, laying on them, or putting your arm around their shoulder stimulates healing. So, for all of you promiscuous people out there, know that you are doing some GOOD in this world! Healing b*tches with your touch. So, hug someone, even if they are shady or you don't really like them, because you are really doing it for yourself.

Love is a high-vibrating, high-frequency, and high-healing form of energy and when you give that to a person who has an infection, illness, or disease, it helps their body holistically heal. Most people don't expect love energy to have a manifesting effect on their physical body, but if emotions are energy and your thoughts and emotions are sent to every single one of your cells via neurotransmitters (molecule messengers,) wouldn't it make sense that love and positive emotional energy strengthen your biology?

Unfortunately, the flip side of that is when you receive (and give) negative, hurtful, and low social energy, it hurts you by elevating your stress response, drains your energy, sometimes causes anxiety, and suppresses your immune system making you more prone to health issues. If you wake up feeling sad and encounter people who say mean, nasty, and hurtful things to you, how do you think that's going to make you feel? Sadder, right? You are either helping people or harming people with your social energy. There's no neutral exchange. No matter what, always remember that what you feel emotional, you are dramatically boosting your immune system up or burning it down. You are either hurting or harming people emotionally, physically, mentally, and biochemically. Love, physical touch, and social support energy will always give your immune system a little recharge to detox terrible toxins, holistically heal, repair your cells, and fight infections, illnesses, and chronic diseases.

Self-Reflection Innerval™

In order to unconsciously activate your relaxation response in your environment, there need to be more safety cues present than danger cues. Where are three places where you feel the safest? Who are three people who make you feel safe? What three things (including pets) make you feel safe?

1. ....

2. ....

3. ....

28 //

E.M.P.O.W.E.R.E.D. HEALTH: 50 DAYS TO COMPLETE REMISSION

I had gone through three different intensive chemo protocols that lasted three weeks each out of the six I was supposed to complete. I had also made a variety of holistic changes that I will go into detail about soon, and now it was time to go in for a PET-CT scan, to see the progress of the rare form of cancer and get an update on my stage and likely prognosis. The PET-CT scan is accompanied by a substantial radiation dose and increased cancer risk. Oncologists downplay the risks of getting them because they say that the risk of complications from cancer is greater than the risks from a mere CT scan. Why would you expose yourself to radiation for a high risk of getting more cancer later and more possible complications?

According to Harvard Medical School, a single chest x-ray exposes a person to about 0.1 mSv (millisievert) or the same amount of ultraviolet radiation people are exposed to naturally from the sun over 10 days. A PET/CT scan exposes you to about 25 mSv of radiation, which is equal to about 8 years of average background radiation exposure.[260] Had I known this beforehand, I would've passed on the PET/CT scan. Nonetheless, before my scan I had posted and joked on social media that morning, wondering what if I went in and the doctor was like "Holy sh*t, you're cured!" Ha, ha.

I stared blankly at my PET-CT scan sheet and tried my hardest to translate and decipher what the scan found, often Googling the terms I wasn't too sure about. The most disruptive statement that stood out to me was in plain English: "The disease has resolved in all areas." At first, it was confusing, I thought to myself, that can't be right, or what does that mean? Maybe it's talking about something else. I was only halfway through the abusive chemo protocol, I still felt awful, and I looked even worse (I thought I did anyway).

To be clear, the doctors had not recommended the chemo treatment to CURE the cancer I was struggling with. Their expectation and the "best-case scenario" was that they were simply elongating what would still be a short and diseased life. So for those who may doubt that this outcome was the result of my own approach, or may write it off saying that the chemo had simply cured me quickly, just know that not even the doctors thought that full recovery was possible, even with the chemo. I wasn't supposed to be superficially cured, let alone respond well to anything, and I was staring at a scan report that said I was superficially cured. They weren't trying for a superficial cure with my treatment plan, they were prolonging my life longer than a week, trying to ease my symptoms and slow the progression of the disease, and it seemed as if all of those outcomes had been achieved and more. I asked a few friends to see if I was crazy because after all I was going through, I probably did go crazy quite a few times! They seemed to confirm that it did indeed say that I was in complete remission or cured. But my doctor never told me that. He just told me "excellent" and led me to book the next round of chemo.

Before the severe anger at this lack of transparency and forced chemo set in, I took another mindful Innerval™ and as soon as I made my decision, a cold wave of defiance swept over me. I was officially over my doctor. I rejected him and his opinions completely. I fired him, or what I thought was firing, because you can't really fire a doctor, but I made it known on social media that he was FIRED. Whatever! I guess it made me feel better at the time. The most important thing to me was, HOLY SH*T I'M F*CKING CURED! I had literally joked about it on social media, and it had become my actual reality. It seemed unreal. But it was very, very real.

Although I changed my mind many times, I had ultimately chosen to go through chemical chemo. After seeing the results of this scan, however, I knew that I could possibly beat it on my own. From there, I switched my focus to detoxing my body from the chemical chemo. Though it may have aided my quick recovery, it also had a number of negative effects on my body. During the chemo, I dramatically changed what I was eating and the way I was thinking about my situation. Later in this chapter, I'll give you the exact program I created with health pillars that allowed me to heal so quickly. To summarize, though, I took herbs and completed other natural therapies without the knowledge of my doctors. Walking my talk of taking a holistic approach, I also had to do some deep-dive trauma release by finally processing, digesting, and touching upon the hidden emotions from my unresolved traumas from childhood and beyond. By the time I reached complete remission in 50 days, my doctors wrote me off as a "spontaneous remission" and said that it wasn't such a big deal that I was in complete remission. They even wanted me to complete MORE chemical chemo rounds and maybe finish the whole treatment. They wanted me to keep on killing my now healthy cells.

There is nothing spontaneous about fighting for your life, taking responsibility for your actions, and doing the intense, deep, and consistent inner and outer work required to holistically heal from any disease, let alone aggressive rare cancer. This was not a spontaneous remission. Doctors like to make cases like mine seem like they are strange, weird, or miraculous. They ignore them completely in order to delegitimize them. We are F*CKING LEGITIMATE and cases like mine simply didn't succumb to the pressures of conventional doctors and their medicine. Can you imagine what it feels like to be told you have a week to live and then reach complete remission in 50 days, only for your doctor to be like "meh, no big deal, come in for your next chemo." Spontaneous remission cases like mine aren't even included in the cure rate statistics of cancer cases. All those fancy statistics that you see on cancer charity websites, EXCLUDE anyone who has healed from cancer naturally or who didn't follow through with the prescribed protocol. They only INCLUDE people who treat cancer with chemical chemo, radiation, or surgery.

ACTIVATE RAPID SELF-HEALING

How did I self-heal so fast? The answer isn't as simple as saying I did this one thing or that one thing. Sorry, life isn't that simple, and your body isn't that reductive. There wasn't one reason that I became sick and expressed cancer, just like there isn't just one way that I was able to activate rapid self-healing. To help you understand what I did so that you can potentially apply the same principles to your own health issue or challenge, I created a coaching program called E.M.P.O.W.E.R.E.D. health, and later I'll go over the details and break down the major components of it. Research shows that there are 9 different interrelated aspects of optimal health and well-being. In addition to the 9 pillars of health I used as holistic guidance, there were three main top-level ideas that I applied to the different pillars of health.

My focus was on me, not on my cancer, my healing ability, and modulating, not boosting my immune system. I used a synergy of strategies. I knew several strategies were more powerful together so I combined as many as I could. I trained my nerves and stimulated my vagus nerve as much as possible to make sure that I stayed strong and anchored in my relaxation response nerve state, my optimal safe, social, and self-healing state. When my stress response was triggered, I knew that would only delay or stop my healing no matter what I was doing, and I would consciously try to leave that state. The power to master your stress, adapt to adversity, and activate rapid self-healing is already inside of you, you just have to train your nerves to use it. Optimal health, fighting chronic health issues, and preventing disease isn't just a pill, a detox cleanse, a yoga class, a tonic, or some ridiculous diet your great-great-grandfather did. It's resetting your energy, rebalancing your inner environment, and doing multiple methods, protocols, and strategies together in synergy.

I used the power of synergy to trigger my own self-healing, and you can too. This principle is used in the real world in multiple industries. Belief, motivation, planning, strategy, action, and execution have the potential to create many desirable outcomes. But if you were to break them up individually how far would you get? If you just had belief, but didn't take action, planned for something, or didn't have the motivation to start and finish? Or if you just took action, but with no plan, belief, or strategy to do whatever you wanted to do? So let's apply this same principle to health and healing. YOU have the power to biologically change how you look, feel, move, and heal, using synergy to reset your energy and rebalance your biology. One strategy, method, or approach is strong by itself, but its power can increase ten-fold when combined with others. Your healing, happiness, holistic health, career, relationships, friendships, and every single aspect of your entire life, all desperately depend on one thing: the state of your energy, which dictates the state of your biology.

So why is it so hard for people to stay healthy and avoid chronic disease? Money. It doesn't talk, it screams like a baby at two in the morning. Most of the things that you need to do to get and stay healthy aren't that profitable. Drugs and sugar-laden foods are powerfully profitable. If the billions of people in the world were walking around healthy, happy, and in harmony, would the medical, fast food, and other industries be making money? F*ck no, they'd probably go out of business and could no longer post superficial social media posts with the hashtag "#blessed". There isn't just one reason why it's hard for you to get to and stay at optimal health, there are several reasons, and it's not just you. Now I'm not saying just give up and lead a lackluster life of laziness, lethargy, and loathing— you're better than that. Otherwise, you wouldn't be right here with me, listening to what I'm laying down. But, look at me now…I am saying that I'm just as tired of the bullsh*t as you are, and I want to help you in the most efficient, effective, and easy-to-follow way possible.

I want to empower you holistically and inspire you to live a happier, healthier, and longer life. To help you easily fulfill your birthright, I created an easy-to-follow roadmap using the 9 pillars of health. I use the word E.M.P.O.W.E.R.E.D. as an acronym to represent the 9 pillars of health. Research shows that these are the 9 essential processes that you should be addressing on your journey to optimal health and wellness. You can't continue to eat the junk, or sleep 4 hours at night, or fill your body with tons of toxins, or have a bunch of emotional turmoil, and still be healthy.

E = Eating

M = Micronutrients

P = Probiotics

O = Oxygen

W = Water

E = Emotions

R = Regeneration

E = Exercise

D = Detox

Here's what the acronym means:

- E - EATING. Nutrition provides the human body with the raw materials, fuel, and information it needs to energize, survive, thrive, and self-heal.

- M - MICRONUTRIENTS. Micronutrients are the vitamins and minerals that the body requires for optimal health. Think of micronutrients as the tiny tools that your cells need to survive, energize, thrive, and self-heal. Because of unhealthy eating habits, most of us are heavily deficient in the basic nutrients that our body needs.

- P - PROBIOTICS/PREBIOTICS/PECTIN. 70% of your immune system is in your gut and your gut bacteria balance and wall lining can either make or break your overall health and well-being.

- O - OXYGEN. Your breathing patterns can either trigger optimal health or fuel dysfunction and disease.

- W - WATER. Water is one of the most critical elements of life. The average adult should be around 60% water, but most become chronically dehydrated and drop to 45 to 50% water creating system dysfunction and chronic health issues.

- E - EMOTIONS. Emotions are energy and directly affect your immunity. Positive emotions and good energy help facilitate health, while negative emotions and bad energy harm health.

- R - REGENERATION. If you don't rest, relax, and recuperate, your body isn't able to get into the parasympathetic nervous state, your safe, social, and self-healing state.

- E - EXERCISE. Exercise and movement help pump toxic fluid from your lymphatic system.

- D – DETOX. Your drainage funnel is a metaphor for your detox pathways that include your cells, organs, lymphatic system, liver, bile ducts, and colon. Every toxin you eat, breathe, and touch gets metabolized through this funnel, including dietary fats and hormones, and these toxins are then excreted out of your body through urine, bile, and stool. The "size" of your funnel is determined by genetics and stress. Although you are born with a specific funnel size, your diet, lifestyle, and environmental factors can expose you to a variety of harmful toxins, which not only "clog" your funnel, but also cause it to get "smaller." This leads to an increased load of toxins AND a decreased ability to filter through these toxins. When your funnel is full or backed up, the toxins cannot leave the body making it hard for you to naturally detox them. Instead, they recirculate through the system, causing toxic burden. This increased toxin load triggers an alarm system, which manifests as bodily symptoms.

All of these pillars are powerful, but I can't stress enough that if I wasn't training my nerves doing different Innervals™, I wouldn't have been in my safe, social, and self-healing state for these things to work at the speed that they did. You could be doing everything right. Eating healthy, sleeping enough, exercising, taking supplements, taking prescription medication, etc but if you don't have a balanced nervous system, you will never heal, or healing will happen at a glacial pace. You can't heal if you're frozen in your stress or shutdown response, and many people are unknowingly stuck, going in circles, or on a plateau. This is one of the reasons why I chose to become a health coach. Not only did I want to fully understand how I triggered my own self-healing, but I wanted to be able to help others spontaneously heal or prevent them from having a chronic health issue at all.

What's a health coach? When you're trying to optimize your health or reverse a chronic health issue, more information isn't always helpful; it can actually be more confusing. A Netflix documentary could be telling you to swear off all meat while several podcasts could be pitching eating only meat to stimulate dramatic healing. The issue for most people isn't the information, the issue is your personal relationship to the information. What most people need is a personalized action plan that takes into account their inner individuality (ID) and someone that can hold them accountable for it. Your blood type, saliva, hormonal levels, micronutrient balance, and gut health are all important factors of your Inner ID. When it comes to your eating experience or "diets," one size does not fit all. A food that energizes me could make you sick or trigger an immune response.

This is where health coaches like me come in. A health coach supports you in creating specific action steps for many areas in your life including nutrition, sleep/regeneration optimization, exercise, relationships, stress reduction, and more. We are an essential member of your medical team, that most people are missing, and that will help you understand the bigger picture with a more holistic (mind, body, emotions, soul) outlook. We guide you in prioritizing the diet and lifestyle factors that will have the largest impact on your health and do it in a very compassionate, efficient, and personalized way.

From Master's degrees in nutrition, registered dietitians, or certifications in health coaching from a variety of accredited organizations, institutes, or universities, health coaches have respected credentials to help you be your holistic best self. A health coach is trained and skilled in behavior change, mindset training, and nutrition. Especially if you're battling chronic health issues, studies show that have a health coach can be a game-changer for you. The reality is that 60 percent of adult Americans have at least one chronic health issue and the majority of them are lifestyle-driven, preventable, and reversible. A healthy sidekick is just the type of motivation and help that some people need to find their way back to optimal health.

In a 2018 systematic literature review conducted by the American Journal of Lifestyle Medicine, of 11 controlled trials investigating the effectiveness of health and wellness coaching, 82 percent of trials found that those who utilized a coach found improvement in nutrition biomarkers and eating behaviors. The most common improvements were seen in weight, blood pressure, and quality of dietary intake.[261] Aside from nutritional improvements, health coaching has been proven to support significant changes in exercise as well. While many older people do their best to exercise, studies show that when people over 60 work with a health coach they are more likely to regularly engage in physical activity and also report secondary improvements in mobility, quality of life, and mood.

According to Parsley Health, for specific health issues, health coaching has shown to be effective in improving outcomes for patients with diabetes, obesity, chronic pain, high cholesterol, and hypertension. Patients working with health coaches are more likely to comply with taking recommended medications, have reduced rates of hospital admissions, and report feeling more empowered in making changes to their health to improve their quality of life.[262]

A health coach can help you with everything from navigating a tricky restaurant menu, to initiating a self-care routine into a busy morning schedule or providing you specific resources for recipes, workouts, or mindfulness programs. As an example, if you were having trouble figuring out which foods were triggering your IBS symptoms or making you feel bloated and constipated, your health coach could run through your daily dietary intake or review a 3-day food journal to help pinpoint triggers for your symptoms. Beyond the creation of tailored goals and the arsenal of personalized resources, you can message your health coach 365 days of the year with any questions, concerns, or updates that may come up. This ensures that you receive the support and accountability needed to maintain inspiration and commitment to the lifestyle changes you're making.

To personalize your experience further, a health coach breaks through the information, misinformation, and noise of all the different recommendations you read about on a daily basis to help you prioritize the changes that will actually yield the most positive results. For example, a health coach can talk you through current wellness trends you may have questions about such as intermittent fasting, ketogenic, paleo, or 100% plant-based diets. Together, you and your health coach can contextualize these practices to your health goals to assess what's ideal for your particular body and routine. Ultimately, the goal is to empower you with the knowledge you need for long-term, sustainable wellness—something that we know can look uniquely different for every person. If you're feeling lost, stuck, frustrated, and like you're going in circles for any health issue you may be facing,

I can help empower you to gracefully get through it. I would advocate for having a health coach in general, but I am also always welcoming new clients to my roster! If you'd like to work with me personally, please feel free to contact me through my website: http://mariogodiva.com.

EYE CIRCLE R MOTOR COMBO. (3 minutes)

1. EYE CIRCLE MOTOR INNERVAL™ // 30 seconds.

Start moving your eyeballs in a big circle to the right as slow as you possibly can. Do this for 30 seconds or 15 circles if you don't have a timer. Relax your eyes back to center before you start the next Innerval™.

2. CORE BREATHING INNERVAL™ // 30 seconds.

Take long, slow, and deep inhales and take longer, slower, and deeper exhales for 30 seconds or 3 times each if you don't have a timer. As you inhale for 3 seconds your core goes out, and as you exhale for 6 seconds your core goes in.

3. Repeat 2 times

STIMULATION. The phrenic nerves, vagus nerves, motor cortex (7), and posterior thoracic nerves.

29 //

RUNNING FROM RELAPSE

For decades I was frozen and had many emotional, mental, and biological layers of a deep freeze. It was Interval Mindfulness™ and its various Innervals™, consistency, and taking a holistic approach that started to thaw me out and pave the way for expeditious self-healing. Even though I rapidly activated self-healing physically, I had to maintain that outcome by constantly focusing on my mental and emotional health. I had to focus on all parts of me or the whole. Just because you may temporarily thaw out doesn't mean that you can't freeze again. Healing is not a one-and-done experience like most people think. That is why a cancer recovery is referred to as remission, because it can return any time. Healing is never a finish line, it's a never-ending hunt with random breaks, and you're the bait. If you have ever battled any type of chronic health issue, addiction, or any other health struggle, it never is really "over"; you'll always be running from relapse. The good news is, the more conscious and healthier your lifestyle is, the further you will stay away from relapse.

Healing takes maintenance, consistency, and sustainability. There's a beauty in all of it when we can live and learn. It seems mundane to spectacular, customary to chaotic, and heartwarming to heartbreaking. It's a journey full of ups and downs, celebrations and disappointments, positive thoughts and negative thoughts, and so much more. Healing isn't sexy, trendy, or fancy. Healing is raw, uncomfortable, unpredictable, and takes constant work. It's extremely important to accept, acknowledge, and truly understand, that no matter what type of healing happens to you or how long you have been on your healing journey, there's always a chance that you can "unheal." We see this all the time in the real world. People view healing as a destination, get there by reaching a certain goal, and then regress often 10 times faster than they healed. People who heal themselves and become sober, only to relapse and head back to rehab, people who heal from a chronic health issue, only to have it sprout back up out of the blue. People that heal from

351

a toxic relationship, then jump right back into another toxic one. What you heal, can always be unhealed faster.

We are born, we live, and then we die. How long we live or the quality of the life that we live is never promised or guaranteed. One major rule of Mother Nature is that when you're unhealthy, you die faster. The only exception to this is when there is some sort of accident or murder that triggers unexpected and sudden death. Whether you're an animal, plant, or human, if you don't have the inner resources AND the external environment to survive, you die, whether you want to die or not. It's really as simple as that. If your health deteriorates without any intervention to reverse the degeneration, you die. We are all guaranteed to die at some point, but quicker death comes to those who indulge in unhealthy lifestyles, habits, and behaviors. This is evidence-based and people know this, yet they still try and negotiate with Mother Nature anyway.[263] When it comes to optimal health, you can't fool, lie, or gaslight Mother Nature. She always knows because your body always keeps the receipts. And when death comes knocking at your door ready to take you home, no amount of excuses, explanations, hiding, denying, or lying is going to stop death from doing what death does.

When you're on the fast track to death, your body is extremely patient and gives you TONS of warning signs, symptoms, lessons, and opportunities to get off that fatal fast track. Sometimes people hear the inner whispers, see the warning signs, learn the lessons, and make dramatic changes to their lifestyle, habits, and behaviors, and most of the time they don't. Sometimes, despite the best care and significant progress made in addressing chronic health issues, they come back. Whether it be cancer, autoimmunity, heart disease, or any other chronic health issue, it can always come back. When this happens, it's called a recurrence or relapse.

It's sadly all too common a story when someone seems to beat cancer only to have it recur and recur again until cancer takes their life. I was worried about this, and as I started my journey back to optimal health, the anxiety and stress were at times crippling and ever constant. As soon as I received the all-clear and left the hospital, guess what I did? I quickly jumped headfirst back into the real world and my old habits in NYC like nothing had happened. Just like I had done before I had cancer, I started shifting between my stress and shutdown responses, going through the motions but never truly being present. I was training clients and teaching classes like nothing was wrong; I was training extremely hard trying to get back the half of my body weight in muscle I lost; I was engaging in social activities, dinners, parties, and events like I was completely fine; and I even found myself at a few music festivals partying the night away. Everything I did was in an effort to cope with my anxiety and stress from my traumatic experiences and my fear of relapse. It felt great at the time! Everyone was so happy to see me and grateful that I didn't lose the struggle with cancer, and so I rode that high, not realizing the habits I was falling into.

Whenever you experience or overcome a chronic health issue, two things have to inevitably change for you to be successful and not relapse. Radical changes to your inner world and your outer environment. I loved NYC with all my heart, but the environment I engaged with in NYC contributed to me becoming sick. The noise, pollution, and never-ending chaos of the city. The always-on, busy, on-the-go nonstop glorified grind and hustle. The flaky, non-committal, and superficial friendships with people who were more concerned about what you could do for them. The fact that you could be making $60,000 a year and still be in poverty from the cost of living in NYC. Being constantly influenced and corrupted by neurotic, panicked, and chaos-addicted people who were unconsciously frozen in their stress response. I could go on and on, but I knew in my gut that if I stayed in NYC, I was going to relapse. The first time around, I ignored my body's inner intelligence and self-feedback signals; this time around, I was hearing what my body was telling me loud and clear. "Get. The. F*ck. Out. Of. Here. Fool!!!" I had to leave NYC. But was I ready to listen?

One of the most prominent people who kept me on my healing journey, even when I repeatedly kept getting off, was my dear friend and naturopath, Dr. Alexa Carlson.[264] The allopathic model of medicine almost killed me and even after I was in complete remission, the doctors wanted to keep treating me. For what? They instilled the fear of cancer recurrence in me and their solution was to just keep filling me full of toxic, expensive, and immune system killing chemical chemo basically for life, to make sure that it never came back. Despite the high risk of me not completely coming back (to life), I knew that training my nerves and taking a holistic approach was directly responsible for my rapid self-healing, and so I set out to find someone to follow up with who didn't want to keep filling me with pills and poison.

I was still training a few clients and two of my main clients, Christine and Patricia, sisters who were successful powerhouses on Wall Street, had always told me about this amazing naturopath, hypnotherapist, spiritual, and well-being doctor Alexa. I heard so many fascinating stories of Dr. Alexa Carlson. She has this quantum biofeedback machine that does remote health screenings and communicates with your cells. In quantum biofeedback, a flow of energy connects every cell, every organ, every thought, and every emotion. The ease or the interference of that flow of energy reflects a profound system of communication that demonstrates the mind/body intelligence. A Quantum Biofeedback machine is an easy-to-operate computer interface that provides safe, gentle, and effective energetic programs. It receives biofeedback messages from your body that shows the root cause of different imbalances. It sends a signal remotely to your cells, your cells respond, and that response is measured against 7,000 different bodily stressors.

Using this machine and program, she can give you the root cause of many health ailments, and release trapped stress and trauma in your cells for healing naturally without chemical prescriptions. It's basically like a remote biological tune-up that makes you feel all tingly inside. She also recommends natural and homeopathic remedies for whatever health challenges you're facing. Symptoms have a root cause, and it's powerful to be able to know exactly what the root cause is of your symptoms so that you can make corrections before those symptoms cascade into something else. Western medicine doesn't treat root causes, it goes after the symptoms which can have people going in circles delaying their healing for the rest of their life. I would hear how Dr. Carlson would remotely destress my clients and they would heal faster, feel better, and think clearer. Her treatment was the perfect complement for my coaching. She was also a spiritual therapist and energy healer that channels to the Divine angelic realm via this angel called Matreail. I know it sounds very woo woo, but I soon came to find out that woo woo or not, she was the real f*cking deal. She's also just a beautiful human being that authentically wants to help people and is really in tune and touch with nature and life, a quality I had scarcely experienced with doctors of western medicine. Quantum biofeedback stress relief, emotional and trauma release therapy, hypnotherapy, quantum therapy, traditional naturopathy, holistic therapist, life coach, angelic channeling, and nutritional counseling are just a few of her specialties and why I call here a one-stop healing shop. Dr. Alexa Carlson became my healing crutch and I talked to her monthly and sometimes twice a month. My healing journey was full of ups and downs. At my lowest points, her approach is what led me to back away from the ledge.

I mention her because of this. No matter who you are or who you think you are, you need some type of authentic support when you're on a healing journey. Whether it be professional, social, relational, or any combination of those, it's imperative that you recognize that authentic healing requires genuine support. Why? Healing isn't easy, it's dark, painful, and miserable. Post-traumatic growth (PTG), the positive, powerful, and life-changing shifts in thinking, living, and relating to the world after experiencing trauma, adversity, or other life challenges doesn't happen in an instant. You aren't going to wake up one day and be like, aha, I'm recovered! Healing and PTG happen in stages and it's kind of like the stock market. It can be trending up or trending down. Some people can say that it's bullish, but there will always be volatility, uncertainty, some dips, and corrections. That's the same process as healing and growing from trauma, adversity, and other life's challenges. Human beings are resilient. We are the product of millions of years of evolution and adaptation; it's what we do. But when it comes to trauma, adversity, and life's challenges, we tend to get frozen, and that hinders our growth potential. The more resourced (inner and outer support) a person is and the less trauma they have experienced as a whole in their lifetime, the more opportunity they have to be resilient and bounce back with ease.

You must have some type of genuine support from a person or group of people who are going to give you more of a big picture view. Even if you feel like you don't "need" support, you have to train yourself to seek support when you feel like it's sometimes too much to bear. Even though I was capable of rapidly self-healing, it took support and a map for me to sustain that healing long term. You already have the tools inside of you, but tools are useless if you don't know how to use them or where you are going on your healing journey. All the tools in the world don't matter if you have no idea where the f*ck you are going or how to put something together! I chose Dr. Alexa Carlson, but you can choose a doctor (preferably functional, holistic, or DO) you trust, therapist, psychologist, or whoever can support you becoming a healthier version of you in the least toxic way. I still talk to her today and highly recommend her as a powerful resource on your healing journey. It can be overwhelming navigating chronic health issues and it's good to get a second or third opinion from someone whose first line of offense isn't to prescribe prescription pills.

HOLISTIC HEALTH

I have mentioned from the beginning of this book that taking a holistic approach to my health gave me the roadmap to rapidly self-healing. But it wasn't until this part of my journey, six months into complete remission and working with Alexa, that I truly learned about and understood what holistic health meant, so I want to share that fuller definition with you now as well. Holistic Health is a whole-person approach to health, happiness, and healing that includes mind, body, emotions, and beliefs. Rather than focusing on illness or certain parts of the body, a holistic approach considers the whole person and how they interact with their environment. Holistic health reminds you that the whole is made up of interconnected and interdependent parts. When one part is disrupted, neglected, or out of balance, it directly affects the other parts. This approach, however, requires that you accept responsibility for your own well-being, and this is where most people go for the "quick fix" pill or strategy. Western medicine doesn't understand the concepts of energy, frequency, and vibration and views things as purely physical, including humans. While the physical aspect is important, we aren't just physical beings. Emotions are one of the biggest and most misunderstood factors that remain unnoticed when it comes to chronic health issues. You can feel your emotional energy in every single cell of your body, yet conventional medicine doesn't acknowledge how it plays a part in your optimal health.

Today we have a national health crisis of invisible enemies. According to the CDC, six in ten adults have a chronic health issue and four in ten have two or more. They are the leading causes of death and disability and the leading drivers of the nation's 3.5 trillion in annual health care costs.[265] Chronic health issues have roots in inflammation, gut issues, nutritional deficiencies, and other physical imbalances. Chronic health issues leave most western doctors at a loss, and patients feel crazy because they have symptoms that are misunderstood. But western medicine doesn't understand that emotions and trauma cause disease. However, Chinese Medicine, Ayurveda, and other eastern modalities have always understood the role of emotions in wellness. Unresolved emotions play a role in chronic pain, chronic illness, and autoimmunity, but there's no blood test for trauma and unresolved emotions. When I encountered over 23 different doctors, not a single one asked about childhood trauma, emotional regulation, unresolved issues, or any inner wounds.

In Western medicine, diagnosis is an ending point when in reality, it should be the holistic starting point. As I've said, your mind, body, and nerves will always inner whisper before they outer scream. I know mine certainly did. Our system wants us to accept a label and use medications to manage it for life. This just disempowers the person, giving little empathy to their unique life experience. When symptoms are interrupting your daily life, it's because these inner whispers are supposed to. They're sending you an SOS message for help. They are your STARTING point and the beginning of an opportunity for self-healing.

We have been conditioned to believe that emotions and unresolved trauma are not part of disease primarily because we can't see them. Western medicine rejects anything that can't be seen, qualified, and measured. But what we can't see also matters. We can't see the sun's rays but know if we're outside for a long time we'll get sunburnt. Trauma and the emotions around it like rage, shame, and resentment are carried not only in our minds but in our bodies. Every single emotional experience you have travels to your body and if you don't process and release the emotional energy, it's stored in your body. Sensations like tightness, tension, or pain, have root causes that stem far beyond the physical, and can often be traced back to emotional triggers as well.

Chronic stress, anxiety, ruminating negativity, resentment, lack of forgiveness, gut issues, weight gain, heart disease, autoimmune issues, chronic pain, fatigue, and constantly feeling stuck are all signs that you are driving your mind, body, and nerves way out of the lines they operate best in. The million-dollar question now is: What are you going to do about it?

Holistic health is when you zoom out and not just look at one thing, it's a massive puzzle that needs to be put back together again so that you can get a better view of a person's inner individuality. This can include looking at many determinants of health like emotional health, environment, physical health, mental health, and looking at their personal beliefs or spiritual health. Who we are, why we are here, and where we are going are some of the puzzle pieces that can be obtained from our mind, body, emotions, and our experiences of life. Our present moment lives are shaped by the stories we tell ourselves and what we have experienced. We all carry layers upon layers of unconscious and conscious patterns, beliefs, emotional traumas, and experiences that shape how we view and show up in the world. Many people are tired of repeating the same patterns, cycles, and re-living the same trauma and experiences, but we don't always know how to step away from what we've always known, into a life of peace, freedom, and a life we love.

One of my favorite quotes from the scholar Hippocrates is: "It's far more important to know what person the disease has, than what disease the person has." This quote makes clear what we should already embrace: that each unique person should be treated as such when their health is being evaluated. Doesn't matter if it's from a medical professional, a functional medicine doctor, naturopathic doctor, or a qualified herbalist. Each person has a multilayered uniqueness to them and their situations. When that is considered, the professional can recommend a holistic and efficient approach to their wellness journey as opposed to the thoughtless one-size-fits-all approach that I experienced again and again.

You are a whole ecosystem with 11 major systems and made up of interrelated parts. Those systems are circulatory, renal/urinary, respiratory, integumentary (skin), endocrine, digestive, skeletal, muscular, nervous, reproductive, and immune/lymphatic systems. Systems biology 101 states that everything is connected to everything and affects everything. Your physical, mental, emotional, and belief aspects depend on each other for survival, balance, and well-being. When one is disrupted a cascade or ripple effect happens to disrupt the others as well. This is why holistic health is so important, because to truly reach optimal wellness in the physical, mental, emotional, and belief senses, we have to be viewing, practicing, and supporting the body as the incredible system it is. A company can't run efficiently without its different systems (HR, accounting, managers, executive, employees, maintenance, front office, etc.). So why approach your body with its hundreds of thousands more employees, departments, and teams a different way?

Holistic health is empowering because it puts the majority of your health in your hands by cultivating self-awareness, self-education, and self-care that helps you make mindful, informed, and healthy choices. And this is exactly where Interval Mindfulness™ plays into holistic health. Optimal health, happiness, and healing takes observation, commitment, and choices. Once you strengthen your self-awareness, you'll understand what works for you, what nourishes you as a whole, and what can trigger different health and life outcomes. What your body craves the most is balance. A holistic health approach helps you navigate your health, happiness, and healing with mindfulness to help motivate, inspire, and guide you back to balance continuously on your life's journey.

The five aspects of holistic health incorporate mental, physical, emotional, belief, and social well-being. This includes your sense of emotional well-being, the health of your body, stress levels, finances, relationships, family, social life, and your belief of connection to the universe, higher self, and/or a supreme being. Holistic health trains you to optimally live the daily human experience. When stress, illness, traffic jams, losses, breakups, and other life challenges are left to their own devices, the tendency is chaos or imbalance. It is holistic health practices like sleep, breathing, nutrition, energy balance, detox, gut health, stress management, and movement that restore balance. When you're doing the inner work and you're conscious about creating balance, your pain goes away, the mind gets clear, and you have more compassion towards yourself and others.

People who don't practice holistic health don't create a sense of wholeness or integration. They often feel disconnected, disintegrated, and divided. By starting to do this inner and outer work on your own, you begin to recognize more easily the many ways people around you are doing the very same thing. Emotional trauma is one of the most overlooked things when it comes to your health, yet science shows us that it's directly and powerfully linked to it. Doing the inner work by loving and caring for yourself will provide many benefits: you have so much more to share as a silent teacher/lover with others in your relationships, even those who are less aware of the world around them. Your holistic approach helps you contribute to the world and all the people whose lives you interact with daily.

The physical, mental, emotional, and belief parts of a human being work cohesively together in order to facilitate balance and well-being for optimal health. However, a holistic approach to health and wellbeing isn't just about herbs, supplements, powders, and potions. It's about eating, exercise, consciousness, emotional wellness, and making good life choices to protect your long-term wellbeing. To be clear, accepting holistic health practices into your life does not necessarily mean casting Western medicine out completely. There have been a few unfortunate incidents reported where people have rejected Western medicine and their health has declined because they were in desperate need of medicine or treatment. Visiting the doctor or taking a prescription are perfectly acceptable practices for holistic health as one small element of a much larger whole approach. The idea is to use medicine only when necessary to avoid excess or getting too far out of balance. For instance, I've shared my experience with antibiotics with you; multiple doctors prescribed me antibiotics, and not only was I allergic to them, but I also didn't realize that although the antibiotics could help relieve an illness immediately, it sent my gut health out of balance for many years to come. Regardless of what your relation to Western medicine has been up to this point, the most important goal is to restore balance from the inside out, starting with your mental health and emotional well-being.

ACCESSING THE CODE

When I tell most people my story, their first response is always "OMG! It was a miracle!" After I display a half-smile, half-grimace, I normally respond with "It wasn't a miracle, it was my will, action, and rebalancing my nervous system." These are three key elements of taking a holistic approach. Calling what happened to me a "miracle" is also insulting to my intelligence. It's a projection of "There's no way he (a Black man) knows how to do that, it must be a miracle."

A miracle implies that I had absolutely nothing to do with my healing, that some supernatural being, powerful prayer, or unknown force magically healed me against my will (and probably in the dead of the night while I slept). I am human and have free will, and if I didn't want to heal myself, I could've said, "F*ck it!" and then let myself die, which I assure you I almost did on many occasions throughout the stages of my fight with chronic disease. Ultimately, no matter how hard you try, you can't heal someone who doesn't want to be healed, and their resistance to healing could be conscious, unconscious, and for the most part, preconditioned.

Being subject to "divine redemption" would also mean that I didn't have the mindset, motivation, and meticulous nature to do it on my own and this doesn't mean I'm not spiritual. If it was a miracle, it would mean that my decisions had nothing to do with it and my body wasn't intelligent enough to heal itself, once it got the signal, directions, or lockbox code from my nerves to do so. More importantly, the idea of a miracle implies that something outside of me had to heal me, instead of something inside of me, and this is how we've been trained to respond to the adversity that we face internally, from a young age.

Western medicine also conditions us to worry, be fearful, and focus on pathology, thus, giving infections, illnesses, and chronic disease power in our minds. They pay no attention to the prevention, the root, or what happens before the pathogenesis or expression of chronic disease. We gladly follow these conventional processes: we go to the doctor and we get an antibiotic, not realizing that antibiotics are a "nuclear approach" that cures short-term symptoms, but promotes long-term sickness by compromising our gut bacteria and immune system. They train us to believe that something on the outside will make us feel better inside. That thing on the outside is pills, procedures, or pathology protocols. When it comes to acute conditions, like a broken arm or getting into a car accident, the "something on the outside" approach may be appropriate, but for chronic conditions which have slowly built up internally over months, years, or decades (as you can clearly see what happened with me), not so much.

On an interesting note, however, besides Google searching, we aren't trained experts in pathology, so why would we question doctors otherwise? We can't and here lies the source of our dependence on conventional medicine. It is not your fault if, up until this point, you have relied solely on conventional medicine because, in our country, this is the standard and other methods are seldom discussed. Your energy flows where your focus goes, and yes, this is the ultimate law of "focused intent" when it comes to shaping our reality. When we are focused on the "outside" things that can heal our insides, our energy flows in that direction, leaving our insides starved of that energy. Why do you think it's so easy to feel "not-so-powerful" in the face of a chronic health issue?

Training people to believe that something on the outside will heal their inside is reckless because it prevents people from being fully accountable for their actions. People know that they can binge-drink, forgo sleep, be unhealthy, and run themselves down to the ground because they know if they get sick or don't feel well, something on the outside will quickly make them feel better on the inside again. What's the incentive to even giving a f*ck about being healthy when they know they can just use a pill, procedure, or protocol to make their pain, anxiety, or sickness go away? What's the incentive if they can use distraction, information, and stimulation to avoid addressing their internal issues?

How many times do you hear about people beating cancer, only for it to make a comeback? How many times do you hear about people battling or managing chronic diseases their whole life because they aren't willing to make the lifestyle overhaul that's necessary for sustained optimal health? Many people don't want to do the inner work or don't have the resources to begin doing so. There are other malevolent reasons cancer and other illnesses reoccur in some people, but anytime you have something chronic, it requires a mental, emotional, physical, and biological lifestyle change. If you make a temporary change to overcome your chronic health issue, your relief from suffering will only be temporary. You can't create a new reality with an old, damaged, and self-sabotaging personality and approach towards your life: you must retrain it.

Our bodies are intelligent, conscious, and highly adaptable but this adaptability goes both ways and can be magnificent or malevolent. Cancer was the malevolent lifestyle adaptation of my habits, choices, and behavior. I wasn't injected with cancer by a thief in the night, I wasn't poisoned with cancer by a rogue foreign country, and I didn't get cancer walking around Area 51 (I think!). Cancer grew within me, because of me and the lifestyle I was leading. I never owned cancer or identified cancer as my own, because it wasn't mine; I did own the choices I made that led to it though. A big part of my healing process was being an adult and taking responsibility for the habits, tendencies, and behavior that got me into that dilemma in the first place. Awareness is the first step and taking responsibility for actions is always the second step to recovering from anything in life. The third step is action to get you where you want to go.

Life Activation Innerval™ (1 minute)

- Awareness (20 seconds). Cultivate awareness in regard to your circumstance. What exactly is going on? How are you truly feeling at this moment? How did you get to this moment and feeling? What chain of events led you to this moment and feeling right now?

- Responsibility (20 seconds). Take responsibility for your actions that brought you to this circumstance. What did you personally do to bring you to this moment and feeling? How did you respond or react to bring you to this moment and feeling? What could you have done differently?

- Action (20 seconds). Take micro-steps to bring you to a healthier, happier, and more harmonized circumstance. Are you willing to accept what happened without a resolution or closure? What can you do to help yourself fully process this experience? What small actions can you take today to help move forward to a better place?

I'm not a wizard, alien, or other higher deity on earth. I don't command any dragons nor am I a Black Jesus—hell, I can't even swim, let alone walk on water! I'm a human being, just like you, who has fallen prey to our deeply dysfunctional, distracted, and delusional world of information, stimulation, and manipulation. Not only that, I'm a Black man in America that has to constantly overcome hundreds of systemic, social, and economic barriers that my white counterparts don't. There was nothing spontaneous about working my ass off, taking a holistic approach to my healing, retraining my preconditioned self, and training my relaxation response to be stronger. Nonetheless, fake fear was used to drive me to action. The several mindful Innervals™ I took while at the hospital were paramount to helping me activate my relaxation response so that I could gain quick insights on self-awareness, self-acceptance, and self-reliance. Instead of thinking I just had one choice, which was to die, every time I shifted into my relaxation response, I was able to access more choices to live. As you would've inferred from my case, part of the problem is our preconditioned self, but remember everything you've ever learned in your life can be unlearned and what's been trained, can be retrained!

Self-Reflection Innerval™

I just talked about how a variety of my habits, choices, and behavior led to the expression of cancer. What three negative habits, choices, and behaviors are you doing now that may lead to the expression of one or several chronic health issues?

_____

_____

_____

30 //

JOURNAL TO LA

I activated rapid self-healing physically, but did that mean that I also emotionally and mentally healed myself completely as well? The answer is no. It's possible to heal from whatever you're going through by stimulating your nerves, but eventually you must engage with the root cause of your challenges which are most likely emotional, mental, or trauma-related. I united my mind, body, and nerves and triggered this symphony of immunity, but I was still on a slippery healing journey that I could easily slip and fall off of. Before I became sick, I was so disconnected from my body that I didn't hear or listen to any of my body's inner whispers and warnings of severe imbalance. But now that I had fully woken up, my inner whispers were louder, eerier, and more haunting, making them impossible to ignore. My inner intelligence was telling me that I needed to do more mentally and emotionally to balance and sustain my healing.

My various Innervals™ helped me activate and strengthen my relaxation response so that I could expeditiously self-heal. They helped greatly at the moment and gave me a strong sense of peace, calm, and grace. But as I jumped headfirst back into my old habits, distractions, and dysfunction, I knew that I was quickly undoing all the mental and emotional resilience I had built up over time. I wanted to be a hot mess and live an unhealthy lifestyle as I had been because it was the cool thing to do and the way to be accepted in NYC social circles, but I didn't want to get sick again. Why does it seem "cool" to be unhealthy? Binge drinking and partying until the wee hours of the morning is a rite of passage in NYC for a lot of sought-after social circles. But most of the time you can't have your cake and eat it too. I knew I needed to take a bigger step and go even deeper. I decided that the most logical next step was to start journaling. Keep doing the binge drinking, partying, and unhealthy behaviors but just write about it to help mitigate the effects of it. I thought this was a brilliant plan! In reality, I was delusional as f*ck trying to desperately cling to my old life. I didn't realize that the lifestyle I had before would have to be left behind if I was to truly move forward.

Do you ever catch yourself stuck in a bad mood, anxious, or struggling with negative thoughts that seemingly come out of nowhere? It's easy to write the day off and if that's what you really want, it's OK every once in a while, to bring your regular schedule to a halt to rest and sulk. You don't need to be positive or happy all the time. It's an emotion like all others that should come and go in waves. You learned one of the best ways to relieve stress in grade school.

Journaling is an incredibly beneficial self-care technique, which doesn't just enhance feelings of happiness, but reduces stress, clarifies thoughts and feelings, and ultimately helps you get to know yourself better.[266] It can be very helpful to implement a journaling practice once you are at the point of your journey when you need to confront some of the emotional root causes of the physical ailments you are encountering. Convert your ruminative thinking to constructive inking. I honestly was never a big journal guy growing up, but I kept seeing the idea pop up and people kept recommending that I try it. Many people thought it would help me cope and process everything that I went through. When you write, you're placing your outer world on pause and taking inventory of your inner world. It can be a very powerful tool to help you understand what's going on inside of you. A lot of the Innervals™ in this book can be used as journal prompts to help you poke around and peel back some of your inner layers.

The journaling process can look different from person to person. I like to journal before bed or the first thing in the morning when I'm the most productive. It can take some time to find the right writing routine for you, but what matters most is that you're allotting time for delving into your mind and uncovering important thoughts and feelings. I have prioritized journaling and have made it an important part of my self-care routine. No matter what kind of crazy thoughts are spinning around in my head, journaling always helps me release tension, ease stress, and elevates my mood. Feeling calm, centered, and capable is literally just a few written sentences or ramblings away. A helpful way to turn your stressful day around is to commit to 5 - 10 minutes to study your feelings. Self-reflection is a superpower, and the more you can get in the habit of doing it via journaling, the more you can recognize specific issues or worries that should be resolved. Once you uncover the root and understand why you're feeling a certain way, you are empowered and then can actually do something about it.

Whenever you activate your stress response, stress hormones like cortisol and epinephrine surge through your body (primarily arms and legs) so that you can do something, like fight or flee a threat. When you take some sort of action like running or fighting, this helps to dissipate those stress hormones and helps you get back into your relaxation response, your safe, calm, and peaceful nerve state. If you're in the middle of a stressful work meeting, you probably can't fight or fly out of there. If you can't do any full-body physical action, the next best thing is to write to help dissipate some of those stress hormones in your arms. Writing stimulates the prefrontal and motor cortex of your brain, also triggering your relaxation response. The most important thing is to take some time, free of distraction, to re-experience the emotions associated with whatever event you're writing about. You don't have to write in an actual journal, although you'll probably get the max benefits that way. Some people, especially tech-savvy people like myself, may prefer and feel more comfortable with typing on a computer or note-taking app on a smartphone than using a physical diary. Do whatever is going to keep you consistent, comfortable, and engaged.

The simple act of describing one's feelings helps people to clear their minds, makes them less anxious, and makes them happier.[267] Many studies show that writing can improve your overall health[268], mental health[269], clear your mind[270], and even improve sleep. This doesn't always mean you can "fix" everything but at a minimum, defining your fears and putting them to paper always makes them less scary and more manageable. If you're new to journaling, I know that one of the biggest roadblocks is not knowing where to start, so hopefully, you'll find a few of these ideas helpful in your own self-care practice.

FEELINGS. How am I really feeling right now?

It may be uncomfortable or seem silly at first, but just try to roll with it. Pour your heart out and really look at how you're feeling right now. If you want to scream or run, write it down. Your journal is your safe space so give yourself permission to do or write whatever you want. If you let your feelings flow without judgment or filter you may discover something about yourself. There is normally a root cause of your feelings, especially negative feelings, and the awareness you gain is the first step to either accepting what you can't control or improving the situation.

CLEAR YOUR MIND. What am I thinking about too much?

One of the greatest acts of self-care is having a quiet, calm, and peaceful mind. Turning down your to-do list, emails, and everything else you've been thinking about is such an exhilarating feeling. Do a mind dump by opening a black page or note app and just let it all go. Get it out of your head and onto paper or in a note-taking app. Write literally everything in your mind until there is nothing left. You may want to give yourself a time limit of nine minutes if you're an overthinker. You'll be tired after this but in a good way.

FORGIVENESS. Who do I need to forgive right now? What do I need to forgive myself for?

Forgiveness doesn't make the other person right; it sets you free. When writing about people and situations you need to forgive, it allows you to view them objectively. It helps you get out of your head and you can show other people, as well as yourself, the kindness they deserve. Imagine that you were having a conversation with family, a friend, or a loved one and they were telling you about the same situation. Write down whatever happened. What would you say to them? Is it easier to be more compassionate and forgiving about the situation?

DREAMS. What are my dreams? What would I do if I wasn't scared of anything right now?

Do you have any big, scary, or far-fetched dreams? What are your passions in life? Do you keep these dreams or passions to yourself because of self-doubt, circumstance, or fear of looking silly? If you do this for too long, your inner child starts to fade away, you start to lose a part of yourself, and you stop expressing your authentic self. You don't need to share them with others if you're not comfortable doing so. Instead, write about them. It's very therapeutic to explore your dreams and ideas in a safe place without fear or judgment. Writing them down can also help you eventually self-generate some of your dreams by working through them.

Journaling helped me greatly, I worked through so many issues and was able to look objectively at what I went through. Not to mention I was able to accurately keep notes and receipts about everything I was going through. It was also helpful to retrace my steps to identify all the layers that resulted in my rapid self-healing. My journaling practice is what ultimately led to the creation of this book. After some suggestions and informative website links from my good friend Tess, a fellow writer, I wanted to write a book. I wanted to not only go deeper with my journaling but writing a book would allow me to help people on a larger scale. What I went through and how I was treated was insane, and I didn't want anyone else to have to go through that. Especially if they were a Black, Brown, or person with another marginalized identity that often gets deprioritized in our healthcare system.

So, in January of 2017, I started a quest to do the unthinkable, write the book that you're reading right now. I thought it could be easy, and my ego quickly got the best of me. After doing some fun google searches and seeing that it typically takes people two, three, or five years or more to write and publish a book, the NYer in me scoffed at that prospect and made a plan to write the book in six months. After all, NYers are highly efficient and we typically do sh*t with more energy, anxiety, and frequency than the average person. After a few more google searches, I fell down the rabbit hole of "writing my dream book" and fell headfirst into the publishing industry that, like many other industries, likes to exploit your dreams for profit. Selling my soul, ownership rights, and the majority of my royalties sounded scary, but at least I would get a book out of it!

Hay House is the world's largest self-help publisher, and many of my mentors like Gabrielle Bernstein, Brendon Burchard, and Dr. Joe Dispenza have published countless books with them. I had my sights set on becoming a Hay House author and I signed up for their Writer's Workshop in Las Vegas on a weekend in April of 2017. That same weekend in LA, I received a VIP ticket to Oprah's Super Soul Sessions 3 taping at UCLA. It was an opportunity to spend an entire day with Oprah! Oprah is one of the most beautiful, compassionate, and inspirational people in the world! Who wouldn't want to do that?!? I knew I had to leave NYC and LA seemed like a better option. People seemed to be super into health and living a healthy lifestyle as spiritual, conscious, and holistic healing modalities were pretty popular. This weekend was a life-changing opportunity to explore living in LA, get the tools I needed to write this book, spend a day with Oprah getting super inspired, and connect with like-minded people. The hustle, bustle, chaos, and fake friendships of NYC were starting to wear me down again, and I felt in my heart that something had to dramatically change if I was going to stay away from relapse.

A former good friend of mine from college, Becca, lived in LA and I would often chat and see her whenever I was on the west coast. She and her husband Mitch had a beautiful two-year-old named Erow, and they often joked about me moving to LA to become their Black Manny. They are millennial parents (went to Burning Man every year for 10 years) and were having a hard time finding an actual nanny that they trusted and liked. It seemed like everything was lining up for me to make the big move, but I was so scared to make the jump. I was terrified of the true death of my ego and preconditioned self of my old habits. The same habits that made me get really sick, that I was routinely indulging in again. I had woken up, but all the people I was surrounding myself with were still subconsciously asleep, adding to the inner sorrow and loneliness. I had outgrown and evolved out of most of my friendships and relationships. Being recently conscious, I knew I had to find my people that were also conscious, woke, and believed in a holistic lifestyle and self-healing. To my pleasant surprise, I was submerged by tons of "my people" when I went to visit LA.

The back-to-back Oprah and Hay House experience during the first weekend of April 2017 was inspiring, uplifting, and truly unforgettable! I don't think I have ever been surrounded by so many inspiring, compassionate, and motivating people at once in my entire life. We not only spent the entire day with Oprah filming, but she also brought along her super friends Glennon Doyle, Gabrielle Bernstein, Tony Robbins, and many others. The energy, vibe, and the love was through the roof. It was like a spiritual church service that lasted all day long, that inspired us all to be better and show up better for the world. The same thing goes for Hay House the next day in Las Vegas. Although a smokey, artificially bright, and shady Las Vegas casino probably wasn't the best choice for a self-help, healing, and writer's conference, we made the best of it. It was so inspiring to hear from some of my favorite authors like Brendon Burchard and Dr. Christiane Northrup, and it was great to meet other aspiring authors and attendees at the conference. I finally felt like I had found my people, and I knew in my heart that I had to commit and make the jump to LA.

The thing with these types of events, however well-intended, is that they are extremely exhilarating and overwhelming. You get an intense high-dose flood of energy, positivity, and feel-good hormones from the events, people, and experiences. It's exciting, inspiring, and super uplifting. You feel invincible, on top of the world, and feel like you can accomplish ANYTHING and passionately pursue your dreams despite whatever obstacles are standing in your way. However, that temporary feeling for most people doesn't really last that long after you leave the event and go back home to your reality, stressors, and everyday life. I was flying high for a good week or so after I went back to NYC, but the reality of how I was going to write and finish a book while suffering from ADHD and still battling off a relapse, all while planning a move to LA quickly sunk me back to reality.

To force myself to write every day, I thought of the brilliant idea of going to a library. I thought that if I was surrounded by books and people who were writing or working, it would help me creatively write and stay motivated. My favorite library was the Stephen A. Schwarzman Library in Bryant Park. And I would show up routinely every single day, even on Sunday, to write my heart away. It took about six months of writing and talking about moving before I finally said "peace out" to NYC and dived headfirst into LA in October 2017. I didn't plan it, I just spontaneously up and left, and found myself in an awful and awkward situation.

All that joking about being a Black Manny actually ended up not being a joke. Becca and Mitch lived in Venice, CA at the time, and I stayed in their spare bedroom which was right next to Erow's room. I did not know how to take care of a baby besides what I had seen on TV, but I was given a crash course by Becca (because Mitch had no clue). It was literally a sitcom comedy. They were white, so you had this big Black buff guy looking after this beautiful and angelic-looking White two-year-old. I looked more like a bodyguard than a Black Manny. The problem was that they basically threw their baby at me because they had never had help before. Part of me understood and I was happy to give them some temporary relief, but I also didn't want to get pigeonholed into being something that I'm not. I'm a Black man in America, and the tendency for some people is to view Black people as inferior and as "the help." I'm intelligent, of course, I would be a good manny, but that's not my destination. It was okay at first, but they weren't paying me to take care of her, they were only offering to let me stay with them. And when you're living in someone's house, it's hard to tell them "no" when they ask you to take care of their child as the live-in Black manny.

My first official Black manny duty was to take Erow to swimming lessons, and I can't swim myself. Luckily, the water wasn't over my head. This Black manny live-in situation worked until it didn't. I was feeling very used and abused, and I wasn't able to really gain ground on writing my book because most of my energy and time was going towards looking after Erow and then recovering from the stress, anxiety, and hypervigilance of looking after her. I love children but this situation was starting to feel like I was a live-in slave. Not to mention that they seemed to have an agenda and would guilt and manipulate me by holding the favor they had done for me over my head. Resentment, anger, and annoyance were building up, and I needed a break. This was not what I had expected when moving to LA.

They had introduced me to Leila Steinberg, a music manager who had a beautiful white German Shepherd mix dog named Detroit. She needed someone to stay at her place for a week or two and watch her dog. I volunteered because at that point I thought taking care of someone else's dog was better and less stressful than a baby! It also gave me my first break and some well-needed space from Becca and Mitch.

Detroit had a next-door neighbor dog friend named Frannie, and I would watch them together sometimes. I loved Detroit and we instantly bonded; he co-regulated me. Shepherds have this uncanny ability to really bond with people. He never left my side. When I was watching Detroit, I noticed that I was always in my relaxation response; I was calm, cool, and collected. I was also always present, mindful, and spontaneously laughing at something that he did. I was truly at peace for the first time in almost two months of being in LA. And that peace was because I was taking care of an animal. This momentary relief made me realize how depressed I had gotten after moving to LA.

Moving to any new place is hard, but LA is harder because it's more of a slow burn. Professionally, no one really knew me and people in LA like to take their time to get to know you and trust you, so it took a while to get clients and even start teaching group fitness classes despite the great business and reputation I had on the other coast. Also, the fitness industry is whitewashed. If you're not White, basic, and all-American looking, you have the hardest time finding clients, getting opportunities, and finding other work. When you're Black, you are really only trying to fill a quota, a sympathy diversity hire, and are often pitted against the other Black people for opportunities, especially in the corporate gym space, where I worked for almost two decades. I watched as several of my all-American white counterparts who moved to LA at the same time as I did get five times the amount of work I did, receive higher pay, greater praise, and more frequent raises. I also don't feel the need to stroke anyone's ego or kiss *ss so that could also be a factor in my slower path to success as well.

I went from being a fitness guru in NYC doing media rounds on TV, being sought after by clients/companies/celebs, and being well-known to becoming a nobody in LA who was treated like sh*t, made to be a slave/Black manny, and had a hard time finding work resulting in financial distress. It was all very humbling yet horrifying at the same time. Once again, I was at what felt like rock bottom. I descended into my shutdown response, a deep, dark, and dysfunctional depression. I had writer's block. I was barely surviving, let alone trying to write. I ended up taking some time off from writing and, at the time, I thought I would never finish.

I became frozen again in my shutdown response shifting into my autopilot survival mode, my personal Groundhog Day movie. The brain needs more energy than any other organ, and this is why we can so easily slip into autopilot as our default way of operating. It allows the brain to conserve energy. Autopilot is a subconscious state that allows you to do things, think thoughts, daydream, and multitask while not being consciously there. We spend about 95% of our daily experience in autopilot mode, our preconditioned self, which is why we are called creatures of habit, reacting in the same ways, thinking the same thoughts, and repeating the same habits. Being on autopilot sometimes isn't necessarily a bad thing, but autopilot is akin to sleepwalking through life as we unconsciously repeat patterns and cycles of our past. My autopilot looked like chronic procrastination, feeling stuck in cycles but wanting to do better, trying to be liked and control the opinions and emotions of the people around me. I was constantly daydreaming and always looking for ways to escape my reality or distract myself from it. Also feeling deeply depressed, overwhelmed, and resentful. I may have overcome cancer, but I spent much longer struggling with the root cause: my emotions and nerve states.

Even though I had awareness of my patterns, struggles, and frustrations and I wanted to be different, I felt stuck, hopeless, and wasn't able to get out of them no matter what I tried to do. At the time, I didn't understand our brain's default programming that so desperately wants us to run on the same conditioning we did in childhood. Most of us are unconsciously hooked, completely, hypnotized by our own stream of endless mental chatter. To make conscious choices to get out of autopilot mode is to "awaken" or wake up. To be "woke", is really to be living a conscious, present, and intentional life. To "awaken" is not a spiritual experience for monks. To awaken is to become aware of our thoughts, emotions, and why we have them. When we awaken, we become able to distance ourselves from our thoughts and see them for what they are. When we are conscious, we then have access to better choices. Rapid self-healing can't be given to us, it must be practiced and trained every day. Be patient, committed, and stay strong. Waking up and healing is a lifelong process of returning home to who we actually are.

CHEST/SPINE SLOW MOTOR COMBO. (3 minutes)
1. CHEST/SPINE SLOW MOTOR INNERVAL™ // 30 seconds.

Twist your chest and spine all the way from the right to left as slow as you possibly can. Do this for 30 seconds or 15 twists if you don't have a timer. Relax your chest and spine back to neutral before you start the next Innerval™.

2. CORE BREATHING INNERVAL™ // 30 seconds.

Take long, slow, and deep inhales and take longer, slower, and deeper exhales for 30 seconds or 3 times each if you don't have a timer. Each inhale should be around 3 seconds and each exhale should be around 6 seconds. As you breathe in, your core goes out, as you breathe out, your core goes in.

3. Repeat 2 times

STIMULATION. The phrenic nerves, vagus nerves, motor cortex (19), and posterior thoracic nerves.

31 //

YOUR INNER WOUNDS

I moved to a new place in LA and continued my west coast grind. Personally, it took me a little over two years to adjust and adapt to LA. And by adjust I mean chill the f*ck out and slow down to the glacial and beachy-vibe pace of most Californians. My Innervals™ and optimistic outlook were keeping me healthy and temporarily propping up my mindset, but I was being deeply overpowered by depression. I was still doing my monthly sessions with Dr. Alexa Carlson, and although they helped pick me up off the ground several times, my motivation tanked and I didn't feel like doing anything. I learned to be so comfortable in my shutdown response that it was hard to notice whenever I slipped into it and became frozen in it.

Motivation is a feeling, and just like other feelings such as happiness, sadness, or anger, it doesn't last. I used to think that most of my job and passion as a coach was to inspire, motivate, and uplift my clients constantly. I soon started to realize that motivation is bullsh*t, and you can't motivate people who simply can't motivate themselves; myself included. You can have all the knowledge, tools, and resources in the world, but if you aren't internally motivated to use them, you really have nothing. If you're frozen, it can be hard to motivate yourself to do even the simplest things that you know that you should be doing.

The root of procrastination is chronic stress. Back then, I let my lack of motivation get me off balance and allowed it to completely derail me. Now, I understand that getting off balance and derailing are two different things, but that can be a hard thing to realize when you're in the thick of a stressed or shut-down nerve state. No matter what you're trying to accomplish or what you're going through, your motivation to do it does not determine your success. How you navigate your motivation ebbing and flowing is what will determine your success. You won't always be motivated to go through, put up with, or deal with sh*t. And when you aren't, you need to back off and honor that. However, don't let your slips turn into slides or allow temporarily backing off to become permanent. I almost did the latter when it came to this very book.

I completely stopped writing because mentally, emotionally, and physically I felt like I couldn't. The trauma of everything I had been through started to disable me again. As I became frozen in my stress and shutdown responses again, I began to think, "what's the point?" and feelings of survivor's remorse kept creeping back in mind. Contrary to what the media likes to portray about depression, I think a large number of people like myself are high functioning in a shutdown or depressed state. We've been so repeatedly traumatized throughout our lives that we essentially train ourselves to exist in shutdown or depression; even though it's not the healthiest nerve state to be in. After about six months of being frozen and depressed living in LA, I wanted to move back to NYC. I tried, I lived, and I was completely over it. I was serious and making concrete plans.

Since I had to do routine check-ups anyway, I decided to find myself a conscious general practitioner who understood that I was going to be my own health care advocate. I was always going to ask questions because I always wanted to be informed about what she thought and why. She recommended that I see this psychiatrist that was in the hospital clinic for the depression I was currently experiencing. I humored her and gave it a chance, and so the saga of doctor's opinions continues. I scheduled an appointment and spent twenty uncomfortable minutes in the office of who I will call "Dr. Wellbutrin". He was a White male, 50s, with stringy, thin, brown hair and glasses. When I walked in, he was hunched over a computer screen. He didn't look at me when I walked in. For the entire time I was in his office, he barely glanced my way about three times. He primarily just stared like he was in a trance at his computer screen. And he typed super loud. It sounded like he was typing on the original mac computer with how loud, clanky, and fast he was typing. Click clock, click clock. He asked me a ton of questions from various times throughout my life and he would shorthand type my answers into his computer. After mentioning that I was experiencing depression and struggling with focus, he started to recommend that I take Wellbutrin. I knew of it only to help people stop smoking, but Wellbutrin is also a "popular" drug to treat depression.

He kept saying it over and over again and kept pushing me to take Wellbutrin even when I was adamant that I didn't want to take antidepressants. How many times should you have to tell a person "no"? Once. "These two good friends take Wellbutrin and it's helped their focus and depression!" He actually said that. What the f*ck does two friends taking Wellbutrin and getting fantastic results have to do with me? He said it so many times that I felt like he was getting a kickback for it. It was the ONLY drug and solution he proposed and scoffed at me when I was asking for more natural or holistic solutions. Here we go again; a White male doctor that doesn't listen to a Black patient and just keeps pushing a pill until he convinces me to say "yes". I said "no" and held my boundary. I left his office furious, filed a complaint against him, and received a response stating "that's just who he is." Feeling super shutdown, deeply triggered, and angry, I went back to my general doctor and she helped me brainstorm some natural solutions to help deal with the deep depression I was experiencing. Because the last time I felt happy and at peace was around an animal, she recommended and prescribed a service animal for me.

I considered it. What did I have to lose besides the depression I was currently experiencing? The next day as I was contemplating moving back to NYC, leaving LA, or simply leaving the planet, I saw that the LA Animal Services shelter was having a "My Furry Valentine" special. I walked in very hopeful, but that hope soon turned into sadness as the vast number of dogs got excited, started barking, and tried to get my attention. I literally wished that I could rescue them all, and it can be hard to make eye contact with some of them sometimes. The first trip was too much. I walked around and was so overwhelmed that after about an hour I simply had to leave. Because I had grown so fond of Detroit the German Shepherd (GSD) I dog sat, I wanted a GSD. Of course, as soon as I told the shelter I wanted a big dog they quickly whisked me away to the pitbull section. I'm a big Black man, so apparently, my first choice is going to be a pit bull! Implicit bias is literally everywhere, truly. I have nothing against pit bulls, but my heart was set on a GSD.

The second trip was better, but still heart-wrenching as I had to navigate the shelter with every single dog jumping up and down and seemingly saying "pick me, pick me". It was on my third trip that I found "Angel". With Angel, it wasn't really "love at first sight" as you hear in many other rescue stories. She was curious but scared of me. She had trauma and was abandoned by her previous owners, and even though she was curious about me, she was very scared of people in general. Nonetheless, I had a gut feeling that she was the one and took a chance on her. I embraced her imperfections, loved her unconditionally, and learned how to train her from the ground up. It turned out she was actually half Siberian Husky and half GSD; a hybrid breed called a Gerberian Shepsky (I just say Shepsky). Medium in size, energetic, and loyal, these pups inherited some of the best qualities from both of their parents. Angel was my safety "anchor" to stay in LA and work through my rough patch, and it's hard to say where I would be today without her pawtervention.

As someone with so much massive trauma that includes abandonment issues, unmet needs, losing immediate family members, and never really growing up feeling safe in any environment, rescuing Angel was the first time I was truly able to have my core needs consistently fulfilled. I spent most of my life frozen, unaware that I even had needs. Now, I was seen, I was heard, and I was able to authentically be myself when I was around her. That's a very shocking statement to me, and it's unfortunately 100% true. She helped to heal some of my inner wounds which had been internally bleeding since my early childhood. Therapist John Bradshaw has dedicated his career to speaking about the "inner child" in people with substance abuse problems. He makes the convincing idea that so many of us end up in toxic relationships because we never addressed the traumas that happened in childhood. This couldn't be truer for me and many other people I know, and I think it far exceeds people with substance abuse problems because unmet needs are a form of little "t" trauma that many people may be unknowingly suffering from.

Every child deserves the essential right to be seen, heard, and authentically express themselves. They deserve to feel secure, safe, protected, and have all their physical needs met like food, water, and a safe home environment. Children also need to be given the freedom to grow, change, and have their emotional needs met as well. Unfortunately, not every child receives this. Safety supersedes physical, it's also personal, emotional, and mental. Being close to your parents, caregivers, or family members, having your needs consistently met, and having your emotional and physical boundaries respected allow you to genuinely feel safe in your family environment. When a child is growing up, it's the emotional and biological responsibility of our parents and family members to create a genuine safe environment for us. However, not all parents accept that responsibility, are aware of that responsibility, or have the capacity to fulfill that responsibility. This isn't placing blame on those parents, most parents are just doing the best they can with knowledge and resources they at that given time.

The concept of the inner child was first proposed by psychologist Carl Jung after he examined his own childlike inner feelings, thoughts, and emotions.[271] Jung suggested that it was this inner part of all of us that influenced all we do and the decisions that we make. When we are connected to our inner child, we feel excited, invigorated, and inspired by life. However, when we are disconnected, we feel lethargic, bored, unhappy, and empty. The inner child holds all the memories and emotions, good or bad, that we experienced. Once wounded, the inner child can negatively influence who we are as adults holding enormous power over our relationships, patterns, and decisions. Inner wounds can keep you frozen, sometimes all through your life. Human beings have three core needs; to be seen, to be heard, and to authentically express ourselves. As children, most of us don't fully have those needs met and this becomes an inner wound. It's our childhood years that our self-image, core beliefs, ability to self-regulate our emotions, and our future relationship dynamics are formed. This is the reason that inner child work can be so powerful and transformative for some people. As you have read, my childhood was filled with deep insecurity and I became frozen in chaotic, unhealthy, and abusive dynamics all throughout my adulthood. As I started to cultivate more awareness, I realized that many of my conditioned actions, behaviors, and habits came from inner wounds that needed to be healed.

Angel is curious, spontaneous, playful, open-minded, and accepting; all core qualities of the inner child. No matter what I'm doing or how I'm feeling, when I'm around her or actively engaging with her, she pulls me into the present moment with her child-like personality and antics. We all have this inner child-like part of ourselves that is free, fun, and capable of awe. However, it can only be accessed when we are in our relaxation response. The inner child is most activated when something touches our past inner wounds and affirms a core belief from that wounding. Things like "I'm broken", "I am not enough", "I'll never find love and be happy" etc. The first micro-step to healing your inner wounds is to acknowledge that there is a part of you that has been wounded. Often as adults, we minimize, ignore, or deflect our inner wounds. It's the inner wounds that create this inner fear in us, and keep us reactively frozen.

I'm talking about inner wounds because they are a little-known form of little "t" trauma, that dysregulates your nervous system and causes you to become frozen. As you start to build awareness, using Interval Mindfulness™ and its various Innervals™, you'll start to thaw out and see this fear in yourself. Once you become aware of it, you can start to cultivate more empathy for all parts of yourself; the healthy, the frozen, and the wounded. You'll also start to see the inner wounds in other people which allows you to be more compassionate and handle challenging people with more grace. To truly heal, you must see the parts of yourself that weren't seen, heard, or able to express your authentic self. I bring up this information about trauma now because it's important to recognize that even after everything I had learned on my journey by the time I got to LA, I was still only at the beginning of my healing journey. I come to you with this story, authentically, to say that the journey of healing from physical and mental trauma does not end, but it can improve. And throughout that whole process, I hope you will be kind, generous, and forgiving with yourself when the journey feels less than linear.

Not only did Angel help with healing some of my inner wounds, but she also helped me shift my focus outside of myself in a healthy way. One of my trauma responses was fawning, a hyper version of people-pleasing that left me chronically depleted because I was always and consistently putting the needs of others first before my own. I didn't even know what my own needs were because I was so focused on everyone else. It's all I knew and what I had been conditioned to do. With Angel, I could put someone else's needs before my own in a healthy way, and that eventually led me back to myself and fully understanding my own needs. I knew I was always going to be running from relapse, and I figured I would get farther with a running buddy. I had to get through this for Angel, I had to ride my waves of motivation for Angel, I had to succeed for Angel and myself. This truly shifted me deeply. I love you Angel with all of my heart, soul, and every fiber in my muscles.

One of the easiest ways for you to heal and get in touch with your inner child is to recreate what you loved to do as a child. Growing up, what did you like to do? Climbing trees, cuddling with teddy bears, watching cartoons, or playing with toys. Consciously make time in your present life for whatever activity you loved to do as a child. When you start looking at your inner wounds and doing inner child work, you could potentially connect to sides of yourself that you never knew existed as an adult. It's important to rediscover our ability to play and explore any silliness or embarrassment that we feel towards it. It may feel a bit weird at first, but it's important to keep an open mind.

Inner Child Self-Reflection Innerval™

Close your eyes and take three long, slow, and deep core breaths. Imagine you're slowly walking downstairs into your safe place. It could be a garden, beach, or any place that makes you feel safe, empowered, and supported. Soak in your safe space. What does it sound like, look like, and smell like?

Invite your younger self in with you and when you see them hug them and make them feel at home. When you're ready, ask your younger self any questions like "when was the first time I/you felt scared?" Wait for their response. When you are done asking them questions, hug them, thank them, and tell them how much you love them. Tell them goodbye as you walk back up the stairs from your safe space to open your eyes in normal consciousness. *What questions do you need to ask your inner child?*

_____

_____

_____

32 //

TRANSCENDING TRAUMA

Things slowly but surely started getting better for me in LA. It was going on two years that I had been living there, and people were starting to get to know me and warm up to me for the most part. I lived mostly in Culver City while I lived in LA. When I left NYC, I was leaving because the city life, pace, vibe, and massive amounts of unresolved trauma-filled people were unhealthy for me. The last thing I wanted to do was leave a place and jump into a smaller version of that city. I resisted moving to downtown, Hollywood, or West Hollywood on purpose because I knew that would be more of the same as feeling like I was in a mini–New York. Culver City was great because it was quiet, full of nature, and was only a mile or two from the beach. If I wanted to experience the city vibe, superficiality, and flakiness in downtown, Hollywood, or WeHo, it was an easy 15-minute (really 45-minute when you factor in LA traffic) drive. My default was peaceful living in Culver City, and this helped me acclimate better to LA.

I was continuously doing the work: I was the healthiest I had ever been, and I looked and felt the best I had ever been. I did it, I thought! I was flying high and slowly my ego started to get the best of me. I started thinking that I had hit my "healing destination" and I was ready to jump headfirst back into the city life of noise, drama, business, and a fast pace that I forgot contributed to me becoming sick in the first place. I felt like I had built up my resilience and I was strong enough to handle anything. I kicked the *ss of rare cancer and I was ready for whatever life can throw at me! It was March 2020 when I moved into a new apartment in Hollywood. I was at Sunset and Highland, literally in the heart of Hollywood by the Walk of Fame. I was excited, it felt good and familiar like NYC, and I was looking forward to exploring more of the part of LA with a true "city feel".

SOCIETAL TRAUMA

Well, the "city feel" ran over me several times. Unless you're a monk, I don't need to go over in much detail what happened in March 2020. The COVID-19 pandemic surprised, disrupted, and stopped the entire world. This massive event of societal trauma not only retraumatized me deeply, but retraumatized billions of people around the globe. It wasn't just a traumatic event, but a catalyst for millions of traumatic events. The pandemic created billions of unique traumatic experiences. This traumatic fallout was more widespread than the virus itself. It also highlighted the many societal, economical, and racial issues that we have always faced to various degrees. Long before the pandemic hit, the bad and breaking news media was drowning out our life balance. The attention economy is designed to keep us constantly engaged in social media, news, and all of the dramas in the world, so this was exacerbated tenfold by the pandemic.

Societal trauma is any type of event, experience, or circumstance that affects us on a mass scale.[272] War, famine, systemic racism, climate change, and cultural isolation are a few examples. During a societal trauma, we all experience the same thing at the same time, but how that trauma is interpreted is a personal experience. We are hardwired for empathy and caring. However, this is also a biological liability. If you look at a lot of the evils in our society, the greed, insecurity, self-harm, and the desire to harm others, you can see that it's a lot of unresolved issues that haven't been identified or addressed. There's a limit to how much stress our system can bear without breaking and without resiliency. People seemed so surprised by how poorly the US was doing compared to other countries around the world. But truthfully, we were a collective hot mess long before the pandemic hit. We were the worst that I've ever seen society functioning physically, mentally, emotionally, biologically, and collectively. Physically incompetent, overloaded with information, malnourished, disconnected, divisive, fear-based, frozen in stress or shutdown response, sleep-deprived, over doctored, hypervigilant, overworked, overeducated, and overentitlted. We barely had a chance to survive anything in that state, let alone a pandemic with a highly contagious virus.

When culture is sick; we are going to be unhealthy. Distance used to have this buffering or numbing effect in how we reacted to trauma, as news spread slowly over time and geographical distance. However, today we have access to all of that instantly, 24/7, right in the palm of our hands. Societal trauma is at an all-time high, and that was the case before the pandemic. The instant access we have to information can enlighten us, but it can also create fear and desperation. Every time we plugin, we are exposing ourselves to potential misinformation and millions of hidden agendas. Whether it's news, advertisements, or internet trolls. We have so much access to technology all the time; it's literally Trauma On Demand. The impact societal trauma has on the mind and body, not just the individual, but all of us is so pervasive that it can be hard to see. Almost like a fish that's unaware of the water in its bowl. We become numb and desensitized to all the pain and bad news that surrounds us. Like it's somehow a normal part of our human story, and it shouldn't be.

Whether you're in the thick of it or watching a traumatic event unfold over and over again on tv or social media, we absorb all of that pain and anxiety into our bodies via our nervous system. It's not uncommon to emerge from these interactions with signs of PTSD. The mental suffering from societal trauma is often more prevalent than that caused by physical injuries. And carrying that trauma with you can be just as painful. We live in such polarized times with large-scale events like pandemics, politics, social issues, economic challenges, or everything all at once. Big events like these have their own inherent impact, but they can amplify the societal traumas that already exist. The pandemic served as a fuse that collectively lit hidden, buried, and forgotten personal trauma bombs in everyone making it easier to become overwhelmed with your own experience.

I've talked about the destructive nature of growing up in a traumatic household. What about growing up in global turmoil? Societal trauma is driven by fear: and fear is driven by not knowing ourselves. Lack of self-awareness. Not knowing ourselves is driven by how we are programmed. It's a weird vicious cycle. When you use Interval Mindfulness™ and its various Innervals™ to help train more awareness, you become empowered to step out, break out, and ask yourself

"Is this in alignment with who I am?" Building awareness is one of the most important things that you can do because it helps you understand who you really are versus what you're consuming. And this is one of the most powerful things that you can do that will help you get unfrozen and change everything.

TRAUMA ON-DEMAND

Trauma is an emotional, and sometimes physical, a scar from something that happened in your past that can change how your mind thinks and how your body works. One of the fastest ways to become frozen is to experience trauma, because trauma radically changes the nervous system. When we acclimate to trauma, it becomes part of who we are and how we interact with the world; for better or worse. Everyone experiences trauma differently, but our response to traumatic events is our resilience. The body is a wondrous symphony of synchronicity of systems that are working together in a life-sustaining harmony. Trauma is an assault on that system that overwhelms its capacity to come back into its own flow. It can happen in an instant or be a prolonged situation. But, in essence, it's something that overwhelms the body's natural intrinsic ability to self-regulate. Collectively we have lost our own innate ability to self-regulate and we desperately rely on external people, things, and substances to co-regulate us through life. Things that are supposed to be crutches until we can properly self-regulate again.

As you have read, trauma is very personal for me. I've experienced trauma in every perceivable way a human could: physical, mental, emotional, and personal trauma. And although it has really sucked and at times seemed overwhelming, the trauma I've experienced has allowed me to create a holistic platform for deep healing, learning, and personal growth. When I look back now at my trauma, I see it as a blessing. The shattering of the beliefs that I held before the trauma was a radical shock to my system. But training awareness, finding resolutions, and adapting to a new normal was food for my soul and one of the first steps to my personal growth. I had to daily feed myself compassion, mindfulness, and hope. I had to relearn to love myself, reconnect to my inner intelligence, and cultivate awareness to see who I really was, not who I thought I was.

Trauma in life is inevitable, and experiencing trauma has nothing to do with your value as a human being. However, unresolved trauma can lead to physical illness and long-lasting emotional and mental issues.[273] But many forms of trauma are more widespread than most people think. According to The National Survey on Drug Use and Health (NSDUH), as of 2017, 46 million adult Americans had a major mood disorder[274] and if the current treatment methodology for that is psychotherapy and medication and people are continuing to get worse, then maybe we aren't asking the right questions or going about it the right way. According to the CDC, more than 60% of adults have experienced trauma as children.[275]

No matter what kind of trauma we experience, the effect it has on our bodies is consistent. Trauma sets our bodies into overdrive and releases chemicals that have helped us survive since the beginning of humanity. Trauma gets stored in our cells and if we hold on to that stress, it can change our bodies and express as pain, headaches, poor posture, poor digestion, and many more inner whispers. Trauma can lead to a person losing their sense of self. Traumatic events, whether big or small, happen to us. You can't change what happened to you, but you can choose to manage what happened and make it a platform for who you want to become in the future. Trauma is an opportunity for deep healing, learning, and personal growth. Finding meaning to your trauma is vital to working through it. Trauma is the nervous system being frozen in a stress response, shutdown response, or the hybrid freeze state. Trauma is the impact of what our bodies survive and can be radically different from one nervous system to the next.

There are actually two paths to trauma, acute life-threatening reactions, probably resulting in a hybrid freeze state, and a chronic disruption of connectedness to self, likely resulting in a flight, fight, or shutdown state. Trauma isn't just some psychological issue that is the result of a traumatic event. It's a fundamental hijacking of the nervous system, which then gets frozen in that state even when the body is otherwise safe and no longer needs defensive behaviors. Traumatic experiences aren't always obvious, and our perception of trauma is just as valid as the trauma itself. Trauma is extremely difficult for any of us and without the skill set to know you don't have a choice to change what happened, but you do have a choice to manage what happened in such a way that it actually becomes a strong platform for who you become in the future.

LITTLE T TRAUMA

Most people associate trauma with big "T" trauma. Big "T" trauma is caused by a specific life-changing event. It can be very frightening, disturbing, and violent, injuring your mind and body like a car accident, mass shooting, or assault. They can leave ruptures in your mind and body if it's not properly healed and worked through. What's not known as widespread of a manner is little "t" trauma. Little T is developmental trauma or small dose trauma that builds up over time. Deep childhood trauma happens when a child witnesses or has overwhelming negative experiences repeatedly and over time. Abuse, neglect, violence, betrayal, etc. Children can experience bouts of sadness, anger, depression, and anxiety and feel that they don't belong anywhere. As adults this can lead to depression, eating disorders, and substance abuse.

The small traumas, even though they aren't as big as the big traumas, slowly build up and start to work their way into our lives, the way we live, the way we relate to ourselves and other people. In some ways, trauma is in the eye of the beholder. If I go through something that I feel was horrible for me, then I might identify that as trauma in my life. There are also traumas that people go through, and they are like "oh it wasn't a big deal. Except it was a big deal because it's impacted their nervous system and they continue to behave in ways and have habits and patterns in life that are a result of early childhood trauma.

Most people have some form of little "t" trauma, but a lot of people don't recognize it because it's not the big "T" trauma, and that's exactly why it's important to discuss in these pages. Trauma sounds like a large and scary word, but most people have it in some form, and acknowledging it will be an important key to freeing oneself from it. There are a lot of people who are intellectual, smart, and high functioning. They can talk about their trauma, other people's trauma, or different theories, but they aren't connected to themselves. They have no idea when you ask, "What are you feeling?" or "What are the sensations in your body?" For me, I didn't know I had trauma until later on in life. That's when I started to investigate because of things that I was experiencing in my adult life that I realized there were some traumas that I had. Just going through the things and unpacking everything that I was feeling in my body physically, emotionally, and personally. And I think that's what was difficult for me. I didn't have a lot of the other things I heard that other people had when it came to childhood trauma.

A lot of times when people have a traumatic experience or they are currently in a place where they are suffering. People will self-blame and judge themselves. There is a lot of resentment, anger, and negative feelings around the experience. If we can take the blame out of the situation, step back a little bit, and not label things as good or bad. This will allow us to approach our lives with more curiosity and not look for blame. It allows us to have a lot more empathy for ourselves and the world around us. And it allows us to have a really deep experience of forgiveness for a traumatic thing that happened in our life.

Little "t" trauma is so prevalent in today's society because people are so unaware of how it's affecting them now. Started in the mid-1990s, the Adverse Childhood Events (ACE) Study of 17,000 adults was done by the CDC and Kaiser Permanente. They uncovered a stunning direct link between childhood trauma, events, and challenges with emotional issues, social problems, and chronic diseases that many people develop in adulthood like depression, lung cancer, heart disease, autoimmune disease, and suicide.[276] This study is powerful because it helps to verify that not only early trauma exists, but that it's an underlying, unknown, and untold traumatic underworld that manifests itself negatively in all phases of adult life. It helps give simple explanations to common intractable physical, social, mental, and emotional problems that people collectively spend billions of dollars to treat without fully understanding why they developed these issues in the first place.

BEHAVIORAL ADAPTATIONS

When you are frozen, your body doesn't think you're frozen; it adapts to you being frozen and those behavioral adaptations could be productive or unproductive. People who experience trauma and get frozen can develop behavioral adaptations, coping strategies, or ways to manage or control their inner turmoil. We tend to lean away from intense, challenging, or difficult thoughts, feelings, and emotions. It's something we do to avoid the discomfort of shifting nerve states. Instead of embracing, and not avoiding, our stress response energy, we engage in some sort of behavior that masks or numbs it. Sound at all familiar? Substance use and abuse, distraction, and addiction to name a few. Some of these things may temporarily relieve the pain and might give us a pseudo sense of relief. But using substances isn't a healthy way to cope with frozen stress response energy. It doesn't help, but it provides relief.

A "behavioral adaptation" is a behavior that we engage in to adapt to frozen stress or shutdown response energy. The frozen defensive or shutdown energy comes from being unable to self-regulate and activate the relaxation response. When we are in these stressed or shutdown states (and the relaxed state), it's really important that we actually feel the experience of our stress or shutdown response nerve state instead of avoiding or repressing it. When we do so, it allows the defensive energy to run its course and discharge. Once this stressed energy is discharged, it makes it easier for the body to self-regulate back into a relaxation response. What most people do is ignore being in a stress response nerve state because frankly, sometimes it f*cking sucks, especially when it's experienced as grief, pain, despair, panic, anxiety, rage, or more. It's hard to engage and embrace those emotions no matter how short they are present for. But they are natural and feeling them is part of the process. You have to feel in order to heal. Feeling challenging emotions isn't easy at first, but the only way out of them is through them. Eventually, we train our capacity to feel them and welcome them the more we embrace, face, and release them.

Pain is part of the process of trauma or being frozen. There's something in our mind that thinks pain and happiness are mutually exclusive. If we have pain, we can't be happy. The opposite of pain isn't happiness, the opposite of pain is no pain or comfort. If I feel this pain, I can't be happy, so I don't want to feel this pain, I don't want to feel. That's trauma running away from feelings; running away from these sensations in our body. Some people have a delayed self-destructive response to their trauma. The path towards healing and becoming unfrozen is making that connection between a behavioral disorder or adaptation such as addiction, substance abuse, relationship problems, suicidal thoughts, and trauma. Breaking through the pain of trauma is a cathartic moment that can be a beautiful and profound experience. But seeing that light is hard when there is so much darkness before it.

Everyone handles trauma differently but look for breakthrough moments that can change your life for the better. Those are the moments we finally recognize and confront the symptoms of our trauma, that's when the journey starts towards healing and getting unstuck. It's usually marked by a common event, hitting rock bottom or a dark night of the soul. Everyone's trauma is as unique as their own individuality, so the paths to overcoming and healing trauma are equally infinite. Talk therapy, physical therapy, spiritual practices, all of these are avenues that one can take to come out whole on the other side of trauma. The paths are infinite and so are the solutions.

Trauma starts out like a weed, if left unchecked it will grow and overtake your being. Our bodies are a record of our life experience and trauma does draw a map for where we need to meet it in order to resolve it. We can rewire our brains so that we can rewrite our lives. It won't always be easy, but it's important to deeply enjoy these human moments in your life without shame. I hope this emboldens you to take those first micro-steps to start defrosting and turning your traumas into triumphs.

HIPS MOTOR COMBO. (3 minutes)
1. HIPS MOTOR INNERVAL™ // 30 seconds.

Move your hips releasing any tension, tightness, or stress. Do this for 30 seconds or count to 30 if you don't have a timer. Relax your hips back to neutral before you start the next Innerval™.

2. CORE BREATHING INNERVAL™ // 30 seconds.

Take long, slow, and deep inhales and take longer, slower, and deeper exhales for 30 seconds or 3 times each if you don't have a timer. Each inhale should be around 3 seconds and each exhale should be around 6 seconds. As you breathe in, your core goes out, as you breathe out, your core goes in.

3. Repeat 2 times

STIMULATION. The phrenic nerves, vagus nerves, motor cortex (20), and posterior thoracic nerves.

33 //

POST TRAUMATIC GROWTH

How am I doing right now? Considering I'm a Black man in America, there are days where all I can do is simply exist. I cannot escape my stress or shut down responses when simply my physical appearance makes walking, running, shopping, or holding an object in my hand, dangerous and a threat to my life. Racism is an experience of separation and an undercurrent of our society. But despite all the additional barriers thrown at me that exponentially increased my struggle, my devastating fall led to an inspiring rise. I'm content, and I look and feel the best I have ever in my life. What I went through made me discover this newfound resilience that I never knew I had before. I'm a more comfortable, conscious, and compassionate human being. I live and express myself authentically and unapologetically. I communicate and uphold my boundaries in all of my relationships, and I disengage with people who aren't healthy for me mentally, emotionally, and physically. Now that I'm on the other side of my traumatic experiences, I have a new sense of purpose and a strong desire to pay it forward. I live in San Diego in Ocean Beach these days. San Diego is a very balanced city to me. It's so diverse, full of pockets of immersive nature, and has endless beautiful beaches. I'm close to the water which is incredibly peaceful for me, and more nature or the city is only ten minutes away.

The interesting thing about all the things that I went through is that yeah, it f*cking sucked. It ruined my life for a long time and it was all very traumatic for me. But through those painful experiences, when I faced them head-on, I acknowledged what happened, deep profound healing came along with it. There's a misconception that trauma is shameful or a sign of weakness, that experiencing trauma of any kind means that we are broken. But in reality, the change we experience from trauma is often the source of our greatest strength. Trauma is the experience, but unresolved trauma is your inability (conscious or unconscious) to process and integrate that experience. Even if you've been traumatized, or experienced any type of physical, mental, or emotional trauma, there's so much that can be done about it, and once that is addressed, profound deep healing, learning, and growth can happen.

I've found that I have also developed this inner sense of neutrality. A new space that I can lean into that feels neutral. Not good or bad, just being. I can now easily become an observer of not only my own thoughts, feelings, and emotions with no attachment but also of the experiences and events of the world. I think this is huge. I never knew that I was capable of being "neutral" or just being. I had always thought that I had to react, respond, and feel a certain way about any and everything that happened to me, others, and in the world. I also possess this uncanny new skill of hedonic adaptation. It's a research-proven tendency of people to revert quickly to stable levels of happiness after a painful or pleasurable event. We live in a society that gives us a daily onslaught of hedonic stimulation at both extremes. It's important to be able to rebalance back to stable levels of happiness after reading the news or seeing a viral video of someone being murdered, especially when that person is murdered because they look like you. It can also be applied to a variety of strong emotional states and could explain why people become accustomed to events they've been repeatedly exposed to.

Human beings are extremely resilient. We are the product of millions of years of evolution and adaptation. It's what we do. But when it comes to trauma, we tend to get frozen and that hinders our potential for post-traumatic growth. We can't control most aspects of life. However, we can control our attitude, intention, and our effort. So, it's hard to understand why things happen especially if it was a traumatic experience. But if you're able to elevate your inner state, to be greater than your outer environment, and this takes training, you have this ability to rise above that. And maybe even potentially be able to find meaning in the most difficult and trying circumstances. And this can happen as easily as changing your nerve state.

As humans, the things that happen to us are just experiences. Whether we view them as good or bad; they are still the same experience. We attach a certain meaning or narrative to them to help us understand or cope. Once you understand that all you have to do is to change your nerve state to change your story, the small changes over time add up to true transformation; it will change your perspective and align to an elevated platform or way of thinking. It will help you get unfrozen or unstuck. You'll realize that you aren't a mess trying to hold together thousands of pieces, but are deeply frozen in patterns that no longer serve you. You realize that not only can you self-regulate when times are good, but that you can do that in any situation. Even throughout some of the most difficult times throughout humanity. I'm living proof that what we think of as traumatic experiences can be turned into a beneficial scenario that can have rippling effects that are hard to understand.

I've come a long way but that doesn't mean I'm perfect or will ever be. Like I've mentioned, this journey is just that, a journey. There's no such thing as a "healing destination" or "cure". These are concepts with moving goalposts because you never stop attaining balance. This world and this country are filled with injustice and existing and taking space as a Black man in America means that my stress response is going to be triggered more easily. I have to operate with some sort of hypervigilance running in the background because of situational circumstances and trying not to piss off people who want to physically harm me just because of what I look like. I also have to exercise patience and resist getting angry when I experience microaggressions or instances of conscious or unconscious bias. That is part of the injustice! Unfortunately, I cannot simply peacefully "exist" in circumstances that White people can easily. It is what it is. What's really helped me come to terms with this overwhelming trauma is a powerful and transformative word: forgiveness. Forgiveness of myself, forgiveness for those who have hurt me, forgiveness for those who have tried to hurt me, forgiveness for society and its archaic, broken, and biased systems, forgiveness for capitalism and all of the unconscious and conscious greed monsters it breeds, forgiveness for life and all that it throws at us. Which is a lot these days. Can a brotha get a break?!? When you are able to forgive yourself and work through the anger, guilt, and shame, there is a sense of relief. An ease of progressing disease. Once you forgive yourself, some of those negative feelings leave you. Forgive yourself for struggling. Forgive yourself for carrying trauma. Your trauma response and behavioral adaptations are your personal ways of coping. Pain is inevitable, but suffering is optional. If you stub your toe, that's pain. But if you're still complaining about stubbing your toe three weeks later, that's suffering.

By slowly and consistently cultivating awareness by practicing Interval Mindfulness™ and its various Innervals™, I have been able to shift the focus from the suffering I experienced to improving myself. It wasn't as easy as flipping a switch, and it requires a commitment to doing the inner work. However, on the other side of my traumas, it's clear to see how that helped me channel the suffering or pain into something productive. My personal post-traumatic growth. We will always keep repeating frozen negative patterns until we face them, feel them, and heal them. All in the name of healing so we can push forward to a fuller, happier, and more connected life. Our own personal "Groundhog Day" for each aspect or lesson that we are too stubborn to learn easily. Once you become aware, face, and embrace your traumas, they will be your pivot moment for greater things in your life. Through your traumas, you'll find your greater purpose, and realize that through those traumatic events, after processing them, dealing with them, and putting them behind you in a healthy way, you can do amazing things.

Once I became unfrozen, I was able to take opportunities to evolve and grow from my experiences. Instead of collapsing or feeling horrible based on the experiences that I went through. Because I was able to make sense of my experiences with my newly trained awareness, I was able to extract the good. I was able to take something that I learned from it and different aspects of my life changed. I began to see life more openly and I was willing to engage with life in a way I hadn't really been able to before. My perception of myself changed. I began to see myself as more capable, strong, and enough. I became a better person because of the challenging times I went through.

Are you frozen? Are you constantly self-soothing yourself? Are you numbing and distracting yourself? If so, how? When you get home is the first thing you do putting on the tv because you desperately don't want to hear what's in your own head? How's your relationship with food? Or are you overeating or undereating?

What are you pretending not to see? Are you pretending not to see that there's trouble in your relationship? Are you pretending not to see that health issue that needs your attention? Are you pretending not to see that you hate your job? To be frozen is many things, but mostly it's to be stuck. To feel stuck in the same patterns, the same responses, and getting the same results. To know that you need to do better and to want to do better; all to end up right back where you started.

To fully transform, we need to stop thinking about what we need to do to change. True transformation, emerging on the other side, climbing out of a black hole, however you need to define it in your mind, comes from when we let go of what is no longer serving us. Transformation is about what we can be; it's about being the change. It's not about what we can do. It's about what we can be. Be the change, live the change, and ultimately, see the change. You start being the change when you get unfrozen.

FORGIVENESS

You are not your traumas; your traumas are simply experiences. It will always be hard to see it at first, but there is always learning, wisdom, and gold in your traumatic experiences; but you have to process them and be willing to look at them from a relaxed state. It's not going to happen right away and each person is unique. Each person will experience it differently and it's important to not re-traumatize ourselves. Talk therapy can be helpful for some people, but picking our scabs and re-wounding ourselves, over and over again, by going back to that initial insult can sometimes be counterproductive. It's also important to deal with what comes up, as it comes up, to the degree that it's coming up. Not make it more than it is or make it less than it is. But allow it and be with, as it is, to the best of your ability. At that moment, with the level of education, maturity, opportunity, and assistance that you have available to you.

A lot of times when people have a traumatic experience or they are currently in a place where they are suffering. A lot of times in their own mind and internally they are thinking "Why me?", "Why did this happen to me?", "Why did someone do this to me?", or "Why was I on that street corner on this day?" And there is a lot of resentment, anger, and negative feelings around the experience. If we can take blame out of the situation and step back a little bit and not label things as good or bad or look for blame. From there, we can begin to approach our life with more curiosity. It allows us to have a lot more empathy for ourselves and the world around us. And it allows us to have a really deep experience of forgiveness for a traumatic thing that happened in our life. Forgiveness is the hardest part of the healing journey. Some people move through forgiveness quickly because it's part of their religion or part of who they are. While others struggle intensely with it. But sometimes, forgiveness is that final hurdle to getting unfrozen and activating rapid self-healing. How does forgiveness help you when you've been traumatized or hurt? It's a way to have acceptance and really move through that grieving process of whatever incident you had. And when you forgive someone, including forgiving parts of yourself, you bring back the power to you.

You get to the other side of your traumas by practicing forgiveness, reframing your beliefs, and cultivating empathy and compassion. Those are the steppingstones to issue resolution. Forgiveness takes a lot of time and it's a process. Forgiveness is being willing to let go of foregone conclusions. Are you willing to let go of the conclusions and assumptions, and willing to look at it as just an experience? When I think about forgiveness, I really think of this concept of empathy. Empathy for self and empathy for others. When I think of empathy, I think we're all people, who are all having an experience in our lives and doing the best we can, at the moment we are in, with what we have been given.

It takes time, it doesn't happen overnight. But every day, everyone has an opportunity to forgive themselves. There's no doubt in my mind that you don't come across an experience, person, thing, something, whether it's through seeing, hearing, smelling, touching, tasting that doesn't trigger something, where you can take that moment and look at yourself and say, I love you. I forgive you. You are beautiful. And you are whole. Everything is training. Training the mind. Letting go is training. Training the mind-body muscle. And most importantly training the thoughts, those voices that come into our mind that don't allow us to forgive, let go, to love, or to move forward. Training the thoughts that keep us frozen, stuck, and going in circles throughout life.

Part of our evolution is to understand that all trauma isn't necessarily bad. It's not a label that we have to put on ourselves. It is an opportunity for us to evolve. Trauma is one of the common threads that connect us and allow us to have authentic empathy for one another because we can personally relate to going through different things. If you are reading this and you are concerned about how your traumas have affected you or concerned about the work you need to do or the support you need to get to help you reach the other side of your traumas, I say to you this: Embrace your traumas and work through them. And when you're comfortable, share your story with others. You never know who you will inspire with your message of overcoming. Your journey towards healing is an honor because you can help other people heal in a way you wouldn't if you didn't have to go through what you went through. Working through trauma is hard work. Sometimes it seems easier to repress, distract, and numb through the pain. But it's a losing game that can cut your life short. The gift of pain is growth: inspirational, personal, and aspirational.

YOU FROZE YOURSELF

I used to identify as being someone who had to learn how to do things the hard way. I'd shrug my shoulders and say, "I'm just stubborn", and continue to bang my head against the wall frozen in the same patterns, habits, and thinking. I genuinely believed the more torturous, painful, chaotic, and demoralizing an experience was, the more worthwhile the outcome would be. That might be true in some instances, but it's not true all the time. We have become so desensitized to trauma, struggle, and suffering, that we secretly crave it and willingly consume it daily. You will never control what happens to you, that's life. What you can control is how you process, recover and integrate that experience; no matter how painful, traumatizing, or tortuous it may have been. When we don't do those things, our bodies will negatively adapt, and we get frozen or stuck.

We don't realize that we become frozen in these patterns because freezing takes time. It's not a switch and happens gradually over time. Often slipping through the conscious awareness of most people. But no matter when or how it happens, it's important to accept and acknowledge that it happened because of your body's responses. This does not mean that it's your fault; it simply means that this is your initial response. Forgive yourself for what you did or how you reacted while you were in survival mode or frozen in your stress or shutdown responses.

You're frozen, not broken. Broken is often a label that people tend to over-identify with. To be broken is hopelessness. Breaking, mostly associated with glass, often results in things breaking into a lot of different pieces that can never be put back together again. What's the first thing we do when we break glass? We throw it away. If someone says and feels like they are broken, they are also probably thinking (consciously or unconsciously) that they deserve to be thrown away or discarded by others. We are a society of labels, but what's disempowering is when we over-identify with labels. I don't want to over-identify with any label, whether it's an objectively great label like "awesome buff guy" or a not-so-flattering label like "angry Black man." When we over-identify with a label, we are robbing ourselves of a million potential other identities and the experiences that could go with them. Try not to collude with the story. Try not to over-identify with the labels, because that's very disempowering.

We've all been conditioned at some point to search outside of ourselves for healing, love, validation, and acceptance in some way. It doesn't matter if you take the red pill or the blue pill, because no pill works without access to the human body. Your body is the catalyst for all things, not the other way around. Many cultural values, family traditions, and work settings reinforce these circumstances. But by always being externally focused on these things in order to regulate ourselves, we can easily get frozen. Stuck going in circles, repeating harmful patterns, ruminating negative feedback loops, and in a deep freeze of self-sabotage, self-loathing, and low self-worth. But these things can be unlearned, undone, and unpacked once you start defrosting by training self-awareness.

Cultivating self-awareness isn't sexy; sorry but I'm not sorry. If you look at any fitness class or athletic practice, nothing they do in there is sexy. The ugly faces, grunting, and all-out effort pushes that make people do the weirdest things (like fart)! But what IS sexy, is the aftermath of that training. What's sexy is watching athletes gracefully execute power moves while they are playing their games or win titles, competitions, and recognition. Or watching people in the world who are healthy, energetic, and magnetic because they consistently exercise, eat healthily, and take care of their mental, emotional, and physical health. I at least make training self-awareness fun, novel, and associative to what you already experience when you take a fitness class or do some other training. It's a real-world practical shift, and not totally conceptual.

No matter what has happened to you, you must understand that you froze yourself. Technically it was your nervous system, but YOUR nervous system; not someone else's. No matter what anyone did to you, no matter how you were abused, hurt, or wronged. No matter what happened YOU FROZE YOURSELF. I'm not saying this to assign blame, point fingers, or name names; I'm saying this to empower you. I had to step up, be an adult, and take responsibility for my actions and responses. If I didn't, I would've never been able to activate my rapid self-healing, least of all accelerate it. That was the initial step of the entire process. Whatever went or is going wrong in your body now was preconditioned by YOU, your choices, and your circumstances. You are a grown *ss adult and should be taking responsibility for YOUR habits, choices, and behavior. No one else. You aren't a victim. Before you start throwing a pity party, you should understand that this very concept is empowering! Anything that's preconditioned by you can ALWAYS be retrained by YOU. If anyone tells you otherwise, it's because they probably profit off of you being a hot mess (no judgment). It's that simple, even though it's not that easy. Thawing out takes time, but when you finally do, it's oh so rewarding.

Another thing that isn't really spoken a lot about it, is that you don't need to always process the trauma or hurt or pain to really feel it or experience it. For some, it may be necessary to re-open certain wounds, feel the hurt and pain again, in order to process and heal. But for other people, just having the awareness of where you're stuck or frozen can be enough to create the shift to self-healing. Just having the awareness of where you got stuck, where it is in your body, where the trauma hurt you or hit you, and having a conversation about it, can be enough to shift you or heal you back into this space of balance.

It's so important that you take responsibility for your own hurt, pain, and unresolved trauma. So many people in this world are walking around with an underlying sense of fear, anger, resentment, guilt, shame, and all the negative emotions that we bury inside that are disturbing. But they're all walking through life thinking "I got this" until a crisis, trauma, accident, or chronic health issue hijacks them. Don't wait until it's too late. Allopathic, naturopathic, and any other -pathic they haven't even created yet to divide the body and to confuse you into thinking self-healing happens differently in different groups, different areas of the body, different parts of the world, at different ages, according to different gene expressions, according to whether your insurance thinks so. Self-healing is only done by you. You froze you, and only you can thaw you. Nobody heals you. Nobody fixes you. Saviors make great plots for movies, but they are BS in real life. Why would you even want to wait for someone to "save" you when you could just save yourself...unless you're codependent. All symptoms, inner whispers, and chronic health issues are your body trying to self-heal. Your body is perfect as it is; nature never makes mistakes. Stop outsourcing your self-healing potential and giving up your power to others.

Passive treatments that quiet your symptoms instead of addressing the root cause isn't healing; it's managing. We all go through different phases in life, and that includes trauma, crisis, and suffering. Trauma, crisis, and suffering isn't a punishment, it's ALWAYS a teaching tool. When you're frozen in a stress response because of it, you will never see that because your priority is survival, not judgment-free thinking. Just like pain, fear, and some of the other things we feel, trauma, crisis, and suffering is a call for action or change.

To truly find trauma, crisis, and suffering as motivating, you really must dismiss, dissolve, and release some of your old, hard, and deep self-limiting beliefs that keep you stuck. How you look, move, feel, and heal is always determined by your lifestyle, behavior, and daily choices. You have the power to proactively make your body run at optimal health. Only YOU can right your reality. It's when you are frozen in reactivity to the world that sh*t hits the fan. Your body's default state is to remain in balance, homeostasis, at all times. It takes a lot of stubbornness, avoidance, and ignorance for you to get chronically sick. Before chronic infection, illness, and disease is an acute infection, illness, and disease. When you look past all the fancy names, the areas, the stages, the duration, the cure rates, how readily you can get infected, and all the other focuses that Western medicine has preconditioned us to focus on, infection, illness, and disease is nothing more than an imbalanced, congested, and stagnant expression of energy that's slow to arrest, reverse, and resolve because of your frozen nerve state.

You experience and perceive energy. Energy flows where your focus goes. At the end of the day, what's making people sick isn't just germs. It's chronic perceived stress, inflammation, poor nutrition, blood sugar balance, processed foods, perpetual fear, herbicides, gut imbalance, EMF exposure, inner wounds, unhealed trauma, heavy metals, overuse of prescription drugs, lack of sunlight, sleep deprivation, shallow breathing, cleaning products, toxic chemicals, and a host of other factors that you will never see, notice, or feel if you're not cultivating self-awareness. You can't fix what you can't see, and you'll never self-heal in the dark. However, by taking baby steps, micro approaches, and cultivating mini moments of awareness with my Interval Mindfulness™ method, you'll effortlessly master your stress, adapt to adversity, and activate rapid self-healing. Now let's get to work together and you better not get #shady.

Sending you love, light, and laughter!

Mario Godiva

P.S. Here's one final Innerval™ combo to close out this book. For bigger, better, and more complex Innerval™ workouts be sure to try the various inner workouts (9 – 21 minutes) on my Video On-Demand library at http://mariogodiva.com

LOVING-KINDNESS 9 INNERVAL™ COMBO. (3 minutes)

1. LOVING-KINDNESS INNERVAL™ // 30 seconds.

Close your eyes; using the finger of your non-dominant hand, write three people that you want to send love, energy, or healing to on your dominant hand. After you write all three people, start drawing a slow circle on your palm and see how long you can spend reliving and feeling the emotions that each person brought up.

2. CORE BREATHING INNERVAL™ // 30 seconds.

Take long, slow, and deep inhales and take longer, slower, and deeper exhales for 30 seconds or 3 cycles (1 inhale/exhale) of breath if you don't have a timer.

3. Repeat 2 times picking 3 new people that you want to send love, energy, or healing wishes to each time you go through the combo.

STIMULATION: Tactile stimulation; prefrontal cortex; visualization; dopamine and serotonin release.

ACKNOWLEDGEMENTS //

I have nothing but endless, deep, and genuine gratitude for the many people who have enriched, empowered, and inspired my life in so many beautiful ways. Thank you to each and every one of you from the bottom of my Godiva heart.

I first and foremost want to thank my wonderful friend Dr. Alexa Carlson. You have walked me off the ledge so many times and helped me heal mentally, emotionally, and physically more than you know. I love you so so much and I'm so grateful for our friendship.

When I first started writing this book, the New Yorker in me thought I could easily do it in six months. Four years later, this labor of love is finally finished.

Writing my first book couldn't have happened without the support of my various editors. I wanted to stop, give up, or take an indefinite break so many times, but I was always inspired to get back on the horse by one of my various editors.

To my very first editor Brendan Fitzgibbons, thank you for helping me overwrite and turn my anger and rage into humor and lightheartedness. It truly set the tone for my voice in this entire work.

To my second editor Pat Barnhart, thank you for working with my short attention span and letting me write and edit chapter by chapter. Also thank you for the nudges to get back on the writing horse every single time that I fell off, which was a lot!

To my third editor Laura Piquero, thank you for helping me create and fine tune the first big picture of my entire manuscript. Your intuitive writing and storytelling helped immensely.

To my fourth editor Dana Alsamsam, thank you for helping me cut down and edit my tendency to overwrite and share too much information. haha Also thank you for making my manuscript more concise, cohesive, and compassionate.

To my fifth and final editor Josh Rapps, thank you for your help with research, fact checking, cites, sources, and my final proofread. You made me feel confident to show this work to the world despite some of the criticism that I know it will face.

To my mommy Monica, rest in power. Your medical martyrdom set the foundation for my resistance and resilience for strictly conventional medical methods.

To my sisters Myeshia, Dominique, and Kishna, thank you for your endless love from afar, support, and adapting as best as you could to our very traumatic childhood.

I thank my many friends (in no order) who encouraged me to write this book and gave me feedback, help, and resources all throughout the process: Alexa, Tess, Kayla, Shauna, and anyone else that isn't named.

To all my holistic health mentors that blazed the trail, hold online summits, and think outside of the Western medicine box. Thank you for your commitment to looking at things from a view that is not mainstream or the primary way of thinking. You have inspired me greatly and although that path can be lonely, your courage for standing up for what you feel is right, health freedom and the freedom to CHOSE, does not go unnoticed.

I also want to thank each and every one of you holding this book. You're holding it because you may be frozen and you're ready to start to defrost to a more peaceful, fulfilling, and present focused life. Self-awareness is your superpower. I'm deeply honored that you want to master your stress, adapt to adversity, and activate rapid self-healing so that you can show up in the world as a better, happier, and healthier YOU.

NOTES & REFERENCES //

1. Morris, Z. S., Wooding, S. & Grant, J. The answer is 17 years, what is the question: Understanding time lags in translational research. *J. R. Soc. Med.* **104**, 510–520 (2011).

2. O'Regan, B. & Hirshberg, C. *Spontaneous Remission: An Annotated Bibliography.* (Institute of Noetic Sciences, 2013).

3. Parasympathetic Summit 2020. *LookUp* https://lookupindiana.org/system-of-care/hamilton/events/parasympathetic-summit-2020 (2020).

4. National Center for Health Statistics (US). Health, United States, 2015: With Special Feature on Racial and Ethnic Health Disparities. 1232 (2016).

5. Hardeman, R. R., Medina, E. M. & Kozhimannil, K. B. Structural Racism and Supporting Black Lives — The Role of Health Professionals. *N. Engl. J. Med.* **375**, 2113–2115 (2016).

6. Choo, E. Easy in, tough out: the dam of health-care racism. *Lancet* **397**, 570 (2021).

7. Krogsbøll, L. T., Hrábjartsson, A. & Gøtzsche, P. C. Spontaneous improvement in randomised clinical trials: Meta-analysis of three-armed trials comparing no treatment, placebo and active intervention. *BMC Med. Res. Methodol.* **9**, (2009).

8. Robson, D. Cancer: The mysterious miracle cases inspiring doctors. *BBC* https://www.bbc.com/future/article/20150306-the-mystery-of-vanishing-cancer (2015).

9. Rohdenburg, G. L. & Wood, F. C. Fluctuations in the growth energy of malignant tumors in man, with especial reference to spontaneous recession. *J. Cancer Res.* **3**, 193–225 (1918).

10. Morton, J. J. & Morton, J. H. Cancer as a chronic disease. *Ann. Surg.* **137**, 683–703 (1953).

11. Cole, W. H. & C, E. T. Spontaneous regression of cancer: preliminary report. *Ann. Surg.* **144**, 366–383 (1956).

12. Barrett, R. *et al.* FISH identifies a KAT6A/CREBBP fusion caused by a cryptic insertional t(8;16) in a case of spontaneously remitting congenital acute myeloid leukemia with a normal karyotype. *Pediatr. Blood Cancer* **64**, (2017).

13. D'Arena, G. *et al.* More on spontaneous regression of chronic lymphocytic leukemia: Two new cases and potential role of lamivudine in a further patient with advanced disease and hepatitis B virus infection. *Leuk. Lymphoma* **55**, 1955–1957 (2014).

14. Udupa, K., Philip, A., Rajendranath, R., Sagar, T. & Majhi, U. Spontaneous regression of primary progressive Hodgkin's lymphoma in a pediatric patient: A case report and review of literature. *Hematol. Oncol. Stem Cell Ther.* **6**, 112–116 (2013).

15. Takahashi, T. *et al.* Spontaneous Regression of Intravascular Large B-Cell Lymphoma and Apoptosis of Lymphoma Cells: A Case Report. *J. Clin. Exp. Hematop.* **55**, 151–156 (2015).

16.   Ito, E. *et al.* Spontaneous breast cancer remission: A case report. *Int. J. Surg. Case Rep.* **25**, 132–136 (2016).

17.   Nakamura, Y. *et al.* Spontaneous remission of a non-small cell lung cancer possibly caused by anti-NY-ESO-1 immunity. *Lung Cancer* **65**, 119–122 (2009).

18.   Kitai, H. *et al.* Spontaneous regression of small cell lung cancer combined with cancer associated retinopathy. *Lung Cancer* **87**, 73–76 (2015).

19.   Balzer, B. L. & Ulbright, T. M. Spontaneous regression of testicular germ cell tumors: An analysis of 42 cases. *Am. J. Surg. Pathol.* **30**, 858–865 (2006).

20.   Lee, T. *et al.* Case: Spontaneous regression of post-radical prostatectomy prostate-specific antigen elevation without adjuvant therapy in a patient with lymph node metastasis. *Can. Urol. Assoc. J.* **11**, E315–E317 (2017).

21.   Katano, A., Takenaka, R., Okuma, K., Yamashita, H. & Nakagawa, K. Repeated episodes of spontaneous regression/progression of cervical adenocarcinoma after adjuvant chemoradiation therapy: A case report. *J. Med. Case Rep.* **9**, 114 (2015).

22.   Parks, A. L., McWhirter, R. M., Evason, K. & Kelley, R. K. Cases of Spontaneous Tumor Regression in Hepatobiliary Cancers: Implications for Immunotherapy? *J. Gastrointest. Cancer* **46**, 161–165 (2015).

23.   Chida, K. *et al.* Spontaneous regression of transverse colon cancer: a case report. *Surg. Case Reports* **3**, 65 (2017).

24.   Pang, C., Sharma, D. & Sankar, T. Spontaneous regression of Merkel cell carcinoma: A case report and review of the literature. *Int. J. Surg. Case Rep.* **7**, 104–108 (2015).

25.   Miller, C. V., Cook, I. S., Jayaramachandran, R. & Tyers, A. G. Spontaneous regression of a conjunctival malignant melanoma. *Orbit* **33**, 139–141 (2014).

26.   Pukel, C. Spontaneous Regression of Cancer: Explanations and Predictions. *Cancer Therapy Advisor* https://www.cancertherapyadvisor.com/home/cancer-topics/general-oncology/spontaneous-regression-of-cancer-explanations-and-predictions/2/ (2017).

27.   Burke, J. Lourdes miracles get a little easier. *The Guardian* https://www.theguardian.com/world/2006/apr/02/religion.france (2006).

28.   Development of the Nervous System. *Lumen Learning* https://courses.lumenlearning.com/boundless-ap/chapter/development-of-the-nervous-system/.

29.   Toledo, C. & Saltsman, K. Genetics by the Numbers. *National Institute of General Medical Sciences* https://www.nigms.nih.gov/education/Inside-Life-Science/Pages/genetics-by-the-numbers.aspx (2012).

30.   Michigan State University. Resiliency on the battlefield: Soldiers with a positive outlook less likely to suffer anxiety, depression. *ScienceDaily* https://www.sciencedaily.com/releases/2011/01/110104101340.htm (2011).

31.   Porges, S. W. *The Polyvagal Theory: Neurophysiological Foundations of Emotions, Attachment, Communication, and Self-regulation.* (W. W. Norton & Company, 2011).

32. Home of Dr. Stephen Porges. https://www.stephenporges.com/.

33. Porges, S. W. Neuroception: A Subconscious System for Detecting Threats and Safety. *Zero Three* 19–24 (2004).

34. Tindle, J. & Tadi, P. *Neuroanatomy, Parasympathetic Nervous System. StatPearls* (StatPearls Publishing, 2020).

35. Alshak, M. N. & M Das, J. *Neuroanatomy, Sympathetic Nervous System. StatPearls* (StatPearls Publishing, 2019).

36. Wagner, D. Polyvagal theory in practice. *Counseling Today* https://ct.counseling.org/2016/06/polyvagal-theory-practice/ (2016).

37. A Bit About Deb. *Rhythm of Regulation* https://www.rhythmofregulation.com/about (2021).

38. Stress effects on the body. *American Psychological Association* https://www.apa.org/topics/stress/body (2018).

39. Kim, H. G., Cheon, E. J., Bai, D. S., Lee, Y. H. & Koo, B. H. Stress and heart rate variability: A meta-analysis and review of the literature. *Psychiatry Investig.* **15**, 235–245 (2018).

40. Tsuji, H. *et al.* Reduced heart rate variability and mortality risk in an elderly cohort: The Framingham heart study. *Circulation* **90**, 878–883 (1994).

41. McGuire, J. Repairing the Nervous System. *Facebook* https://www.facebook.com/repairingthenervoussystem/photos/a.101643378001844/261923938640453/?type=3 (2021).

42. About Dan. https://drdansiegel.com/.

43. Walford, M. Trauma and the Nervous System. *Rise Up* https://www.bodywisefoundation.org/blog/bodywisefoundation/nervous-system-trauma (2017).

44. Graham, L. The Neuroscience of Resilience: Nervous System Regulation. *LoveAndLifeToolbox* https://loveandlifetoolbox.com/the-neuroscience-of-resilience-nervous-system-regulation/ (2010).

45. Villines, Z. & Han, S. What does the frontal lobe do? *MedicalNewsToday* https://www.medicalnewstoday.com/articles/318139 (2017).

46. Arnsten, A. F. T. Stress signalling pathways that impair prefrontal cortex structure and function. *Nat. Rev. Neurosci.* **10**, 410–422 (2009).

47. Graham, L. *Resilience: Powerful Practices for Bouncing Back from Disappointment, Difficulty, and Even Disaster.* (New World Library, 2018).

48. Graham, L. The Neuroscience of Resilience. *Linda Graham, MFT* https://lindagraham-mft.net/the-neuroscience-of-resilience/ (2010).

49. The Power to Heal Yourself. *The Holistic Psychologist* https://theholisticpsychologist.com/.

50. Stress and Your Gut. *Gastrointestinal Society* https://badgut.org/information-centre/a-z-digestive-topics/stress-and-your-gut/ (2007).

51.   Hyman, M. 10 Strategies to Reverse Autoimmune Disease. *Dr. Hyman Blog* https://drhyman.com/blog/2015/07/24/10-strategies-to-reverse-autoimmune-disease/ (2015).

52.   Kippola, P. *Beat Autoimmune: The 6 Keys to Reverse Your Condition and Reclaim Your Health.* (Citadel Press, 2019).

53.   Toxic Chemicals. *Natural Resources Defense Council* https://www.nrdc.org/issues/toxic-chemicals.

54.   Chemicals in the human body. *The World Counts* https://www.theworldcounts.com/challenges/toxic-exposures/polluted-bodies/chemicals-in-the-human-body/story (2021).

55.   Pizzorno, J. Conventional laboratory tests to assess toxin burden. *Integr. Med.* **14**, 8–16 (2015).

56.   Bennett, J. W. & Klich, M. Mycotoxins. *Clin. Microbiol. Rev.* **16**, 497–516 (2003).

57.   De Vocht, F. 'Dirty electricity': What, where, and should we care. *J. Expo. Sci. Environ. Epidemiol.* **20**, 399–405 (2010).

58.   Cryan, J. F. *et al.* The microbiota-gut-brain axis. *Physiol. Rev.* **99**, 1877–2013 (2019).

59.   Paterni, I., Granchi, C. & Minutolo, F. Risks and benefits related to alimentary exposure to xenoestrogens. *Crit. Rev. Food Sci. Nutr.* **57**, 3384–3404 (2017).

60.   Banks, W. A. *et al.* Lipopolysaccharide-induced blood-brain barrier disruption: Roles of cyclooxygenase, oxidative stress, neuroinflammation, and elements of the neurovascular unit. *J. Neuroinflammation* **12**, (2015).

61.   Chaudhuri, J. *et al.* The Role of Advanced Glycation End Products in Aging and Metabolic Diseases: Bridging Association and Causality. *Cell Metab.* **28**, 337–352 (2018).

62.   Vighi, G., Marcucci, F., Sensi, L., Di Cara, G. & Frati, F. Allergy and the gastrointestinal system. *Clin. Exp. Immunol.* **153**, 3–6 (2008).

63.   Chon, M. Deepak Chopra and J Balvin Are Hosting A Free Bilingual 21-Day Meditation Experience. *Oprah Daily* https://www.oprahdaily.com/life/health/a32947147/deepak-chopra-j-balvin-meditation-bilingual/ (2020).

64.   Tolle, E. The First Step of Conscious Manifestation | Conscious Manifestation 2020. *YouTube* https://www.youtube.com/watch?v=HCvdfM6FV1Y (2020).

65.   Bernstein, G. My Top 5 Manifesting Secrets. *Dear Gabby* https://gabbybernstein.com/top-5-manifesting-secrets/ (2017).

66.   Jean-Philippe, M. Iyanla Vanzant Weighs in on Infidelity, Splitting the Bill, and More For 'In Our O-Pinion'. *Oprah Daily* https://www.oprahdaily.com/entertainment/tv-movies/a26589692/iyanla-vanzant-advice-in-our-opinion/ (2019).

67.   Jean-Philippe, M. 5 Oprah Quotes That Have All the Wisdom You'll Ever Need. *Oprah Daily* (2019).

68.   Jennings, R. Shut up, I'm manifesting! *Vox* https://www.vox.com/the-goods/21524975/manifesting-does-it-really-work-meme (2020).

69. Oettingen, G., Mayer, D. & Portnow, S. Pleasure Now, Pain Later: Positive Fantasies About the Future Predict Symptoms of Depression. *Psychol. Sci.* **27**, 345–353 (2016).

70. Kim, H. & Newman, M. G. The paradox of relaxation training: Relaxation induced anxiety and mediation effects of negative contrast sensitivity in generalized anxiety disorder and major depressive disorder. *J. Affect. Disord.* **259**, 271–278 (2019).

71. Waxenbaum, J. A. & Varacallo, M. *Anatomy, Autonomic Nervous System. StatPearls* (StatPearls Publishing, 2019).

72. Salazar-Muñoz, Y. *et al.* Classification and Assessment of the Patelar Reflex Response through Biomechanical Measures. *J. Healthc. Eng.* **2019**, (2019).

73. Ross, V. Numbers: The Nervous System, From 268-MPH Signals to Trillions of Synapses. *Discover* https://www.discovermagazine.com/health/numbers-the-nervous-system-from-268-mph-signals-to-trillions-of-synapses.

74. Habituation, Sensitization, and Potentiation. *Lumen Learning* https://courses.lumenlearning.com/boundless-psychology/chapter/biological-basis-of-learning/ (2021).

75. Vagus Nerve Overview. *Healthline* (2018).

76. Schwerdtfeger, A. R. & Scheel, S. M. Self-esteem fluctuations and cardiac vagal control in everyday life. *Int. J. Psychophysiol.* **83**, 328–335 (2012).

77. Browne, S. J. What The Vagus Nerve Is And How To Stimulate It For Better Mental Health. *Forbes* https://www.forbes.com/sites/womensmedia/2021/04/15/what-the-vagus-nerve-is-and-how-to-stimulate-it-for-better-mental-health/?sh=3c1f12796250 (2021).

78. Gastroparesis. *Cedars Sinai* https://www.cedars-sinai.org/health-library/diseases-and-conditions/g/gastroparesis.html.

79. Bonaz, B. Is-there a place for vagus nerve stimulation in inflammatory bowel diseases? *Bioelectron. Med.* **4**, 1–9 (2018).

80. Bosmans, G. *et al.* Vagus nerve stimulation dampens intestinal inflammation in a murine model of experimental food allergy. *Allergy Eur. J. Allergy Clin. Immunol.* **74**, 1748–1759 (2019).

81. Underwood, E. Newly detailed nerve links between brain and other organs shape thoughts, memories, and feelings. *Science* https://www.sciencemag.org/news/2021/06/newly-detailed-nerve-links-between-brain-and-other-organs-shape-thoughts-memories-and (2021).

82. Breit, S., Kupferberg, A., Rogler, G. & Hasler, G. Vagus nerve as modulator of the brain-gut axis in psychiatric and inflammatory disorders. *Front. Psychiatry* **9**, (2018).

83. Zakrajsek, L. What Happens in Vagus: Jump-start Recovery by Increasing Vagal Tone. *National Institute for Fitness & Sport* https://www.nifs.org/blog/what-happens-in-vagus-jump-start-recovery-by-increasing-vagal-tone (2020).

84. Simon-Thomas, E. R. Measuring Compassion in the Body. *Greater Good Magazine* https://greatergood.berkeley.edu/article/item/measuring_compassion_in_the_body (2015).

85. Coote, J. H. & White, M. J. CrossTalk proposal: Bradycardia in the trained athlete is attributable to high vagal tone. *Journal of Physiology* vol. 593 1745–1747 (2015).

86. Adelson, R. Stimulating the vagus nerve: memories are made of this. *Am. Psychol. Assoc.* **34**, 36 (2004).

87. Kok, B. E. *et al.* How Positive Emotions Build Physical Health: Perceived Positive Social Connections Account for the Upward Spiral Between Positive Emotions and Vagal Tone. *Psychol. Sci.* **24**, 1123–1132 (2013).

88. Howland, R. H. Vagus Nerve Stimulation. *Curr. Behav. Neurosci. Reports* **1**, 64–73 (2014).

89. Horeis, M. The vagus nerve: your secret weapon in fighting stress. *Allied Services* https://www.allied-services.org/news/2020/june/the-vagus-nerve-your-secret-weapon-in-fighting-s/ (2020).

90. Impact of COVID-19 on minoritized and marginalized communities. *American Medical Association* https://www.ama-assn.org/delivering-care/health-equity/impact-covid-19-minoritized-and-marginalized-communities (2020).

91. Brar, K. Trauma porn: Misguided 'activism' on social media harms more than it helps. *The Butler Collegian* https://thebutlercollegian.com/2020/09/trauma-porn-misguided-activism-on-social-media-harms-more-than-it-helps/ (2020).

92. ACSM Fitness Trends. *The American College of Sports Medicine* https://www.acsm.org/read-research/trending-topics-resource-pages/acsm-fitness-trends (2021).

93. Gillen, J. B. *et al.* Twelve weeks of sprint interval training improves indices of cardiometabolic health similar to traditional endurance training despite a five-fold lower exercise volume and time commitment. *PLoS One* **11**, e0154075 (2016).

94. Taylor, J., McLean, L., Korner, A., Stratton, E. & Glozier, N. Mindfulness and yoga for psychological trauma: systematic review and meta-analysis. *Journal of Trauma and Dissociation* vol. 21 536–573 (2020).

95. Carlson, L. E. Mindfulness-Based Interventions for Physical Conditions: A Narrative Review Evaluating Levels of Evidence. *ISRN Psychiatry* **2012**, 1–21 (2012).

96. Uddin, L. Q. Cognitive and behavioural flexibility: neural mechanisms and clinical considerations. *Nat. Rev. Neurosci.* **22**, 167–179 (2021).

97. Stress, Addiction, and Neuroplasticity –How the Brain Changes. *National Institute for the Clinical Application of Behavioral Medicine* https://www.nicabm.com/stress-addiction-and-neuroplasticity/.

98. Mecking, O. The Case for Doing Nothing. *New York Times* https://www.nytimes.com/2019/04/29/smarter-living/the-case-for-doing-nothing.html (2019).

99. Oppong, T. The Science of Silence: How Solitude Enriches Creative Work. *Inc.* https://www.inc.com/thomas-oppong/the-science-of-silence-how-solitude-enriches-creative-work.html (2017).

100. Use of Yoga and Meditation Becoming More Popular in U.S. *Centers for Disease Control and Prevention* https://www.cdc.gov/nchs/pressroom/nchs_press_releases/2018/201811_Yoga_Meditation.htm (2018).

101. About the Religious Landscape Study. *Pew Research Center* https://www.pewforum.org/about-the-religious-landscape-study/ (2014).

102. Rakicevic, M. 27 Meditation Statistics for Your Well-Being in 2021. *DisturbMeNote* https://disturbmenot.co/meditation-statistics/ (2021).

103. Engleberg, B. R. For Some People, Relaxing Makes Anxiety Worse. *Paper Gown* https://thepapergown.zocdoc.com/some-anxious-people-get-more-anxious-when-they-try-to-relax/ (2020).

104. Hofmann, S. G., Sawyer, A. T., Witt, A. A. & Oh, D. The Effect of Mindfulness-Based Therapy on Anxiety and Depression: A Meta-Analytic Review. *J. Consult. Clin. Psychol.* **78**, 169–183 (2010).

105. Tseng, J. & Poppenk, J. Brain meta-state transitions demarcate thoughts across task contexts exposing the mental noise of trait neuroticism. *Nat. Commun. 2020 111* **11**, 1–12 (2020).

106. Powell, A. When science meets mindfulness. *The Harvard Gazette* https://news.harvard.edu/gazette/story/2018/04/harvard-researchers-study-how-mindfulness-may-change-the-brain-in-depressed-patients/ (2018).

107. Creswell, J. D., Pacilio, L. E., Lindsay, E. K. & Brown, K. W. Brief mindfulness meditation training alters psychological and neuroendocrine responses to social evaluative stress. *Psychoneuroendocrinology* **44**, 1–12 (2014).

108. The Twelve Core Life Skills. *Life Skills and Citizenship Education Initiative* https://www.unicef.org/mena/media/6186/file/Twelve Core Life Skills for MENA_EN.pdf .pdf (2015).

109. Celeste Campbell, PsyD. *BrainLine* https://www.brainline.org/author/celeste-campbell-psyd (2021).

110. Ackerman, C. E. What is Neuroplasticity? A Psychologist Explains [+14 Exercises]. *PositivePsychology* https://positivepsychology.com/neuroplasticity/ (2021).

111. Kempermann, G. Why new neurons? Possible functions for adult hippocampal neurogenesis. *J. Neurosci.* **22**, 635–638 (2002).

112. Vemuri, P. *et al.* Association of lifetime intellectual enrichment with cognitive decline in the older population. *JAMA Neurol.* **71**, 1017–1024 (2014).

113. Sigmund Freud (1856-1939). *GoodTherapy* https://www.goodtherapy.org/famous-psychologists/sigmund-freud.html (2015).

114. Otgaar, H. *et al.* The Return of the Repressed: The Persistent and Problematic Claims of Long-Forgotten Trauma. *Perspect. Psychol. Sci.* **14**, 1072–1095 (2019).

115. Allan, P. How to Snap Back to Reality when 'Escapism' Becomes "Avoidance". *LifeHacker*

417

https://lifehacker.com/how-to-snap-back-to-reality-when-escapism-becomes-av-1723091630 (2015).

116.   McCorry, L. K. Physiology of the autonomic nervous system. *Am. J. Pharm. Educ.* **71**, 78 (2007).

117.   Fisher, J. P., Young, C. N. & Fadel, P. J. Central sympathetic overactivity: Maladies and mechanisms. *Auton. Neurosci. Basic Clin.* **148**, 5–15 (2009).

118.   Tawakol, A. *et al.* Relation between resting amygdalar activity and cardiovascular events: a longitudinal and cohort study. *Lancet* **389**, 834–845 (2017).

119.   Rege, S. & Graham, J. How Stress Increases the Risk of Cardiovascular Disease (CVD). *Psych Scene* https://psychscenehub.com/psychinsights/stress-increases-risk-cardiovascular-disease-cvd/ (2020).

120.   Bruce, M. A., Griffith, D. M. & Thorpe, R. J. Stress and the kidney. *Adv. Chronic Kidney Dis.* **22**, 46–53 (2015).

121.   Siddiqui, A., Madhu, S. V., Sharma, S. B. & Desai, N. G. Endocrine stress responses and risk of type 2 diabetes mellitus. *Stress* **18**, 498–506 (2015).

122.   Scott, K. A., Melhorn, S. J. & Sakai, R. R. Effects of Chronic Social Stress on Obesity. *Curr. Obes. Rep.* **1**, 16–25 (2012).

123.   Chandola, T., Brunner, E. & Marmot, M. Chronic stress at work and the metabolic syndrome: Prospective study. *Br. Med. J.* **332**, 521–524 (2006).

124.   Hemmerle, A. M., Herman, J. P. & Seroogy, K. B. Stress, depression and Parkinson's disease. *Exp. Neurol.* **233**, 79–86 (2012).

125.   Trapp, R. Leaders Need To Take The Compassionate Route To Performance. *Forbes* https://www.forbes.com/sites/rogertrapp/2019/04/24/leaders-need-to-take-the-compassionate-route-to-performance/?sh=3a2442174307 (2019).

126.   Pappas, S. What's in a Fat Cell? *Live Science* https://www.livescience.com/62218-whats-in-a-fat-cell.html (2018).

127.   Lanese, N. Fight or Flight: The Sympathetic Nervous System. *Live Science* https://www.livescience.com/65446-sympathetic-nervous-system.html (2019).

128.   Mariotti, A. The effects of chronic stress on health: New insights into the molecular mechanisms of brain-body communication. *Futur. Sci. OA* **1**, (2015).

129.   Kenney, M. J. & Ganta, C. K. Autonomic nervous system and immune system interactions. *Compr. Physiol.* **4**, 1177–1200 (2014).

130.   Lakin, R. *et al.* Changes in heart rate and its regulation by the autonomic nervous system do not differ between forced and voluntary exercise in mice. *Front. Physiol.* **9**, 841 (2018).

131.   Porges, S. W. The polyvagal perspective. *Biol. Psychol.* **74**, 116–143 (2007).

132.   Peterson, C. Many animals play dead—and not just to avoid getting eaten. *National Geographic* https://www.nationalgeographic.com/animals/article/many-animals-play-dead-not-just-to-avoid-predators (2021).

133.   Porges, S. W. The polyvagal theory: New insights into adaptive reactions of the autonomic

nervous system. *Cleve. Clin. J. Med.* **76**, S86 (2009).

134. Sunseri, J. Building Safety Anchors. https://www.justinlmft.com/.

135. Tan, S. Y. & Yip, A. Hans Selye (1907-1982): Founder of the stress theory. *Singapore Med. J.* **59**, 170–171 (2018).

136. Schreiber, L. R. N., Odlaug, B. L. & Grant, J. E. The overlap between binge eating disorder and substance use disorders: Diagnosis and neurobiology. *J. Behav. Addict.* **2**, 191 (2013).

137. Hanna, H. His Stress, Her Stress. *The American Institute of Stress* https://www.stress.org/his-stress-her-stress (2017).

138. Doane, L. D. & Adam, E. K. Loneliness and Cortisol: Momentary, Day-to-day, and Trait Associations. *Psychoneuroendocrinology* **35**, 430 (2010).

139. Furman, D. *et al.* Chronic inflammation in the etiology of disease across the life span. *Nat. Med.* **25**, 1822–1832 (2019).

140. Inflammation as a core feature in people with depression. *Science Media Centre* https://www.sciencemediacentre.org/inflammation-as-a-core-feature-in-people-with-depression/ (2021).

141. Professor Cathryn Lewis. *King's College London* https://www.kcl.ac.uk/people/cathryn-lewis.

142. Nella, D., Panagopoulou, E., Galanis, N., Montgomery, A. & Benos, A. Consequences of Job Insecurity on the Psychological and Physical Health of Greek Civil Servants. *Biomed Res. Int.* **2015**, (2015).

143. Thomas, R. M., Hotsenpiller, G. & Peterson, D. A. Acute psychosocial stress reduces cell survival in adult hippocampal neurogenesis without altering proliferation. *J. Neurosci.* **27**, 2734–2743 (2007).

144. Hathaway, B. Even in the healthy, stress causes brain to shrink, Yale study shows. *Yale News* https://news.yale.edu/2012/01/09/even-healthy-stress-causes-brain-shrink-yale-study-shows (2012).

145. Conrad, C. D. A critical review of chronic stress effects on spatial learning and memory. *Prog. Neuro-Psychopharmacology Biol. Psychiatry* **34**, 742–755 (2010).

146. Chetty, S. *et al.* Stress and glucocorticoids promote oligodendrogenesis in the adult hippocampus. *Mol. Psychiatry* **19**, 1275–1283 (2014).

147. Yang, L. *et al.* The Effects of Psychological Stress on Depression. *Curr. Neuropharmacol.* **13**, 494–504 (2015).

148. McGonigal, K. How to make stress your friend. *TED* https://www.ted.com/talks/kelly_mcgonigal_how_to_make_stress_your_friend/details?language=en (2013).

149. Keller, A. *et al.* Does the perception that stress affects health matter? The association with health and mortality. *Heal. Psychol.* **31**, 677–684 (2012).

150. Zaccaro, A. *et al.* How Breath-Control Can Change Your Life: A Systematic Review on

Psycho-Physiological Correlates of Slow Breathing. *Front. Hum. Neurosci.* **12**, 353 (2018).

151. Ma, X. *et al.* The effect of diaphragmatic breathing on attention, negative affect and stress in healthy adults. *Front. Psychol.* **8**, 874 (2017).

152. Gerritsen, R. J. S. & Band, G. P. H. Breath of Life: The Respiratory Vagal Stimulation Model of Contemplative Activity. *Front. Hum. Neurosci.* **12**, 9 (2018).

153. B, O., H, A. & O, S. Oral breathing in patients with sleep-related breathing disorders. *Acta Otolaryngol.* **122**, 651–654 (2002).

154. van der Velden, V. H. & Hulsmann, A. R. Autonomic innervation of human airways: structure, function, and pathophysiology in asthma. *Neuroimmunomodulation* **6**, 145–159 (1999).

155. Crecinto, C., Efthemeou, T., Boffelli, P. T. & Navalta, J. W. A. Effects of Nasal or Oral Breathing on Anaerobic Power Output and Metabolic Responses. *Int. J. Exerc. Sci.* **10**, 506 (2017).

156. Berman, J. Could nasal breathing improve athletic performance? *Washington Post* https://www.washingtonpost.com/lifestyle/wellness/when-it-comes-to-breathing-during-exercise-youre-probably-doing-it-wrong/2019/01/23/b4d3c338-1e59-11e9-8b59-

157. KJ, L., CA, P., YB, L., HK, K. & CK, K. EEG signals during mouth breathing in a working memory task. *Int. J. Neurosci.* **130**, 425–434 (2020).

158. Furness, J. B., Callaghan, B. P., Rivera, L. R. & Cho, H. J. The enteric nervous system and gastrointestinal innervation: Integrated local and central control. *Adv. Exp. Med. Biol.* **817**, 39–71 (2014).

159. Michael D. Gershon, MD. *Columbia University Department of Pathology and Cell Biology* https://www.pathology.columbia.edu/profile/michael-d-gershon-md.

160. Gershon, M. D. The thoughtful bowel. *Acta Physiol.* **228**, e13331 (2020).

161. Hadhazy, A. Think Twice: How the Gut's 'Second Brain' Influences Mood and Well-Being. *Scientific American* https://www.scientificamerican.com/article/gut-second-brain/ (2020).

162. Ramirez, J. *et al.* Antibiotics as Major Disruptors of Gut Microbiota. *Front. Cell. Infect. Microbiol.* **10**, 731 (2020).

163. Yale University. How a single cell gives rise to the 37 trillion cells in an average adult. *ScienceDaily* https://www.sciencedaily.com/releases/2021/03/210318142451.htm (2021).

164. Fischetti, M. & Christiansen, J. Our Bodies Replace Billions of Cells Every Day. *Scientific American* https://www.scientificamerican.com/article/our-bodies-replace-billions-of-cells-every-day/ (2021).

165. Rynders, C. A. *et al.* Effectiveness of Intermittent Fasting and Time-Restricted Feeding Compared to Continuous Energy Restriction for Weight Loss. *Nutrients* **11**, (2019).

166. What is septic shock? *Healthline* https://www.healthline.com/health/septic-shock (2016).

167. Tressler, C. Sham charity operators turn the Big C into a Big Con. *Federal Trade Comission* https://www.consumer.ftc.gov/blog/2015/05/sham-charity-operators-turn-big-

c-big-con (2015).

168.   Parkin, J. & Cohen, B. An overview of the immune system. *Lancet* **357**, 1777–1789
         (2001).

169.   The Immune System. *Johns Hopkins Medicine*
         https://www.hopkinsmedicine.org/health/conditions-and-diseases/the-immune-system.

170.   How does the immune system work? *InformedHealth* (2020).

171.   Overview of the Immune System. *National Institute of Allergy and Infectious Diseases* (2013).

172.   Blach-Olszewska, Z. & Leszek, J. Mechanisms of over-activated innate immune system
         regulation in autoimmune and neurodegenerative disorders. *Neuropsychiatr. Dis. Treat.* **3**,
         365 (2007).

173.   Childs, C. E., Calder, P. C. & Miles, E. A. Diet and Immune Function. *Nutrients* **11**,
         (2019).

174.   L, M. & T, V. de W. Food processing, gut microbiota and the globesity problem. *Crit.
         Rev. Food Sci. Nutr.* **60**, 1769–1782 (2020).

175.   Vighi, G., Marcucci, F., Sensi, L., Di Cara, G. & Frati, F. Allergy and the gastrointestinal
         system. *Clin. Exp. Immunol.* **153**, 3–6 (2008).

176.   Bredesen, D. E. Reversal of cognitive decline: A novel therapeutic program. *Aging
         (Albany. NY).* **6**, 707–717 (2014).

177.   L, O. *et al.* T-cell activation in patients with irritable bowel syndrome. *Am. J. Gastroenterol.*
         104, 1205–1212 (2009).

178.   Abelson, R. Drug Sales Bring Huge Profits, And Scrutiny, to Cancer Doctors. *New York
         Times* https://www.nytimes.com/2003/01/26/us/drug-sales-bring-huge-profits-and-
         scrutiny-to-cancer-doctors.html (2003).

179.   Panagioti, M. *et al.* Prevalence, severity, and nature of preventable patient harm across
         medical care settings: Systematic review and meta-analysis. *BMJ* **366**, (2019).

180.   Study Suggests Medical Errors Now Third Leading Cause of Death in the U.S. . *Johns
         Hopkins Medicine*
         https://www.hopkinsmedicine.org/news/media/releases/study_suggests_medical_errors_no
         w_third_leading_cause_of_death_in_the_us (2016).

181.   Corbie-Smith, G., Thomas, S. B., Williams, M. V. & Moody-Ayers, S. Attitudes and
         beliefs of African Americans toward participation in medical research. *J. Gen. Intern. Med.*
         14, 537–546 (1999).

182.   Scharf, D. P. *et al.* More than Tuskegee: Understanding mistrust about research
         participation. *J. Health Care Poor Underserved* **21**, 879–897 (2010).

183.   Jiang, T. *et al.* Apple-Derived Pectin Modulates Gut Microbiota, Improves Gut Barrier
         Function, and Attenuates Metabolic Endotoxemia in Rats with Diet-Induced Obesity.
         Nutrients **8**, 126 (2016).

184.   MA, el-N. & RT, Y. Study of antimicrobial action of pectin. I. Antibacterial and
         antifungal activities of pectin. *Planta Med.* **18**, 201–209 (1970).

185.   Singh, V., Yeoh, B. S. & Vijay-Kumar, M. Fermentable Fiber Pectin Improves Intestinal
         Inflammation by Modulating Gut Microbial Metabolites and Inflammasome Activity.
         Curr. Dev. Nutr. **4**, 1535–1535 (2020).

186.   D, G., A, C. & K, E. The effects of diet on inflammation: emphasis on the metabolic
         syndrome. *J. Am. Coll. Cardiol.* **48**, 677–685 (2006).

187.   Lv, X. *et al.* Citrus fruits as a treasure trove of active natural metabolites that potentially
         provide benefits for human health. *Chem. Cent. J.* **9**, (2015).

188.   S, C. *et al.* Chemopreventive Agents and Inhibitors of Cancer Hallmarks: May Citrus
         Offer New Perspectives? *Nutrients* **8**, (2016).

189.   Vitamin C Fact Sheet for Consumers. *National Institutes of Health*
         https://ods.od.nih.gov/factsheets/VitaminC-Consumer/ (2021).

190.   H, H. & E, C. Vitamin C for preventing and treating the common cold. *Cochrane database
         Syst. Rev.* **2013**, (2013).

191.   Fiedor, J. & Burda, K. Potential Role of Carotenoids as Antioxidants in Human Health
         and Disease. *Nutrients* **6**, 466 (2014).

192.   Beta-Carotene. *Kaiser Permanente*
         https://wa.kaiserpermanente.org/kbase/topic.jhtml?docId=hn-2804006 (2015).

193.   Rahmani, A. H., shabrmi, F. M. Al & Aly, S. M. Active ingredients of ginger as potential
         candidates in the prevention and treatment of diseases via modulation of biological
         activities. *Int. J. Physiol. Pathophysiol. Pharmacol.* **6**, 125 (2014).

194.   Lakhan, S. E., Ford, C. T. & Tepper, D. Zingiberaceae extracts for pain: a systematic
         review and meta-analysis. *Nutr. J.* **14**, (2015).

195.   M, P. *et al.* The effect of ginger supplementation on lipid profile: A systematic review and
         meta-analysis of clinical trials. *Phytomedicine* **43**, 28–36 (2018).

196.   J, B., F, A., MC, G., ID, N. & AJ, S. Allicin: chemistry and biological properties.
         Molecules **19**, 12591–12618 (2014).

197.   Garlic . *National Center for Complementary and Integrative Health*
         https://www.nccih.nih.gov/health/garlic (2020).

198.   Pham-Huy, L. A., He, H. & Pham-Huy, C. Free Radicals, Antioxidants in Disease and
         Health. *Int. J. Biomed. Sci.* **4**, 89 (2008).

199.   Kamath, A. B. *et al.* Antigens in tea-beverage prime human Vγ2Vδ2 T cells in vitro and
         in vivo for memory and nonmemory antibacterial cytokine responses. *PNAS* **100**, 6009–
         6014 (2003).

200.   Nance, C. L., Mata, M., McMullen, A., McMaster, S. & Shearer, W. T. Regulation Of
         Innate Immune Recognition Of Viral Infection By Epigallocatechin Gallate. *J. Allergy
         Clin. Immunol.* **133**, AB246 (2014).

201.   Chacko, S. M., Thambi, P. T., Kuttan, R. & Nishigaki, I. Beneficial effects of green tea:
         A literature review. *Chin. Med.* **5**, 13 (2010).

202.   Suarez-Arroyo, I. J. *et al.* Anti-Tumor Effects of Ganoderma lucidum (Reishi) in

Inflammatory Breast Cancer in In Vivo and In Vitro Models. *PLoS One* **8**, 57431 (2013).

203. Matsuzaki, H. *et al.* Antidepressant-like effects of a water-soluble extract from the culture medium of Ganoderma lucidum mycelia in rats. *BMC Complement. Altern. Med.* **13**, 1–8 (2013).

204. Huang, H.-T. *et al.* Hericium erinaceus mycelium and its small bioactive compounds promote oligodendrocyte maturation with an increase in myelin basic protein. *Sci. Rep.* **11**, 1–13 (2021).

205. Nagano, M. *et al.* Reduction of depression and anxiety by 4 weeks Hericium erinaceus intake. *Biomed. Res.* **31**, 231–237 (2010).

206. Park, Y. K., Lee, H. B., Jeon, E. J., Jung, H. S. & Kang, H. M. Chaga mushroom extract inhibits oxidative DNA damage in human lymphocytes as assessed by comet assay. *BioFactors* **21**, 109–112 (2004).

207. Liang, L., Zhang, Z., Sun, W. & Wang, Y. Effect of the Inonotus obliquus polysaccharides on blood lipid metabolism and oxidative stress of rats fed high-fat diet in vivo. *Proc. 2009 2nd Int. Conf. Biomed. Eng. Informatics, BMEI 2009* (2009)

208. Kim, S. H. *et al.* Edible Mushrooms Reduce Atherosclerosis in Ldlr-/- Mice Fed a High-Fat Diet. *J. Nutr.* **149**, 1377–1384 (2019).

209. Kabir, Y., Yamaguchi, M. & Kimura, S. Effect of shiitake (Lentinus edodes) and maitake (Grifola frondosa) mushrooms on blood pressure and plasma lipids of spontaneously hypertensive rats. *J. Nutr. Sci. Vitaminol. (Tokyo).* **33**, 341–346 (1987).

210. McFarlin, B. K. et al. Reduced inflammatory and muscle damage biomarkers following oral supplementation with bioavailable curcumin. *BBA Clin.* **5**, 72 (2016).

211. Zorofchian Moghadamtousi, S. et al. A review on antibacterial, antiviral, and antifungal activity of curcumin. BioMed Res. (2014)

212. Tripoli, E. *et al.* The phenolic compounds of olive oil: structure, biological activity and beneficial effects on human health. *Nutr. Res. Rev.* **18**, 98–112 (2005).

213. Servili, M. *et al.* Phenolic compounds in olive oil: antioxidant, health and organoleptic activities according to their chemical structure. *Inflammopharmacology* **17**, 76–84 (2009).

214. Jurado-Ruiz, E. *et al.* Extra virgin olive oil diet intervention improves insulin resistance and islet performance in diet-induced diabetes in mice. *Sci. Rep.* **9**, 1–13 (2019).

215. Lucas, L., Russell, A. & Keast, R. Molecular mechanisms of inflammation. Anti-inflammatory benefits of virgin olive oil and the phenolic compound oleocanthal. *Curr. Pharm. Des.* **17**, 754–768 (2011).

216. Leech, J. 11 Proven Benefits of Olive Oil. *Healthline* https://www.healthline.com/nutrition/11-proven-benefits-of-olive-oil (2018).

217. Aranow, C. Vitamin D and the Immune System. *J. Investig. Med.* **59**, 881 (2011).

218. Liu, M.-J. *et al.* ZIP8 Regulates Host Defense through Zinc-Mediated Inhibition of NF-κB. *Cell Rep.* **3**, 386–400 (2013).

219. Aranow, C. Vitamin D and the Immune System. *J. Investig. Med.* **59**, 881 (2011).

220. Prasad, A. S. Zinc is an Antioxidant and Anti-Inflammatory Agent: Its Role in Human Health. *Front. Nutr.* **1**, (2014).

221. Zinc. *National Institutes of Health* https://ods.od.nih.gov/factsheets/Zinc-HealthProfessional/ (2021).

222. Melchart, D., Linde, K., Worku, F., Bauer, R. & Wagner, H. Immunomodulation with echinacea - a systematic review of controlled clinical trials. *Phytomedicine* **1**, 245–254 (1994).

223. Shah, S. A., Sander, S., White, C. M., Rinaldi, M. & Coleman, C. I. Evaluation of echinacea for the prevention and treatment of the common cold: a meta-analysis. *Lancet Infect. Dis.* **7**, 473–480 (2007).

224. Raman, R. Echinacea: Benefits, Uses, Side Effects and Dosage. *Healthline* https://www.healthline.com/nutrition/echinacea (2018).

225. Rondanelli, M. *et al.* The effect and safety of highly standardized Ginger (Zingiber officinale) and Echinacea (Echinacea angustifolia) extract supplementation on inflammation and chronic pain in NSAIDs poor responders. A pilot study in subjects with knee arthrosis. *Nat. Prod. Res.* **31**, 1309–1313 (2017).

226. Ulbricht, C. *et al.* An evidence-based systematic review of elderberry and elderflower (Sambucus nigra) by the Natural Standard Research Collaboration. *J. Diet. Suppl.* **11**, 80–120 (2014).

227. Sidor, A. & Gramza-Michałowska, A. Advanced research on the antioxidant and health benefit of elderberry (Sambucus nigra) in food – a review. *J. Funct. Foods* **18**, 941–958 (2015).

228. Hawkins, J., Baker, C., Cherry, L. & Dunne, E. Black elderberry (Sambucus nigra) supplementation effectively treats upper respiratory symptoms: A meta-analysis of randomized, controlled clinical trials. *Complement. Ther. Med.* **42**, 361–365 (2019).

229. Semeco, A. 7 Proven Health Benefits of Ginseng. *Healthline* https://www.healthline.com/nutrition/ginseng-benefits#TOC_TITLE_HDR_1 (2018).

230. Im, D.-S. & Nah, S. Y. Yin and Yang of ginseng pharmacology: ginsenosides vs gintonin. *Acta Pharmacol. Sin.* **34**, 1367–1373 (2013).

231. Kang, S. & Min, H. Ginseng, the 'Immunity Boost': The Effects of Panax ginseng on Immune System. *J. Ginseng Res.* **36**, 354 (2012).

232. Hjalmarsdottir, F. 17 Science-Based Benefits of Omega-3 Fatty Acids. *Healthline* https://www.healthline.com/nutrition/17-health-benefits-of-omega-3 (2018).

233. Meixner, M. Astragalus: An Ancient Root With Health Benefits. *Healthline* https://www.healthline.com/nutrition/astragalus (2018).

234. Hyman, M. Glutathione: The Mother of All Antioxidants. *Huffington Post* https://www.huffpost.com/entry/glutathione-the-mother-of_b_530494 (2011).

235. Kerksick, C. & Willoughby, D. The Antioxidant Role of Glutathione and N-Acetyl-Cysteine Supplements and Exercise-Induced Oxidative Stress. *J. Int. Soc. Sport. Nutr. 2005*

22 **2**, 1–7 (2005).

236.   Jones, D. P. *et al.* Glutathione in foods listed in the National Cancer Institute's Health Habits and History Food Frequency Questionnaire. *Nutr. Cancer* **17**, 57–75 (1992).

237.   Segerstrom, S. C. & Miller, M. E. Psychological stress and the human immune system: a meta-analytic study of 30 years of inquiry. *Psychol. Bull.* **130**, 601–630 (2004).

238.   Nieman, D. C. & Wentz, L. M. The compelling link between physical activity and the body's defense system. *J. Sport Heal. Sci.* **8**, 201–217 (2019).

239.   Simpson, R., Kunz, H., Agha, N. & Graff, R. Exercise and the Regulation of Immune Functions. *Prog. Mol. Biol. Transl. Sci.* **135**, 355–380 (2015).

240.   Cohen, S. *et al.* Chronic stress, glucocorticoid receptor resistance, inflammation, and disease risk. *Proc. Natl. Acad. Sci. U. S. A.* **109**, 5995–5999 (2012).

241.   Carlsson, E., Frostell, A., Ludvigsson, J. & Maria Faresjö. Psychological stress in children may alter the immune response. *J. Immunol.* **192**, 2071–2081 (2014).

242.   Morey, J. N., Boggero, I. A., Scott, A. B. & Segerstrom, S. C. Current Directions in Stress and Human Immune Function. *Curr. Opin. Psychol.* **5**, 13 (2015).

243.   Prather, A. A., Janicki-Deverts, D., Hall, M. H. & Cohen, S. Behaviorally Assessed Sleep and Susceptibility to the Common Cold. *Sleep* **38**, 1353–1359 (2015).

244.   Besedovsky, L., Lange, T. & Born, J. Sleep and immune function. *Pflugers Arch.* **463**, 121 (2012).

245.   Besedovsky, L., Lange, T. & Haack, M. The Sleep-Immune Crosstalk in Health and Disease. *Physiol. Rev.* **99**, 1325–1380 (2019).

246.   Mullington, J. M., Simpson, N. S., Meier-Ewert, H. K. & Haack, M. Sleep loss and inflammation. *Best Pract. Res. Clin. Endocrinol. Metab.* **24**, 775–784 (2010).

247.   Alcohol does not protect against COVID-19; access should be restricted during lockdown. *World Health Organization* https://www.euro.who.int/en/health-topics/disease-prevention/alcohol-use/news/news/2020/04/alcohol-does-not-protect-against-covid-19-access-should-be-restricted-during-lockdown (2020).

248.   The Ria Team. How Does Alcohol Affect Your Metabolism? *Ria Health* https://riahealth.com/2021/03/01/how-does-alcohol-affect-your-metabolism/ (2021).

249.   Ries, J. How Alcohol Can Affect Your Immune System. *Healthline* https://www.healthline.com/health-news/can-alcohol-hurt-your-immune-system-during-covid-19-outbreak (2020).

250.   Johnson, R. J., Sánchez-Lozada, L. G., Andrews, P. & Lanaspa, M. A. Perspective: A Historical and Scientific Perspective of Sugar and Its Relation with Obesity and Diabetes. *Adv. Nutr.* **8**, 412–422 (2017).

251.   Linendoll, W. 75% of Americans are chronically dehydrated, are you drinking enough water? *Good Morning America* https://www.goodmorningamerica.com/wellness/video/75-americans-chronically-dehydrated-drinking-water-71169567 (2020).

252.   Hill, P. L., Allemand, M. & Roberts, B. W. Examining the Pathways between Gratitude

and Self-Rated Physical Health across Adulthood. *Pers. Individ. Dif.* **54**, 92 (2013).

253.   The Genetics of Cancer. *National Cancer Institute* (2017).

254.   Green, J. & Shellenberger, R. The healing energy of love. *Altern. Ther. Health Med.* **2**, 46–56 (1996).

255.   Blue, A. Having a Partner Present – or in Mind – May Keep Blood Pressure Down. *University of Arizona News* https://news.arizona.edu/story/having-partner-present-or-mind-may-keep-blood-pressure-down (2019).

256.   Kaiser Permanente. Women with more social connections have higher breast cancer survival, study shows. *ScienceDaily* https://www.sciencedaily.com/releases/2016/12/161213115055.htm (2016).

257.   Gillespie, L. It Takes Two: The Role of Co-Regulation in Building Self-Regulation Skills. *Zero to Three* https://www.zerotothree.org/resources/1777-it-takes-two-the-role-of-co-regulation-in-building-self-regulation-skills.

258.   Nicholson, N. How Hardwired Is Human Behavior? *Harvard Business Review* https://hbr.org/1998/07/how-hardwired-is-human-behavior (1998).

259.   KM, G., SS, G., J, A. & KC, L. Effects of partner support on resting oxytocin, cortisol, norepinephrine, and blood pressure before and after warm partner contact. *Psychosom. Med.* **67**, 531–538 (2005).

260.   Radiation risk from medical imaging. *Harvard Health Publishing* (2020).

261.   Kennel, J. Health and Wellness Coaching Improves Weight and Nutrition Behaviors. *Am. J. Lifestyle Med.* **12**, 448–450 (2018).

262.   Johnston, K. Why A Health Coach Is Key to Your Success. *Parsley Health* https://www.parsleyhealth.com/blog/what-is-a-health-coach/ (2020).

263.   Murray, C. J. L. *et al.* The state of US health, 1990-2016: Burden of diseases, injuries, and risk factors among US states. *JAMA* **319**, 1444–1472 (2018).

264.   Dahra, A. The Language of Love & Light: Open up Your Channels. *The Language of Love and Light* https://www.thelanguageofloveandlight.com/ (2016).

265.   National Center for Chronic Disease Prevention and Health Promotion (NCCDPHP). *Centers for Disease Control and Prevention* https://www.cdc.gov/chronicdisease/index.htm.

266.   Spera, S. P., Buhrfeind, E. D. & Pennebaker, J. W. Expressive Writing and Coping with Job Loss. *Acad. Manag. J.* **37**, 722–733 (1994).

267.   Willis, J. The Brain-Based Benefits of Writing for Math and Science Learning. *Edutopia* https://www.edutopia.org/blog/writing-executive-function-brain-research-judy-willis (2011).

268.   Wapner, J. Blogging--It's Good for You. *Scientific American* https://www.scientificamerican.com/article/the-healthy-type/ (2008).

260.   Baikie, K. A. & Wilhelm, K. Emotional and physical health benefits of expressive writing. *Adv. Psychiatr. Treat.* **11**, 338–346 (2005).

270.   King, L. A. The health benefits of writing about life goals. *Personal. Soc. Psychol. Bull.* **27**,

798–807 (2001).

271.   Davis, S. The Wounded Inner Child. *The Foundation for Post-Traumatic Healing and Complex Trauma Research* https://cptsdfoundation.org/2020/07/13/the-wounded-inner-child/ (2020).

272.   Bjornsson, A. S. *et al.* Social trauma and its association with posttraumatic stress disorder and social anxiety disorder. *J. Anxiety Disord.* **72**, (2020).

273.   Min, M. O., Minnes, S., Kim, H. & Singer, L. T. Pathways linking childhood maltreatment and adult physical health. *Child Abus. Negl.* **37**, 361–373 (2013).

274.   Mental Health By the Numbers. *Alliance on Mental Illness* https://www.nami.org/mhstats.

275.   Houry, D. Identifying, Preventing, and Treating Childhood Trauma. *Centers for Disease Control and Prevention* https://www.cdc.gov/washington/testimony/2019/t20190711.htm (2019).

276.   About the CDC-Kaiser ACE Study. *Centers for Disease Control and Prevention* https://www.cdc.gov/violenceprevention/aces/about.html.